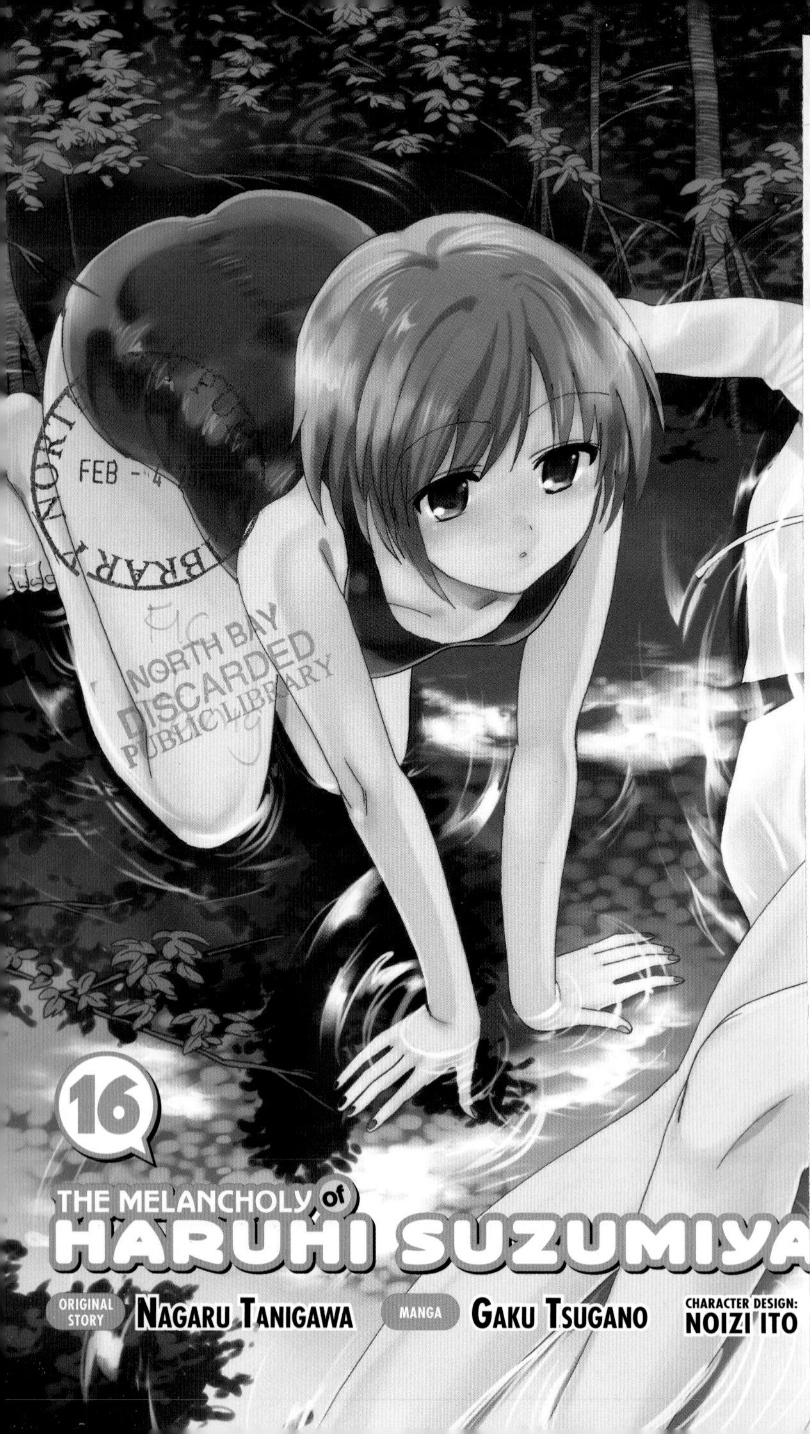

16

THE MELANCHOLY of HARUHI SUZUMIYA

ORIGINAL STORY NAGARU TANIGAWA

MANGA GAKU TSUGANO

CHARACTER DESIGN: NOIZI ITO

CONTENTS

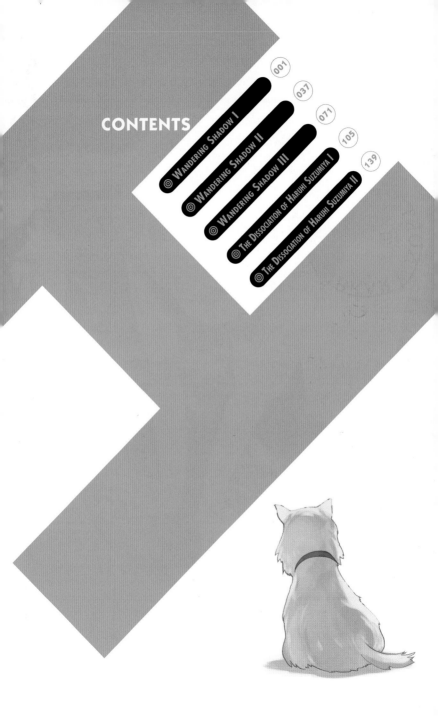

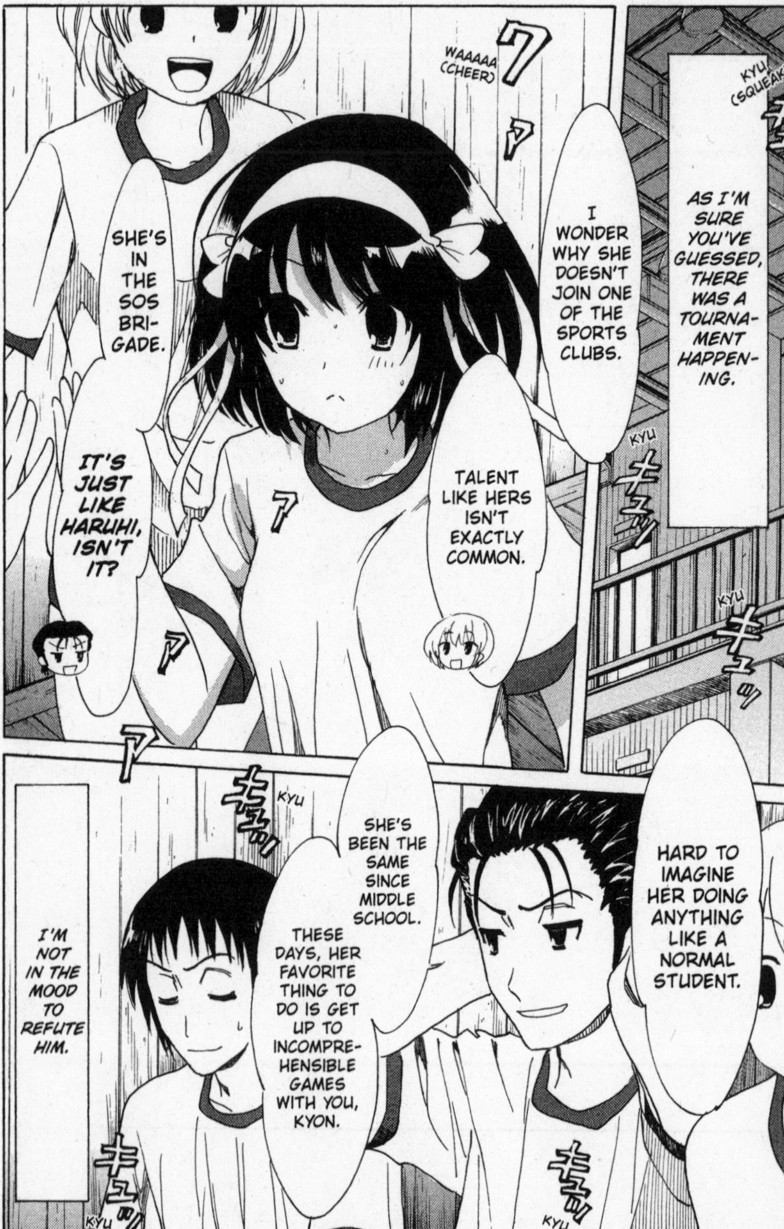
KYU (SQUEAK)
AS I'M SURE YOU'VE GUESSED, THERE WAS A TOURNAMENT HAPPENING.
KYU
KYU
WAAAAA (CHEER)
I WONDER WHY SHE DOESN'T JOIN ONE OF THE SPORTS CLUBS.
TALENT LIKE HERS ISN'T EXACTLY COMMON.
SHE'S IN THE SOS BRIGADE.
IT'S JUST LIKE HARUHI, ISN'T IT?
HARD TO IMAGINE HER DOING ANYTHING LIKE A NORMAL STUDENT.
SHE'S BEEN THE SAME SINCE MIDDLE SCHOOL.
KYU
THESE DAYS, HER FAVORITE THING TO DO IS GET UP TO INCOMPREHENSIBLE GAMES WITH YOU, KYON.
I'M NOT IN THE MOOD TO REFUTE HIM.
KYU
KYU

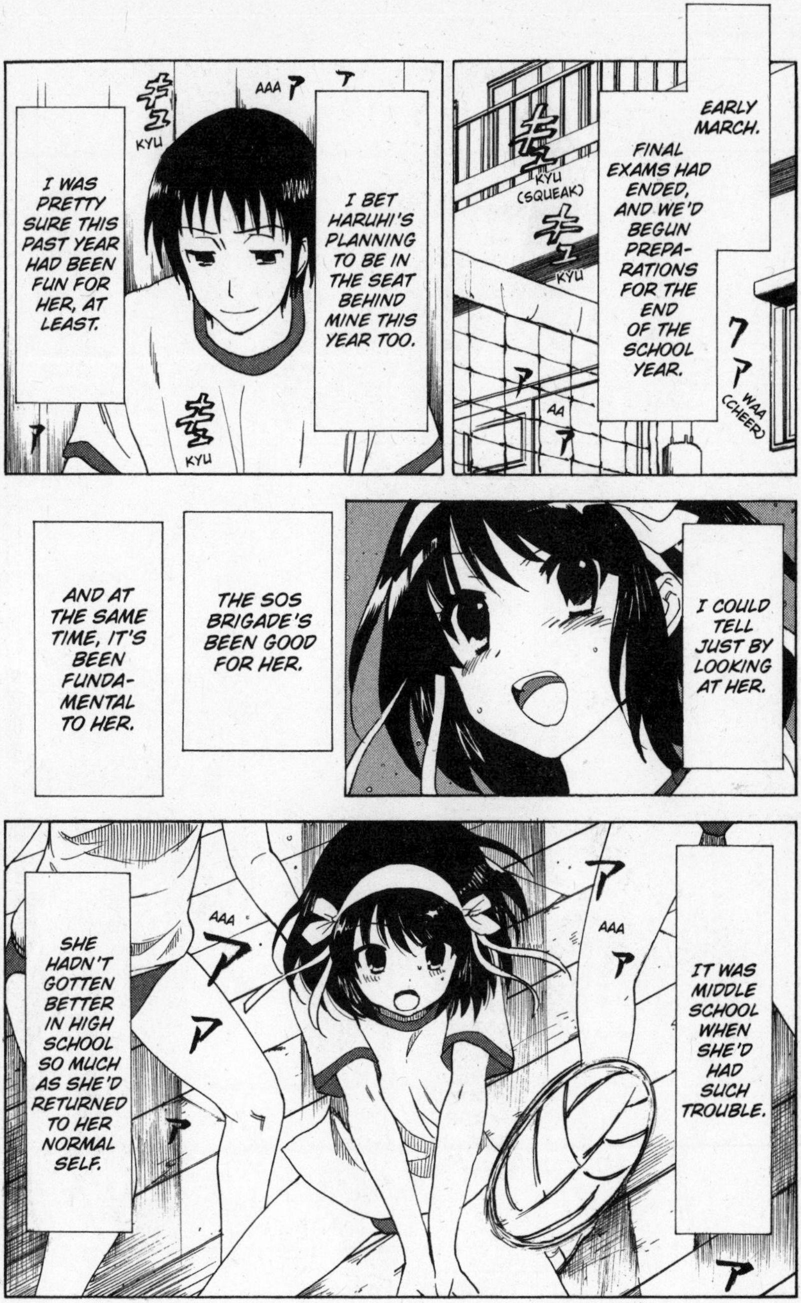
EARLY MARCH.
FINAL EXAMS HAD ENDED, AND WE'D BEGUN PREPARATIONS FOR THE END OF THE SCHOOL YEAR.
KYU (SQUEAK)
KYU
WAA (CHEER)
AA
I BET HARUHI'S PLANNING TO BE IN THE SEAT BEHIND MINE THIS YEAR TOO.
AAA
KYU
I WAS PRETTY SURE THIS PAST YEAR HAD BEEN FUN FOR HER, AT LEAST.
KYU
I COULD TELL JUST BY LOOKING AT HER.
THE SOS BRIGADE'S BEEN GOOD FOR HER.
AND AT THE SAME TIME, IT'S BEEN FUNDAMENTAL TO HER.
IT WAS MIDDLE SCHOOL WHEN SHE'D HAD SUCH TROUBLE.
AAA
AAA
SHE HADN'T GOTTEN BETTER IN HIGH SCHOOL SO MUCH AS SHE'D RETURNED TO HER NORMAL SELF.

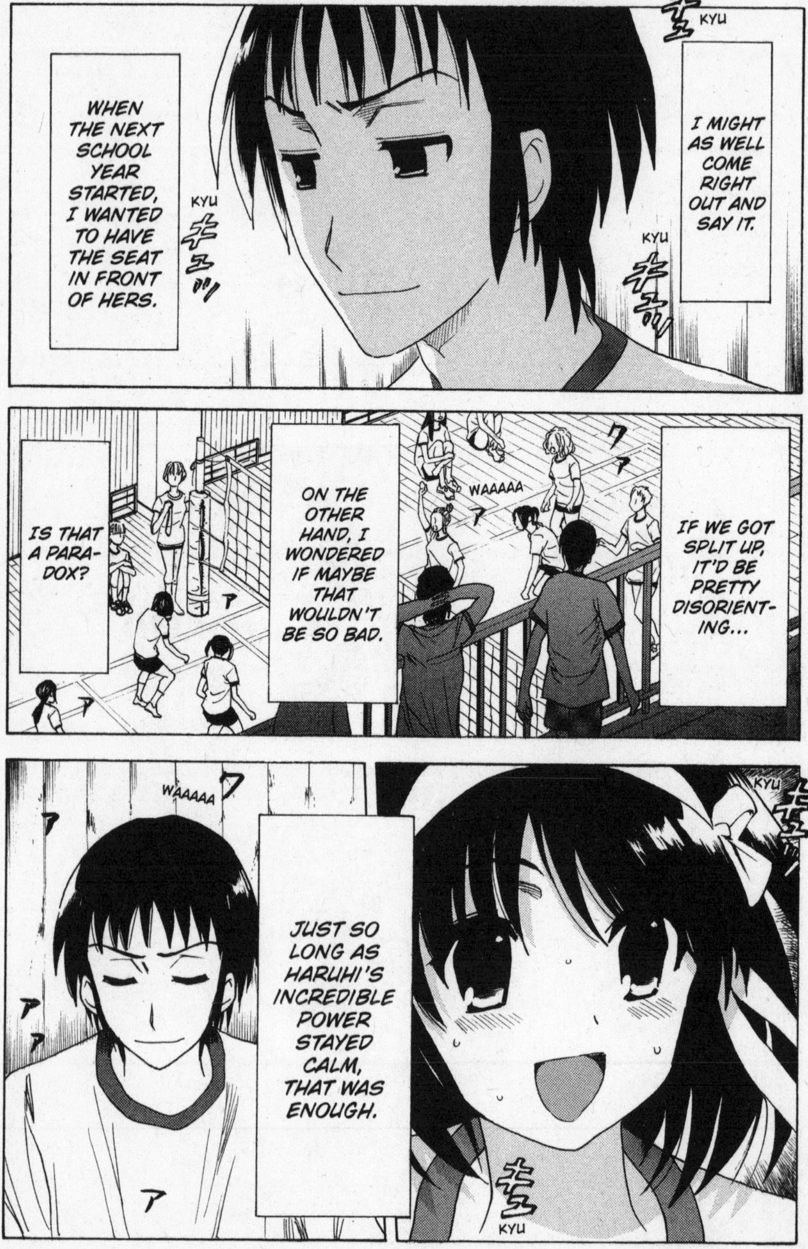
KYU
I MIGHT AS WELL COME RIGHT OUT AND SAY IT.
KYU
KYU
WHEN THE NEXT SCHOOL YEAR STARTED, I WANTED TO HAVE THE SEAT IN FRONT OF HERS.
IF WE GOT SPLIT UP, IT'D BE PRETTY DISORIENT-ING...
WAAAAA
ON THE OTHER HAND, I WONDERED IF MAYBE THAT WOULDN'T BE SO BAD.
IS THAT A PARA-DOX?
KYU
JUST SO LONG AS HARUHI'S INCREDIBLE POWER STAYED CALM, THAT WAS ENOUGH.
KYU
WAAAAA

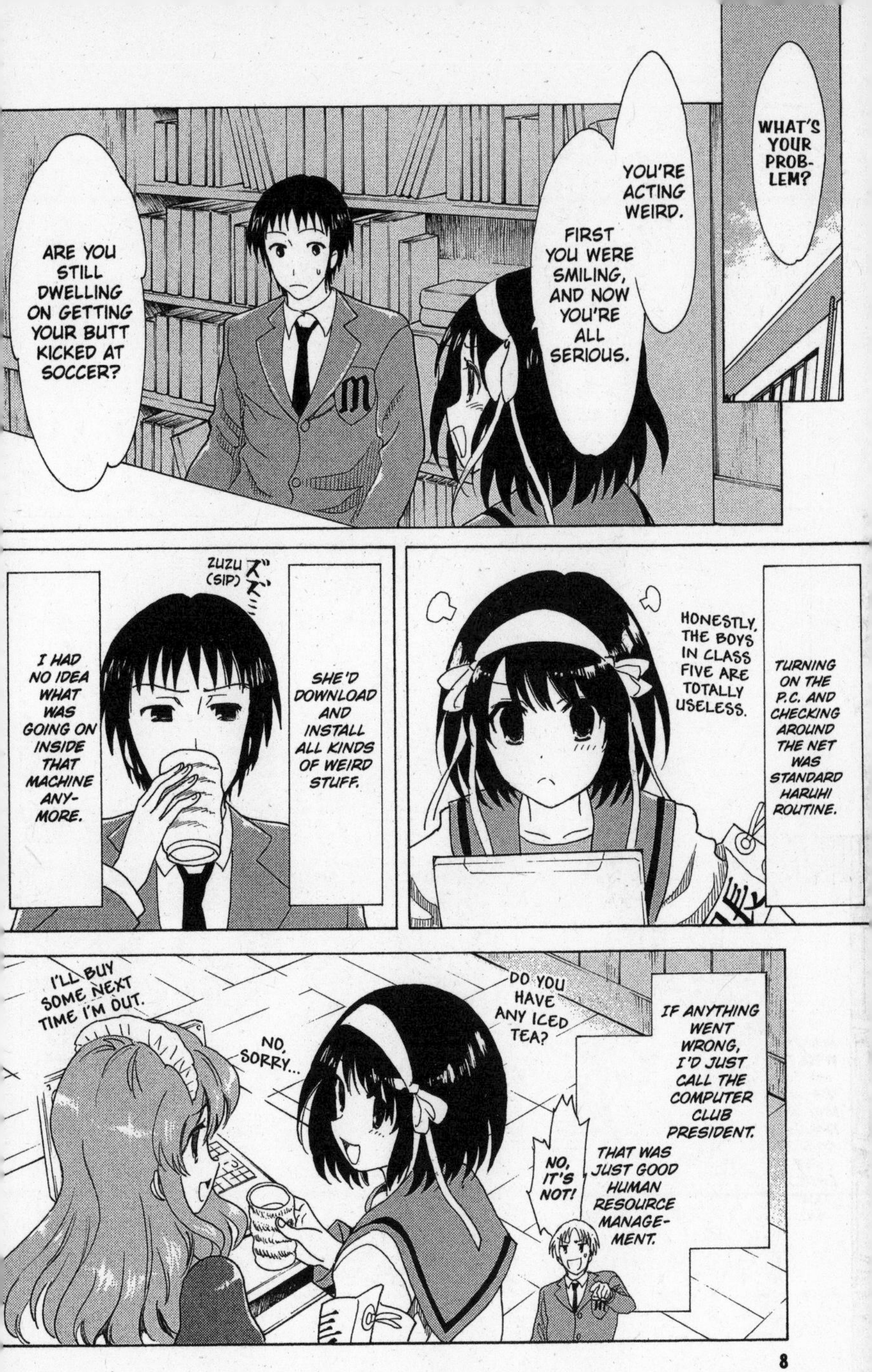
WHAT'S YOUR PROBLEM?
YOU'RE ACTING WEIRD.
FIRST YOU WERE SMILING, AND NOW YOU'RE ALL SERIOUS.
ARE YOU STILL DWELLING ON GETTING YOUR BUTT KICKED AT SOCCER?
TURNING ON THE P.C. AND CHECKING AROUND THE NET WAS STANDARD HARUHI ROUTINE.
HONESTLY, THE BOYS IN CLASS FIVE ARE TOTALLY USELESS.
SHE'D DOWNLOAD AND INSTALL ALL KINDS OF WEIRD STUFF.
ZUZU (SIP)
I HAD NO IDEA WHAT WAS GOING ON INSIDE THAT MACHINE ANY-MORE.
IF ANYTHING WENT WRONG, I'D JUST CALL THE COMPUTER CLUB PRESIDENT.
THAT WAS JUST GOOD HUMAN RESOURCE MANAGE-MENT.
NO, IT'S NOT!
DO YOU HAVE ANY ICED TEA?
NO, SORRY...
I'LL BUY SOME NEXT TIME I'M OUT.

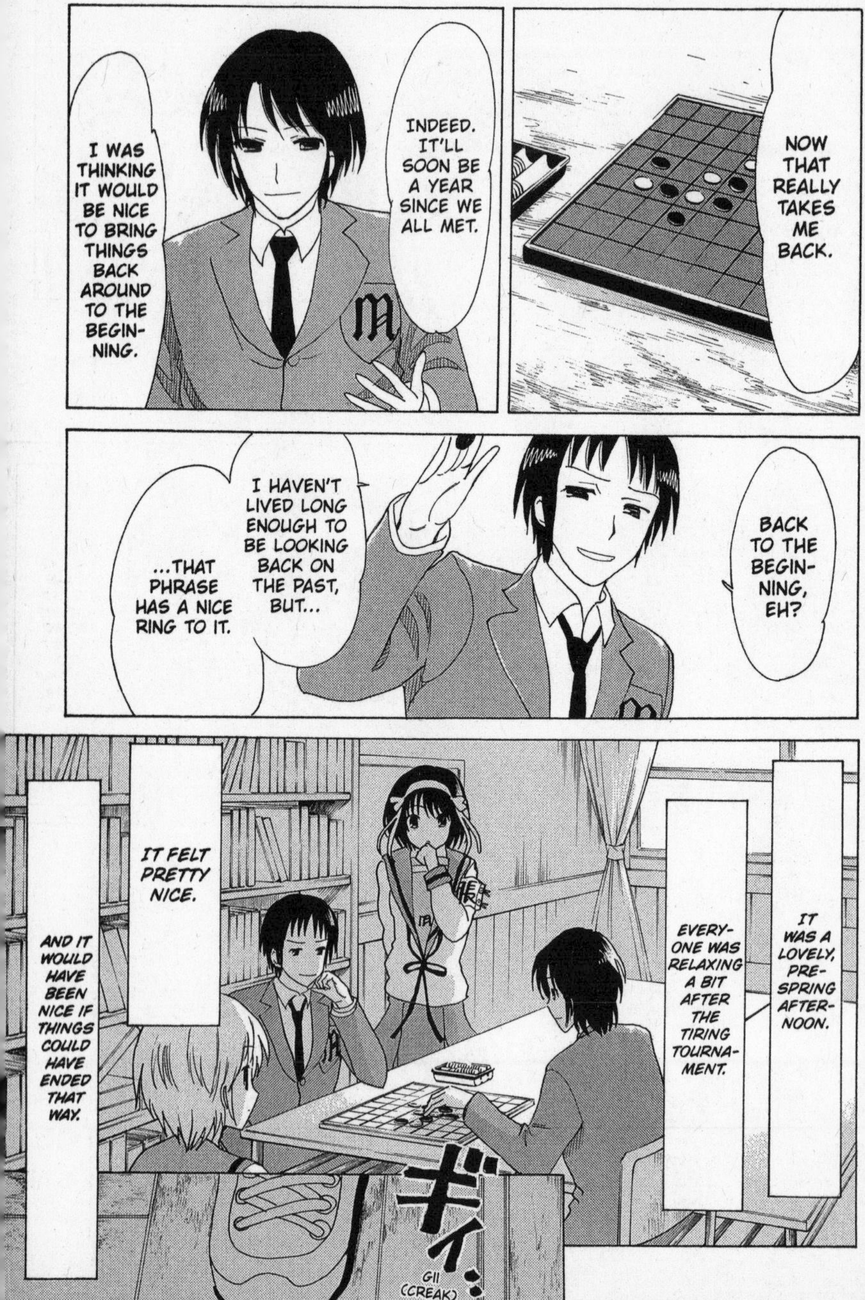
NOW THAT REALLY TAKES ME BACK.
INDEED. IT'LL SOON BE A YEAR SINCE WE ALL MET.
I WAS THINKING IT WOULD BE NICE TO BRING THINGS BACK AROUND TO THE BEGINNING.
BACK TO THE BEGINNING, EH?
I HAVEN'T LIVED LONG ENOUGH TO BE LOOKING BACK ON THE PAST, BUT...
...THAT PHRASE HAS A NICE RING TO IT.
IT WAS A LOVELY, PRE-SPRING AFTERNOON.
EVERYONE WAS RELAXING A BIT AFTER THE TIRING TOURNAMENT.
IT FELT PRETTY NICE.
AND IT WOULD HAVE BEEN NICE IF THINGS COULD HAVE ENDED THAT WAY.
ギイ…
GII (CREAK)

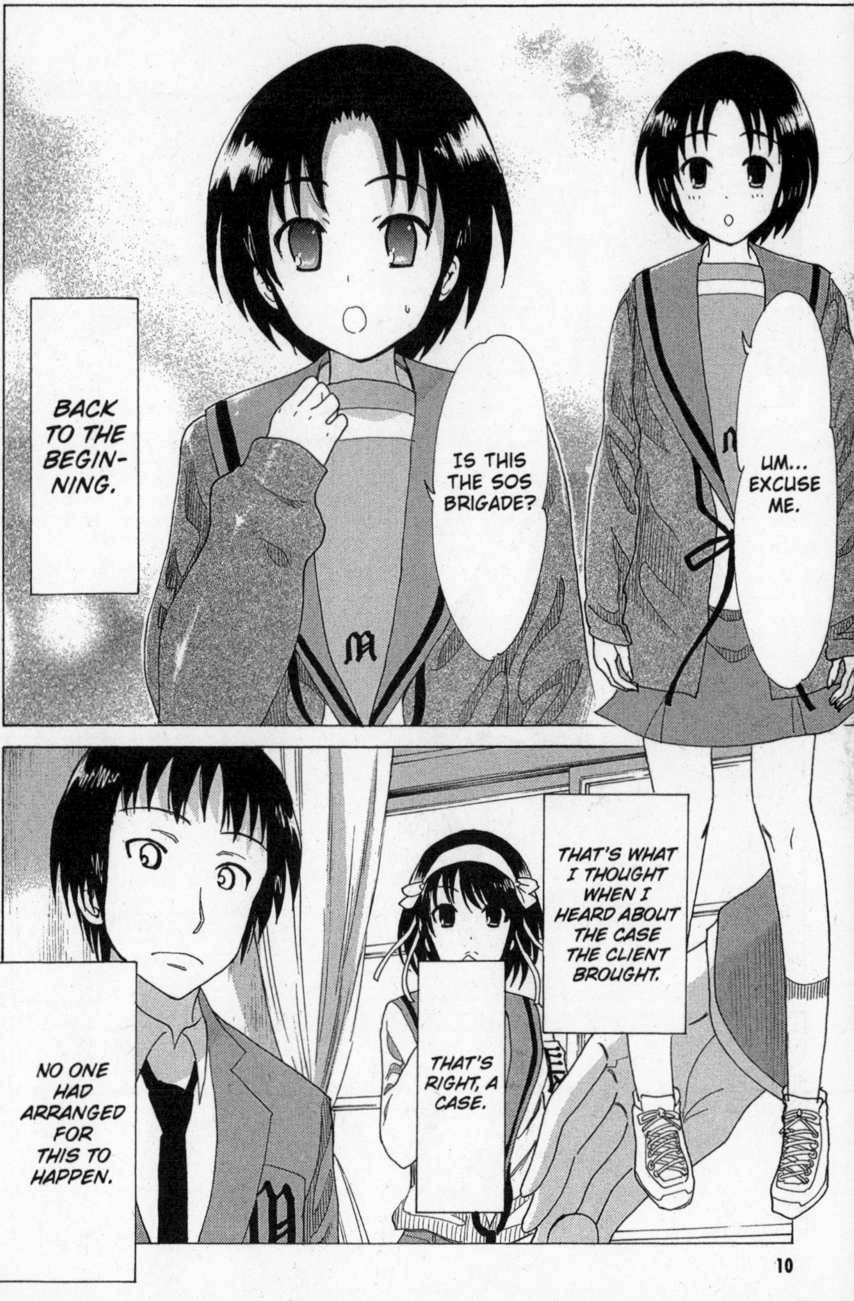
UM... EXCUSE ME.
IS THIS THE SOS BRIGADE?
BACK TO THE BEGIN-NING.
THAT'S WHAT I THOUGHT WHEN I HEARD ABOUT THE CASE THE CLIENT BROUGHT.
THAT'S RIGHT, A CASE.
NO ONE HAD ARRANGED FOR THIS TO HAPPEN.

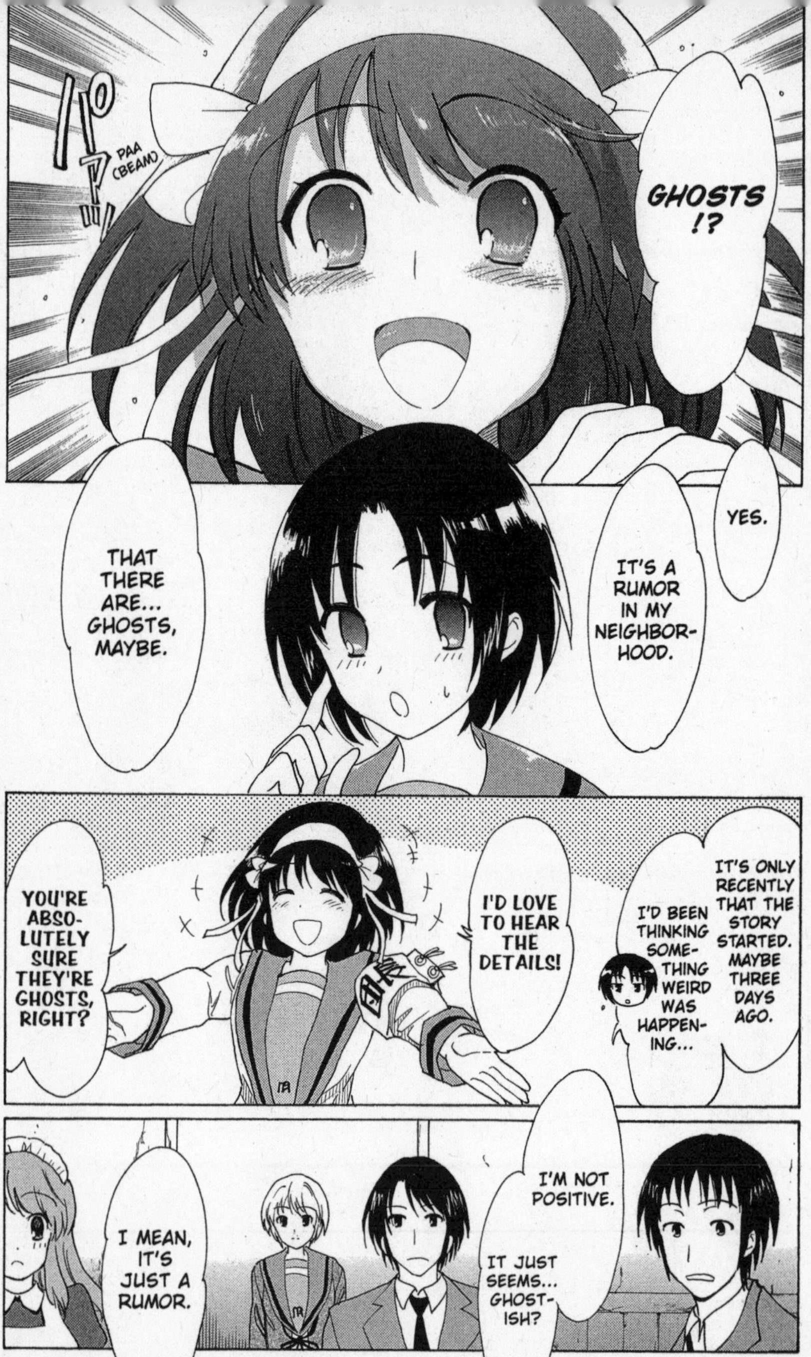
GHOSTS!?
PAA (BEAM)
YES.
IT'S A RUMOR IN MY NEIGHBOR-HOOD.
THAT THERE ARE... GHOSTS, MAYBE.
IT'S ONLY RECENTLY THAT THE STORY STARTED. MAYBE THREE DAYS AGO.
I'D BEEN THINKING SOME-THING WEIRD WAS HAPPEN-ING...
I'D LOVE TO HEAR THE DETAILS!
YOU'RE ABSO-LUTELY SURE THEY'RE GHOSTS, RIGHT?
I'M NOT POSITIVE.
IT JUST SEEMS... GHOST-ISH?
I MEAN, IT'S JUST A RUMOR.

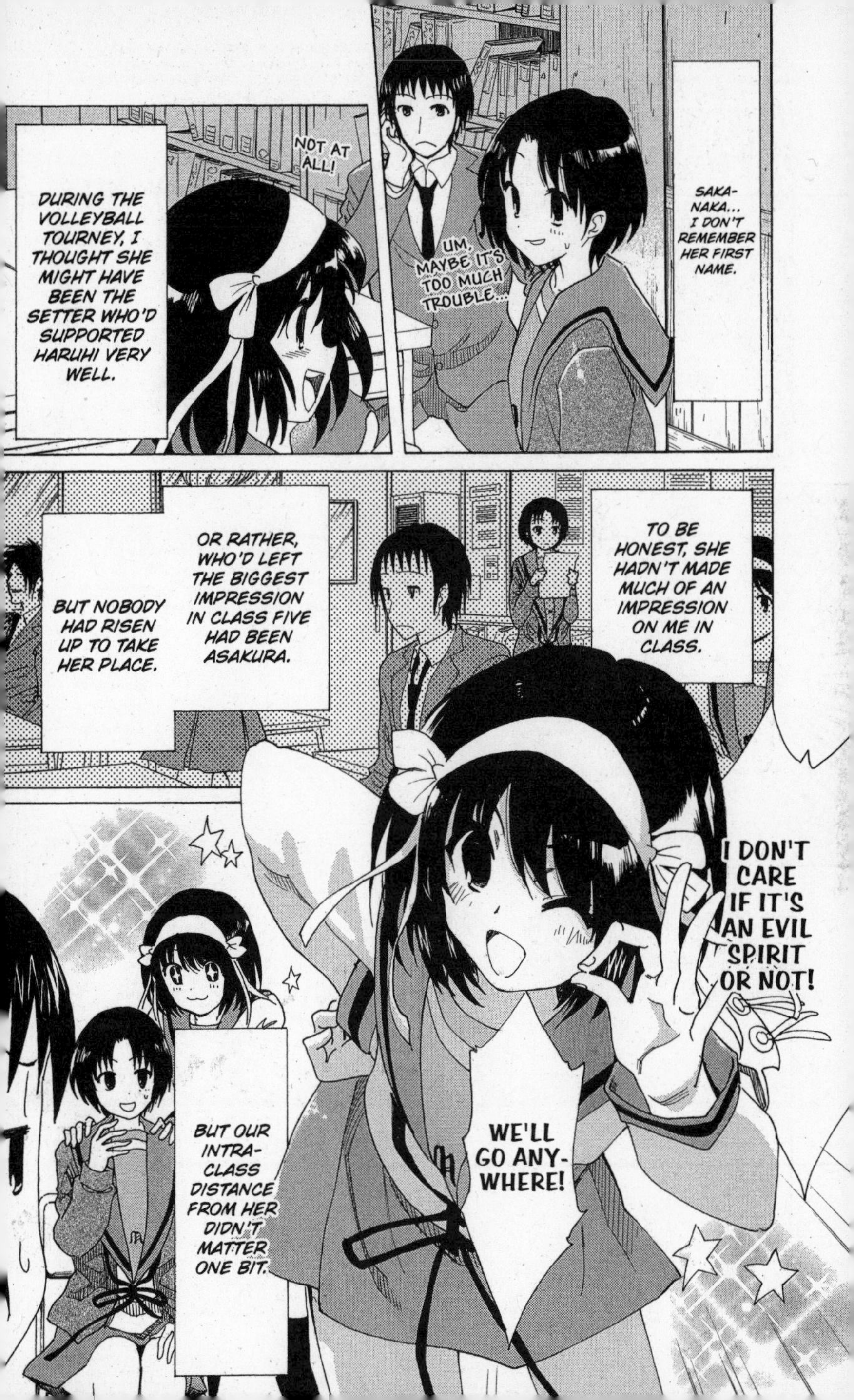
SAKA-NAKA... I DON'T REMEMBER HER FIRST NAME.
UM, MAYBE IT'S TOO MUCH TROUBLE...
NOT AT ALL!
DURING THE VOLLEYBALL TOURNEY, I THOUGHT SHE MIGHT HAVE BEEN THE SETTER WHO'D SUPPORTED HARUHI VERY WELL.
TO BE HONEST, SHE HADN'T MADE MUCH OF AN IMPRESSION ON ME IN CLASS.
OR RATHER, WHO'D LEFT THE BIGGEST IMPRESSION IN CLASS FIVE HAD BEEN ASAKURA.
BUT NOBODY HAD RISEN UP TO TAKE HER PLACE.
I DON'T CARE IF IT'S AN EVIL SPIRIT OR NOT!
WE'LL GO ANY-WHERE!
BUT OUR INTRA-CLASS DISTANCE FROM HER DIDN'T MATTER ONE BIT.

FLYER: SOS BRIGADE DECLARATION OF PRINCIPLES. WE, THE SOS BRIGADE, ARE SEARCHING FOR THE WORLD'S MYSTERIES. PEOPLE WHO'VE EXPERIENCED MYSTERIOUS PHENOMENA IN THE PAST, ARE CURRENTLY EXPERIENCING MYSTERIOUS PHENOMENA, OR PLAN TO EXPERIENCE MYSTERIOUS PHENOMENA IN THE FUTURE SHOULD COME TO US FOR A CONSULTATION. WE WILL HELP YOU FIND RESOLUTION.

SFX: GOSO (RUMMAGE)

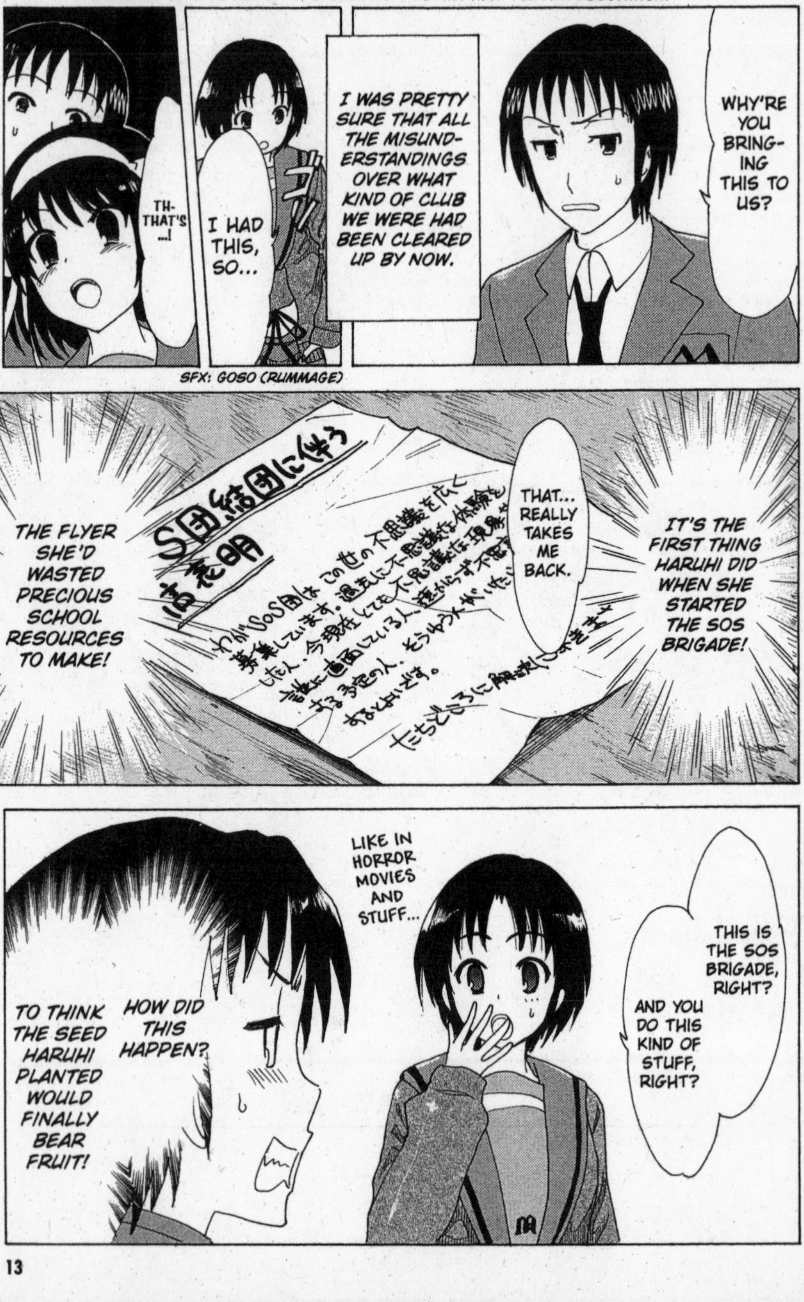
WHY'RE YOU BRINGING THIS TO US?
I WAS PRETTY SURE THAT ALL THE MISUNDERSTANDINGS OVER WHAT KIND OF CLUB WE WERE HAD BEEN CLEARED UP BY NOW.
I HAD THIS, SO...
TH-THAT'S...!
IT'S THE FIRST THING HARUHI DID WHEN SHE STARTED THE SOS BRIGADE!
THAT... REALLY TAKES ME BACK.
THE FLYER SHE'D WASTED PRECIOUS SCHOOL RESOURCES TO MAKE!
THIS IS THE SOS BRIGADE, RIGHT?
AND YOU DO THIS KIND OF STUFF, RIGHT?
LIKE IN HORROR MOVIES AND STUFF...
HOW DID THIS HAPPEN?
TO THINK THE SEED HARUHI PLANTED WOULD FINALLY BEAR FRUIT!

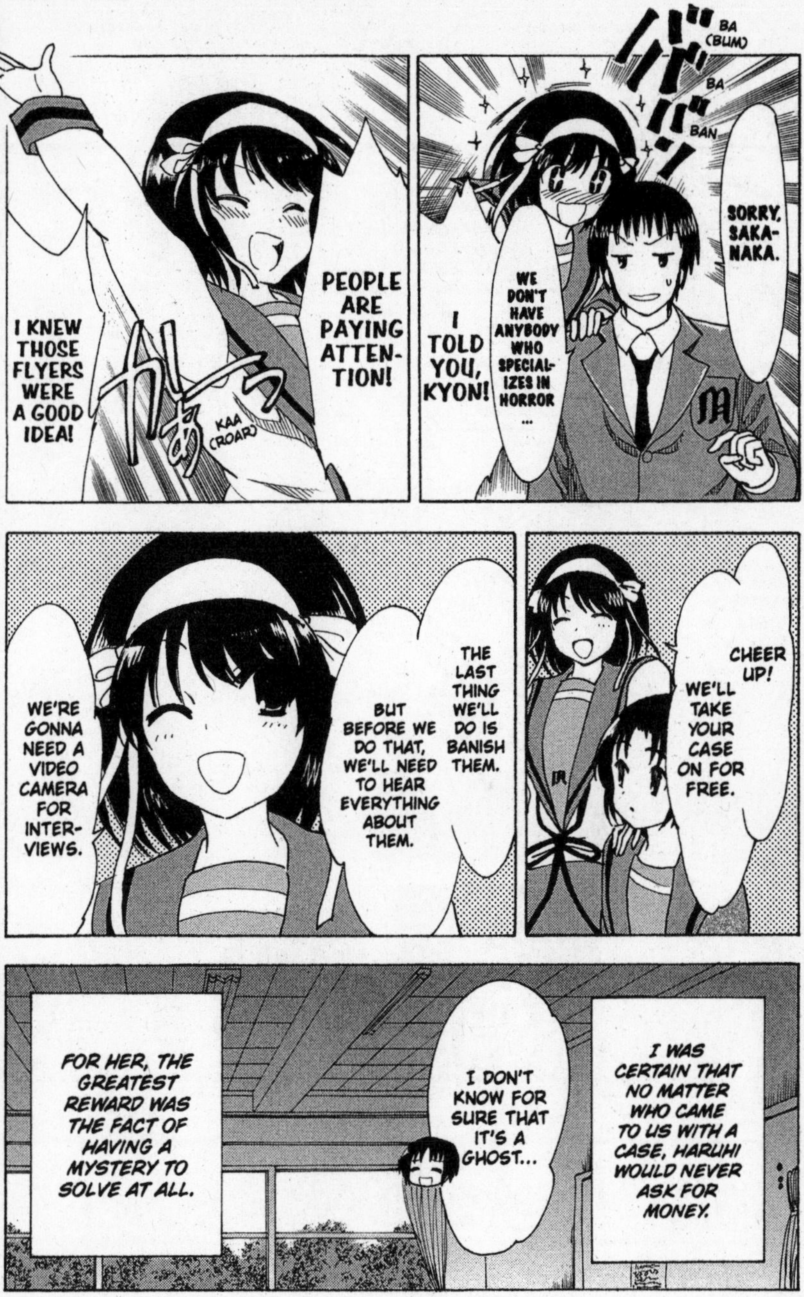
BA (BUM)
BA
BAN
SORRY, SAKANAKA.
WE DON'T HAVE ANYBODY WHO SPECIALIZES IN HORROR...
I TOLD YOU, KYON!
PEOPLE ARE PAYING ATTENTION!
I KNEW THOSE FLYERS WERE A GOOD IDEA!
KAA (ROAR)
CHEER UP!
WE'LL TAKE YOUR CASE ON FOR FREE.
THE LAST THING WE'LL DO IS BANISH THEM.
BUT BEFORE WE DO THAT, WE'LL NEED TO HEAR EVERYTHING ABOUT THEM.
WE'RE GONNA NEED A VIDEO CAMERA FOR INTERVIEWS.
I WAS CERTAIN THAT NO MATTER WHO CAME TO US WITH A CASE, HARUHI WOULD NEVER ASK FOR MONEY.
I DON'T KNOW FOR SURE THAT IT'S A GHOST...
FOR HER, THE GREATEST REWARD WAS THE FACT OF HAVING A MYSTERY TO SOLVE AT ALL.

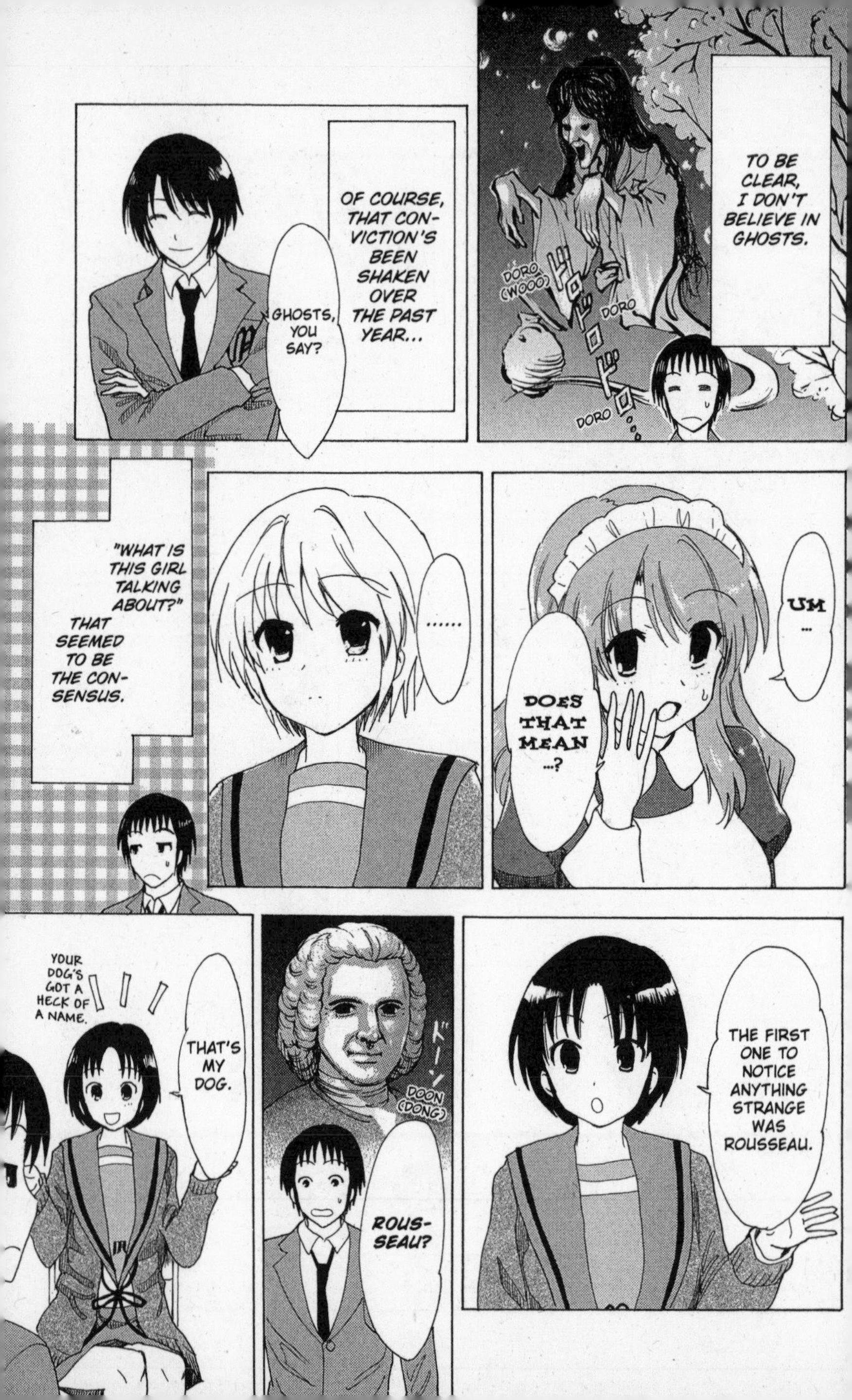
TO BE CLEAR, I DON'T BELIEVE IN GHOSTS.
DORO (WOOO)
DORO
DORO
OF COURSE, THAT CONVICTION'S BEEN SHAKEN OVER THE PAST YEAR...
GHOSTS, YOU SAY?
UM ...
DOES THAT MEAN ...?
......
"WHAT IS THIS GIRL TALKING ABOUT?" THAT SEEMED TO BE THE CONSENSUS.
THE FIRST ONE TO NOTICE ANYTHING STRANGE WAS ROUSSEAU.
DOON (DONG)
ROUSSEAU?
THAT'S MY DOG.
YOUR DOG'S GOT A HECK OF A NAME.

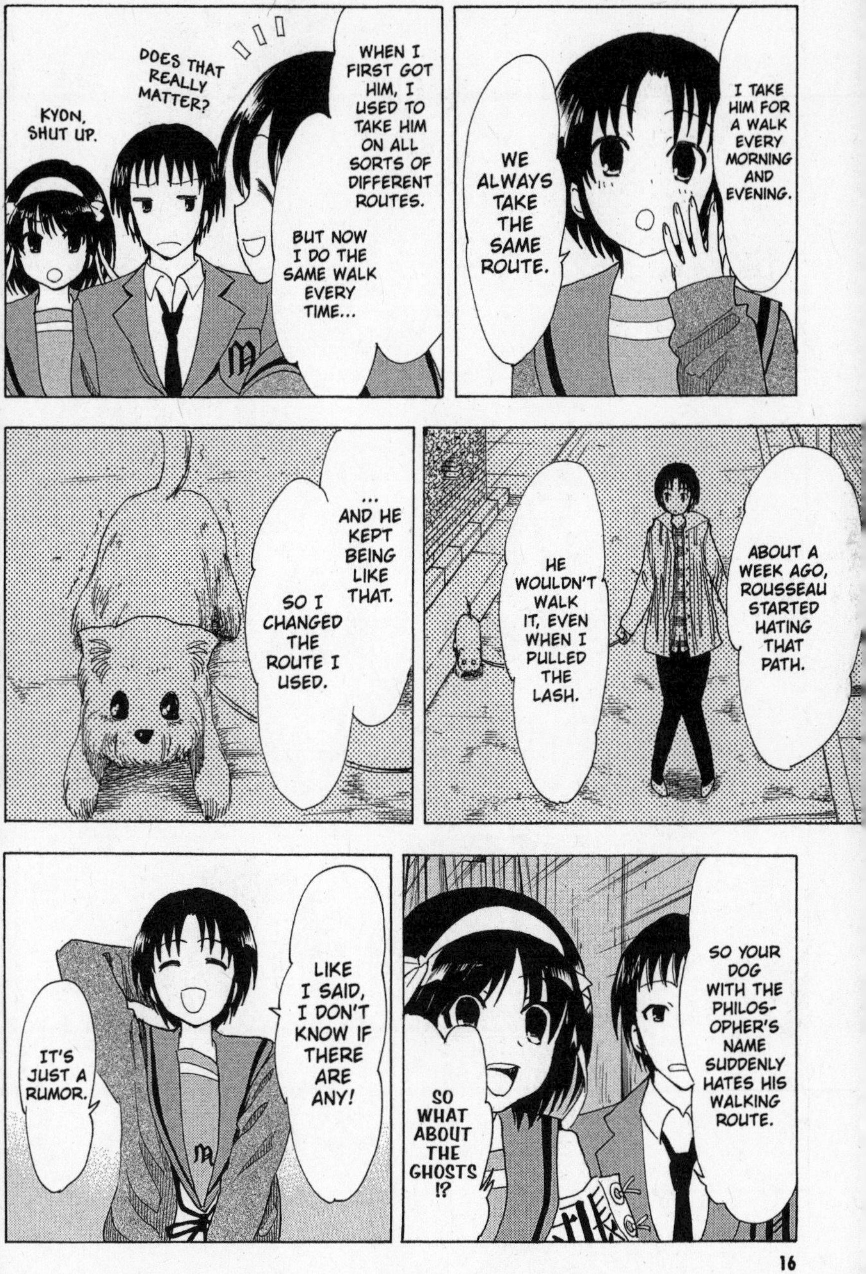
I TAKE HIM FOR A WALK EVERY MORNING AND EVENING.
WE ALWAYS TAKE THE SAME ROUTE.
WHEN I FIRST GOT HIM, I USED TO TAKE HIM ON ALL SORTS OF DIFFERENT ROUTES.
BUT NOW I DO THE SAME WALK EVERY TIME...
DOES THAT REALLY MATTER?
KYON, SHUT UP.
ABOUT A WEEK AGO, ROUSSEAU STARTED HATING THAT PATH.
HE WOULDN'T WALK IT, EVEN WHEN I PULLED THE LASH.
... AND HE KEPT BEING LIKE THAT.
SO I CHANGED THE ROUTE I USED.
SO YOUR DOG WITH THE PHILOS-OPHER'S NAME SUDDENLY HATES HIS WALKING ROUTE.
SO WHAT ABOUT THE GHOSTS !?
LIKE I SAID, I DON'T KNOW IF THERE ARE ANY!
IT'S JUST A RUMOR.

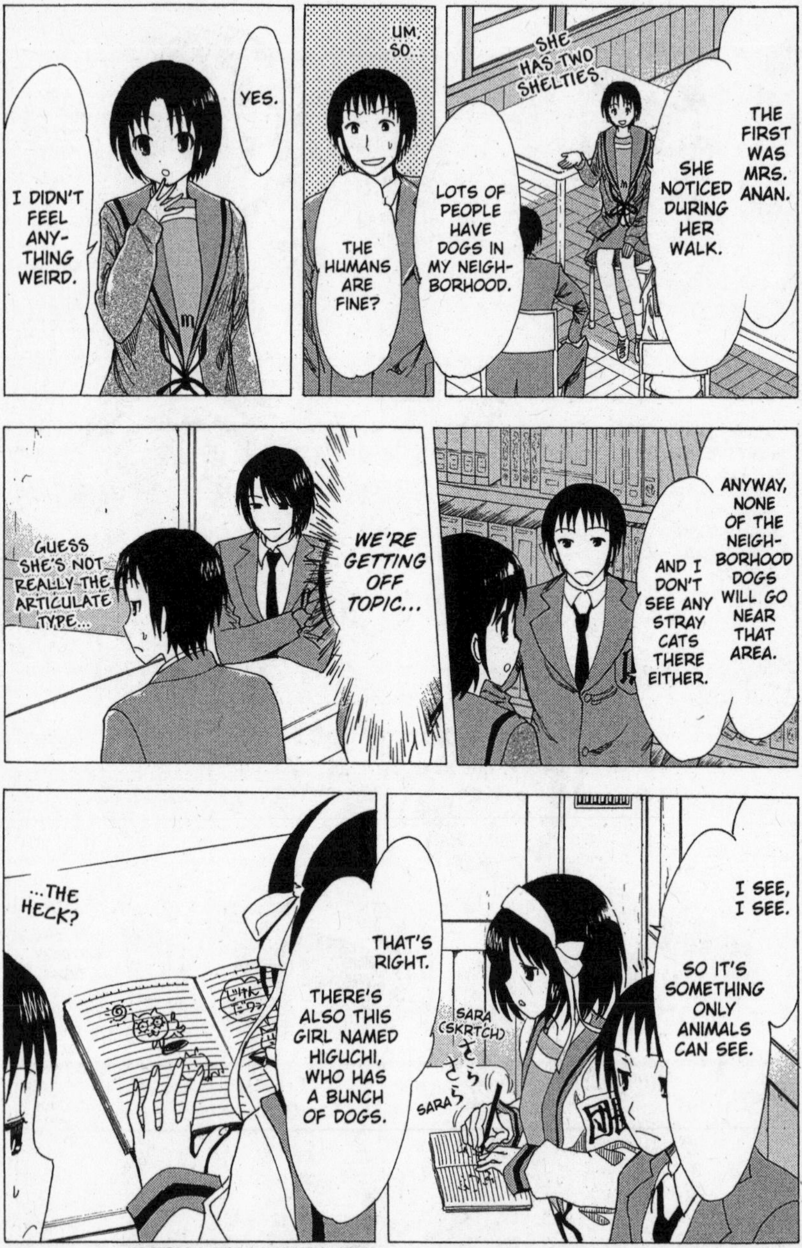
THE FIRST WAS MRS. ANAN.
SHE NOTICED DURING HER WALK.
SHE HAS TWO SHELTIES.
UM, SO...
LOTS OF PEOPLE HAVE DOGS IN MY NEIGHBORHOOD.
THE HUMANS ARE FINE?
YES.
I DIDN'T FEEL ANYTHING WEIRD.
ANYWAY, NONE OF THE NEIGHBORHOOD DOGS WILL GO NEAR THAT AREA.
AND I DON'T SEE ANY STRAY CATS THERE EITHER.
WE'RE GETTING OFF TOPIC...
GUESS SHE'S NOT REALLY THE ARTICULATE TYPE...
I SEE, I SEE.
SO IT'S SOMETHING ONLY ANIMALS CAN SEE.
SARA (SKRTCH)
SARA
THAT'S RIGHT.
THERE'S ALSO THIS GIRL NAMED HIGUCHI, WHO HAS A BUNCH OF DOGS.
...THE HECK?

NOTEBOOK: IT'S A MYSTERY, WOOF!

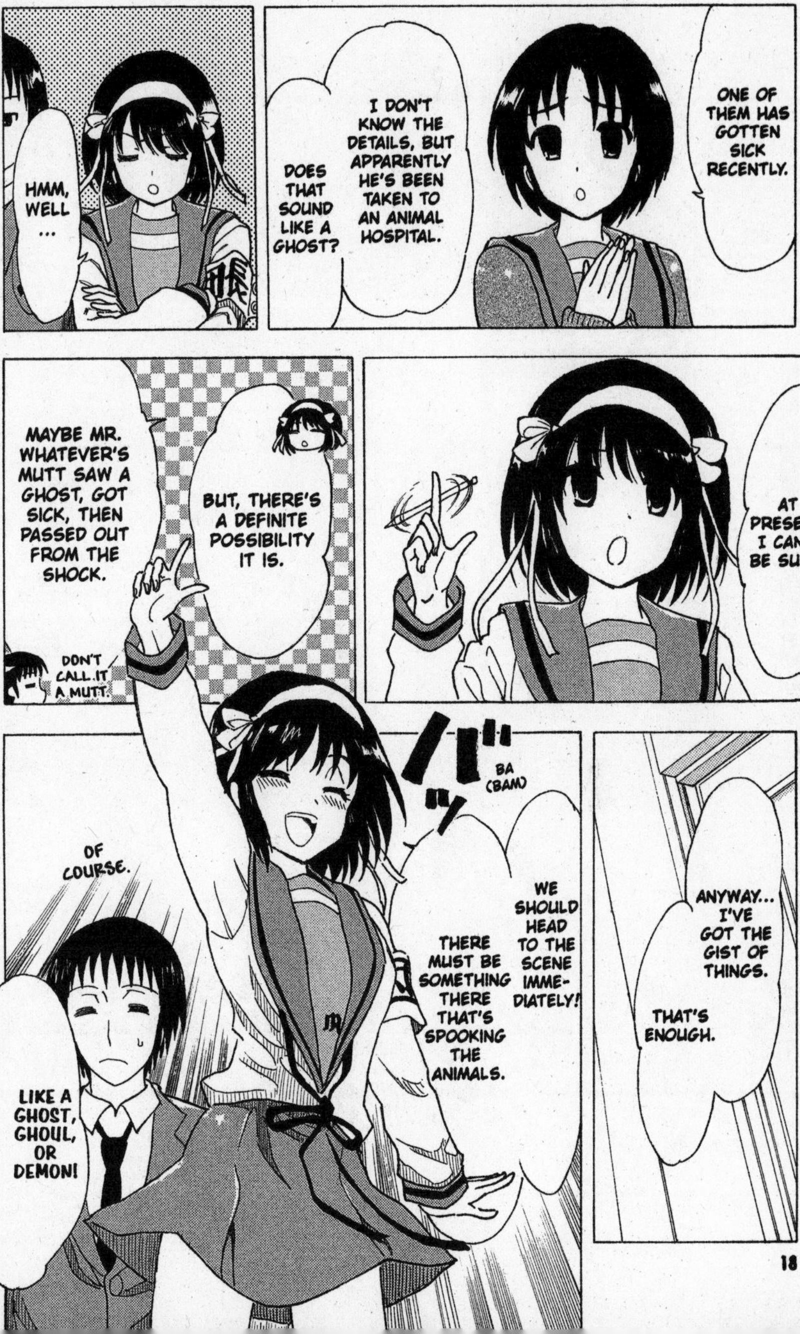
ONE OF THEM HAS GOTTEN SICK RECENTLY.
I DON'T KNOW THE DETAILS, BUT APPARENTLY HE'S BEEN TAKEN TO AN ANIMAL HOSPITAL.
DOES THAT SOUND LIKE A GHOST?
HMM, WELL ...
AT PRESENT, I CAN'T BE SURE.
BUT, THERE'S A DEFINITE POSSIBILITY IT IS.
MAYBE MR. WHATEVER'S MUTT SAW A GHOST, GOT SICK, THEN PASSED OUT FROM THE SHOCK.
DON'T CALL IT A MUTT.
ANYWAY... I'VE GOT THE GIST OF THINGS.
THAT'S ENOUGH.
BA (BAM)
WE SHOULD HEAD TO THE SCENE IMMEDIATELY!
THERE MUST BE SOMETHING THERE THAT'S SPOOKING THE ANIMALS.
OF COURSE.
LIKE A GHOST, GHOUL, OR DEMON!

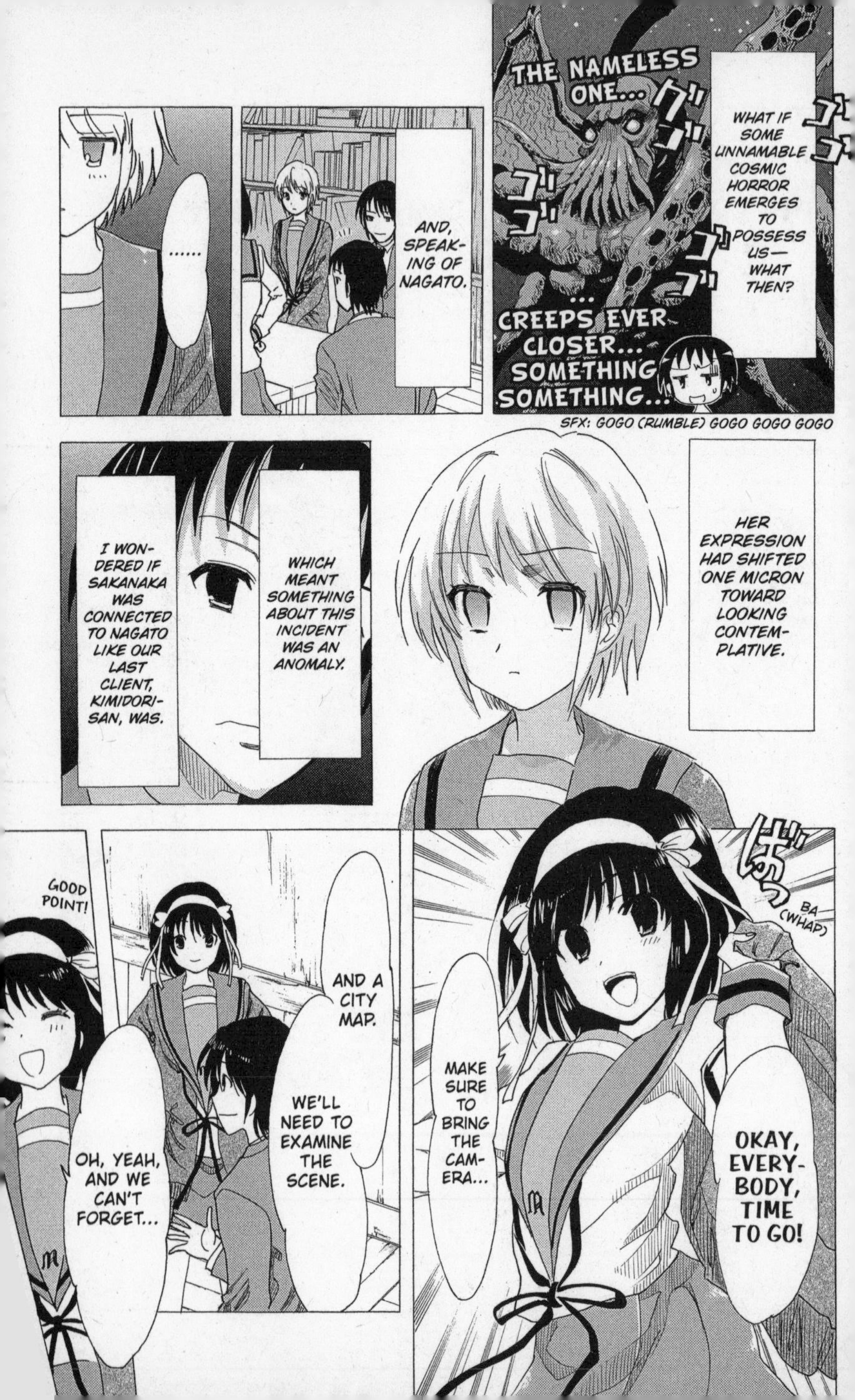
WHAT IF SOME UNNAMABLE COSMIC HORROR EMERGES TO POSSESS US—WHAT THEN?
THE NAMELESS ONE...
...CREEPS EVER CLOSER... SOMETHING SOMETHING...
SFX: GOGO (RUMBLE) GOGO GOGO GOGO
AND, SPEAKING OF NAGATO.
......
HER EXPRESSION HAD SHIFTED ONE MICRON TOWARD LOOKING CONTEMPLATIVE.
WHICH MEANT SOMETHING ABOUT THIS INCIDENT WAS AN ANOMALY.
I WONDERED IF SAKANAKA WAS CONNECTED TO NAGATO LIKE OUR LAST CLIENT, KIMIDORI-SAN, WAS.
BA (WHAP)
OKAY, EVERYBODY, TIME TO GO!
MAKE SURE TO BRING THE CAMERA...
AND A CITY MAP.
WE'LL NEED TO EXAMINE THE SCENE.
GOOD POINT!
OH, YEAH, AND WE CAN'T FORGET...

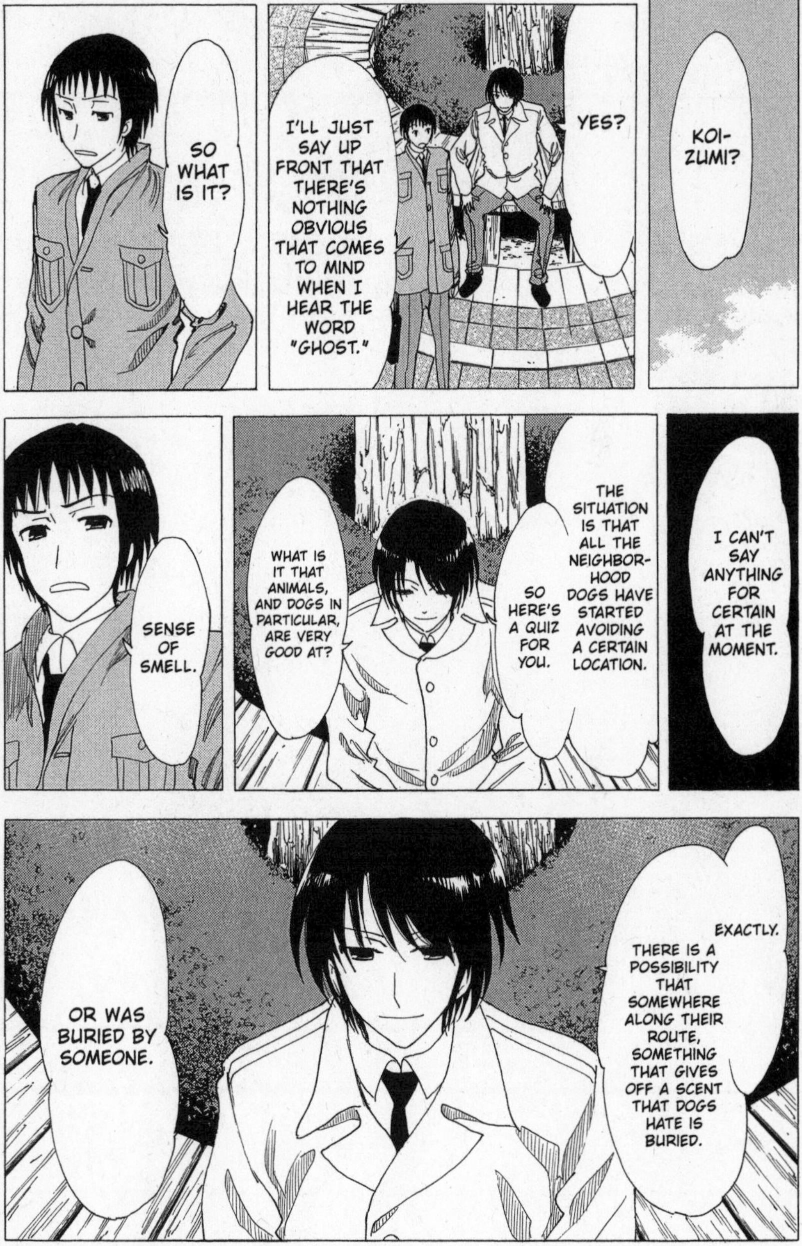
KOI-ZUMI?
YES?
I'LL JUST SAY UP FRONT THAT THERE'S NOTHING OBVIOUS THAT COMES TO MIND WHEN I HEAR THE WORD "GHOST."
SO WHAT IS IT?
I CAN'T SAY ANYTHING FOR CERTAIN AT THE MOMENT.
THE SITUATION IS THAT ALL THE NEIGHBOR-HOOD DOGS HAVE STARTED AVOIDING A CERTAIN LOCATION.
SO HERE'S A QUIZ FOR YOU.
WHAT IS IT THAT ANIMALS, AND DOGS IN PARTICULAR, ARE VERY GOOD AT?
SENSE OF SMELL.
EXACTLY.
THERE IS A POSSIBILITY THAT SOMEWHERE ALONG THEIR ROUTE, SOMETHING THAT GIVES OFF A SCENT THAT DOGS HATE IS BURIED.
OR WAS BURIED BY SOMEONE.

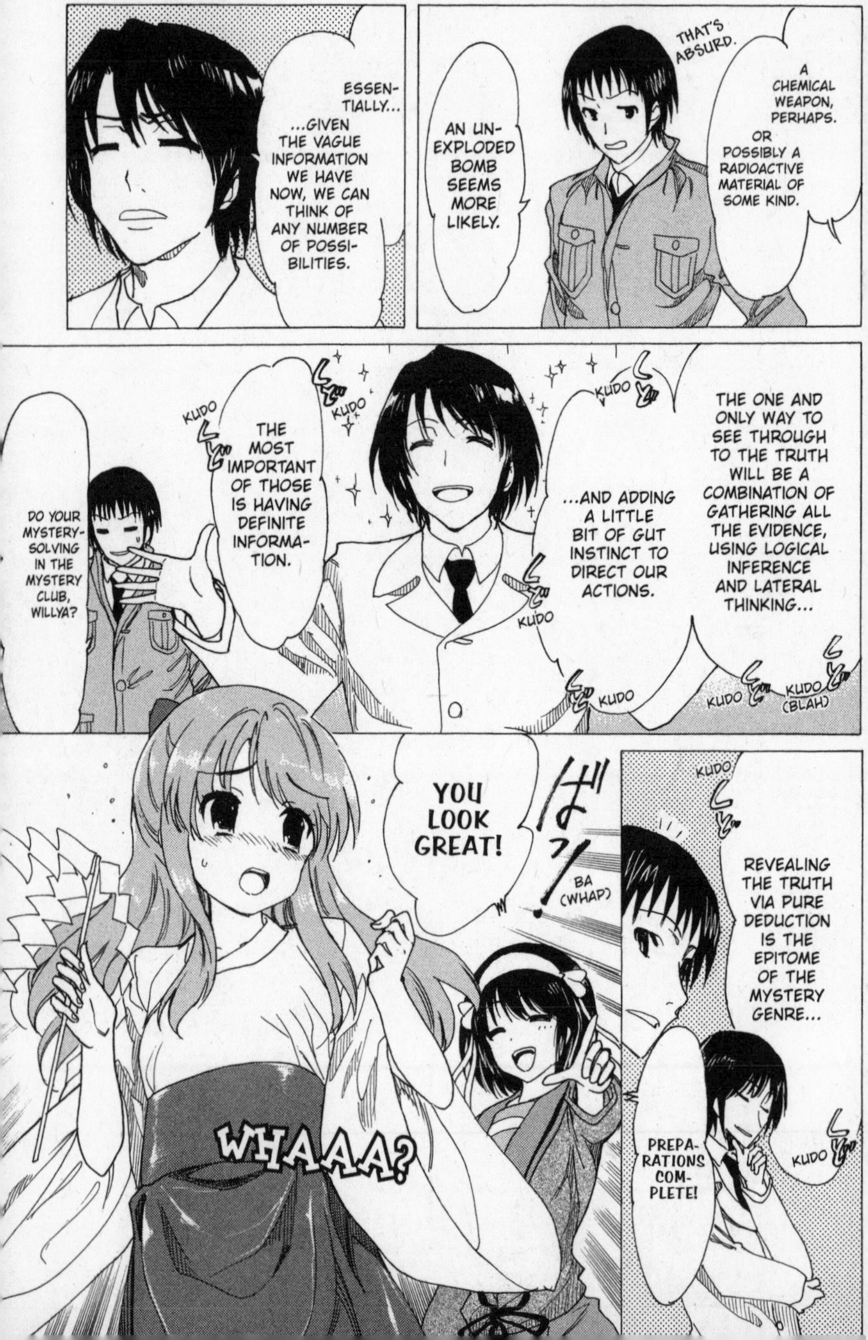
THAT'S ABSURD.
A CHEMICAL WEAPON, PERHAPS.
OR POSSIBLY A RADIOACTIVE MATERIAL OF SOME KIND.
AN UN-EXPLODED BOMB SEEMS MORE LIKELY.
ESSEN-TIALLY...
...GIVEN THE VAGUE INFORMATION WE HAVE NOW, WE CAN THINK OF ANY NUMBER OF POSSI-BILITIES.
THE ONE AND ONLY WAY TO SEE THROUGH TO THE TRUTH WILL BE A COMBINATION OF GATHERING ALL THE EVIDENCE, USING LOGICAL INFERENCE AND LATERAL THINKING...
KUDO (BLAH)
KUDO
KUDO
...AND ADDING A LITTLE BIT OF GUT INSTINCT TO DIRECT OUR ACTIONS.
KUDO
KUDO
KUDO
THE MOST IMPORTANT OF THOSE IS HAVING DEFINITE INFORMA-TION.
KUDO
DO YOUR MYSTERY-SOLVING IN THE MYSTERY CLUB, WILLYA?
KUDO
REVEALING THE TRUTH VIA PURE DEDUCTION IS THE EPITOME OF THE MYSTERY GENRE...
KUDO
PREPA-RATIONS COM-PLETE!
BA (WHAP)
YOU LOOK GREAT!
WHAAAA?

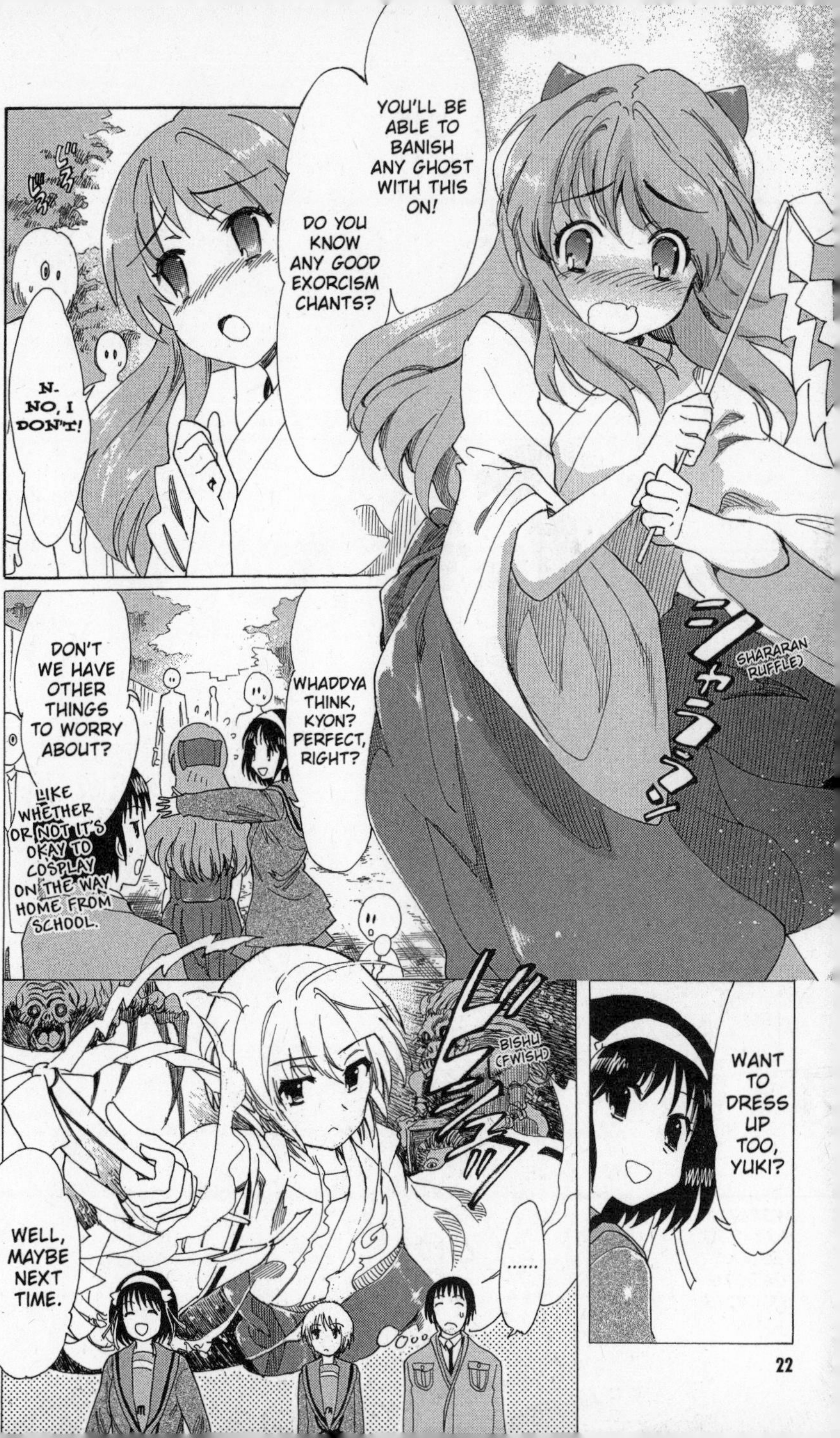
YOU'LL BE ABLE TO BANISH ANY GHOST WITH THIS ON!
DO YOU KNOW ANY GOOD EXORCISM CHANTS?
N- NO, I DON'T!
SHARARAN (RUFFLE)
WHADDYA THINK, KYON? PERFECT, RIGHT?
DON'T WE HAVE OTHER THINGS TO WORRY ABOUT?
LIKE WHETHER OR NOT IT'S OKAY TO COSPLAY ON THE WAY HOME FROM SCHOOL.
WANT TO DRESS UP TOO, YUKI?
BISHU (FWISH)
......
WELL, MAYBE NEXT TIME.

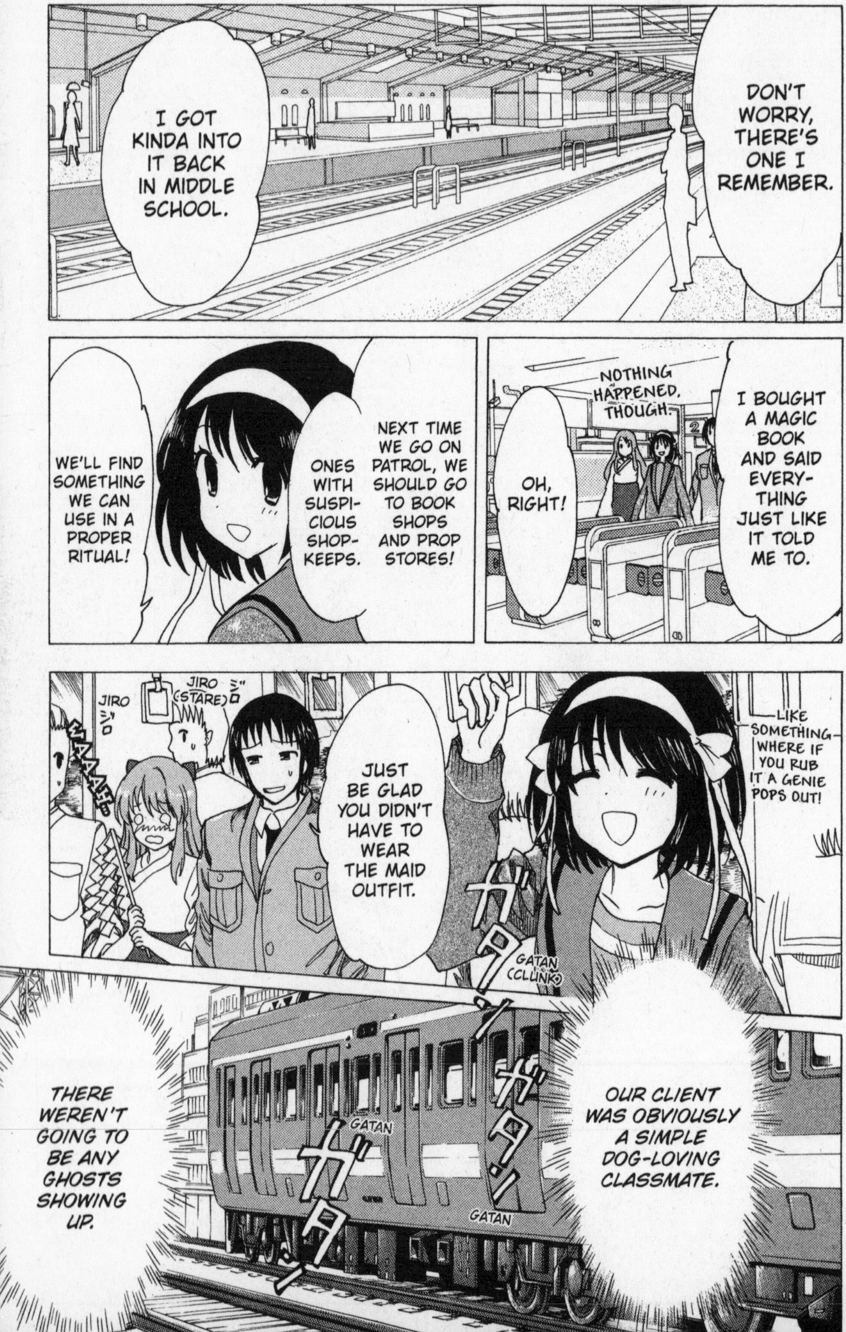
DON'T WORRY, THERE'S ONE I REMEMBER.
I GOT KINDA INTO IT BACK IN MIDDLE SCHOOL.
I BOUGHT A MAGIC BOOK AND SAID EVERYTHING JUST LIKE IT TOLD ME TO.
NOTHING HAPPENED, THOUGH.
OH, RIGHT!
NEXT TIME WE GO ON PATROL, WE SHOULD GO TO BOOK SHOPS AND PROP STORES!
ONES WITH SUSPICIOUS SHOPKEEPS.
WE'LL FIND SOMETHING WE CAN USE IN A PROPER RITUAL!
LIKE SOMETHING WHERE IF YOU RUB IT A GENIE POPS OUT!
JUST BE GLAD YOU DIDN'T HAVE TO WEAR THE MAID OUTFIT.
JIRO (STARE)
JIRO
GATAN (CLUNK)
OUR CLIENT WAS OBVIOUSLY A SIMPLE DOG-LOVING CLASSMATE.
GATAN
GATAN
THERE WEREN'T GOING TO BE ANY GHOSTS SHOWING UP.

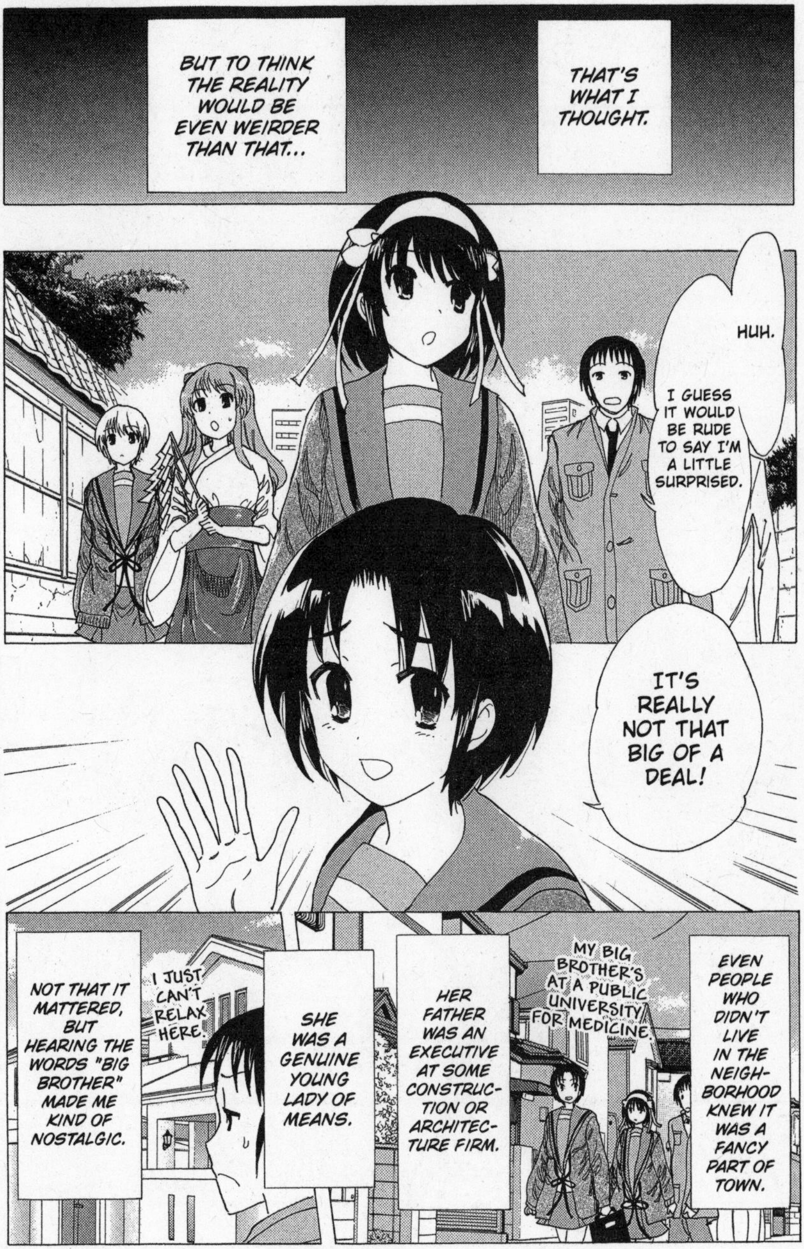
THAT'S WHAT I THOUGHT.
BUT TO THINK THE REALITY WOULD BE EVEN WEIRDER THAN THAT...
HUH.
I GUESS IT WOULD BE RUDE TO SAY I'M A LITTLE SURPRISED.
IT'S REALLY NOT THAT BIG OF A DEAL!
EVEN PEOPLE WHO DIDN'T LIVE IN THE NEIGHBORHOOD KNEW IT WAS A FANCY PART OF TOWN.
MY BIG BROTHER'S AT A PUBLIC UNIVERSITY FOR MEDICINE.
HER FATHER WAS AN EXECUTIVE AT SOME CONSTRUCTION OR ARCHITECTURE FIRM.
SHE WAS A GENUINE YOUNG LADY OF MEANS.
I JUST CAN'T RELAX HERE.
NOT THAT IT MATTERED, BUT HEARING THE WORDS "BIG BROTHER" MADE ME KIND OF NOSTALGIC.

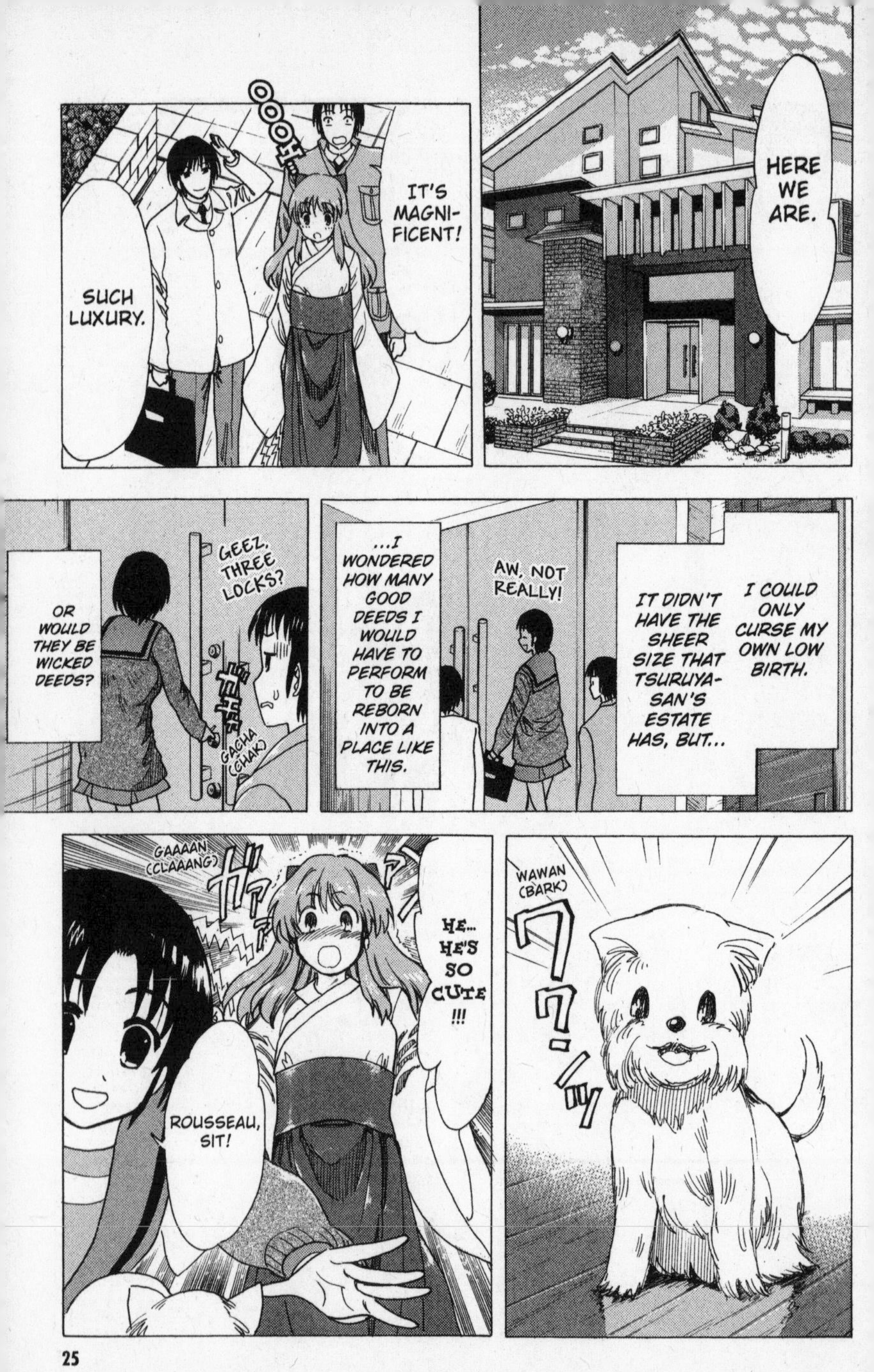
HERE WE ARE.
OOOOH
IT'S MAGNI-FICENT!
SUCH LUXURY.
IT DIDN'T HAVE THE SHEER SIZE THAT TSURUYA-SAN'S ESTATE HAS, BUT...
I COULD ONLY CURSE MY OWN LOW BIRTH.
AW, NOT REALLY!
...I WONDERED HOW MANY GOOD DEEDS I WOULD HAVE TO PERFORM TO BE REBORN INTO A PLACE LIKE THIS.
GEEZ, THREE LOCKS?
GACHA (CHAK)
OR WOULD THEY BE WICKED DEEDS?
WAWAN (BARK)
HE... HE'S SO CUTE!!!
GAAAAN (CLAAANG)
ROUSSEAU, SIT!

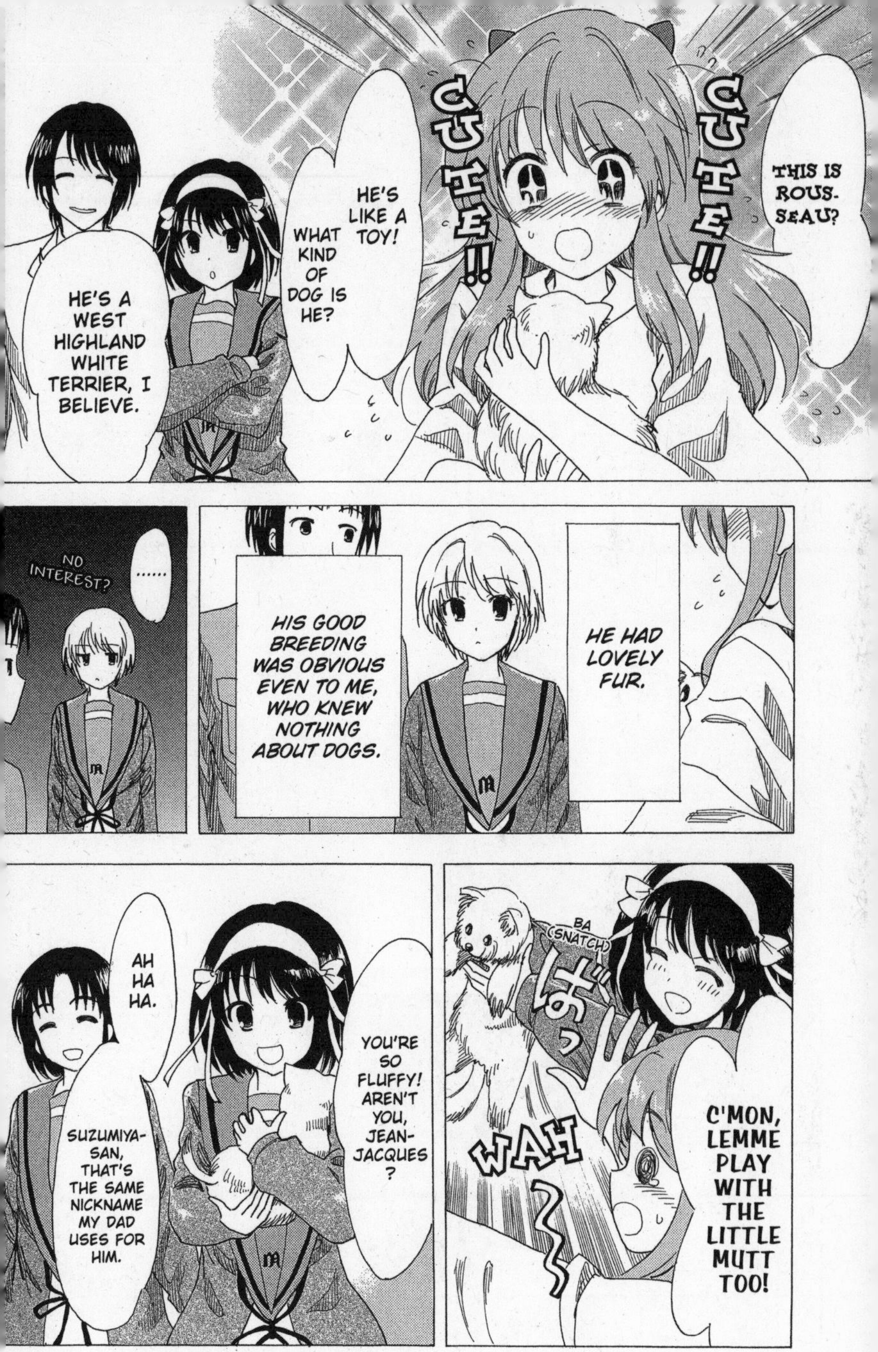
THIS IS ROUS-SEAU?
CUTE!!
CUTE!!
HE'S LIKE A TOY!
WHAT KIND OF DOG IS HE?
HE'S A WEST HIGHLAND WHITE TERRIER, I BELIEVE.
HE HAD LOVELY FUR.
HIS GOOD BREEDING WAS OBVIOUS EVEN TO ME, WHO KNEW NOTHING ABOUT DOGS.
......
NO INTEREST?
C'MON, LEMME PLAY WITH THE LITTLE MUTT TOO!
BA (SNATCH)
ばっ
WAH
YOU'RE SO FLUFFY! AREN'T YOU, JEAN-JACQUES?
AH HA HA.
SUZUMIYA-SAN, THAT'S THE SAME NICKNAME MY DAD USES FOR HIM.

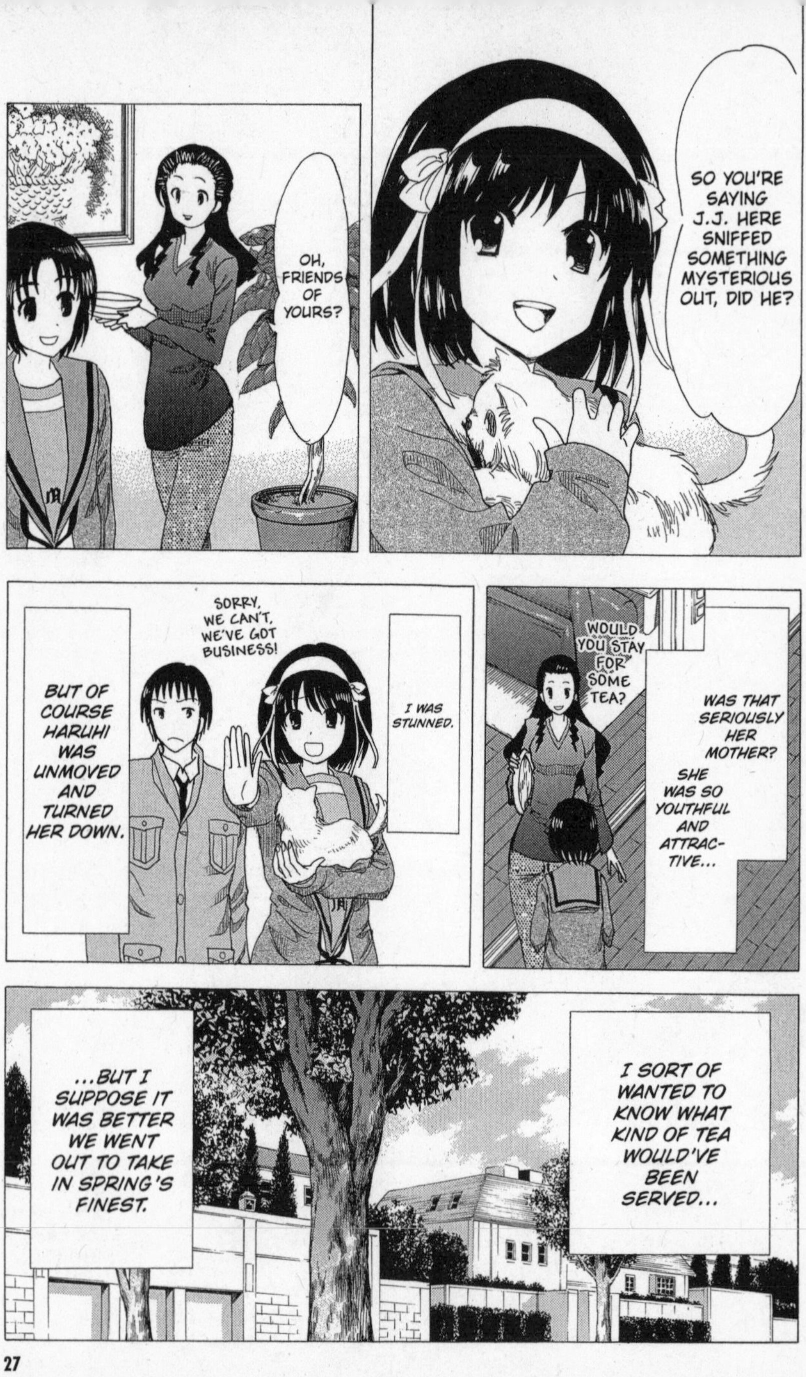
SO YOU'RE SAYING J.J. HERE SNIFFED SOMETHING MYSTERIOUS OUT, DID HE?
OH, FRIENDS OF YOURS?
WOULD YOU STAY FOR SOME TEA?
WAS THAT SERIOUSLY HER MOTHER?
SHE WAS SO YOUTHFUL AND ATTRACTIVE...
I WAS STUNNED.
SORRY, WE CAN'T, WE'VE GOT BUSINESS!
BUT OF COURSE HARUHI WAS UNMOVED AND TURNED HER DOWN.
I SORT OF WANTED TO KNOW WHAT KIND OF TEA WOULD'VE BEEN SERVED...
...BUT I SUPPOSE IT WAS BETTER WE WENT OUT TO TAKE IN SPRING'S FINEST.

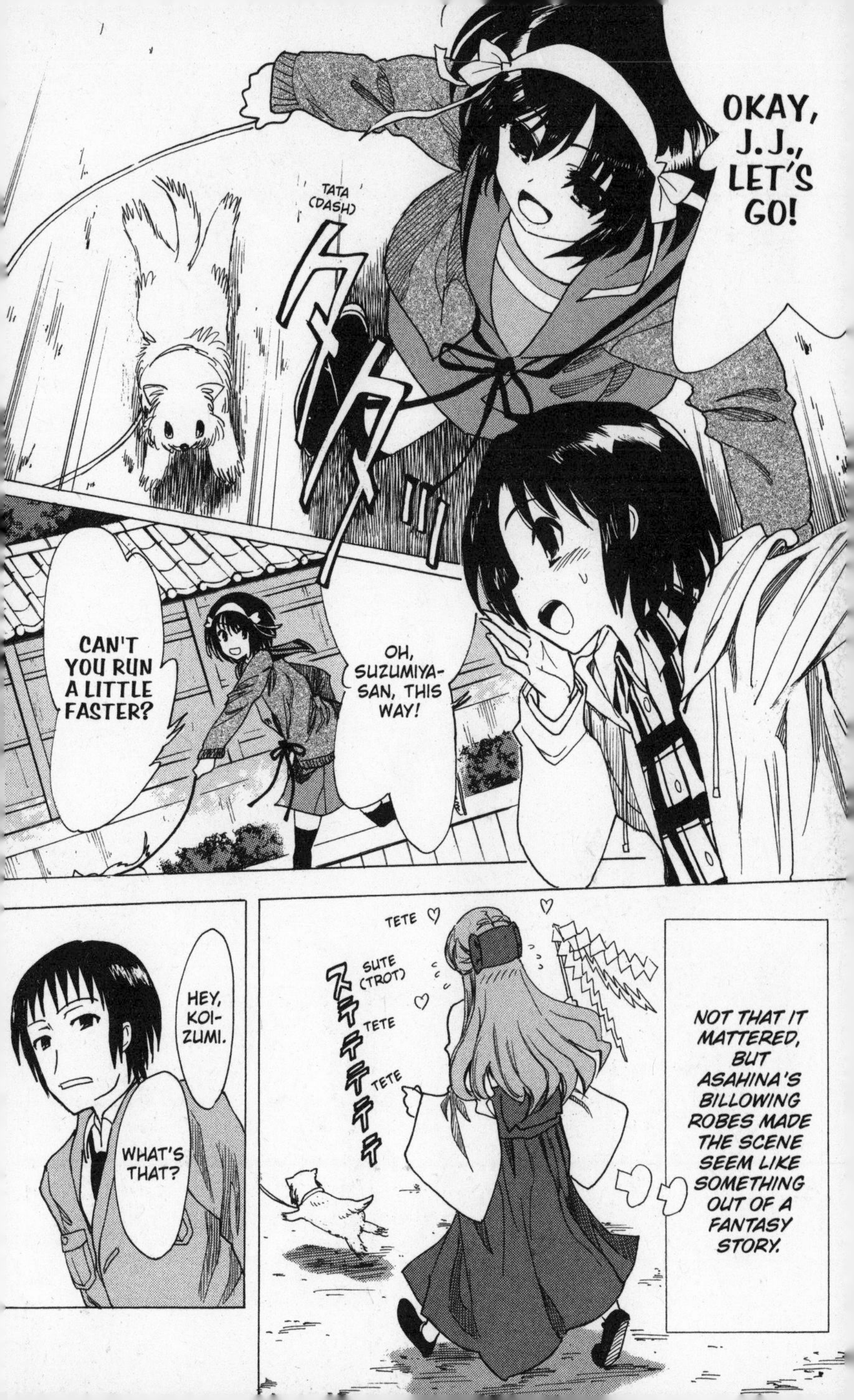
OKAY, J.J., LET'S GO!
TATA (DASH)
OH, SUZUMIYA-SAN, THIS WAY!
CAN'T YOU RUN A LITTLE FASTER?
NOT THAT IT MATTERED, BUT ASAHINA'S BILLOWING ROBES MADE THE SCENE SEEM LIKE SOMETHING OUT OF A FANTASY STORY.
TETE
SUTE (TROT)
TETE
TETE
HEY, KOI-ZUMI.
WHAT'S THAT?

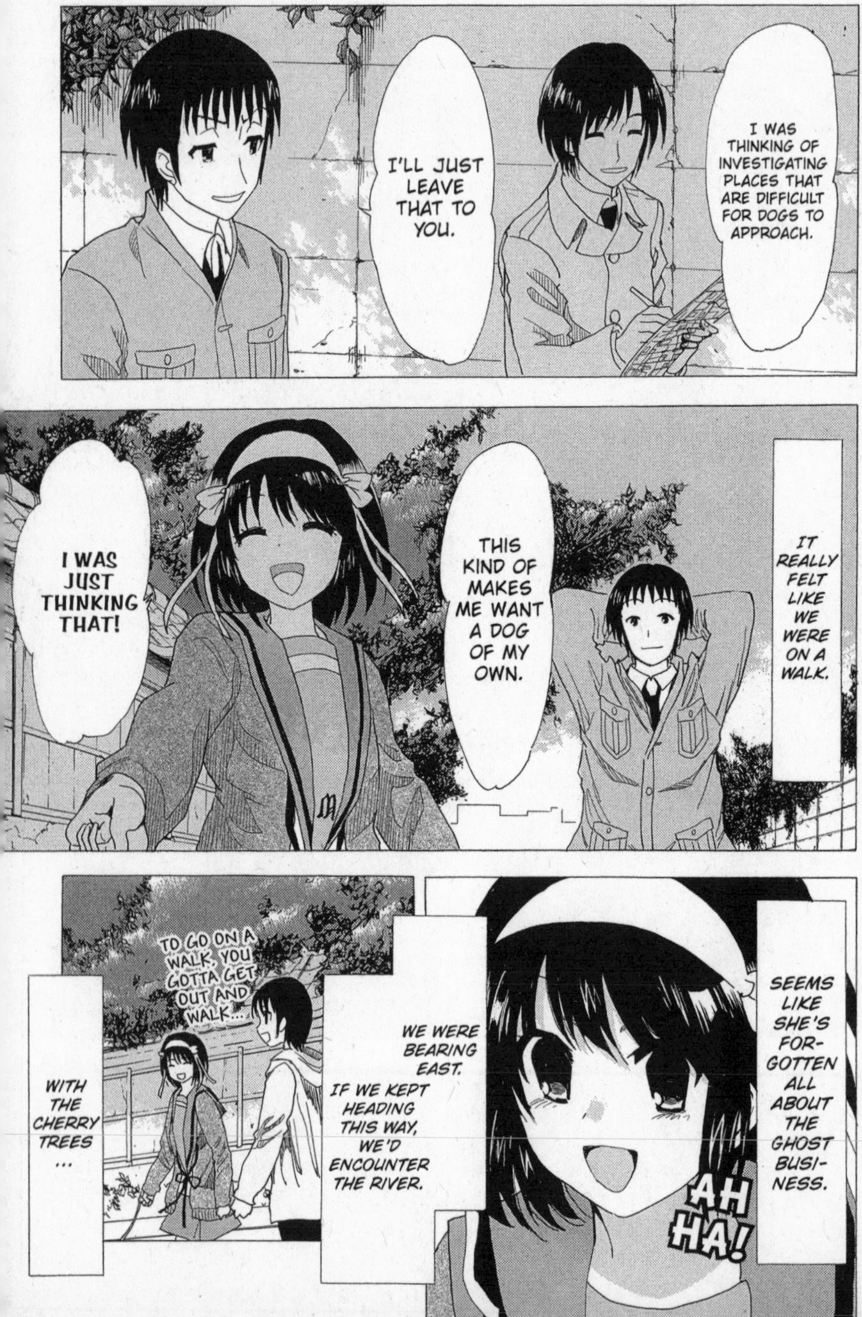

I WAS THINKING OF INVESTIGATING PLACES THAT ARE DIFFICULT FOR DOGS TO APPROACH.
I'LL JUST LEAVE THAT TO YOU.
IT REALLY FELT LIKE WE WERE ON A WALK.
THIS KIND OF MAKES ME WANT A DOG OF MY OWN.
I WAS JUST THINKING THAT!
SEEMS LIKE SHE'S FOR-GOTTEN ALL ABOUT THE GHOST BUSI-NESS.
AH HA!
WE WERE BEARING EAST. IF WE KEPT HEADING THIS WAY, WE'D ENCOUNTER THE RIVER.
TO GO ON A WALK, YOU GOTTA GET OUT AND WALK...
WITH THE CHERRY TREES ...

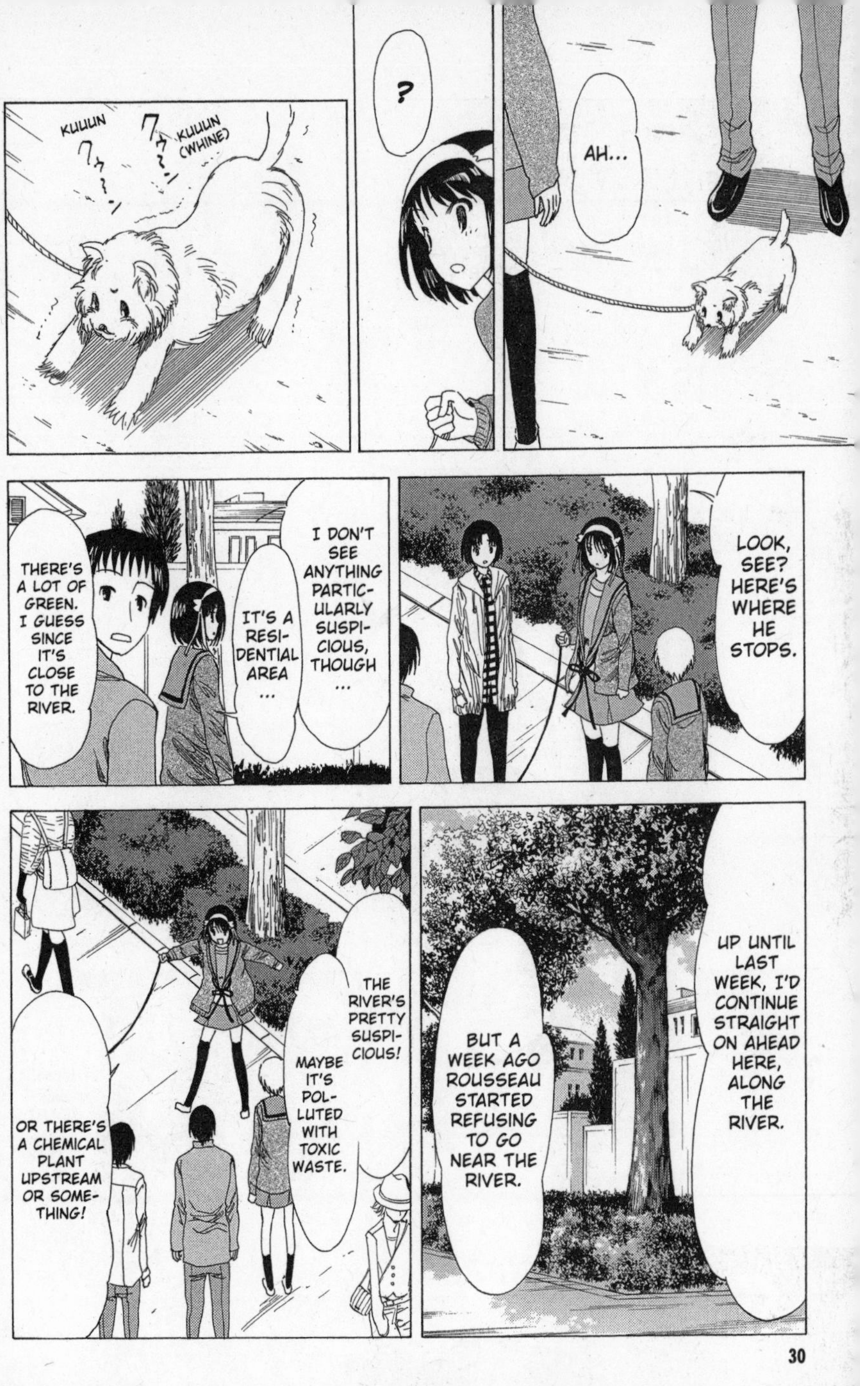
AH...
?
KUUUN (WHINE)
KUUUN
LOOK, SEE? HERE'S WHERE HE STOPS.
I DON'T SEE ANYTHING PARTICULARLY SUSPICIOUS, THOUGH...
IT'S A RESIDENTIAL AREA...
THERE'S A LOT OF GREEN. I GUESS SINCE IT'S CLOSE TO THE RIVER.
UP UNTIL LAST WEEK, I'D CONTINUE STRAIGHT ON AHEAD HERE, ALONG THE RIVER.
BUT A WEEK AGO ROUSSEAU STARTED REFUSING TO GO NEAR THE RIVER.
THE RIVER'S PRETTY SUSPICIOUS!
MAYBE IT'S POLLUTED WITH TOXIC WASTE.
OR THERE'S A CHEMICAL PLANT UPSTREAM OR SOMETHING!

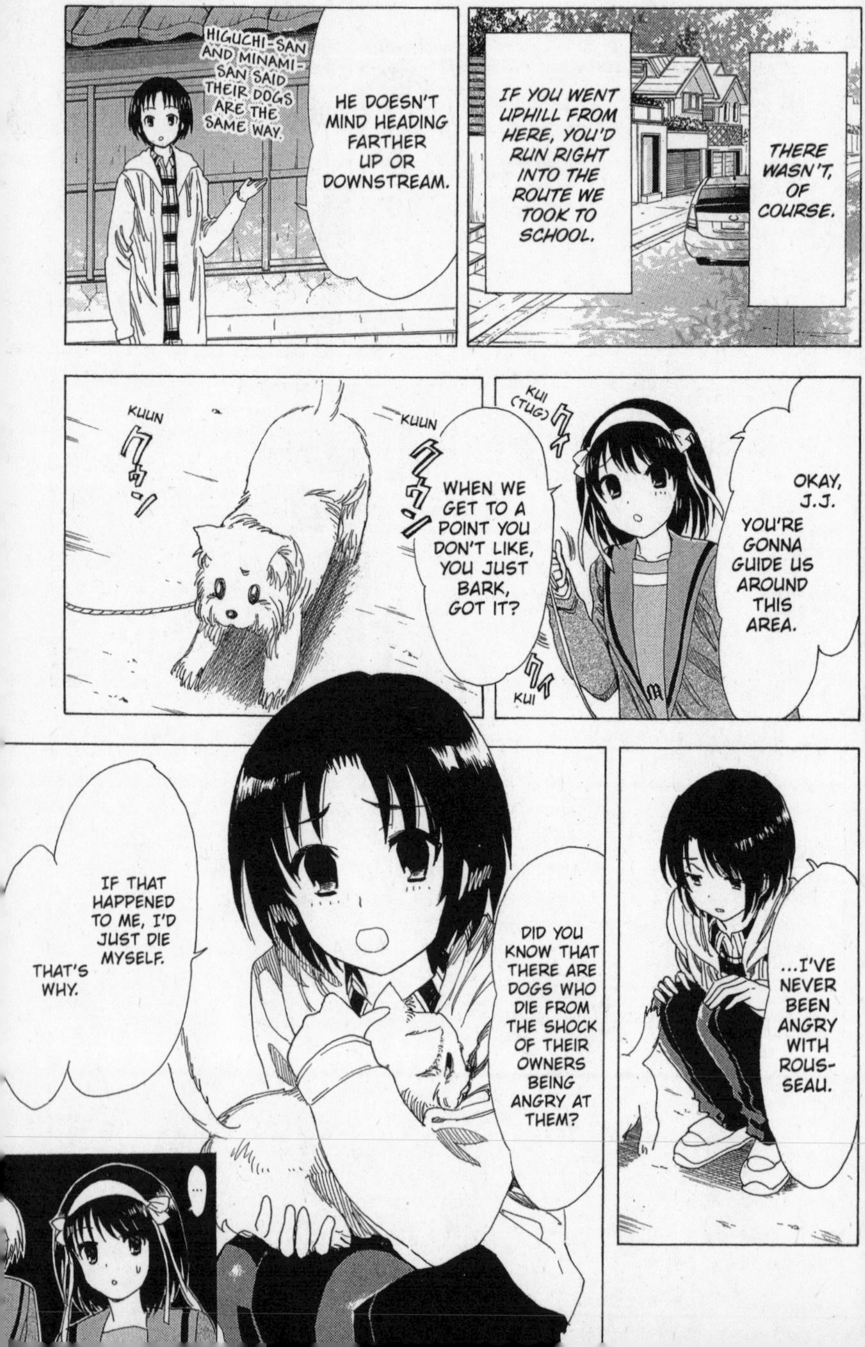
THERE WASN'T, OF COURSE.
IF YOU WENT UPHILL FROM HERE, YOU'D RUN RIGHT INTO THE ROUTE WE TOOK TO SCHOOL.
HE DOESN'T MIND HEADING FARTHER UP OR DOWNSTREAM.
HIGUCHI-SAN AND MINAMI-SAN SAID THEIR DOGS ARE THE SAME WAY.
OKAY, J.J.
YOU'RE GONNA GUIDE US AROUND THIS AREA.
KUI (TUG)
WHEN WE GET TO A POINT YOU DON'T LIKE, YOU JUST BARK, GOT IT?
KUI
KUUN
KUUN
...I'VE NEVER BEEN ANGRY WITH ROUS-SEAU.
DID YOU KNOW THAT THERE ARE DOGS WHO DIE FROM THE SHOCK OF THEIR OWNERS BEING ANGRY AT THEM?
IF THAT HAPPENED TO ME, I'D JUST DIE MYSELF.
THAT'S WHY.
...

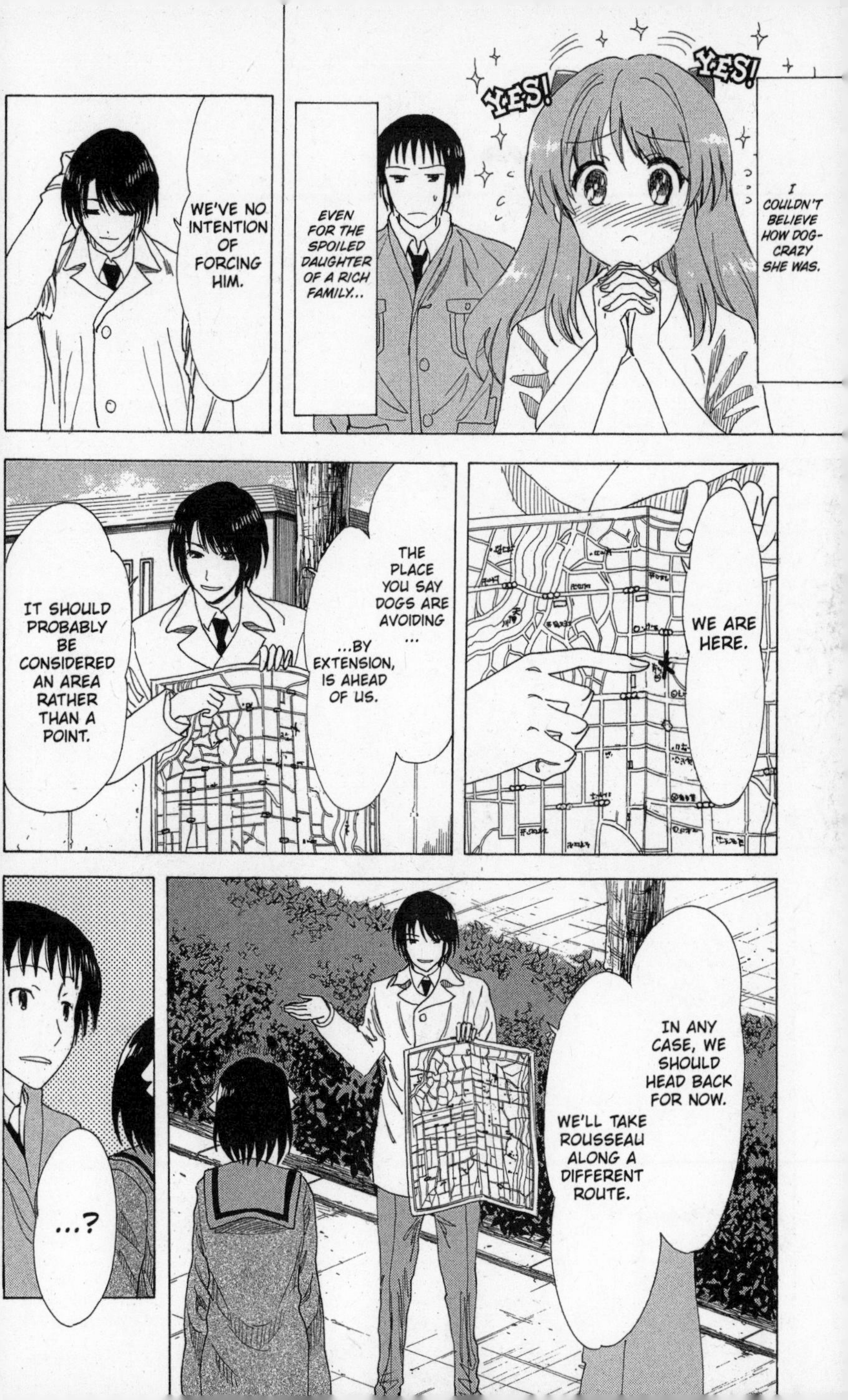
YES!
YES!
I COULDN'T BELIEVE HOW DOG-CRAZY SHE WAS.
EVEN FOR THE SPOILED DAUGHTER OF A RICH FAMILY...
WE'VE NO INTENTION OF FORCING HIM.
WE ARE HERE.
THE PLACE YOU SAY DOGS ARE AVOIDING ...
...BY EXTENSION, IS AHEAD OF US.
IT SHOULD PROBABLY BE CONSIDERED AN AREA RATHER THAN A POINT.
IN ANY CASE, WE SHOULD HEAD BACK FOR NOW.
WE'LL TAKE ROUSSEAU ALONG A DIFFERENT ROUTE.
...?

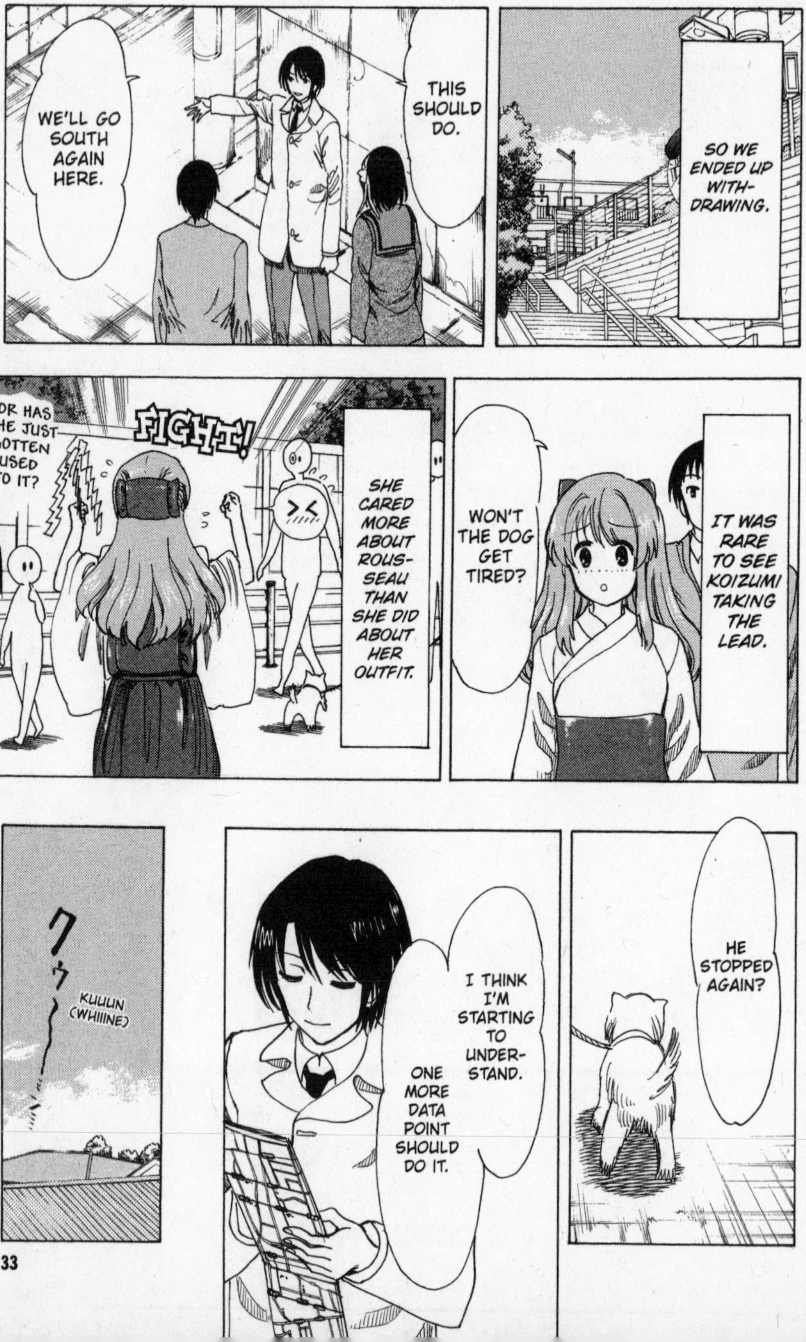
SO WE ENDED UP WITH-DRAWING.
THIS SHOULD DO.
WE'LL GO SOUTH AGAIN HERE.
IT WAS RARE TO SEE KOIZUMI TAKING THE LEAD.
WON'T THE DOG GET TIRED?
SHE CARED MORE ABOUT ROUS-SEAU THAN SHE DID ABOUT HER OUTFIT.
FIGHT!
OR HAS SHE JUST GOTTEN USED TO IT?
HE STOPPED AGAIN?
I THINK I'M STARTING TO UNDER-STAND.
ONE MORE DATA POINT SHOULD DO IT.
クゥ～
KUUUN (WHIIINE)

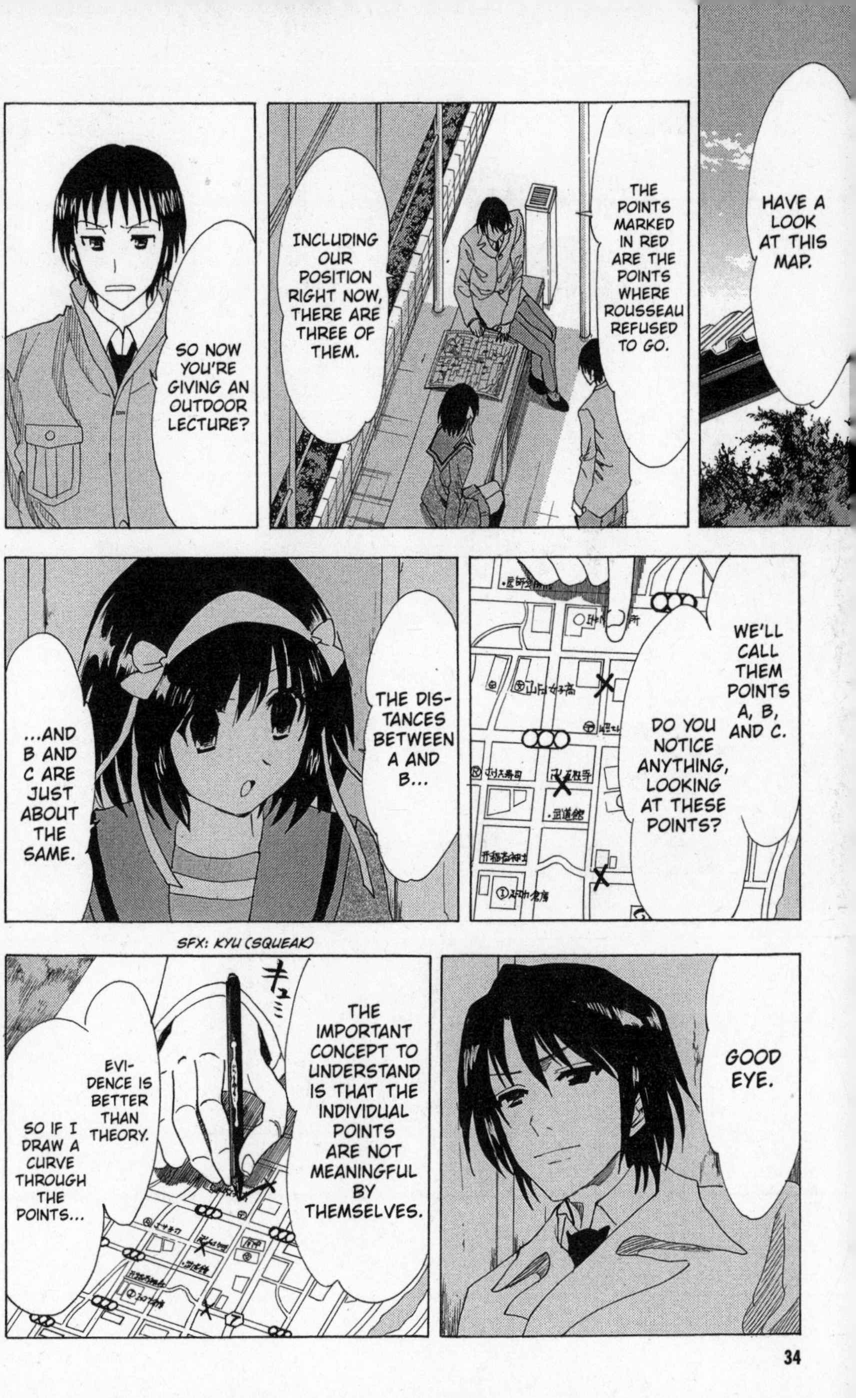
HAVE A LOOK AT THIS MAP.
THE POINTS MARKED IN RED ARE THE POINTS WHERE ROUSSEAU REFUSED TO GO.
INCLUDING OUR POSITION RIGHT NOW, THERE ARE THREE OF THEM.
SO NOW YOU'RE GIVING AN OUTDOOR LECTURE?
WE'LL CALL THEM POINTS A, B, AND C.
DO YOU NOTICE ANYTHING, LOOKING AT THESE POINTS?
THE DIS-TANCES BETWEEN A AND B...
...AND B AND C ARE JUST ABOUT THE SAME.
GOOD EYE.
SFX: KYU (SQUEAK)
THE IMPORTANT CONCEPT TO UNDERSTAND IS THAT THE INDIVIDUAL POINTS ARE NOT MEANINGFUL BY THEMSELVES.
EVI-DENCE IS BETTER THAN THEORY.
SO IF I DRAW A CURVE THROUGH THE POINTS...

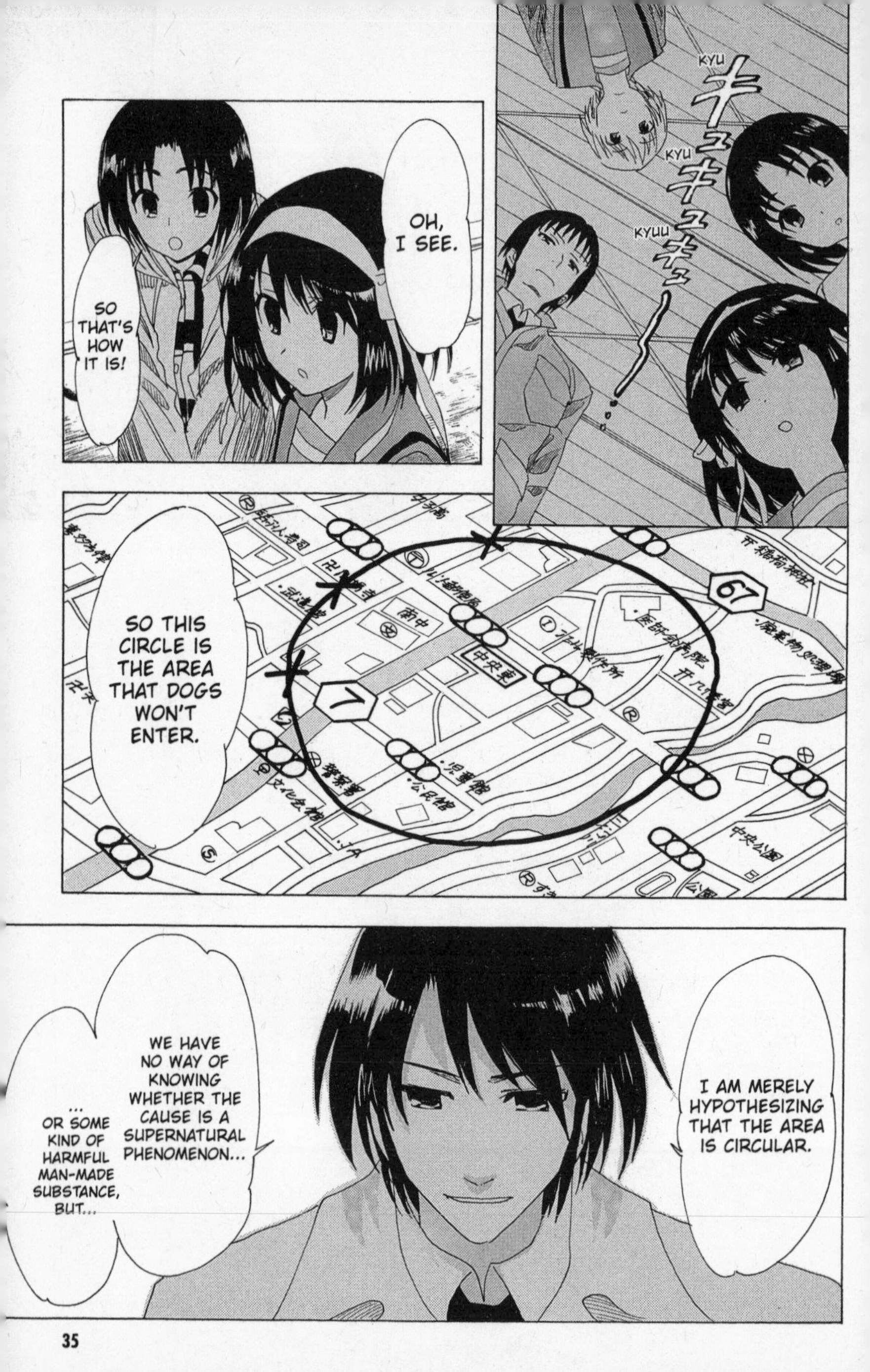
KYU
KYU
KYUU
OH, I SEE.
SO THAT'S HOW IT IS!
SO THIS CIRCLE IS THE AREA THAT DOGS WON'T ENTER.
67
7
中央東
警察署
公民館
児童館
中央公園
I AM MERELY HYPOTHESIZING THAT THE AREA IS CIRCULAR.
WE HAVE NO WAY OF KNOWING WHETHER THE CAUSE IS A SUPERNATURAL PHENOMENON...
... OR SOME KIND OF HARMFUL MAN-MADE SUBSTANCE, BUT...

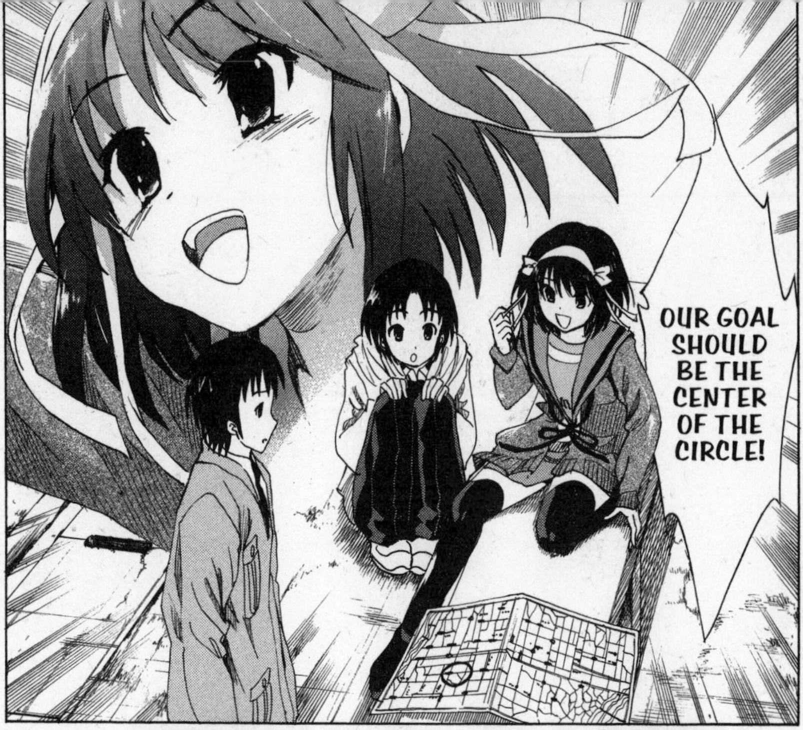
OUR GOAL SHOULD BE THE CENTER OF THE CIRCLE!

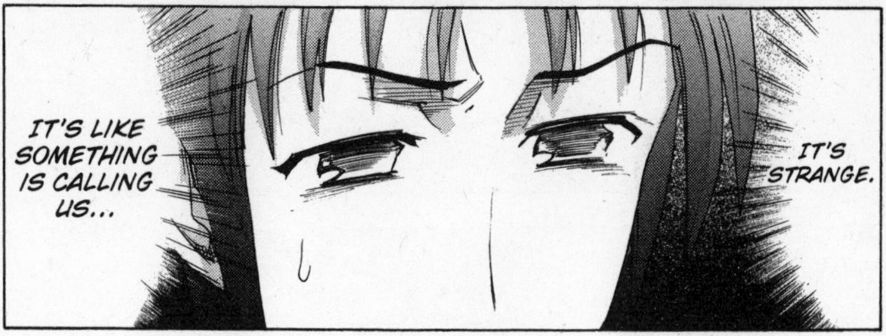
IT'S STRANGE.
IT'S LIKE SOMETHING IS CALLING US...

WE CAN'T STOP EVEN THOUGH HER EXCELLENCY THE BRIGADE CHIEF IS HERE...

...OR MAYBE BECAUSE OF THAT.

WANDERING SHADOW I : END

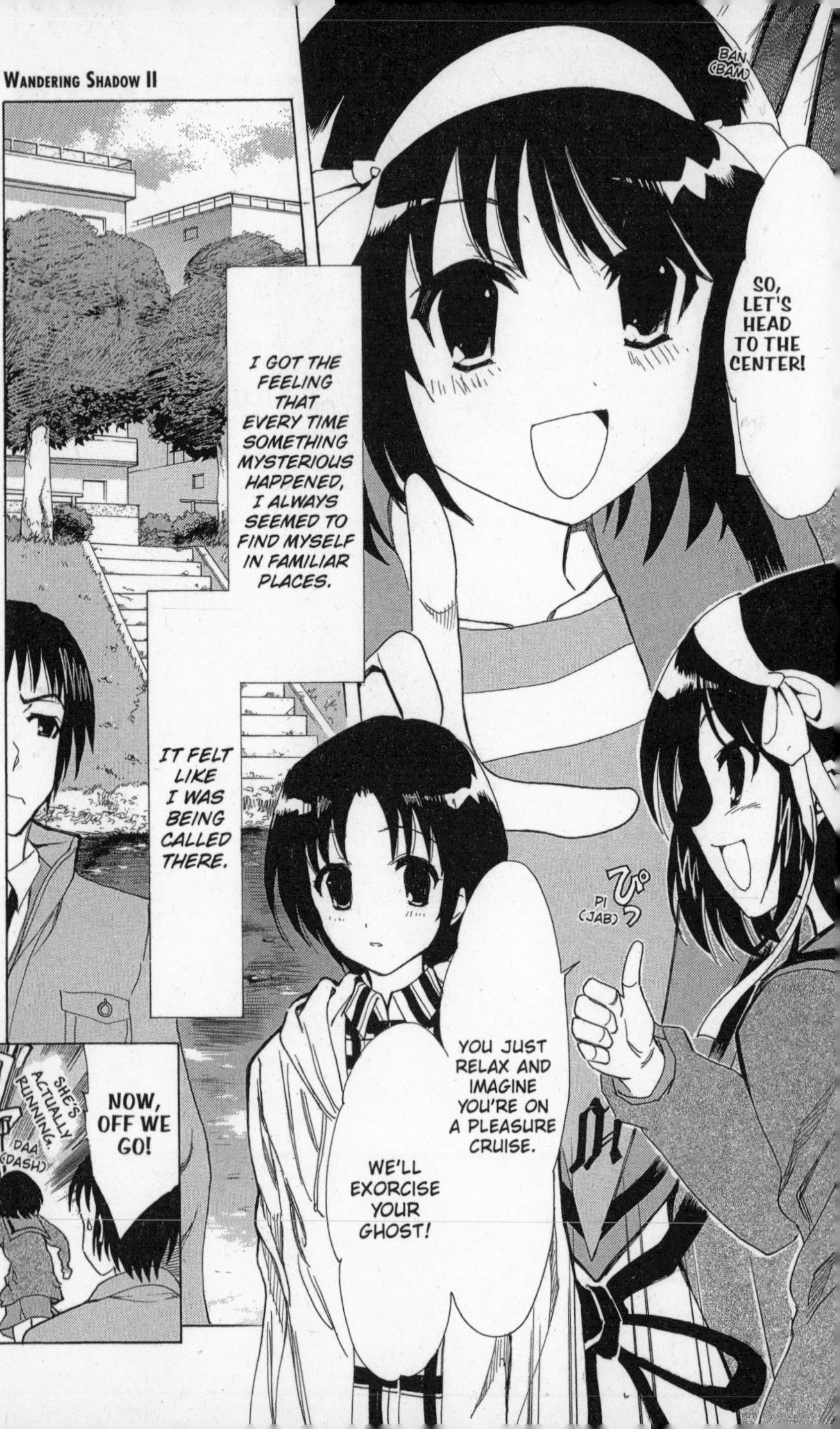
BAN (BAM)
SO, LET'S HEAD TO THE CENTER!
I GOT THE FEELING THAT EVERY TIME SOMETHING MYSTERIOUS HAPPENED, I ALWAYS SEEMED TO FIND MYSELF IN FAMILIAR PLACES.
IT FELT LIKE I WAS BEING CALLED THERE.
PI (JAB)
YOU JUST RELAX AND IMAGINE YOU'RE ON A PLEASURE CRUISE.
WE'LL EXORCISE YOUR GHOST!
NOW, OFF WE GO!
SHE'S ACTUALLY RUNNING.
DAA (DASH)

◎ Wandering Shadow II

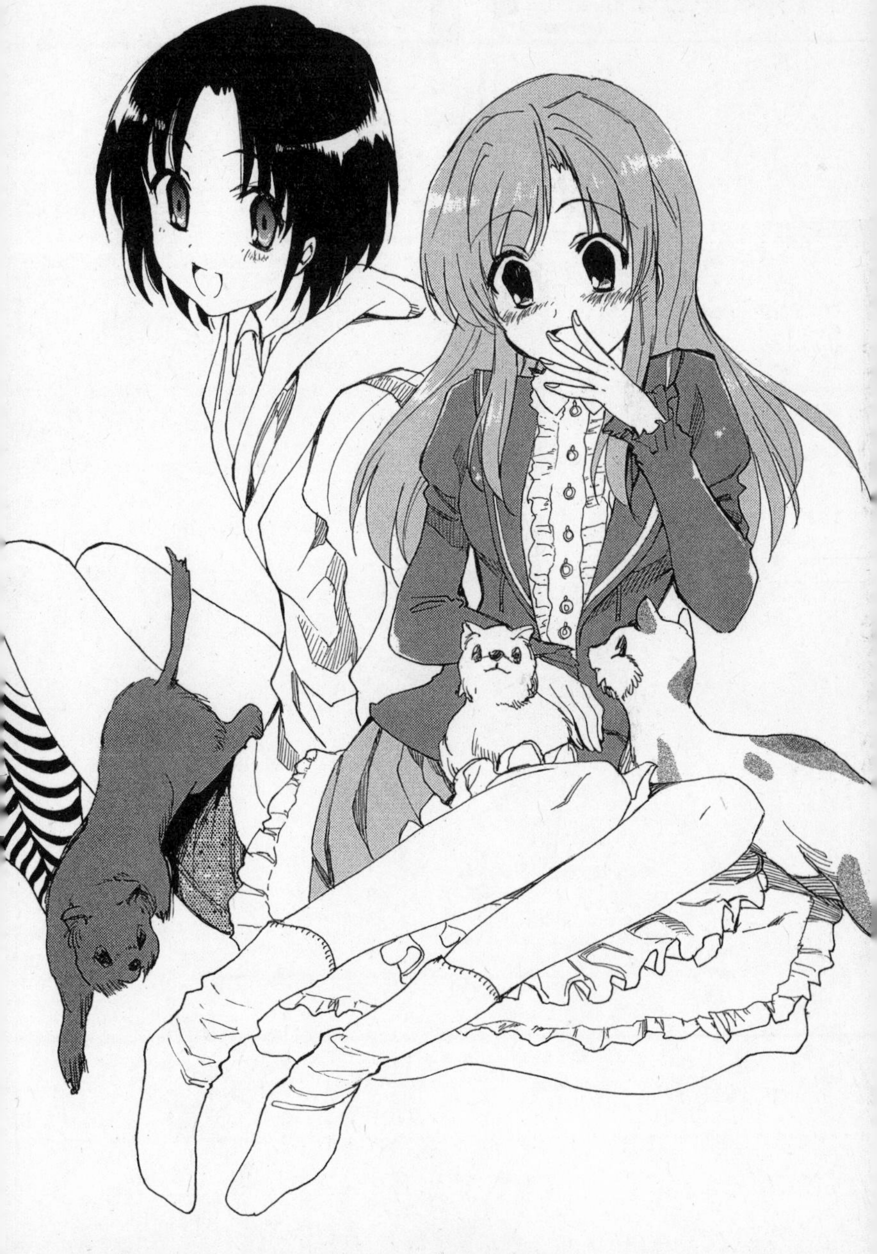

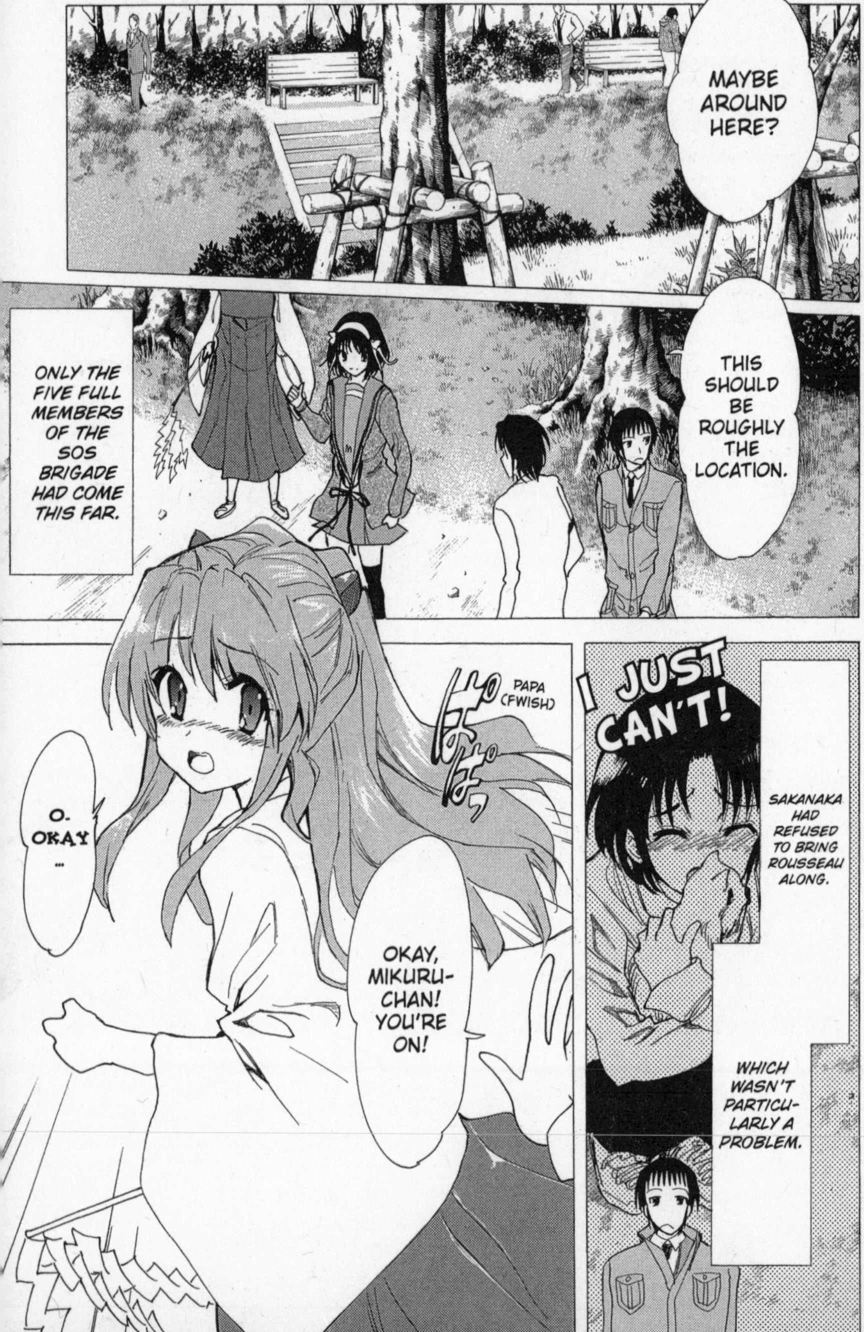
MAYBE AROUND HERE?
THIS SHOULD BE ROUGHLY THE LOCATION.
ONLY THE FIVE FULL MEMBERS OF THE SOS BRIGADE HAD COME THIS FAR.
I JUST CAN'T!
SAKANAKA HAD REFUSED TO BRING ROUSSEAU ALONG.
WHICH WASN'T PARTICULARLY A PROBLEM.
ぱぱっ
PAPA (FWISH)
OKAY, MIKURU-CHAN! YOU'RE ON!
O. OKAY ...

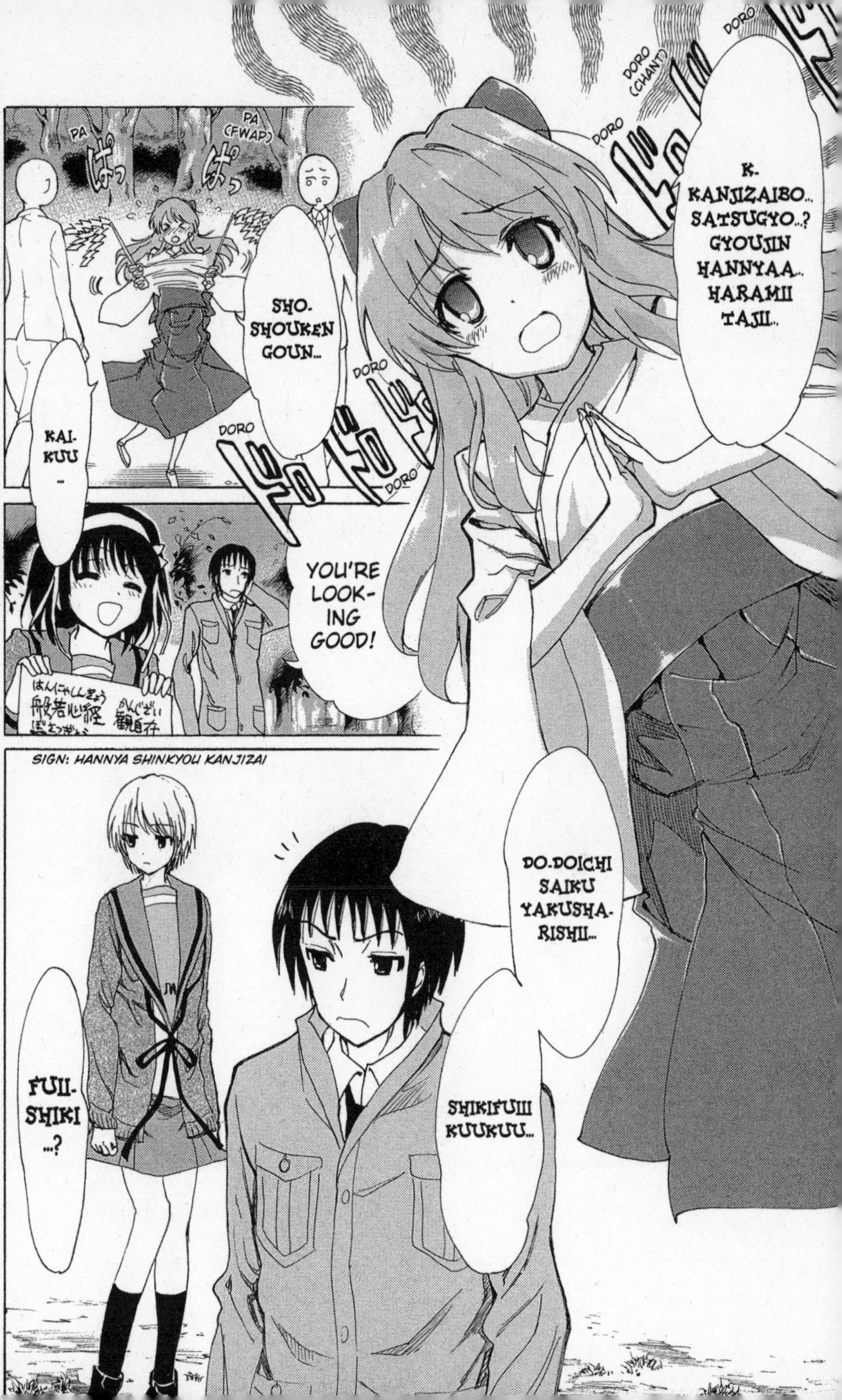
DORO
DORO (CHANT)
DORO
K. KANJIZAIBO... SATSUGYO...? GYOUJIN HANNYAA... HARAMII TAJII...
PA (FWAP)
ぱっ
PA
ぱっ
SHO-SHOUKEN GOUN...
DORO
DORO
DORO
KAI-KUU...
YOU'RE LOOK-ING GOOD!
はんにゃしんぎょう 般若心経 かんじざい 観自在
SIGN: HANNYA SHINKYOU KANJIZAI
DO-DOICHI SAIKU YAKUSHA-RISHII...
SHIKIFUIII KUUKUU...
FUII-SHIKI...?

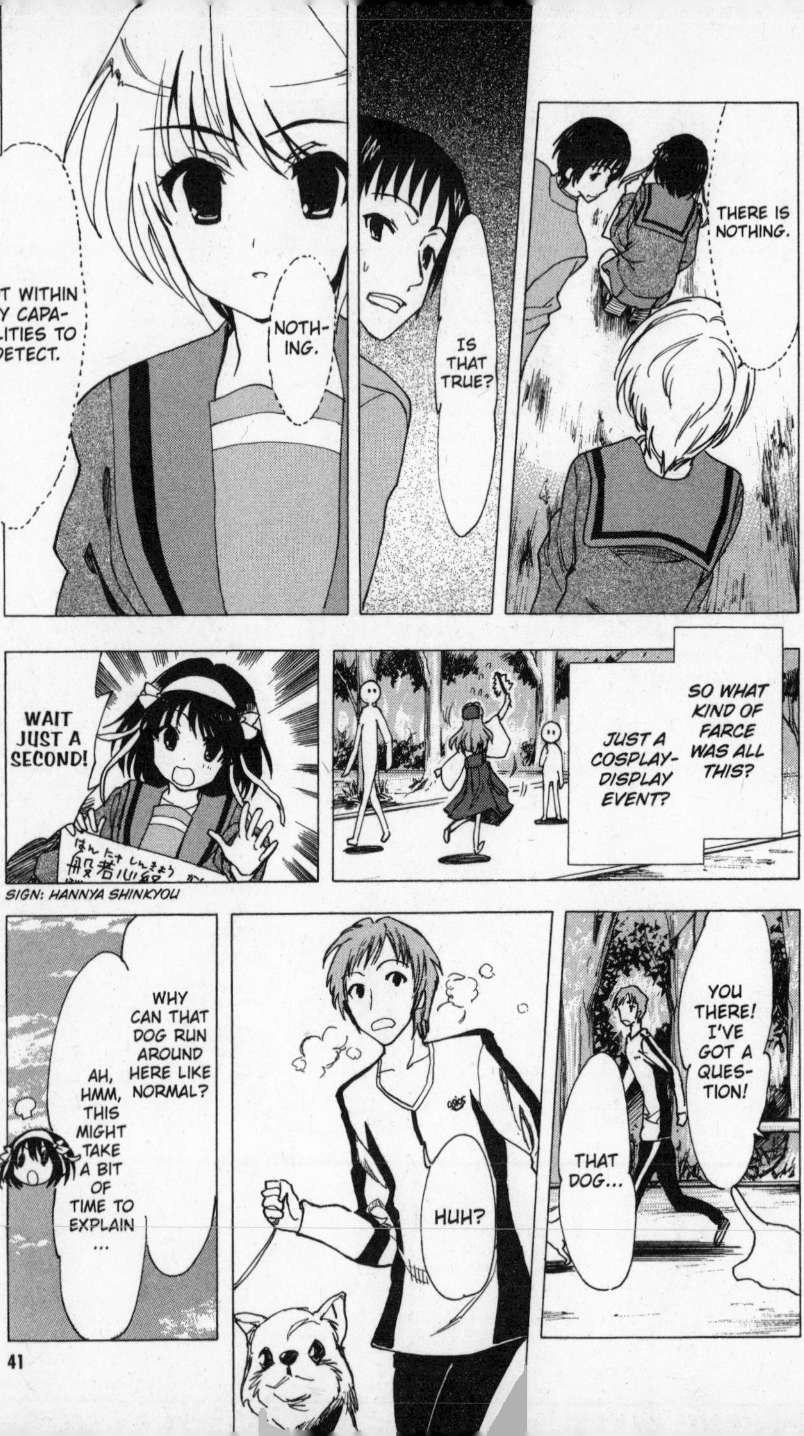
THERE IS NOTHING.
IS THAT TRUE?
NOTHING.
NOT WITHIN MY CAPABILITIES TO DETECT.
SO WHAT KIND OF FARCE WAS ALL THIS?
JUST A COSPLAY-DISPLAY EVENT?
WAIT JUST A SECOND!
SIGN: HANNYA SHINKYOU
YOU THERE! I'VE GOT A QUESTION!
THAT DOG...
HUH?
WHY CAN THAT DOG RUN AROUND HERE LIKE NORMAL?
AH, HMM, THIS MIGHT TAKE A BIT OF TIME TO EXPLAIN...

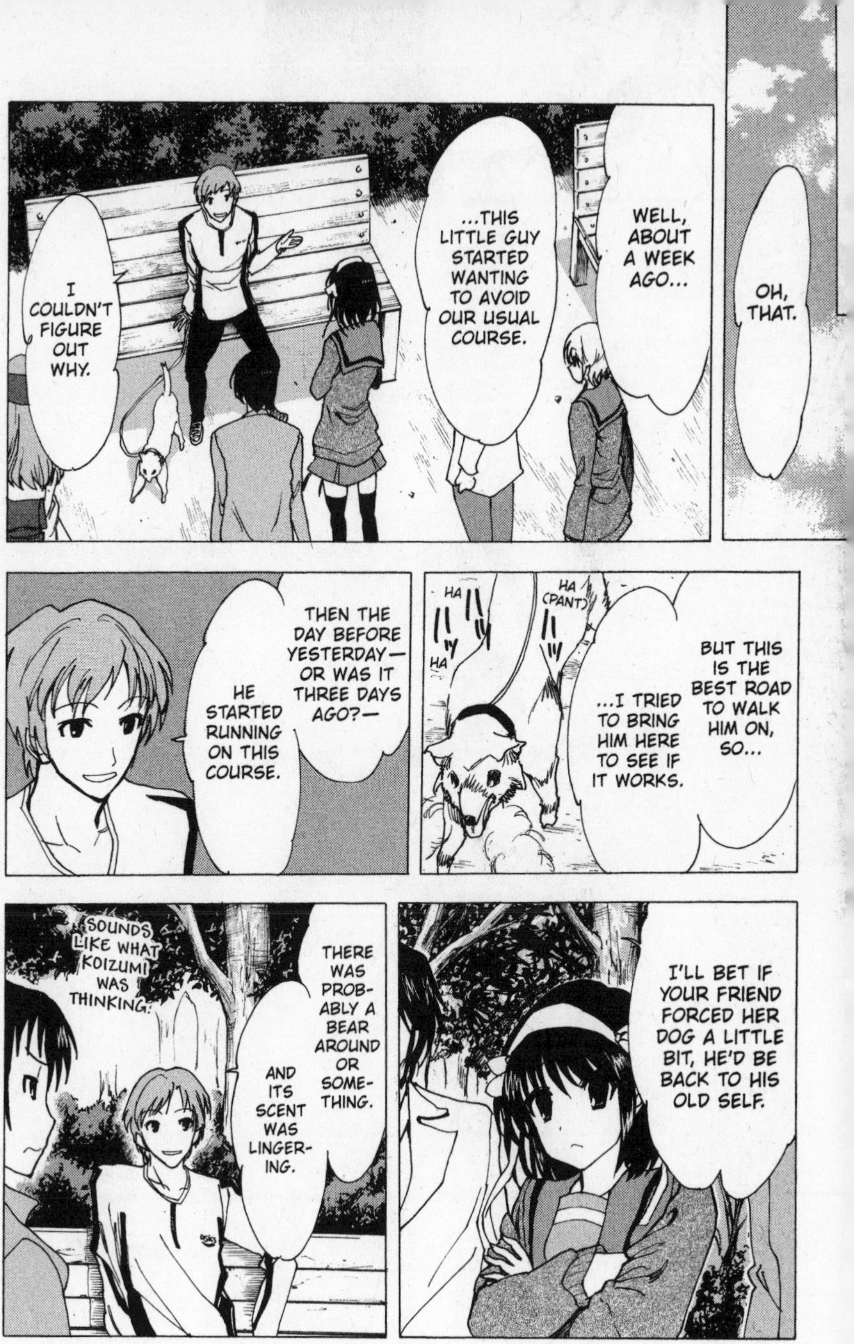
OH, THAT.
WELL, ABOUT A WEEK AGO...
...THIS LITTLE GUY STARTED WANTING TO AVOID OUR USUAL COURSE.
I COULDN'T FIGURE OUT WHY.
HA (PANT)
HA
HA
BUT THIS IS THE BEST ROAD TO WALK HIM ON, SO...
...I TRIED TO BRING HIM HERE TO SEE IF IT WORKS.
THEN THE DAY BEFORE YESTERDAY—OR WAS IT THREE DAYS AGO?—
HE STARTED RUNNING ON THIS COURSE.
I'LL BET IF YOUR FRIEND FORCED HER DOG A LITTLE BIT, HE'D BE BACK TO HIS OLD SELF.
THERE WAS PROBABLY A BEAR AROUND OR SOMETHING.
AND ITS SCENT WAS LINGERING.
SOUNDS LIKE WHAT KOIZUMI WAS THINKING.

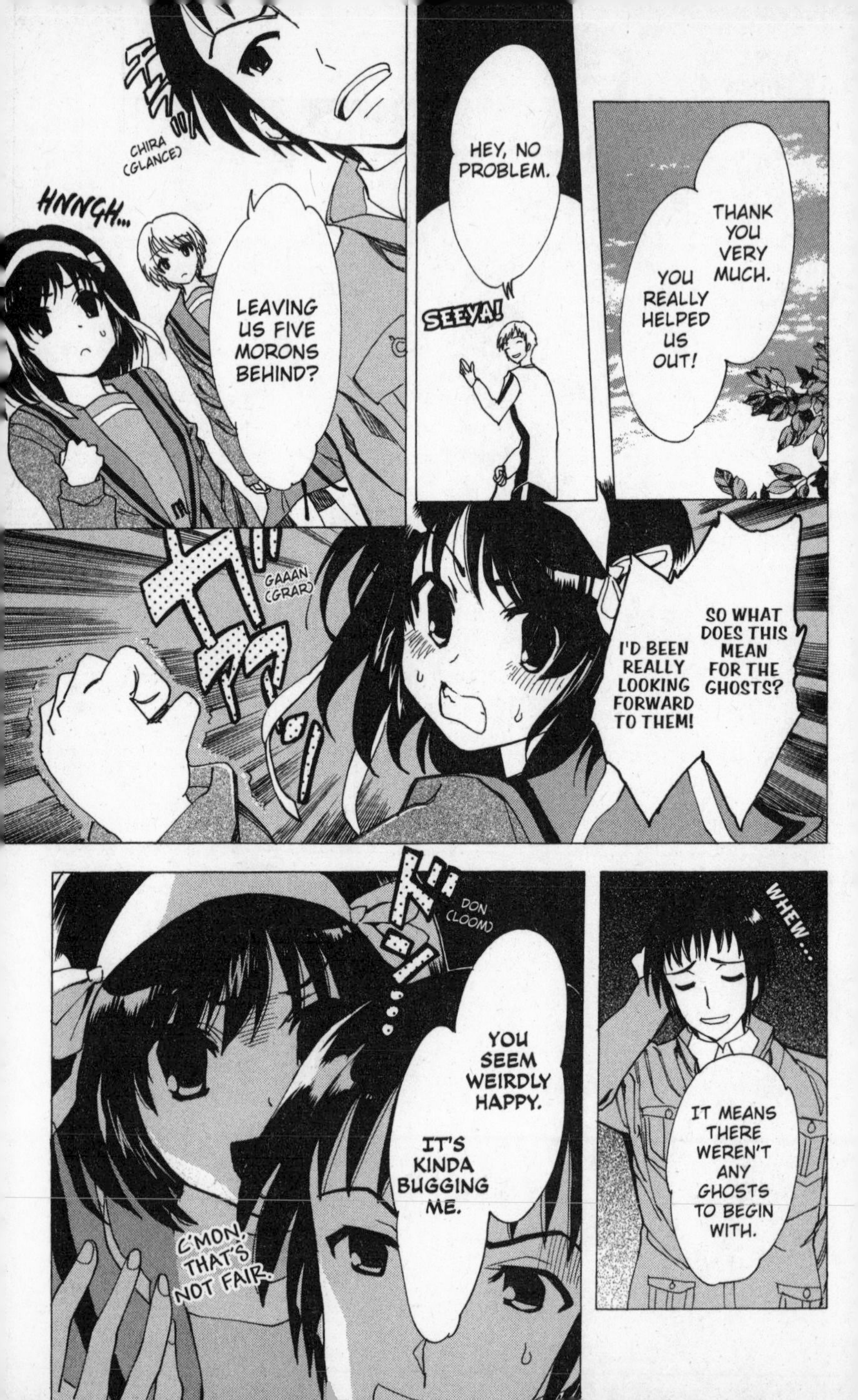
THANK YOU VERY MUCH.
YOU REALLY HELPED US OUT!
HEY, NO PROBLEM.
SEEYA!
CHIRA (GLANCE)
LEAVING US FIVE MORONS BEHIND?
HNNGH...
SO WHAT DOES THIS MEAN FOR THE GHOSTS?
I'D BEEN REALLY LOOKING FORWARD TO THEM!
GAAAN (GRAR)
WHEW...
IT MEANS THERE WEREN'T ANY GHOSTS TO BEGIN WITH.
DON (LOOM)
YOU SEEM WEIRDLY HAPPY.
IT'S KINDA BUGGING ME.
C'MON, THAT'S NOT FAIR.

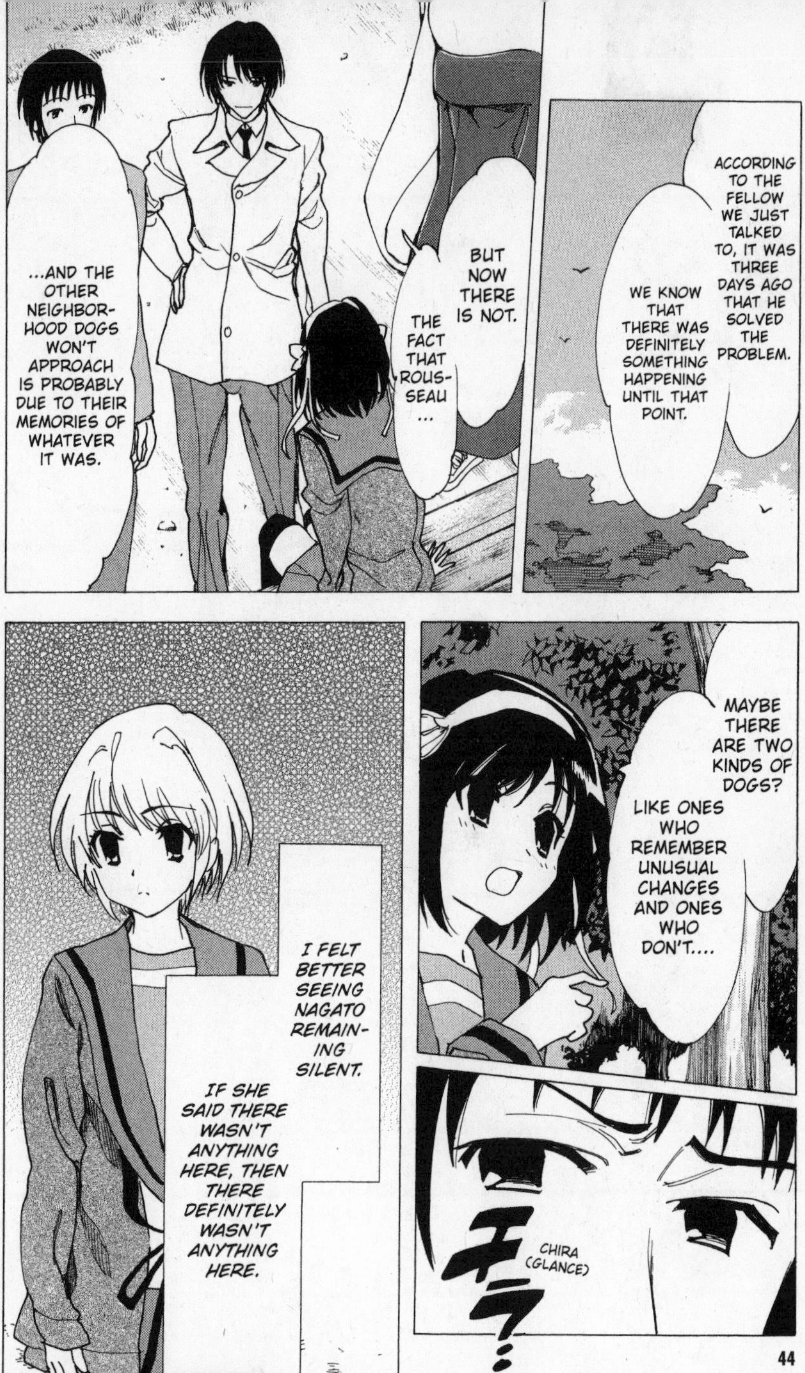
ACCORDING TO THE FELLOW WE JUST TALKED TO, IT WAS THREE DAYS AGO THAT HE SOLVED THE PROBLEM.
WE KNOW THAT THERE WAS DEFINITELY SOMETHING HAPPENING UNTIL THAT POINT.
BUT NOW THERE IS NOT.
THE FACT THAT ROUSSEAU...
...AND THE OTHER NEIGHBORHOOD DOGS WON'T APPROACH IS PROBABLY DUE TO THEIR MEMORIES OF WHATEVER IT WAS.
MAYBE THERE ARE TWO KINDS OF DOGS?
LIKE ONES WHO REMEMBER UNUSUAL CHANGES AND ONES WHO DON'T....
チラ…
CHIRA (GLANCE)
I FELT BETTER SEEING NAGATO REMAINING SILENT.
IF SHE SAID THERE WASN'T ANYTHING HERE, THEN THERE DEFINITELY WASN'T ANYTHING HERE.

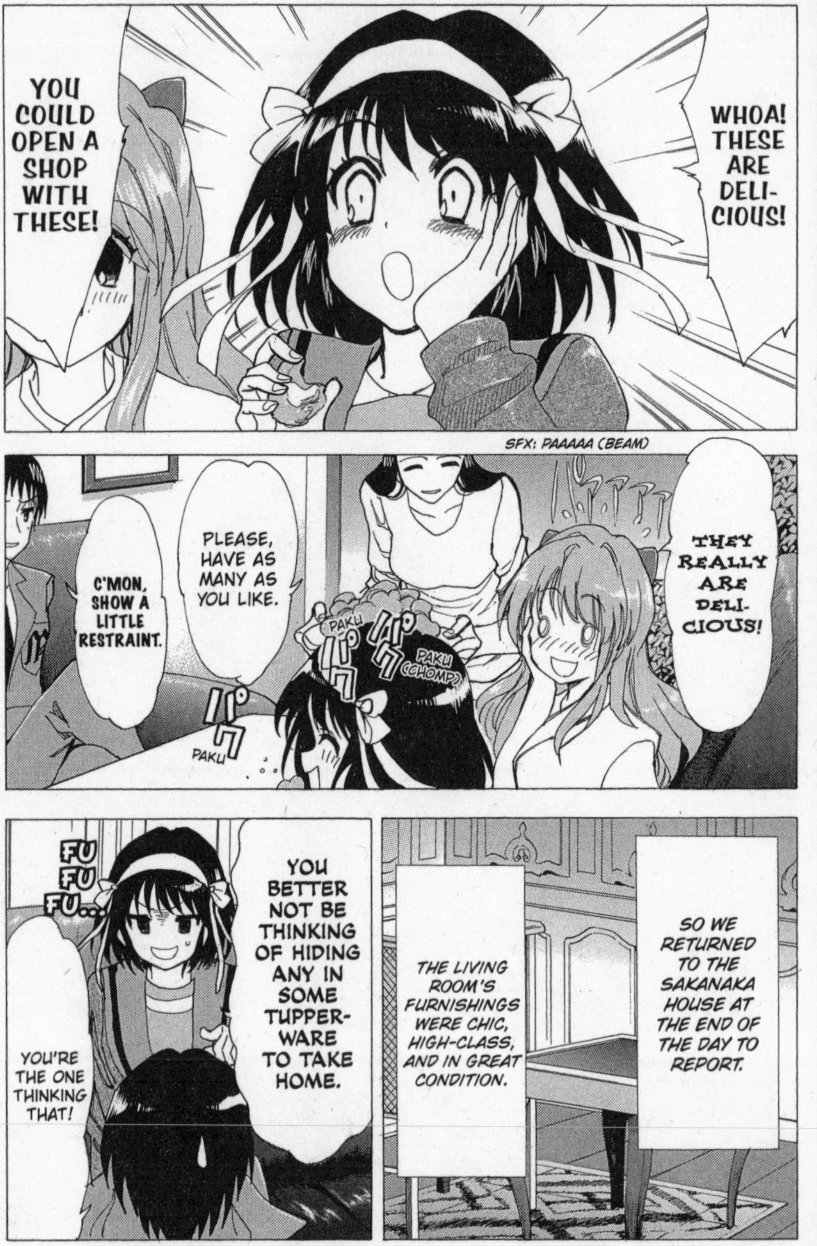
WHOA! THESE ARE DELICIOUS!
YOU COULD OPEN A SHOP WITH THESE!
SFX: PAAAAA (BEAM)
THEY REALLY ARE DELICIOUS!
PAKU
PAKU (CHOMP)
PAKU
PLEASE, HAVE AS MANY AS YOU LIKE.
C'MON, SHOW A LITTLE RESTRAINT.
SO WE RETURNED TO THE SAKANAKA HOUSE AT THE END OF THE DAY TO REPORT.
THE LIVING ROOM'S FURNISHINGS WERE CHIC, HIGH-CLASS, AND IN GREAT CONDITION.
YOU BETTER NOT BE THINKING OF HIDING ANY IN SOME TUPPER-WARE TO TAKE HOME.
FU FU FU...
YOU'RE THE ONE THINKING THAT!

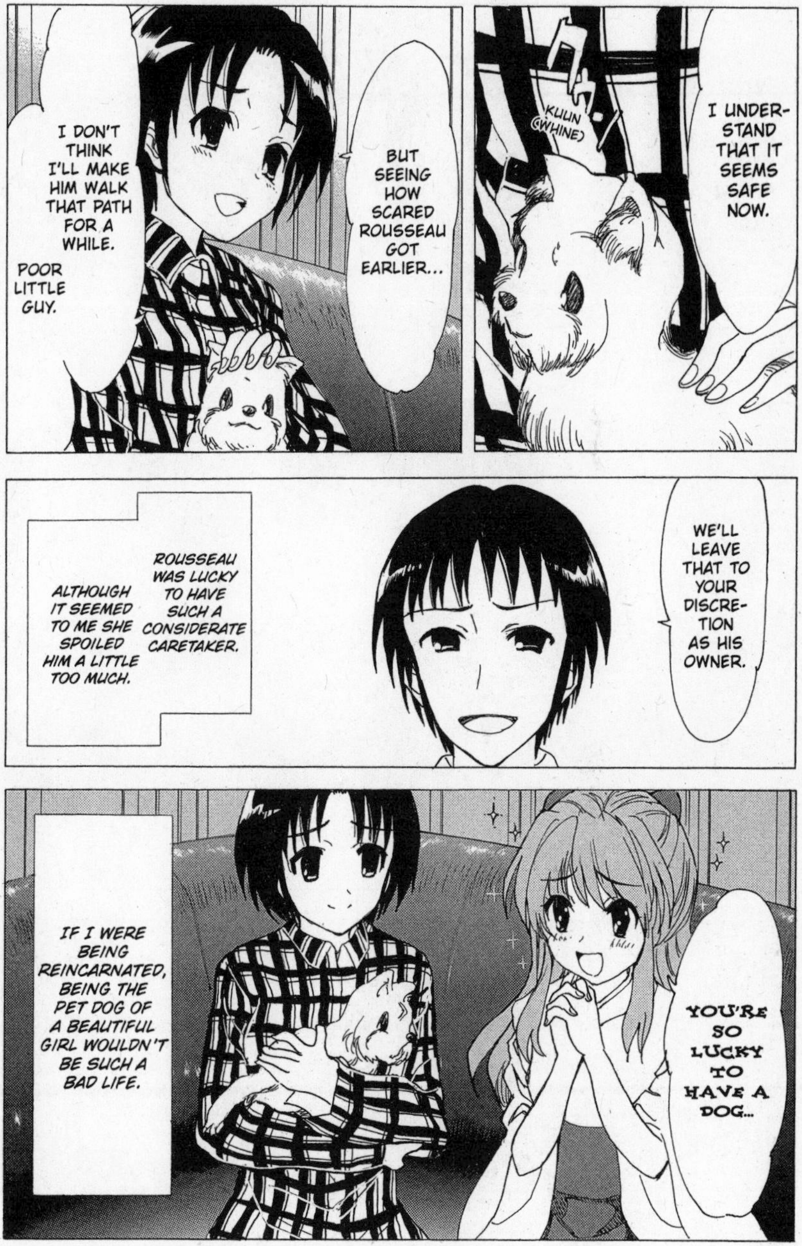
I UNDERSTAND THAT IT SEEMS SAFE NOW.
KUUN (WHINE)
BUT SEEING HOW SCARED ROUSSEAU GOT EARLIER...
I DON'T THINK I'LL MAKE HIM WALK THAT PATH FOR A WHILE.
POOR LITTLE GUY.
WE'LL LEAVE THAT TO YOUR DISCRETION AS HIS OWNER.
ROUSSEAU WAS LUCKY TO HAVE SUCH A CONSIDERATE CARETAKER.
ALTHOUGH IT SEEMED TO ME SHE SPOILED HIM A LITTLE TOO MUCH.
YOU'RE SO LUCKY TO HAVE A DOG...
IF I WERE BEING REINCARNATED, BEING THE PET DOG OF A BEAUTIFUL GIRL WOULDN'T BE SUCH A BAD LIFE.

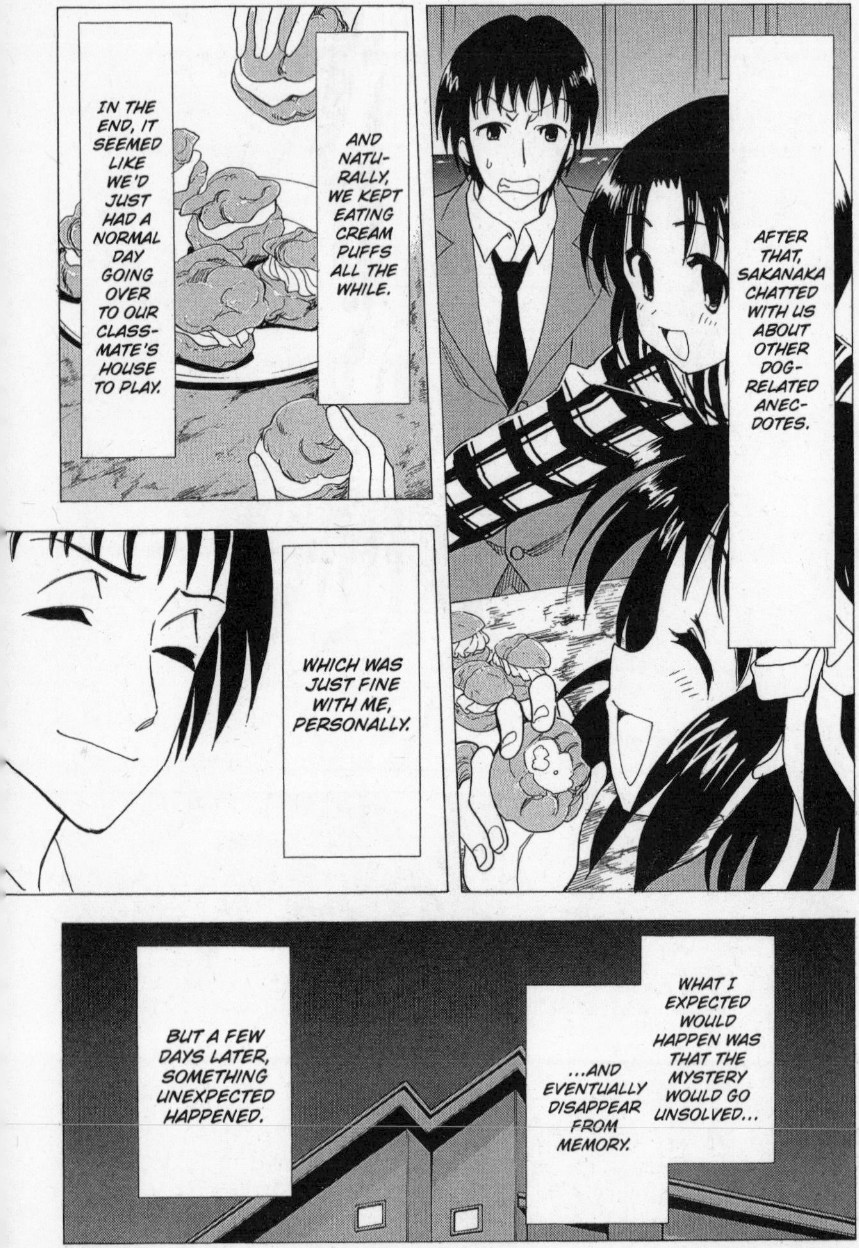
AFTER THAT, SAKANAKA CHATTED WITH US ABOUT OTHER DOG-RELATED ANEC-DOTES.
AND NATU-RALLY, WE KEPT EATING CREAM PUFFS ALL THE WHILE.
IN THE END, IT SEEMED LIKE WE'D JUST HAD A NORMAL DAY GOING OVER TO OUR CLASS-MATE'S HOUSE TO PLAY.
WHICH WAS JUST FINE WITH ME, PERSONALLY.
WHAT I EXPECTED WOULD HAPPEN WAS THAT THE MYSTERY WOULD GO UNSOLVED...
...AND EVENTUALLY DISAPPEAR FROM MEMORY.
BUT A FEW DAYS LATER, SOMETHING UNEXPECTED HAPPENED.

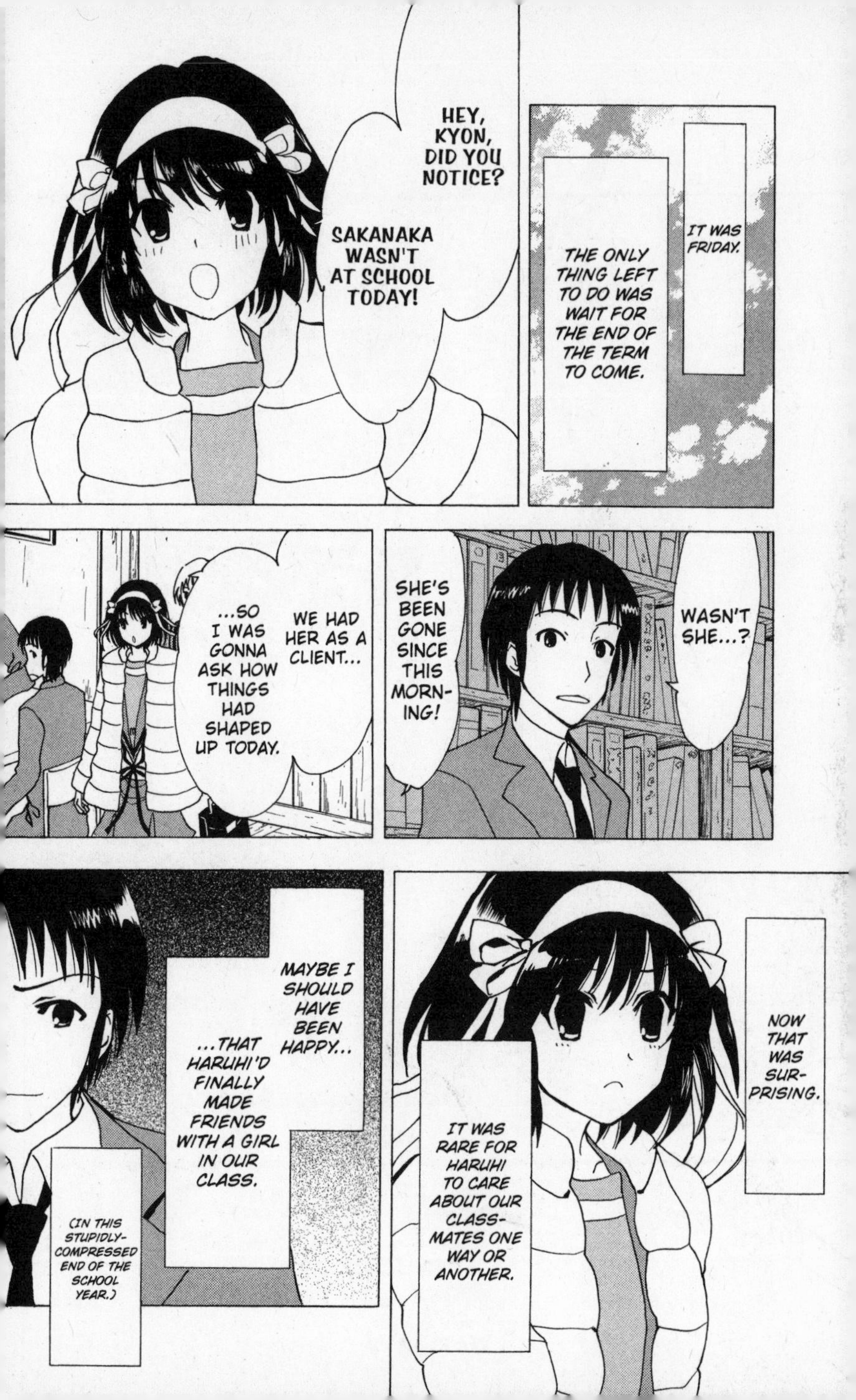
IT WAS FRIDAY.
THE ONLY THING LEFT TO DO WAS WAIT FOR THE END OF THE TERM TO COME.
HEY, KYON, DID YOU NOTICE?
SAKANAKA WASN'T AT SCHOOL TODAY!
WASN'T SHE...?
SHE'S BEEN GONE SINCE THIS MORNING!
WE HAD HER AS A CLIENT...
...SO I WAS GONNA ASK HOW THINGS HAD SHAPED UP TODAY.
NOW THAT WAS SURPRISING.
IT WAS RARE FOR HARUHI TO CARE ABOUT OUR CLASSMATES ONE WAY OR ANOTHER.
MAYBE I SHOULD HAVE BEEN HAPPY...
...THAT HARUHI'D FINALLY MADE FRIENDS WITH A GIRL IN OUR CLASS.
(IN THIS STUPIDLY-COMPRESSED END OF THE SCHOOL YEAR.)

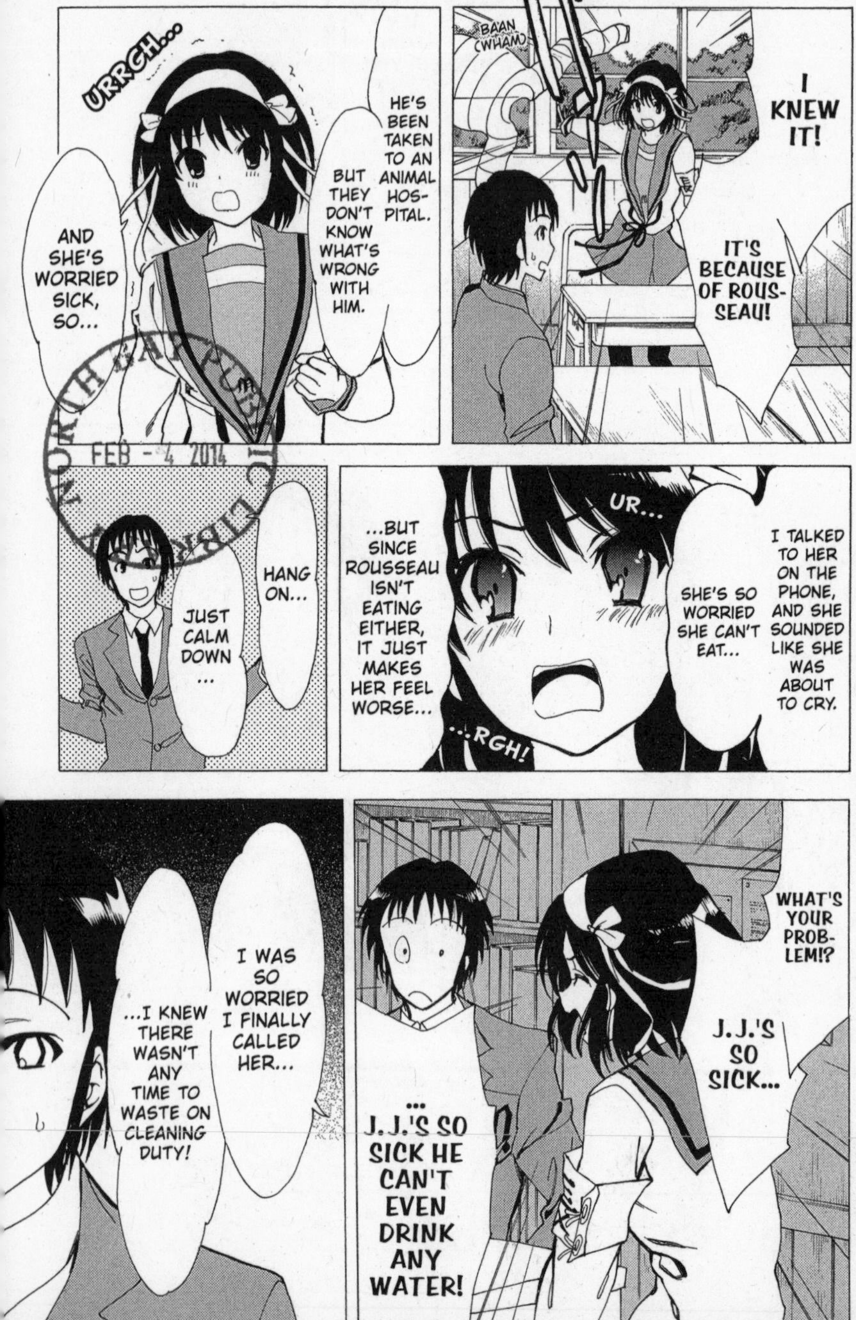
BA'AN (WHAM)
I KNEW IT!
IT'S BECAUSE OF ROUSSEAU!
HE'S BEEN TAKEN TO AN ANIMAL HOSPITAL.
BUT THEY DON'T KNOW WHAT'S WRONG WITH HIM.
AND SHE'S WORRIED SICK, SO...
URRGH...
I TALKED TO HER ON THE PHONE, AND SHE SOUNDED LIKE SHE WAS ABOUT TO CRY.
SHE'S SO WORRIED SHE CAN'T EAT...
UR...
...BUT SINCE ROUSSEAU ISN'T EATING EITHER, IT JUST MAKES HER FEEL WORSE...
...RGH!
HANG ON...
JUST CALM DOWN...
WHAT'S YOUR PROBLEM!?
J.J.'S SO SICK...
...J.J.'S SO SICK HE CAN'T EVEN DRINK ANY WATER!
I WAS SO WORRIED I FINALLY CALLED HER...
...I KNEW THERE WASN'T ANY TIME TO WASTE ON CLEANING DUTY!

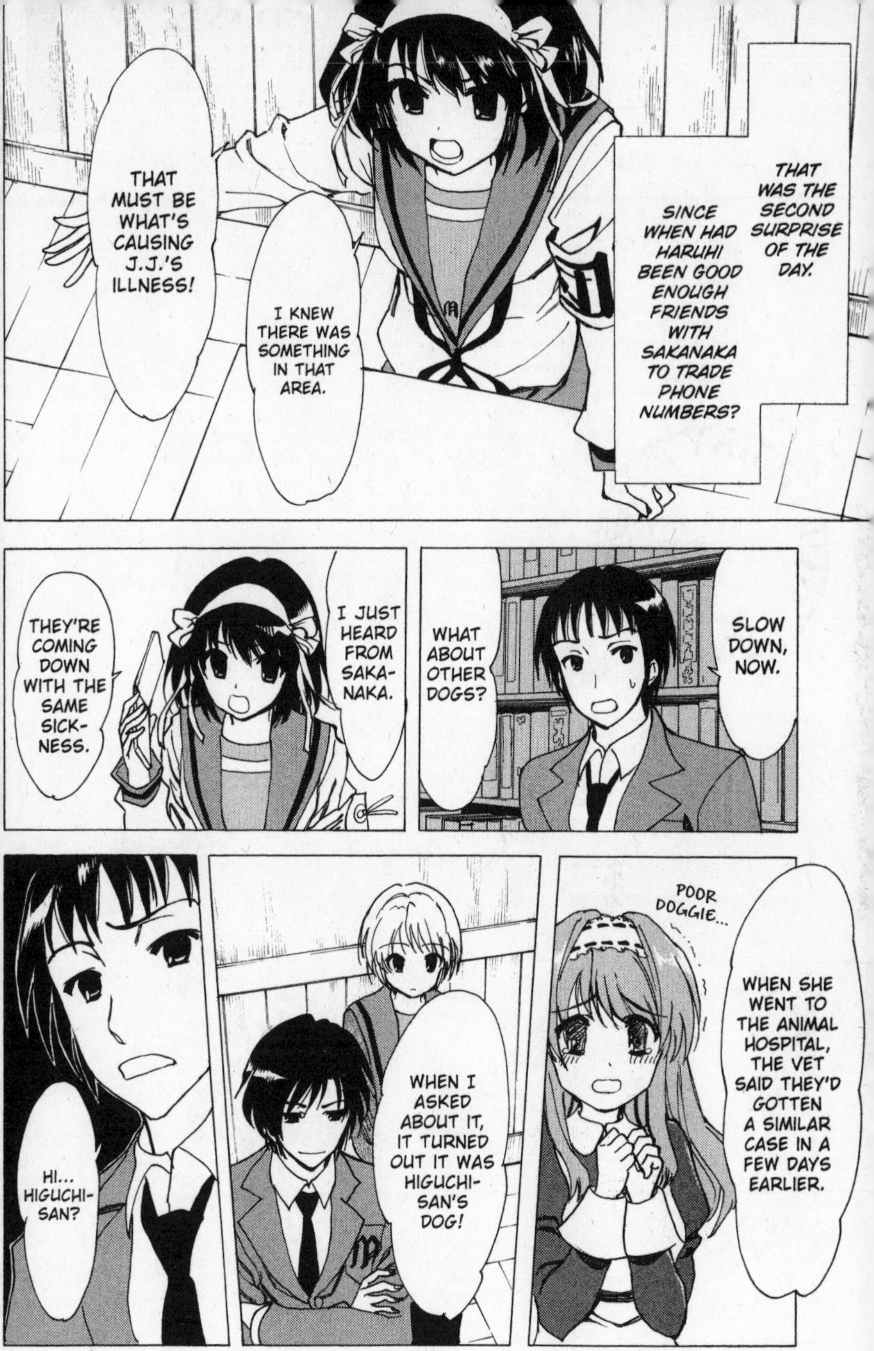
THAT WAS THE SECOND SURPRISE OF THE DAY.
SINCE WHEN HAD HARUHI BEEN GOOD ENOUGH FRIENDS WITH SAKANAKA TO TRADE PHONE NUMBERS?
I KNEW THERE WAS SOMETHING IN THAT AREA.
THAT MUST BE WHAT'S CAUSING J.J.'S ILLNESS!
SLOW DOWN, NOW.
WHAT ABOUT OTHER DOGS?
I JUST HEARD FROM SAKA-NAKA.
THEY'RE COMING DOWN WITH THE SAME SICK-NESS.
POOR DOGGIE...
WHEN SHE WENT TO THE ANIMAL HOSPITAL, THE VET SAID THEY'D GOTTEN A SIMILAR CASE IN A FEW DAYS EARLIER.
WHEN I ASKED ABOUT IT, IT TURNED OUT IT WAS HIGUCHI-SAN'S DOG!
HI... HIGUCHI-SAN?

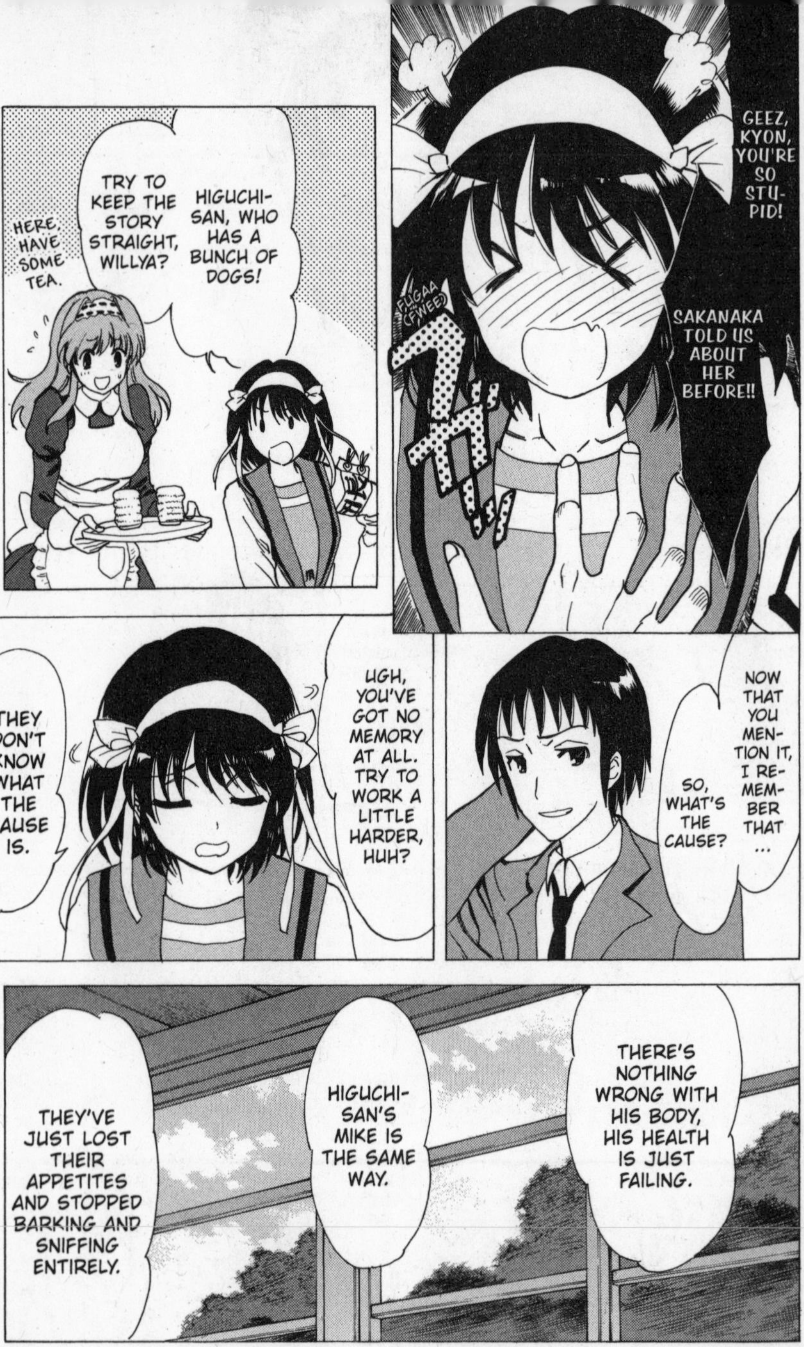
GEEZ, KYON, YOU'RE SO STUPID!
SAKANAKA TOLD US ABOUT HER BEFORE!!
FUGAA (FWEE)
HIGUCHI-SAN, WHO HAS A BUNCH OF DOGS!
TRY TO KEEP THE STORY STRAIGHT, WILLYA?
HERE, HAVE SOME TEA.
NOW THAT YOU MENTION IT, I REMEMBER THAT ...
SO, WHAT'S THE CAUSE?
UGH, YOU'VE GOT NO MEMORY AT ALL. TRY TO WORK A LITTLE HARDER, HUH?
THEY DON'T KNOW WHAT THE CAUSE IS.
THERE'S NOTHING WRONG WITH HIS BODY, HIS HEALTH IS JUST FAILING.
HIGUCHI-SAN'S MIKE IS THE SAME WAY.
THEY'VE JUST LOST THEIR APPETITES AND STOPPED BARKING AND SNIFFING ENTIRELY.

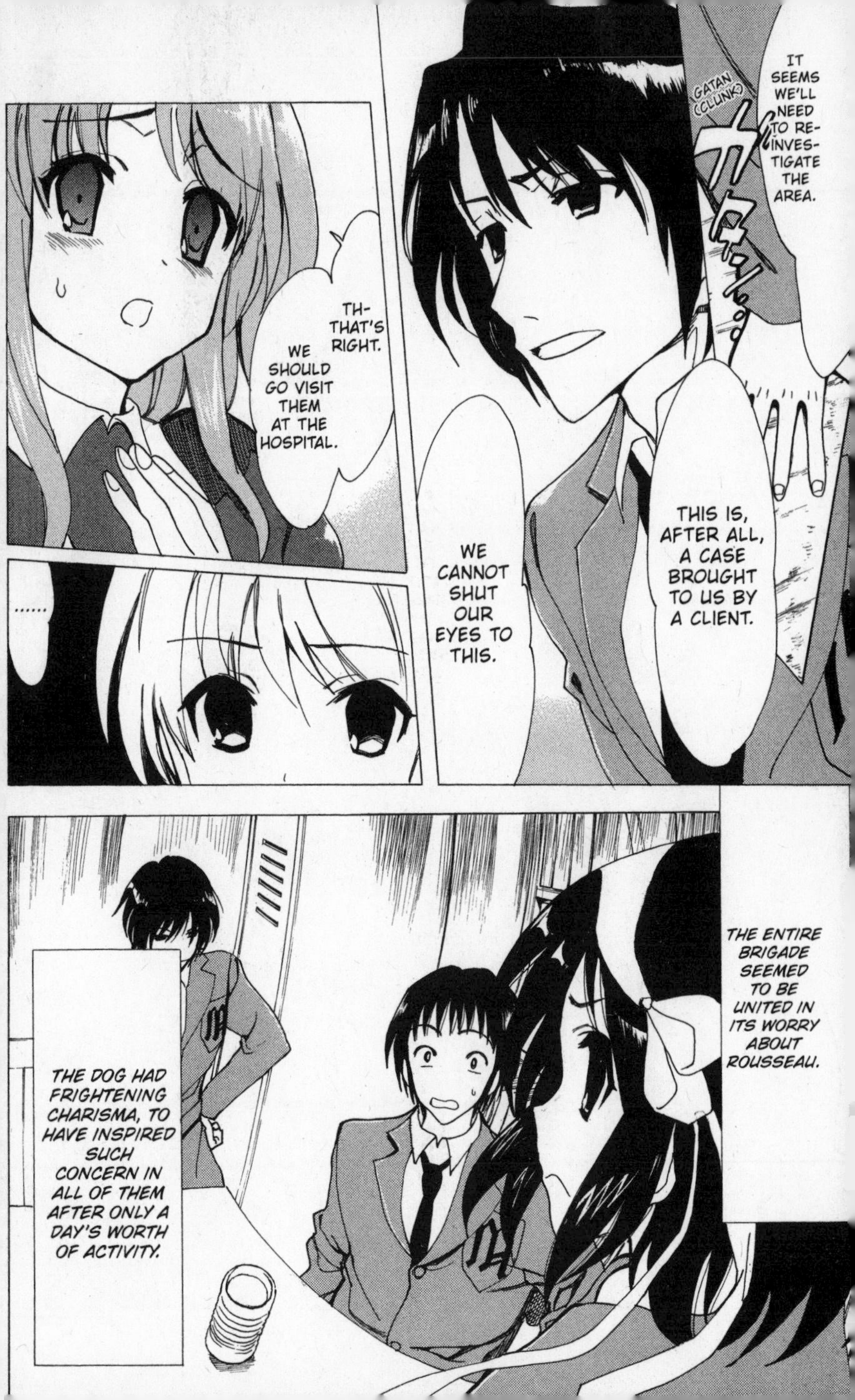
GATAN (CLUNK)
IT SEEMS WE'LL NEED TO RE-INVESTIGATE THE AREA.
THIS IS, AFTER ALL, A CASE BROUGHT TO US BY A CLIENT.
WE CANNOT SHUT OUR EYES TO THIS.
TH-THAT'S RIGHT.
WE SHOULD GO VISIT THEM AT THE HOSPITAL.
......
THE ENTIRE BRIGADE SEEMED TO BE UNITED IN ITS WORRY ABOUT ROUSSEAU.
THE DOG HAD FRIGHTENING CHARISMA, TO HAVE INSPIRED SUCH CONCERN IN ALL OF THEM AFTER ONLY A DAY'S WORTH OF ACTIVITY.

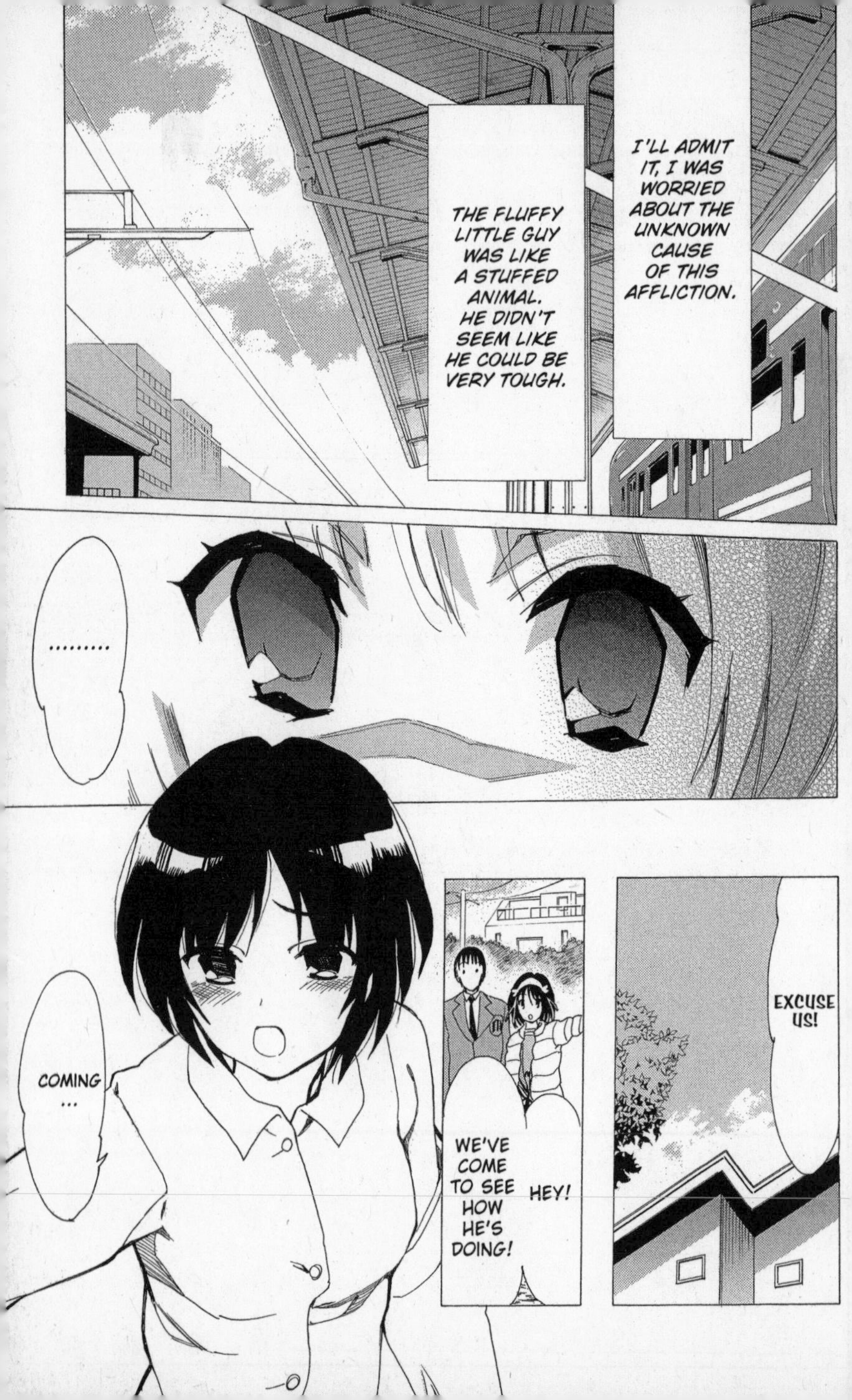
I'LL ADMIT IT, I WAS WORRIED ABOUT THE UNKNOWN CAUSE OF THIS AFFLICTION.
THE FLUFFY LITTLE GUY WAS LIKE A STUFFED ANIMAL. HE DIDN'T SEEM LIKE HE COULD BE VERY TOUGH.
....
EXCUSE US!
HEY!
WE'VE COME TO SEE HOW HE'S DOING!
COMING ...

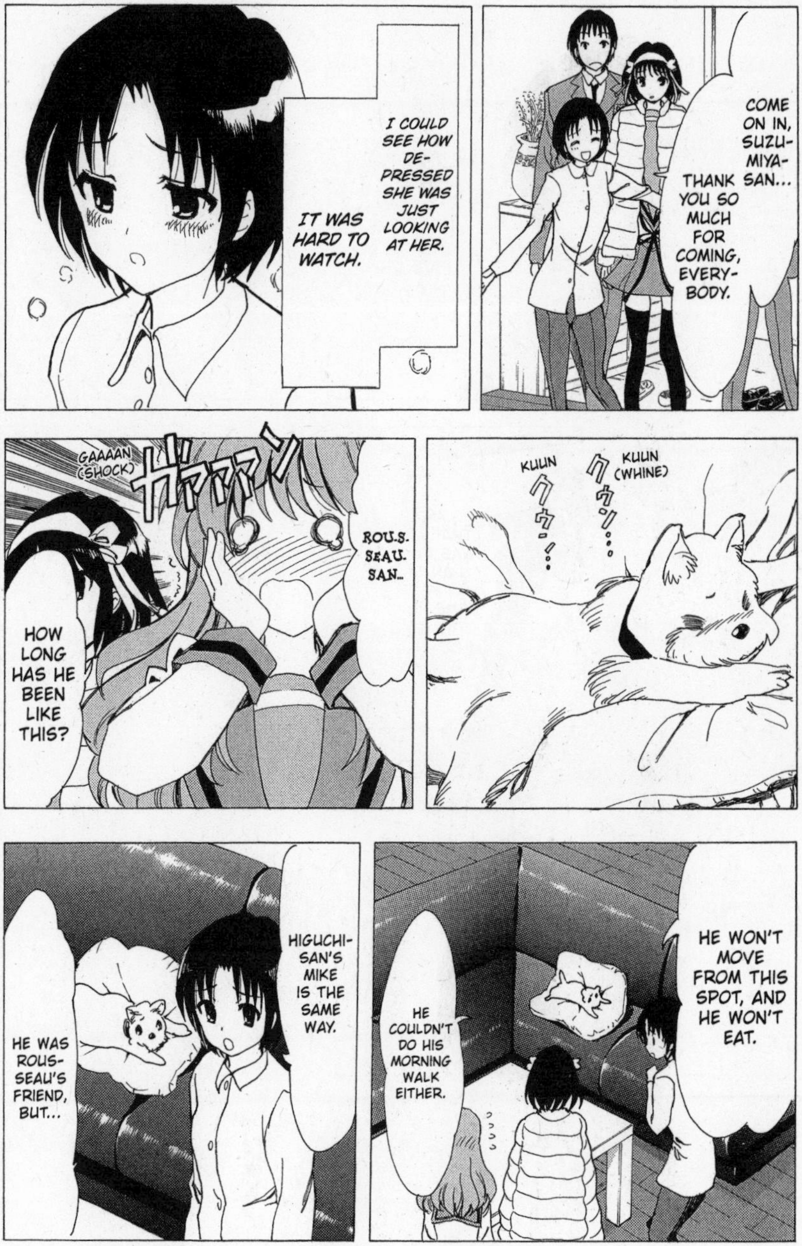

COME ON IN, SUZUMIYA-SAN...
THANK YOU SO MUCH FOR COMING, EVERYBODY.
I COULD SEE HOW DEPRESSED SHE WAS JUST LOOKING AT HER.
IT WAS HARD TO WATCH.
KUUN (WHINE)
KUUN
GAAAAN (SHOCK)
ROUS.SEAU.SAN...
HOW LONG HAS HE BEEN LIKE THIS?
HE WON'T MOVE FROM THIS SPOT, AND HE WON'T EAT.
HE COULDN'T DO HIS MORNING WALK EITHER.
HIGUCHI-SAN'S MIKE IS THE SAME WAY.
HE WAS ROUSSEAU'S FRIEND, BUT...

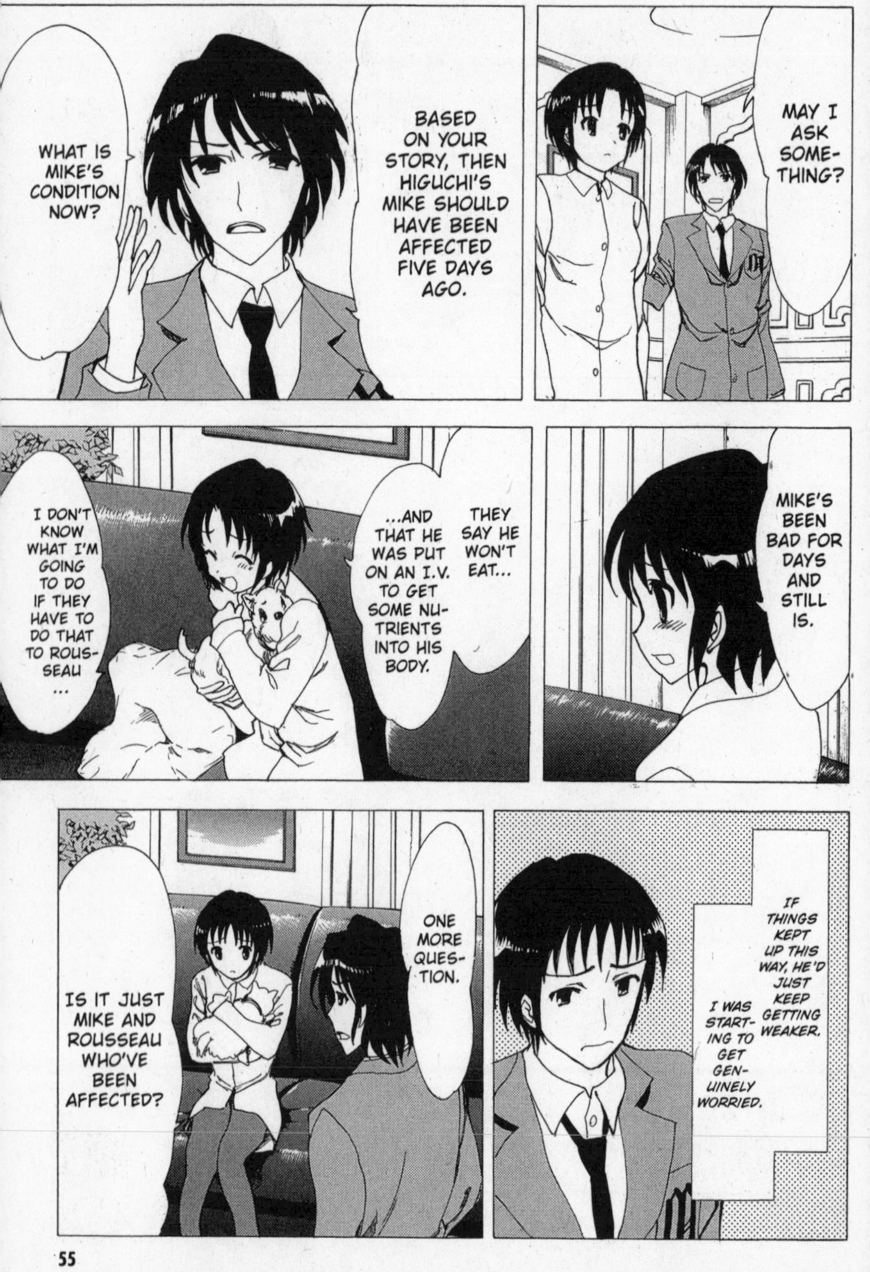
MAY I ASK SOMETHING?
BASED ON YOUR STORY, THEN HIGUCHI'S MIKE SHOULD HAVE BEEN AFFECTED FIVE DAYS AGO.
WHAT IS MIKE'S CONDITION NOW?
MIKE'S BEEN BAD FOR DAYS AND STILL IS.
THEY SAY HE WON'T EAT...
...AND THAT HE WAS PUT ON AN I.V. TO GET SOME NUTRIENTS INTO HIS BODY.
I DON'T KNOW WHAT I'M GOING TO DO IF THEY HAVE TO DO THAT TO ROUSSEAU...
IF THINGS KEPT UP THIS WAY, HE'D JUST KEEP GETTING WEAKER.
I WAS STARTING TO GET GENUINELY WORRIED.
ONE MORE QUESTION.
IS IT JUST MIKE AND ROUSSEAU WHO'VE BEEN AFFECTED?

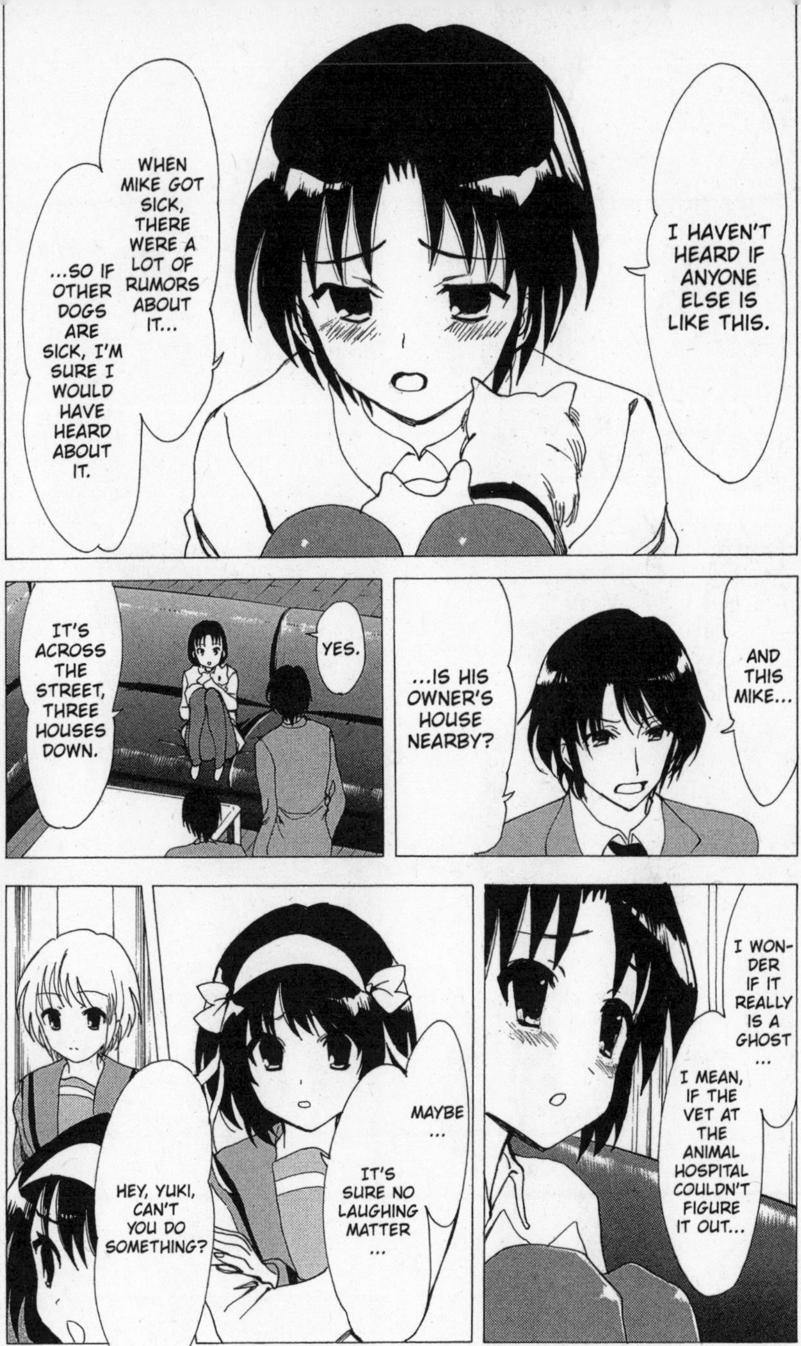
I HAVEN'T HEARD IF ANYONE ELSE IS LIKE THIS.
WHEN MIKE GOT SICK, THERE WERE A LOT OF RUMORS ABOUT IT...
...SO IF OTHER DOGS ARE SICK, I'M SURE I WOULD HAVE HEARD ABOUT IT.
AND THIS MIKE...
...IS HIS OWNER'S HOUSE NEARBY?
YES.
IT'S ACROSS THE STREET, THREE HOUSES DOWN.
I WON-DER IF IT REALLY IS A GHOST...
I MEAN, IF THE VET AT THE ANIMAL HOSPITAL COULDN'T FIGURE IT OUT...
MAYBE...
IT'S SURE NO LAUGHING MATTER...
HEY, YUKI, CAN'T YOU DO SOMETHING?

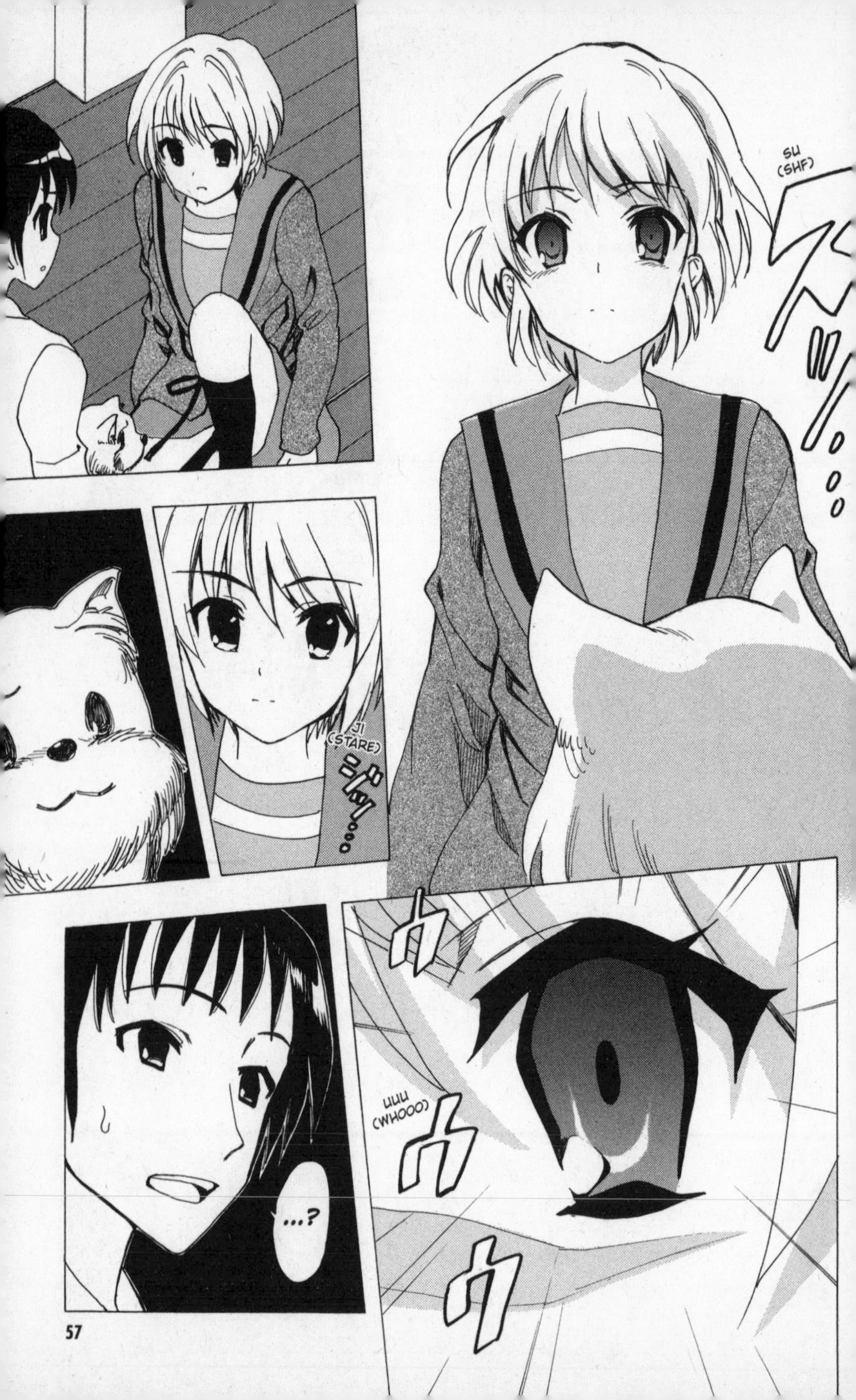
SU (SHF)
JI (STARE)
UUU (WHOOO)
...?

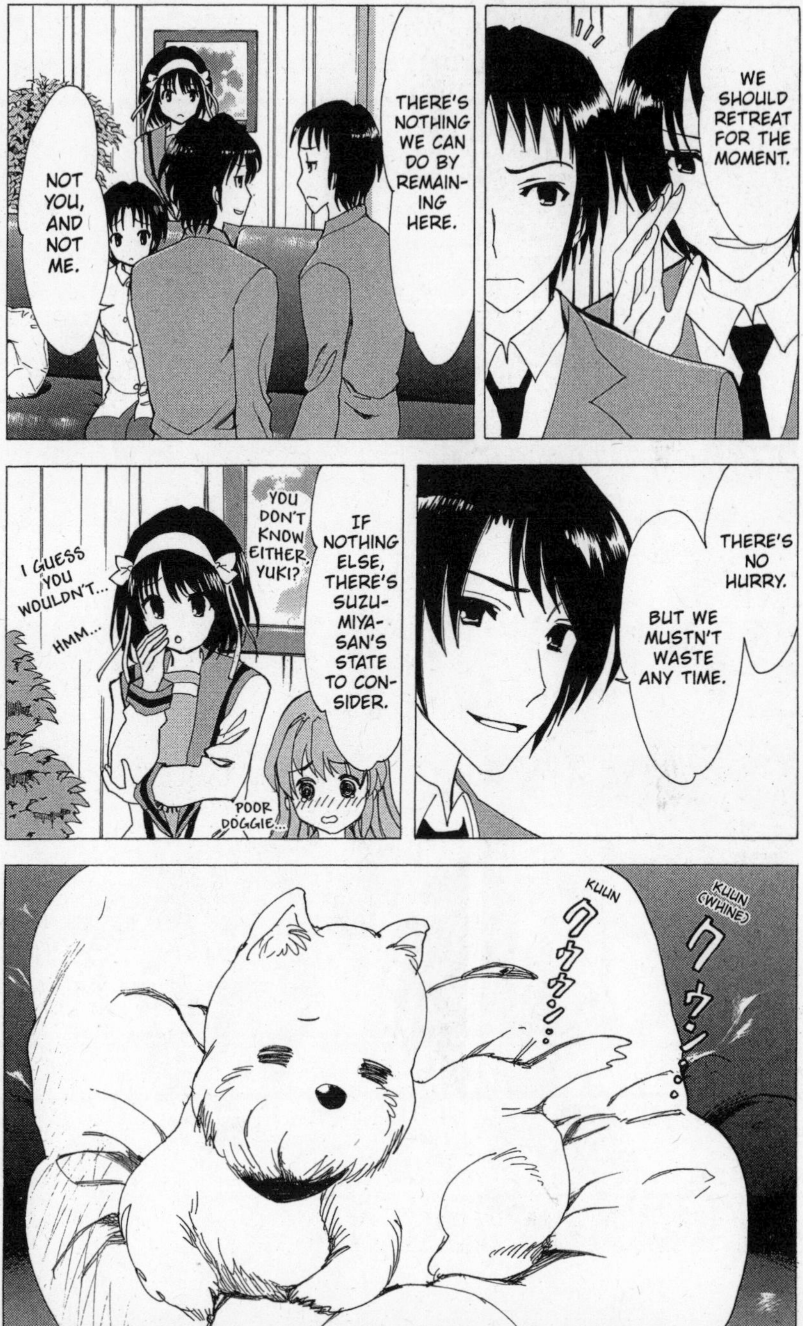
WE SHOULD RETREAT FOR THE MOMENT.
THERE'S NOTHING WE CAN DO BY REMAINING HERE.
NOT YOU, AND NOT ME.
THERE'S NO HURRY.
BUT WE MUSTN'T WASTE ANY TIME.
IF NOTHING ELSE, THERE'S SUZUMIYA-SAN'S STATE TO CONSIDER.
YOU DON'T KNOW EITHER, YUKI?
I GUESS YOU WOULDN'T...
HMM...
POOR DOGGIE...
KUUN (WHINE)
クウーン。。
KUUN
クウウン。。

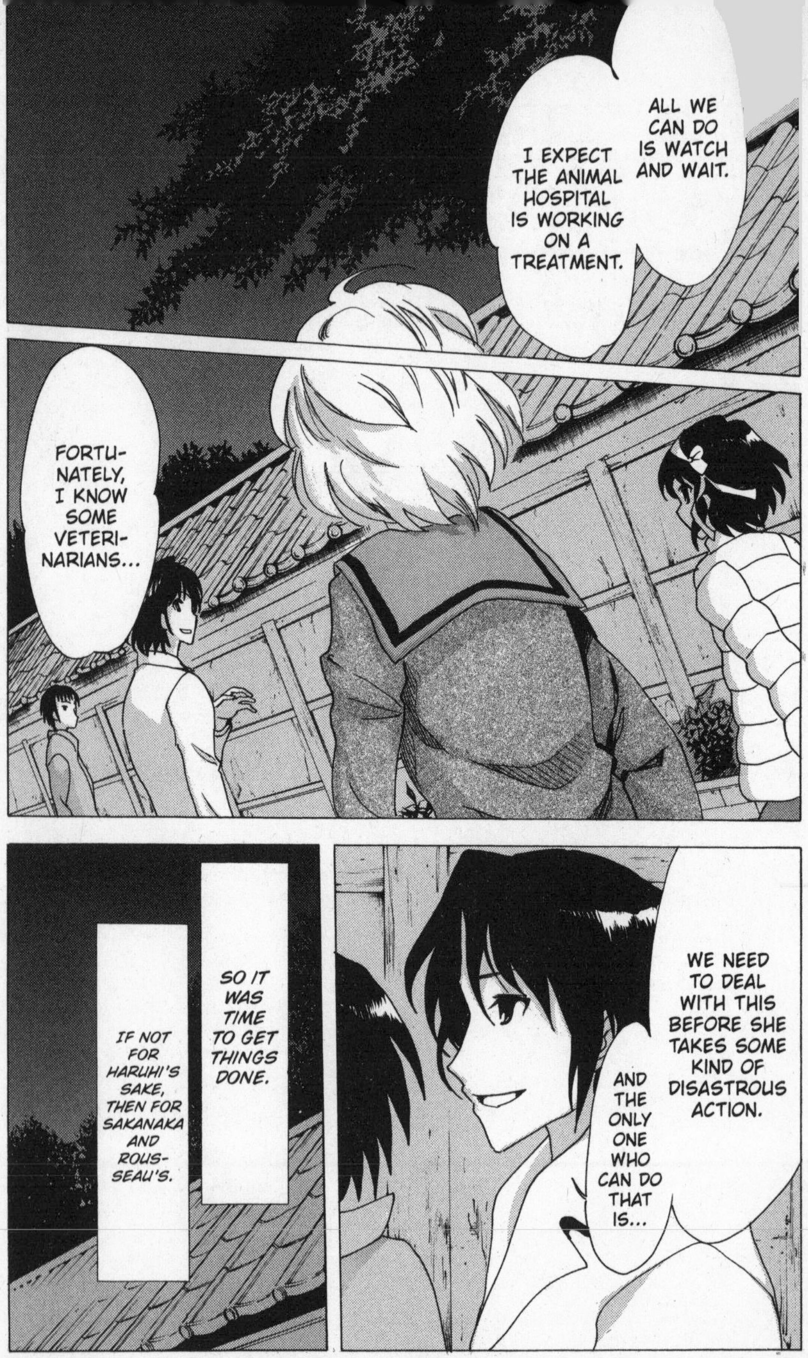
ALL WE CAN DO IS WATCH AND WAIT.
I EXPECT THE ANIMAL HOSPITAL IS WORKING ON A TREATMENT.
FORTU-NATELY, I KNOW SOME VETERI-NARIANS...
WE NEED TO DEAL WITH THIS BEFORE SHE TAKES SOME KIND OF DISASTROUS ACTION.
AND THE ONLY ONE WHO CAN DO THAT IS...
SO IT WAS TIME TO GET THINGS DONE.
IF NOT FOR HARUHI'S SAKE, THEN FOR SAKANAKA AND ROUS-SEAU'S.

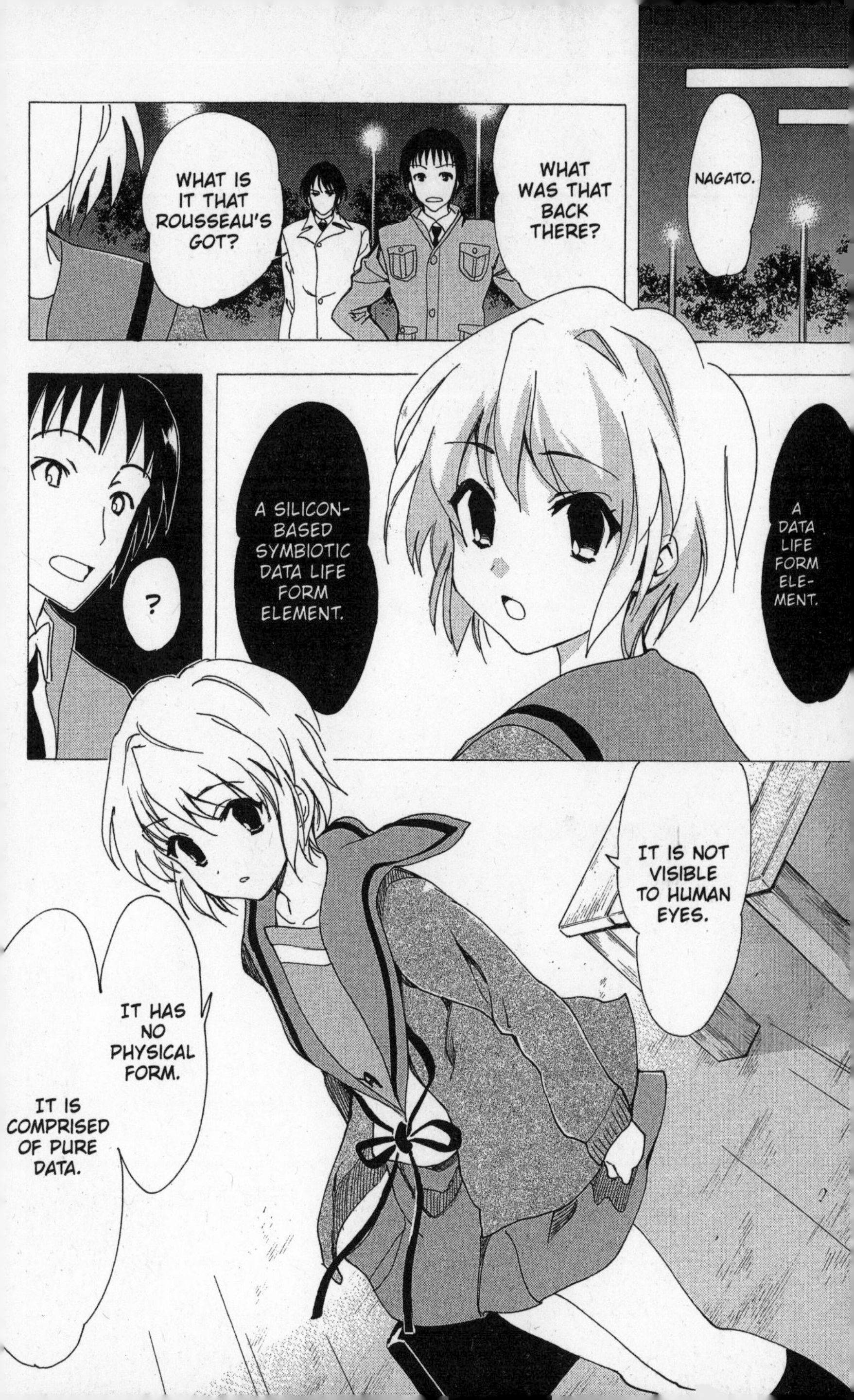
NAGATO.
WHAT WAS THAT BACK THERE?
WHAT IS IT THAT ROUSSEAU'S GOT?
A DATA LIFE FORM ELE-MENT.
A SILICON-BASED SYMBIOTIC DATA LIFE FORM ELEMENT.
?
IT IS NOT VISIBLE TO HUMAN EYES.
IT HAS NO PHYSICAL FORM.
IT IS COMPRISED OF PURE DATA.

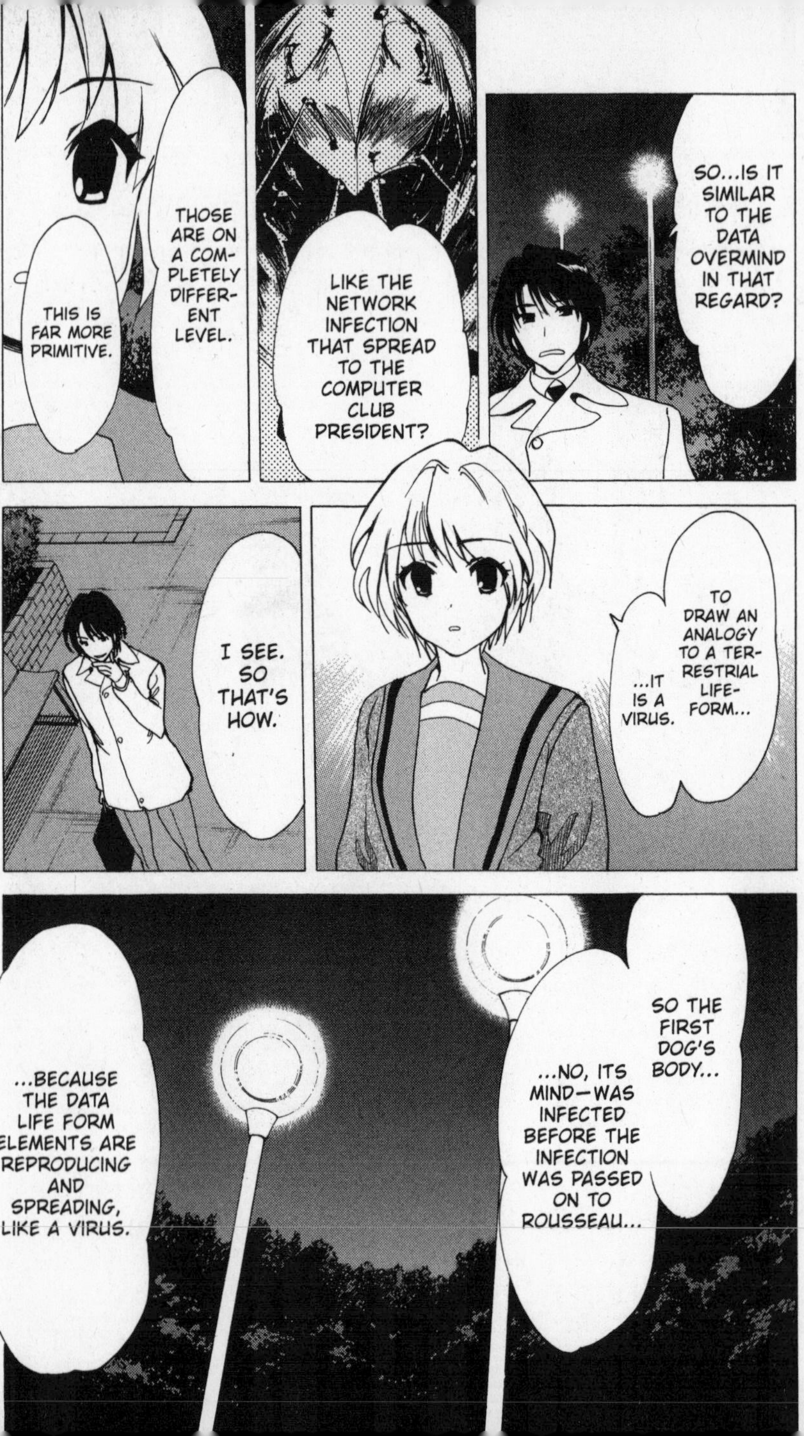

SO...IS IT SIMILAR TO THE DATA OVERMIND IN THAT REGARD?
LIKE THE NETWORK INFECTION THAT SPREAD TO THE COMPUTER CLUB PRESIDENT?
THOSE ARE ON A COMPLETELY DIFFERENT LEVEL.
THIS IS FAR MORE PRIMITIVE.
TO DRAW AN ANALOGY TO A TERRESTRIAL LIFE-FORM...
...IT IS A VIRUS.
I SEE. SO THAT'S HOW.
SO THE FIRST DOG'S BODY...
...NO, ITS MIND—WAS INFECTED BEFORE THE INFECTION WAS PASSED ON TO ROUSSEAU...
...BECAUSE THE DATA LIFE FORM ELEMENTS ARE REPRODUCING AND SPREADING, LIKE A VIRUS.

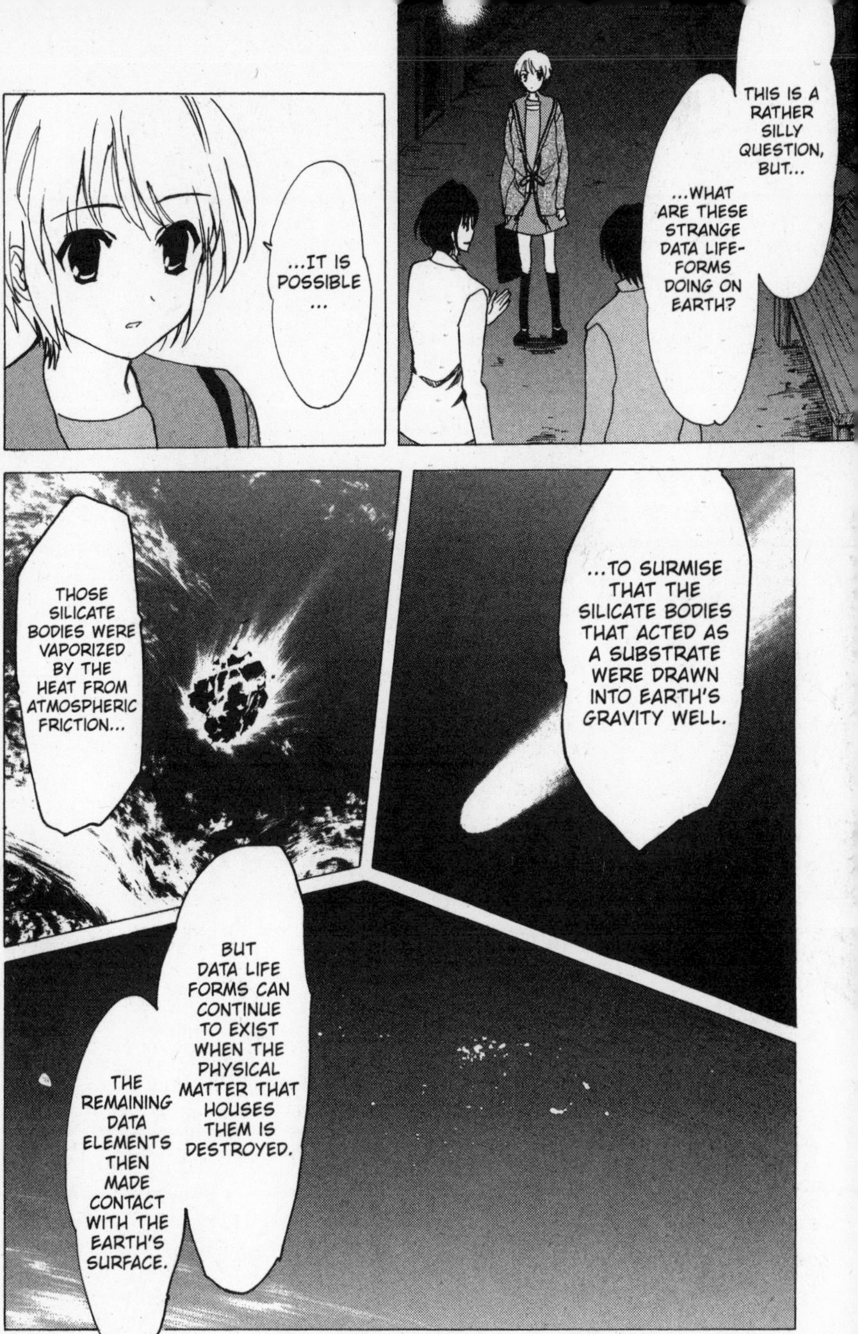
THIS IS A RATHER SILLY QUESTION, BUT...
...WHAT ARE THESE STRANGE DATA LIFE-FORMS DOING ON EARTH?
...IT IS POSSIBLE ...
...TO SURMISE THAT THE SILICATE BODIES THAT ACTED AS A SUBSTRATE WERE DRAWN INTO EARTH'S GRAVITY WELL.
THOSE SILICATE BODIES WERE VAPORIZED BY THE HEAT FROM ATMOSPHERIC FRICTION...
BUT DATA LIFE FORMS CAN CONTINUE TO EXIST WHEN THE PHYSICAL MATTER THAT HOUSES THEM IS DESTROYED.
THE REMAINING DATA ELEMENTS THEN MADE CONTACT WITH THE EARTH'S SURFACE.

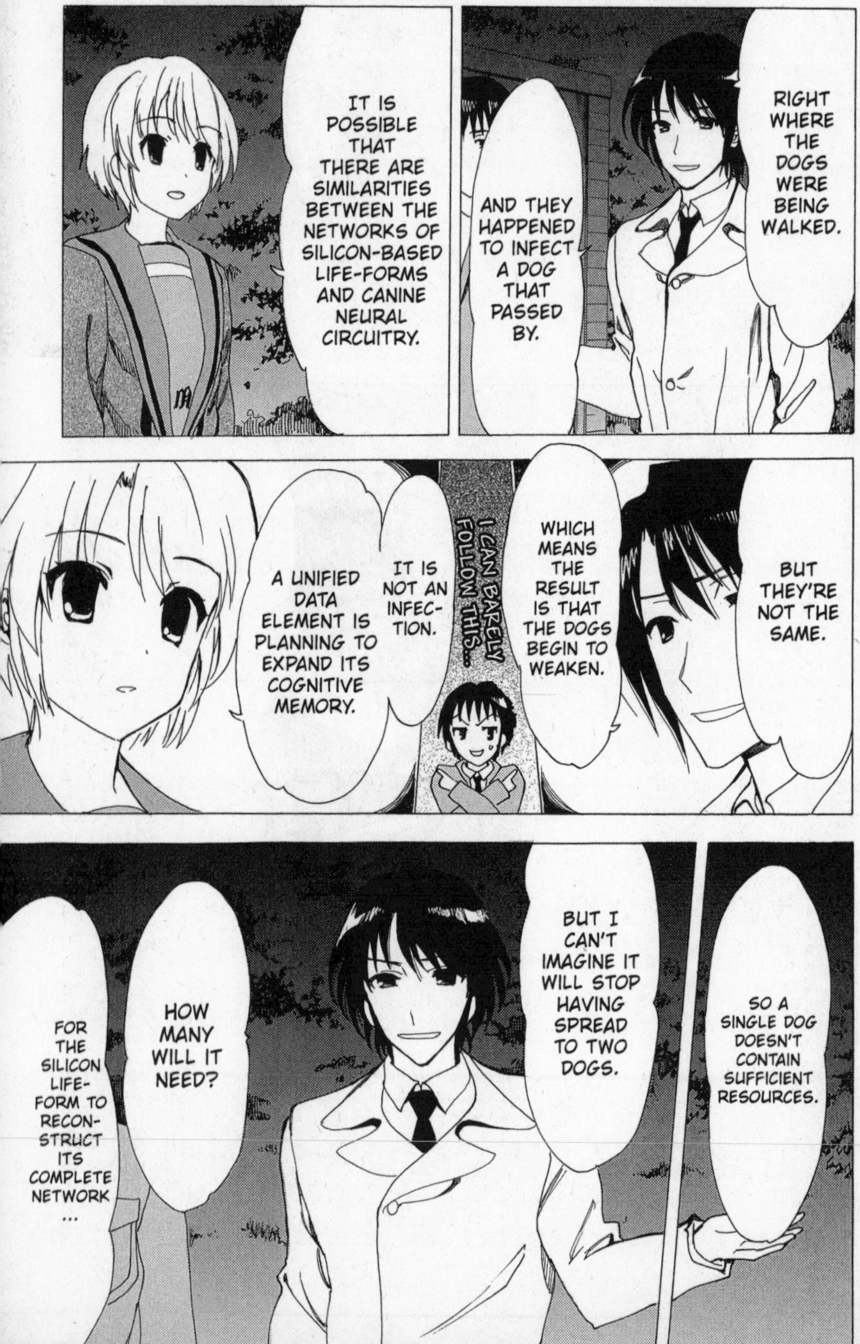
RIGHT WHERE THE DOGS WERE BEING WALKED.
AND THEY HAPPENED TO INFECT A DOG THAT PASSED BY.
IT IS POSSIBLE THAT THERE ARE SIMILARITIES BETWEEN THE NETWORKS OF SILICON-BASED LIFE-FORMS AND CANINE NEURAL CIRCUITRY.
BUT THEY'RE NOT THE SAME.
WHICH MEANS THE RESULT IS THAT THE DOGS BEGIN TO WEAKEN.
I CAN BARELY FOLLOW THIS...
IT IS NOT AN INFEC-TION.
A UNIFIED DATA ELEMENT IS PLANNING TO EXPAND ITS COGNITIVE MEMORY.
SO A SINGLE DOG DOESN'T CONTAIN SUFFICIENT RESOURCES.
BUT I CAN'T IMAGINE IT WILL STOP HAVING SPREAD TO TWO DOGS.
HOW MANY WILL IT NEED?
FOR THE SILICON LIFE-FORM TO RECON-STRUCT ITS COMPLETE NETWORK ...

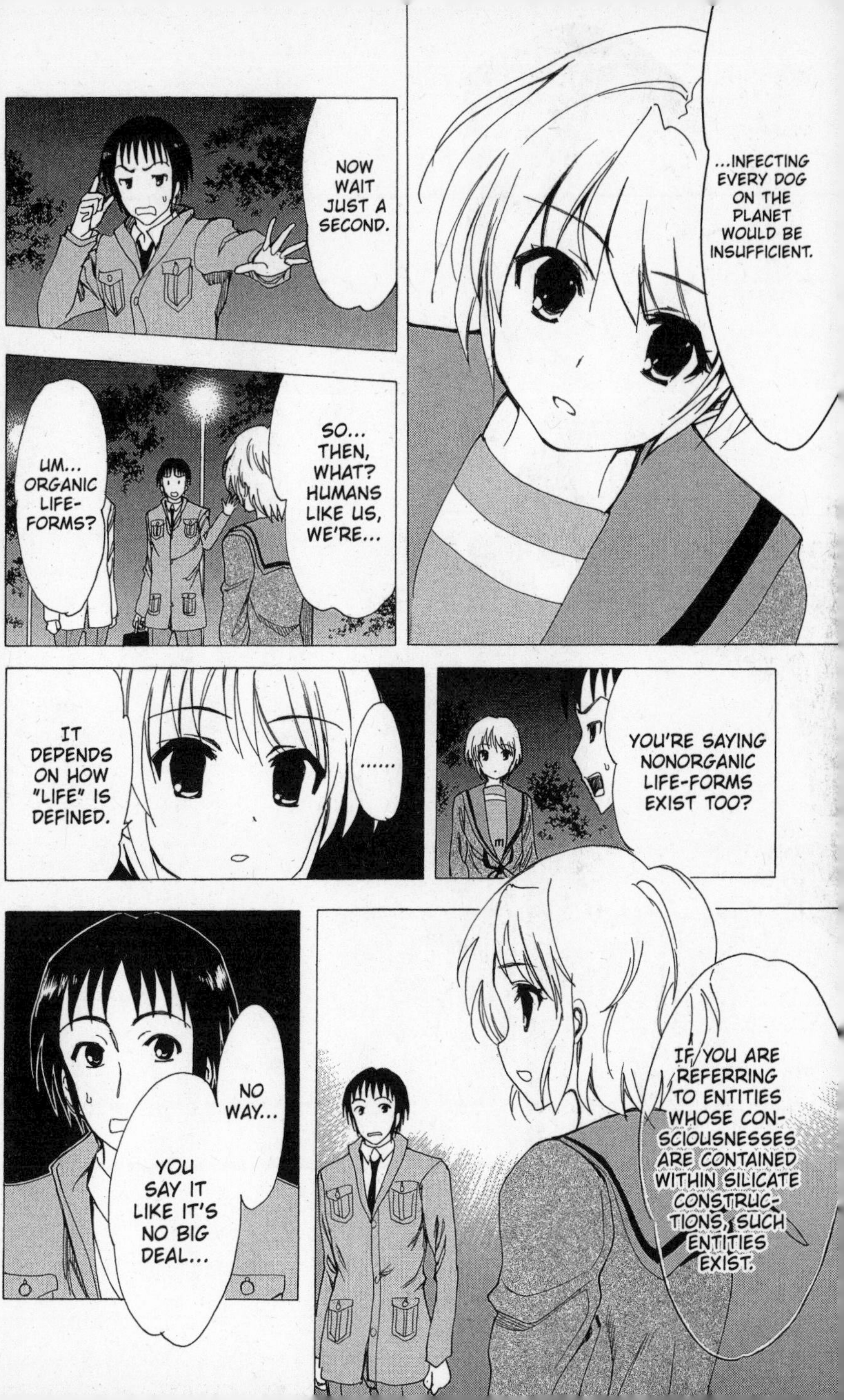
...INFECTING EVERY DOG ON THE PLANET WOULD BE INSUFFICIENT.
NOW WAIT JUST A SECOND.
SO... THEN, WHAT? HUMANS LIKE US, WE'RE...
UM... ORGANIC LIFE-FORMS?
YOU'RE SAYING NONORGANIC LIFE-FORMS EXIST TOO?
......
IT DEPENDS ON HOW "LIFE" IS DEFINED.
IF YOU ARE REFERRING TO ENTITIES WHOSE CONSCIOUSNESSES ARE CONTAINED WITHIN SILICATE CONSTRUCTIONS, SUCH ENTITIES EXIST.
NO WAY...
YOU SAY IT LIKE IT'S NO BIG DEAL...

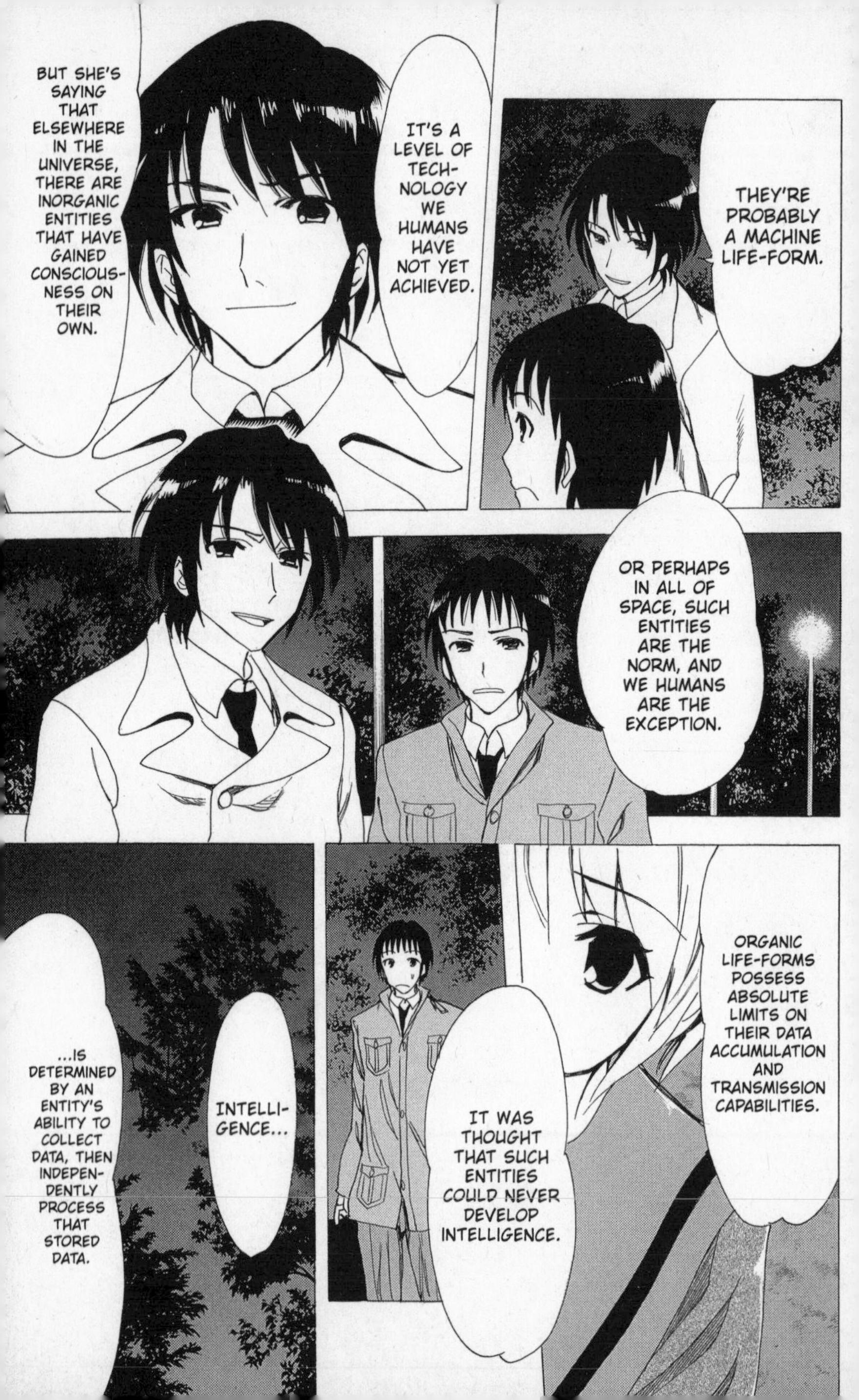
THEY'RE PROBABLY A MACHINE LIFE-FORM.
IT'S A LEVEL OF TECH-NOLOGY WE HUMANS HAVE NOT YET ACHIEVED.
BUT SHE'S SAYING THAT ELSEWHERE IN THE UNIVERSE, THERE ARE INORGANIC ENTITIES THAT HAVE GAINED CONSCIOUS-NESS ON THEIR OWN.
OR PERHAPS IN ALL OF SPACE, SUCH ENTITIES ARE THE NORM, AND WE HUMANS ARE THE EXCEPTION.
ORGANIC LIFE-FORMS POSSESS ABSOLUTE LIMITS ON THEIR DATA ACCUMULATION AND TRANSMISSION CAPABILITIES.
IT WAS THOUGHT THAT SUCH ENTITIES COULD NEVER DEVELOP INTELLIGENCE.
INTELLI-GENCE...
...IS DETERMINED BY AN ENTITY'S ABILITY TO COLLECT DATA, THEN INDEPEN-DENTLY PROCESS THAT STORED DATA.

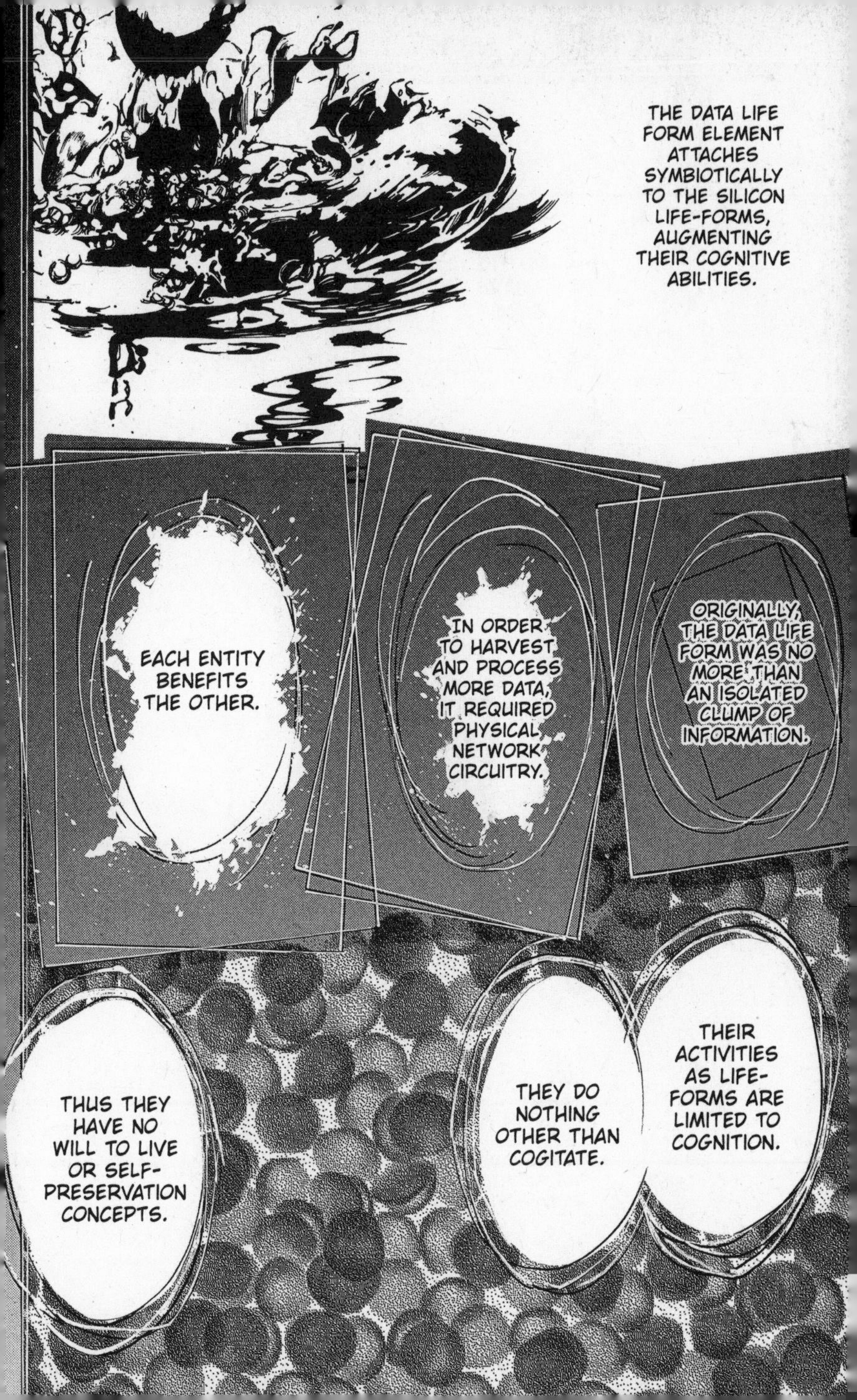
THE DATA LIFE FORM ELEMENT ATTACHES SYMBIOTICALLY TO THE SILICON LIFE-FORMS, AUGMENTING THEIR COGNITIVE ABILITIES.
ORIGINALLY, THE DATA LIFE FORM WAS NO MORE THAN AN ISOLATED CLUMP OF INFORMATION.
IN ORDER TO HARVEST AND PROCESS MORE DATA, IT REQUIRED PHYSICAL NETWORK CIRCUITRY.
EACH ENTITY BENEFITS THE OTHER.
THEIR ACTIVITIES AS LIFE-FORMS ARE LIMITED TO COGNITION.
THEY DO NOTHING OTHER THAN COGITATE.
THUS THEY HAVE NO WILL TO LIVE OR SELF-PRESERVATION CONCEPTS.

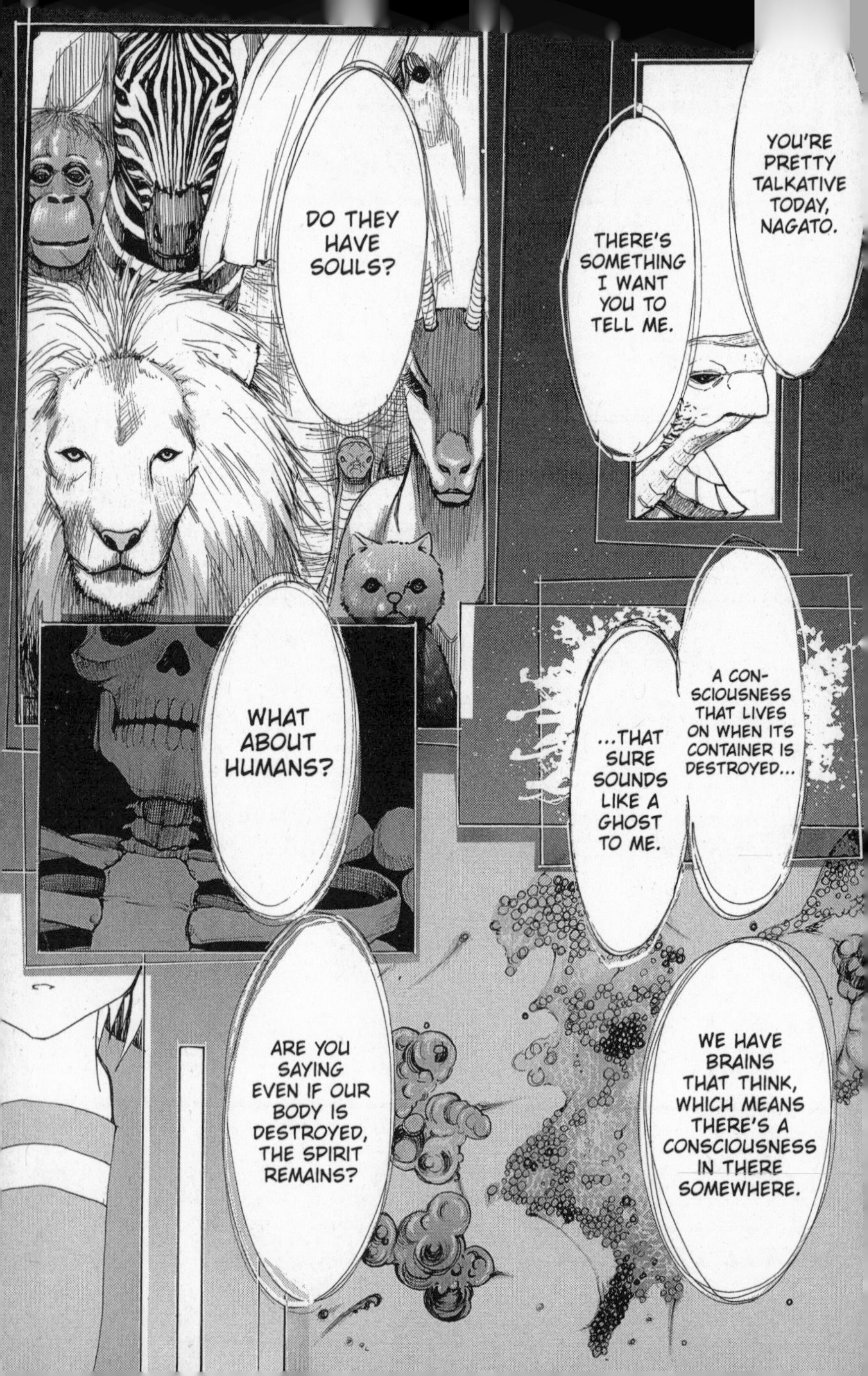
YOU'RE PRETTY TALKATIVE TODAY, NAGATO.
THERE'S SOMETHING I WANT YOU TO TELL ME.
DO THEY HAVE SOULS?
A CON-SCIOUSNESS THAT LIVES ON WHEN ITS CONTAINER IS DESTROYED...
...THAT SURE SOUNDS LIKE A GHOST TO ME.
WHAT ABOUT HUMANS?
WE HAVE BRAINS THAT THINK, WHICH MEANS THERE'S A CONSCIOUSNESS IN THERE SOMEWHERE.
ARE YOU SAYING EVEN IF OUR BODY IS DESTROYED, THE SPIRIT REMAINS?

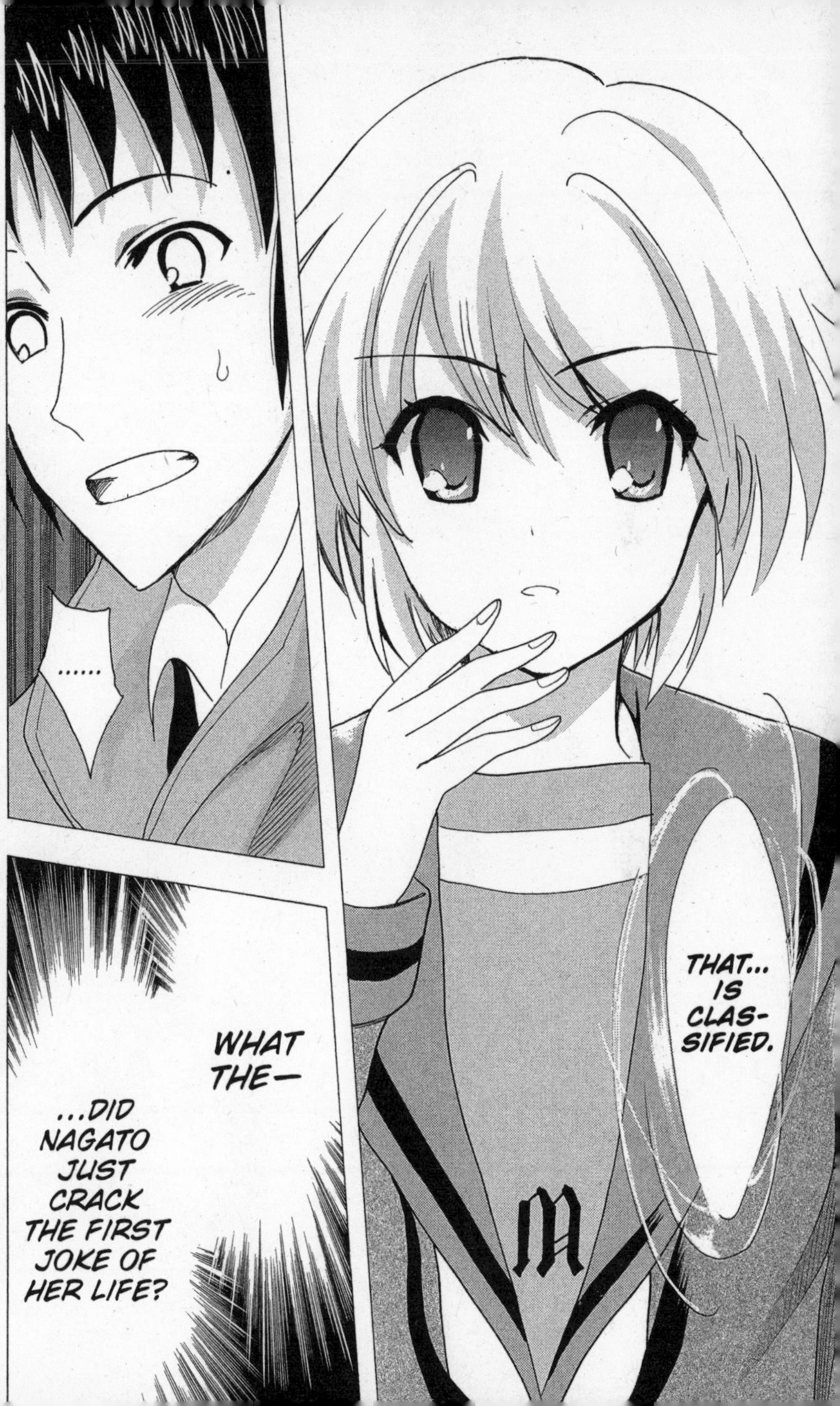
THAT... IS CLAS-SIFIED.
......
WHAT THE—
...DID NAGATO JUST CRACK THE FIRST JOKE OF HER LIFE?

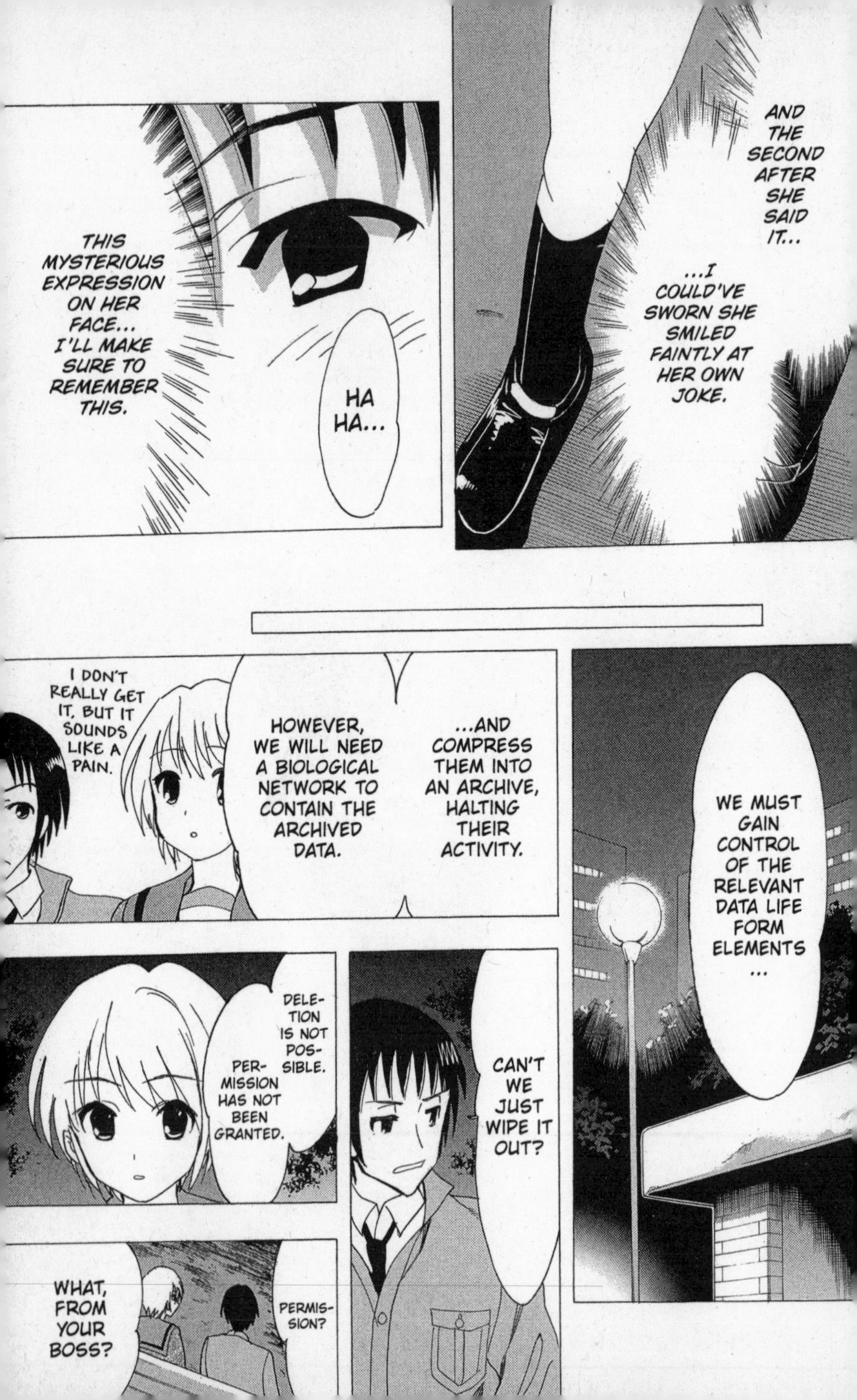
AND THE SECOND AFTER SHE SAID IT...
...I COULD'VE SWORN SHE SMILED FAINTLY AT HER OWN JOKE.
HA HA...
THIS MYSTERIOUS EXPRESSION ON HER FACE... I'LL MAKE SURE TO REMEMBER THIS.
WE MUST GAIN CONTROL OF THE RELEVANT DATA LIFE FORM ELEMENTS ...
...AND COMPRESS THEM INTO AN ARCHIVE, HALTING THEIR ACTIVITY.
HOWEVER, WE WILL NEED A BIOLOGICAL NETWORK TO CONTAIN THE ARCHIVED DATA.
I DON'T REALLY GET IT, BUT IT SOUNDS LIKE A PAIN.
CAN'T WE JUST WIPE IT OUT?
DELETION IS NOT POSSIBLE.
PERMISSION HAS NOT BEEN GRANTED.
PERMISSION?
WHAT, FROM YOUR BOSS?

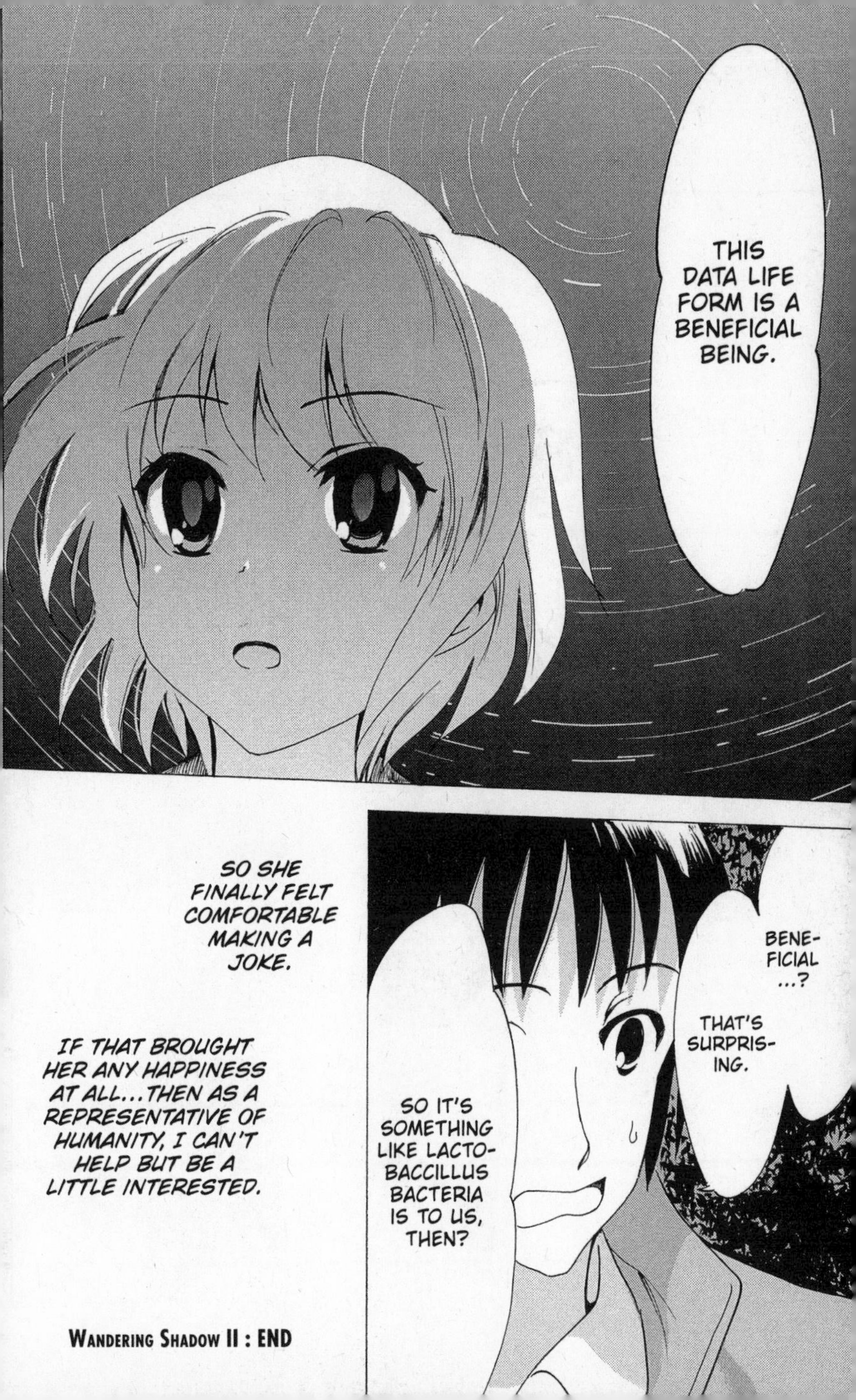
THIS DATA LIFE FORM IS A BENEFICIAL BEING.
BENE-FICIAL ...?
THAT'S SURPRIS-ING.
SO IT'S SOMETHING LIKE LACTO-BACCILLUS BACTERIA IS TO US, THEN?
SO SHE FINALLY FELT COMFORTABLE MAKING A JOKE.
IF THAT BROUGHT HER ANY HAPPINESS AT ALL...THEN AS A REPRESENTATIVE OF HUMANITY, I CAN'T HELP BUT BE A LITTLE INTERESTED.

Wandering Shadow II : END

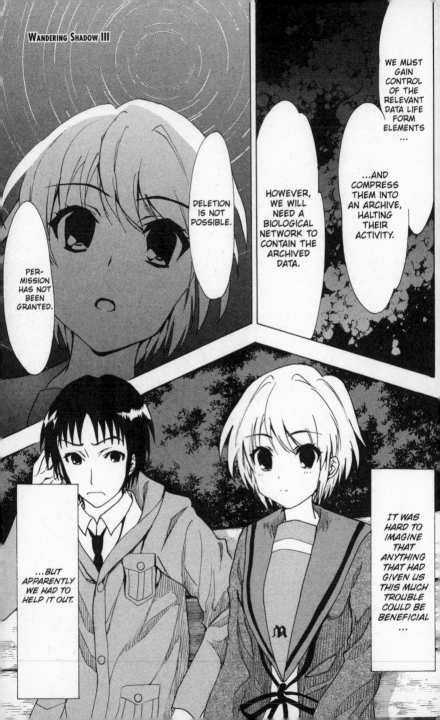

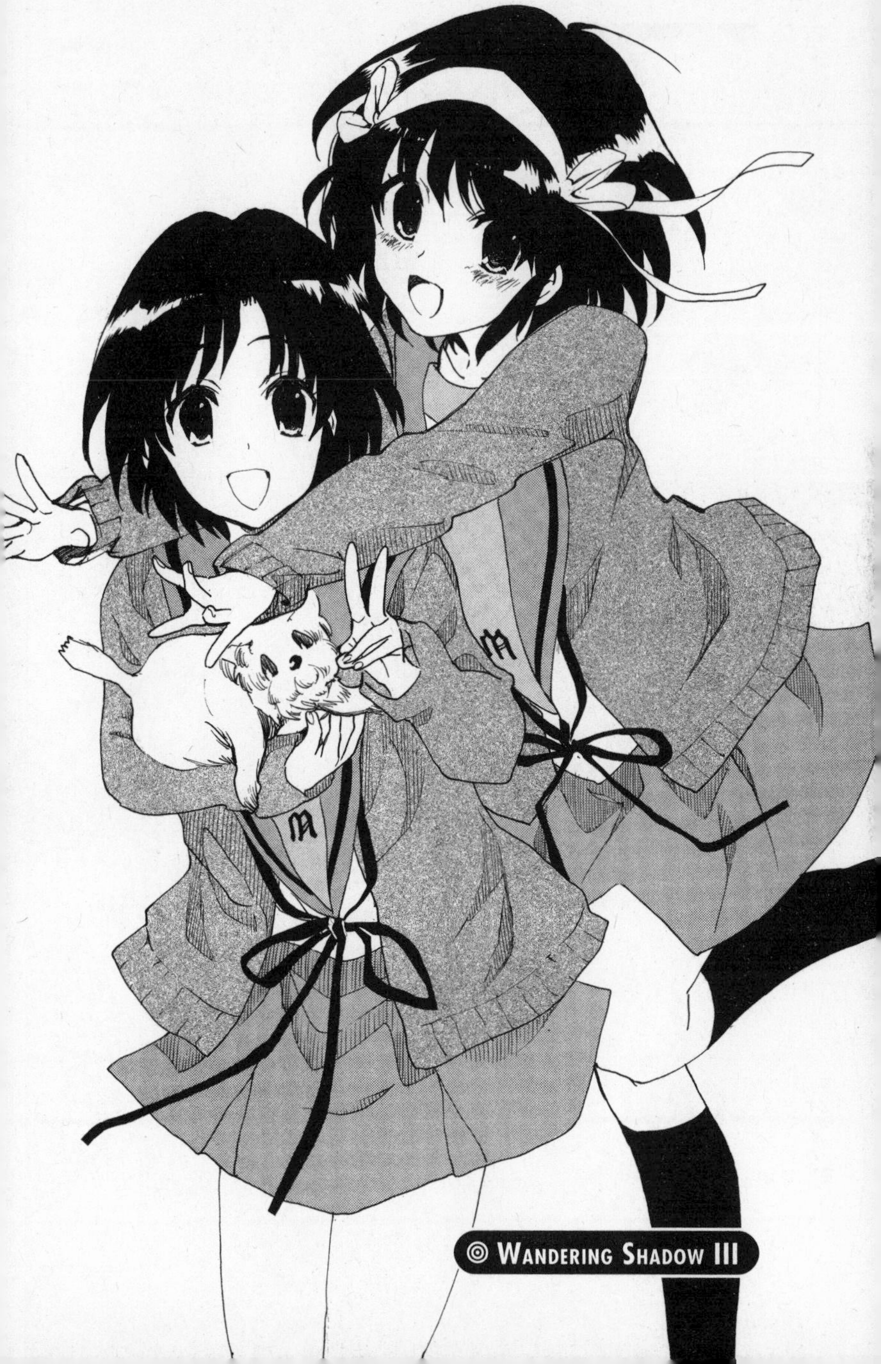

◎ WANDERING SHADOW III

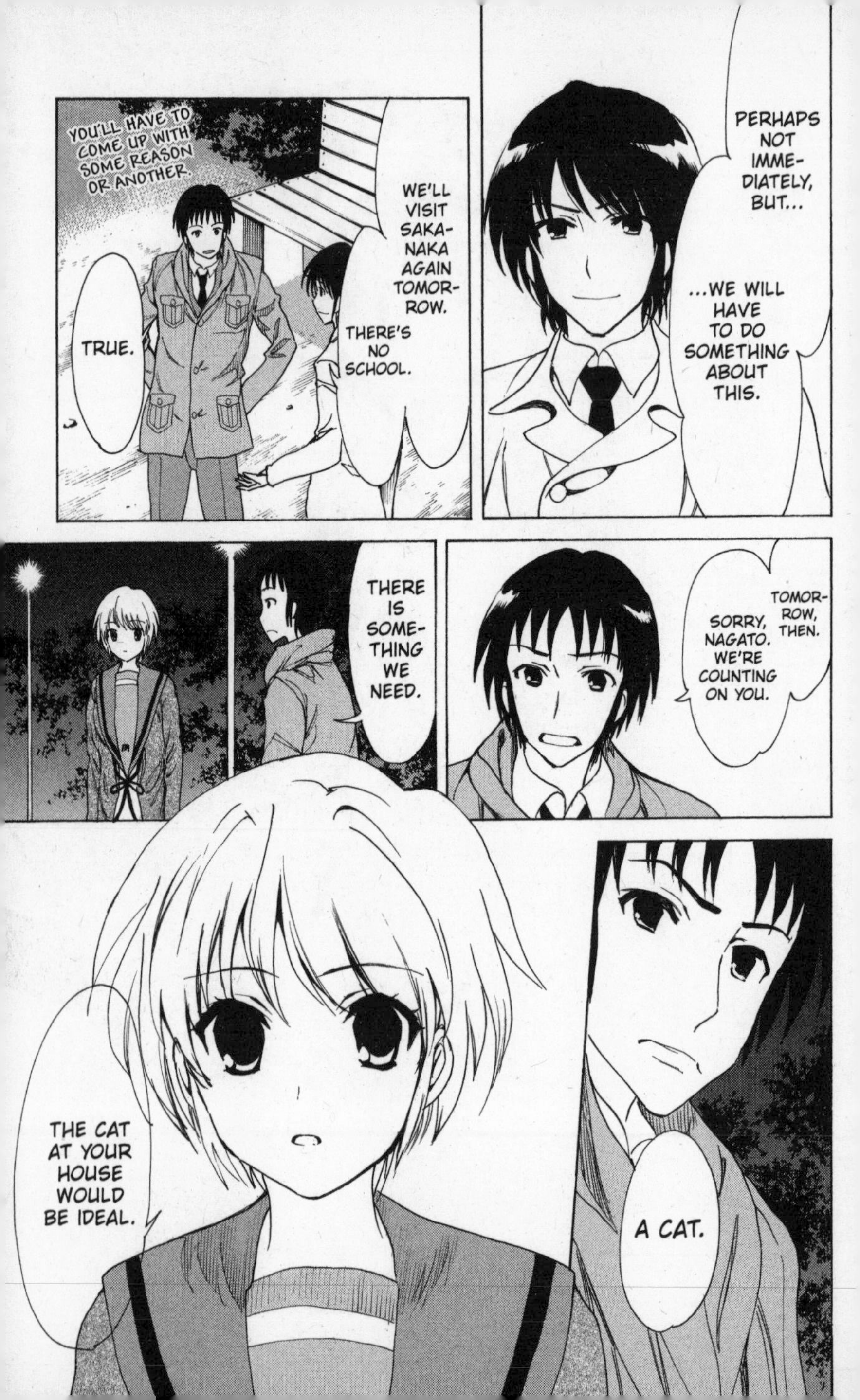
PERHAPS NOT IMMEDIATELY, BUT...
...WE WILL HAVE TO DO SOMETHING ABOUT THIS.
WE'LL VISIT SAKANAKA AGAIN TOMORROW.
THERE'S NO SCHOOL.
YOU'LL HAVE TO COME UP WITH SOME REASON OR ANOTHER.
TRUE.
TOMORROW, THEN.
SORRY, NAGATO. WE'RE COUNTING ON YOU.
THERE IS SOMETHING WE NEED.
A CAT.
THE CAT AT YOUR HOUSE WOULD BE IDEAL.

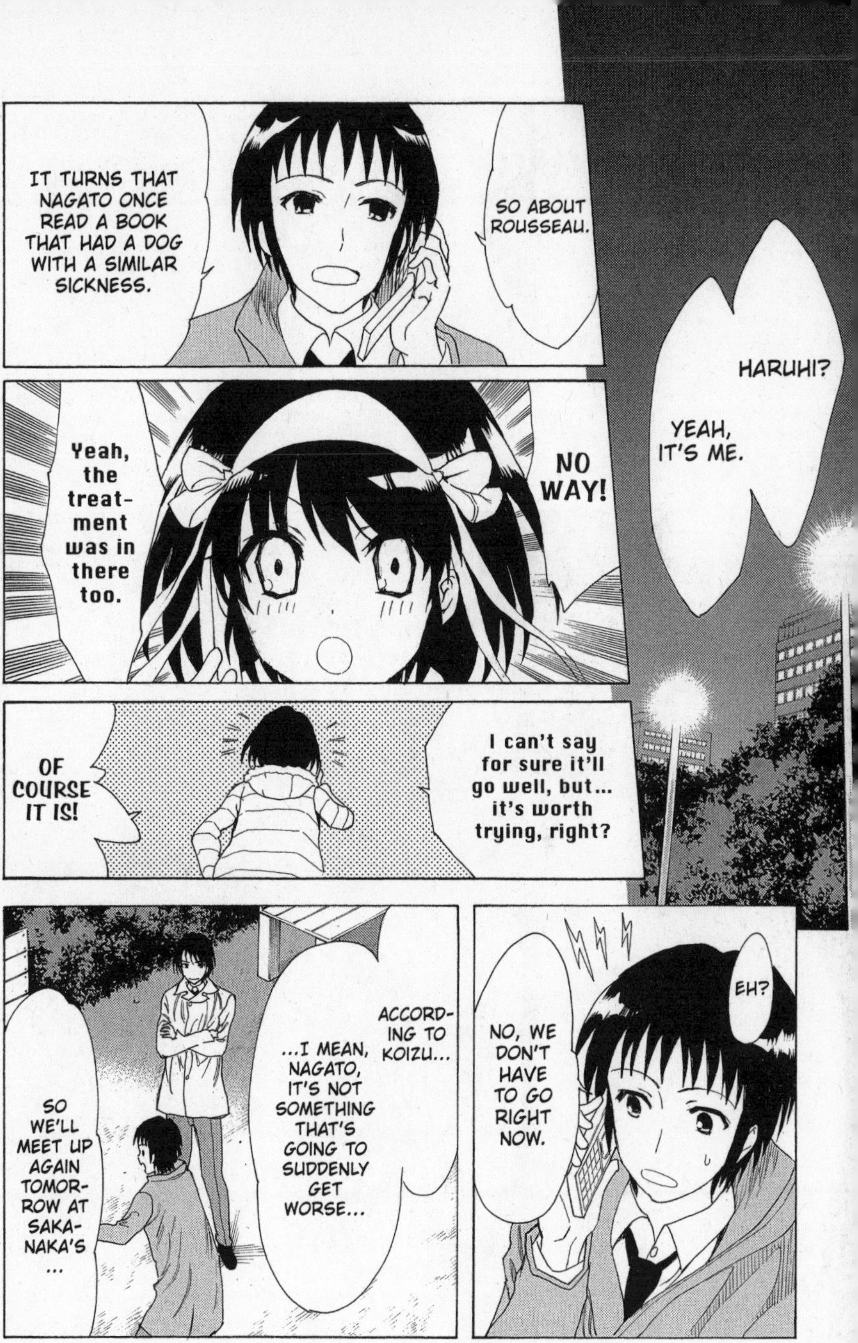
HARUHI?
YEAH, IT'S ME.
SO ABOUT ROUSSEAU.
IT TURNS THAT NAGATO ONCE READ A BOOK THAT HAD A DOG WITH A SIMILAR SICKNESS.
NO WAY!
Yeah, the treat-ment was in there too.
I can't say for sure it'll go well, but... it's worth trying, right?
OF COURSE IT IS!
EH?
NO, WE DON'T HAVE TO GO RIGHT NOW.
ACCORD-ING TO KOIZU...
...I MEAN, NAGATO, IT'S NOT SOMETHING THAT'S GOING TO SUDDENLY GET WORSE...
SO WE'LL MEET UP AGAIN TOMOR-ROW AT SAKA-NAKA'S ...

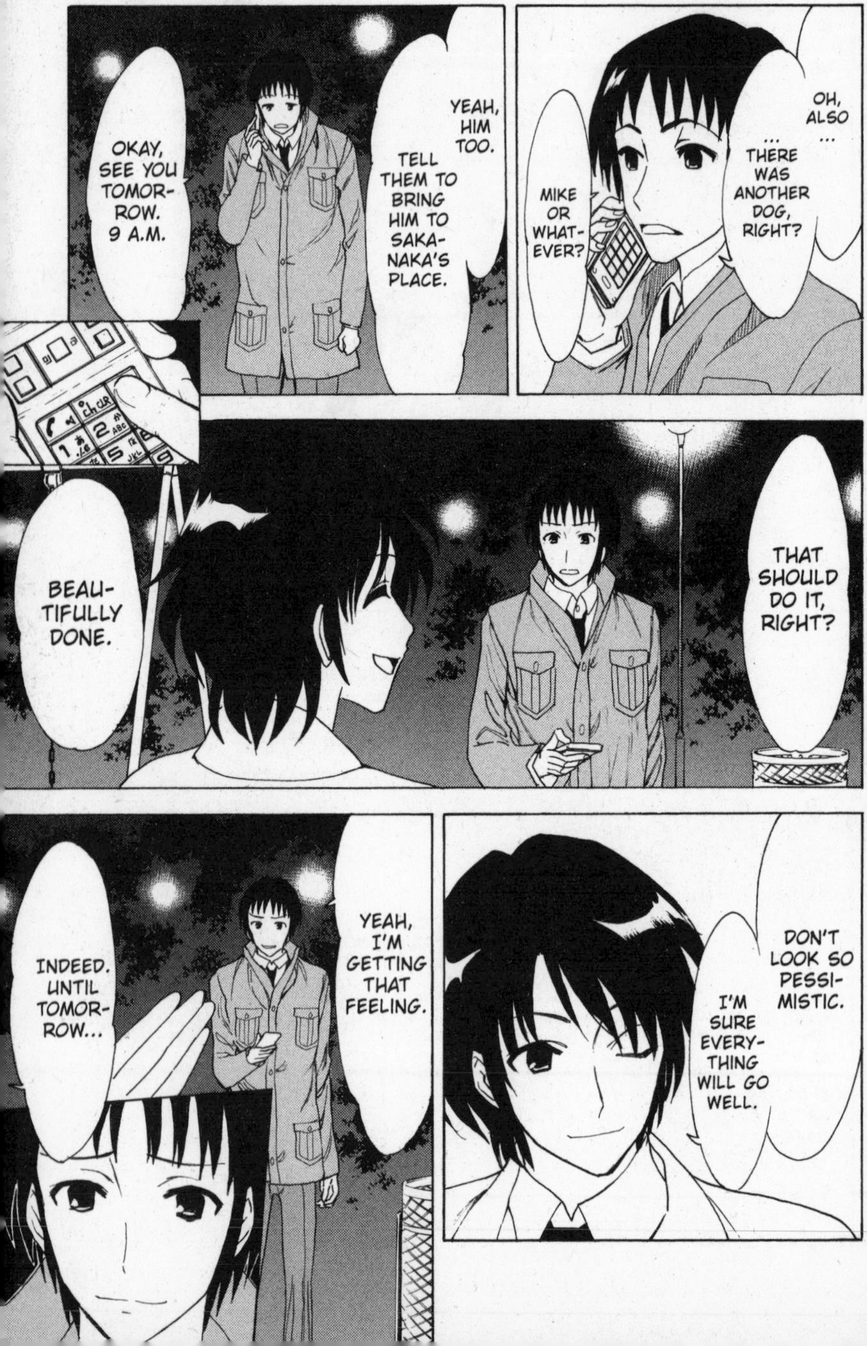
OH, ALSO ... ... THERE WAS ANOTHER DOG, RIGHT?
MIKE OR WHAT-EVER?
YEAH, HIM TOO.
TELL THEM TO BRING HIM TO SAKA-NAKA'S PLACE.
OKAY, SEE YOU TOMOR-ROW. 9 A.M.
THAT SHOULD DO IT, RIGHT?
BEAU-TIFULLY DONE.
DON'T LOOK SO PESSI-MISTIC.
I'M SURE EVERY-THING WILL GO WELL.
YEAH, I'M GETTING THAT FEELING.
INDEED. UNTIL TOMOR-ROW...

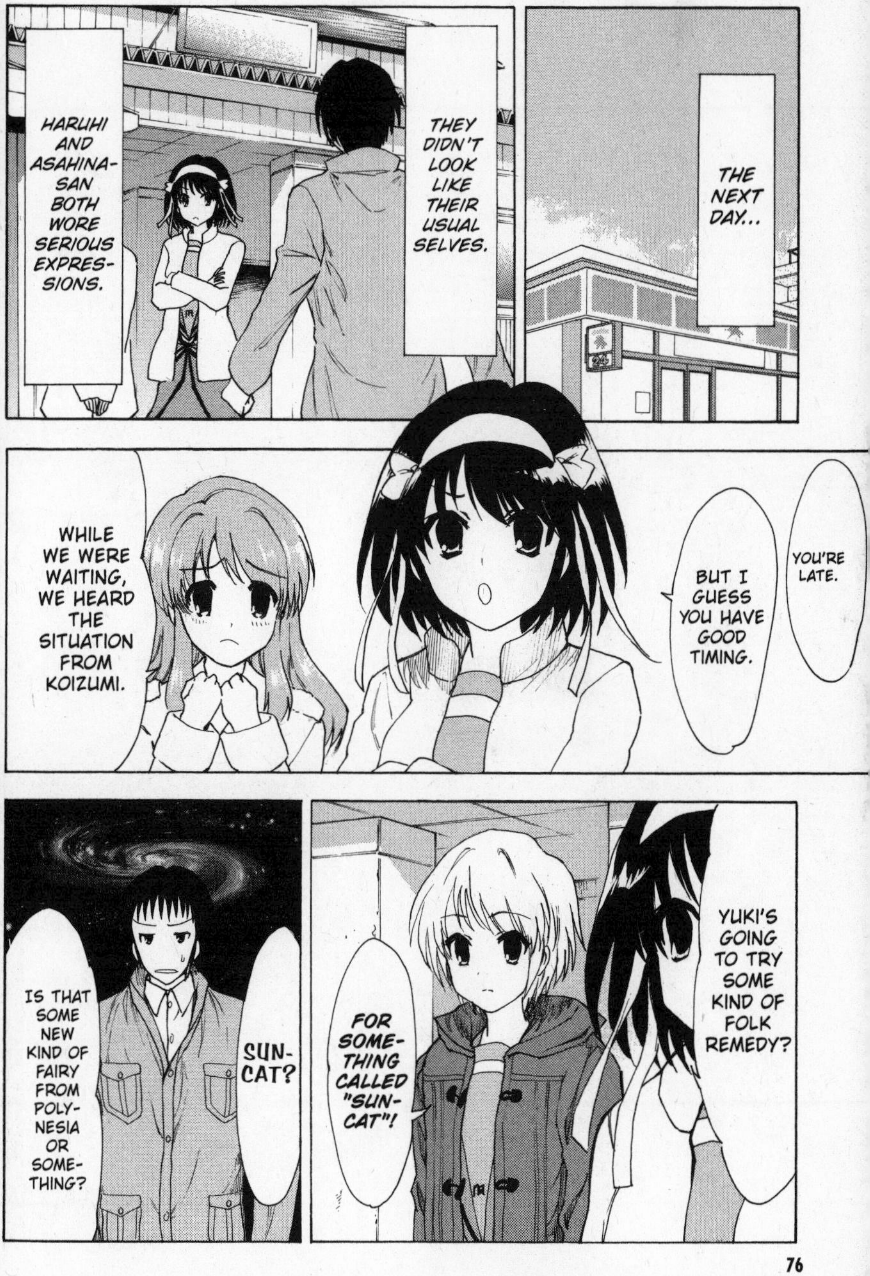
THE NEXT DAY...
THEY DIDN'T LOOK LIKE THEIR USUAL SELVES.
HARUHI AND ASAHINA-SAN BOTH WORE SERIOUS EXPRESSIONS.
YOU'RE LATE.
BUT I GUESS YOU HAVE GOOD TIMING.
WHILE WE WERE WAITING, WE HEARD THE SITUATION FROM KOIZUMI.
YUKI'S GOING TO TRY SOME KIND OF FOLK REMEDY?
FOR SOMETHING CALLED "SUN-CAT"!
SUN-CAT?
IS THAT SOME NEW KIND OF FAIRY FROM POLYNESIA OR SOMETHING?

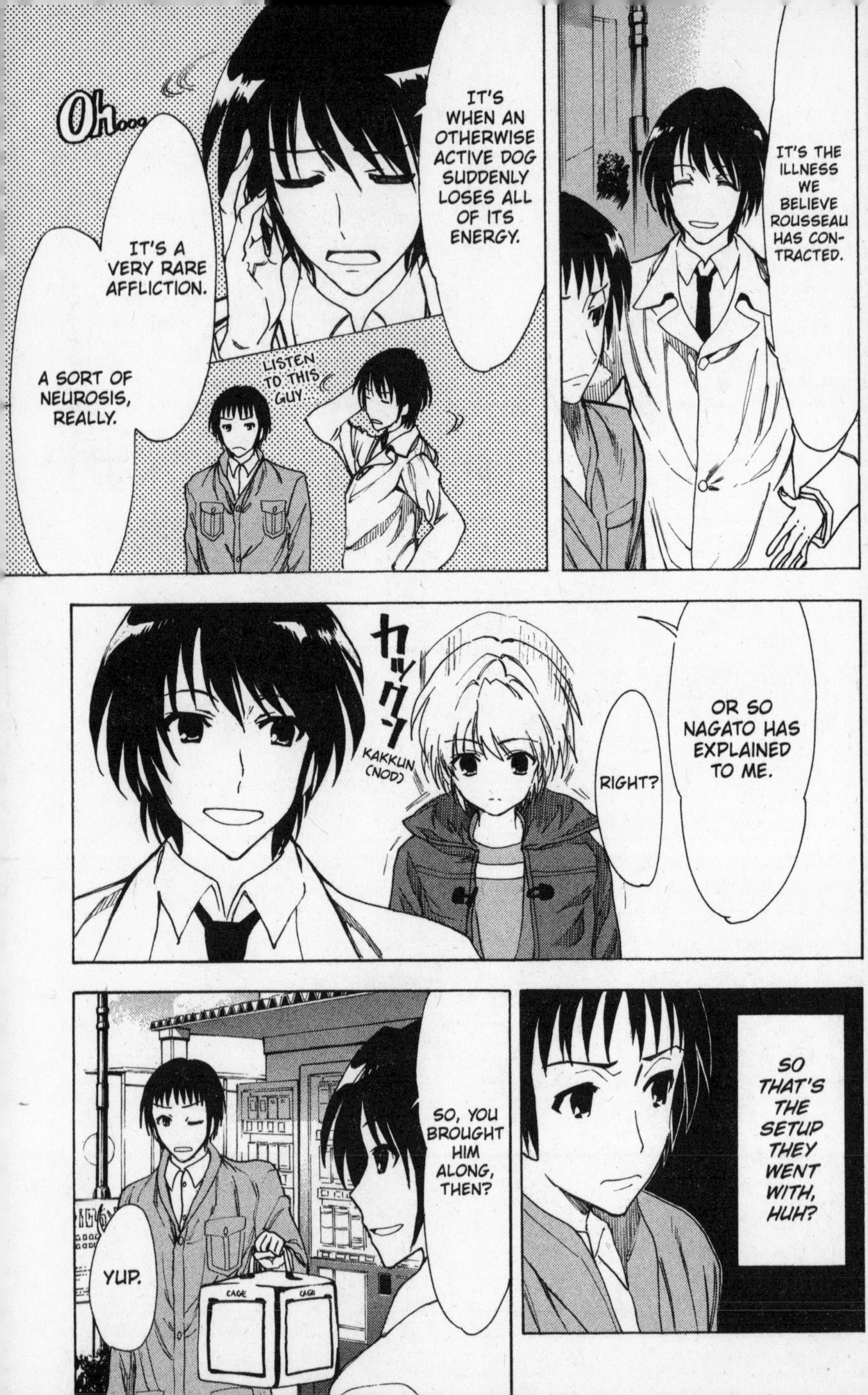
IT'S THE ILLNESS WE BELIEVE ROUSSEAU HAS CONTRACTED.
IT'S WHEN AN OTHERWISE ACTIVE DOG SUDDENLY LOSES ALL OF ITS ENERGY.
Oh...
IT'S A VERY RARE AFFLICTION.
A SORT OF NEUROSIS, REALLY.
LISTEN TO THIS GUY.
OR SO NAGATO HAS EXPLAINED TO ME.
RIGHT?
KAKKUN (NOD)
SO THAT'S THE SETUP THEY WENT WITH, HUH?
SO, YOU BROUGHT HIM ALONG, THEN?
YUP.
CAGE
CAGE

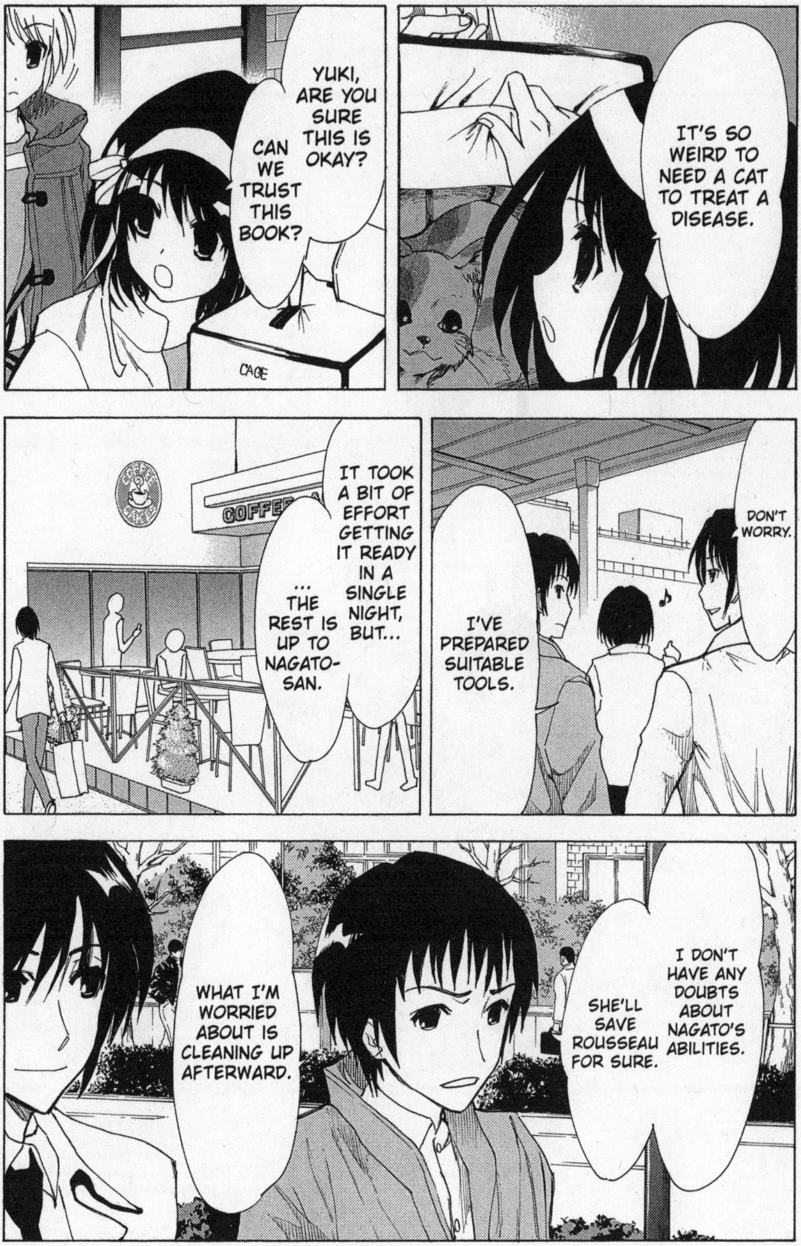
IT'S SO WEIRD TO NEED A CAT TO TREAT A DISEASE.
YUKI, ARE YOU SURE THIS IS OKAY?
CAN WE TRUST THIS BOOK?
CAGE
DON'T WORRY.
I'VE PREPARED SUITABLE TOOLS.
IT TOOK A BIT OF EFFORT GETTING IT READY IN A SINGLE NIGHT, BUT...
... THE REST IS UP TO NAGATO-SAN.
I DON'T HAVE ANY DOUBTS ABOUT NAGATO'S ABILITIES.
SHE'LL SAVE ROUSSEAU FOR SURE.
WHAT I'M WORRIED ABOUT IS CLEANING UP AFTERWARD.

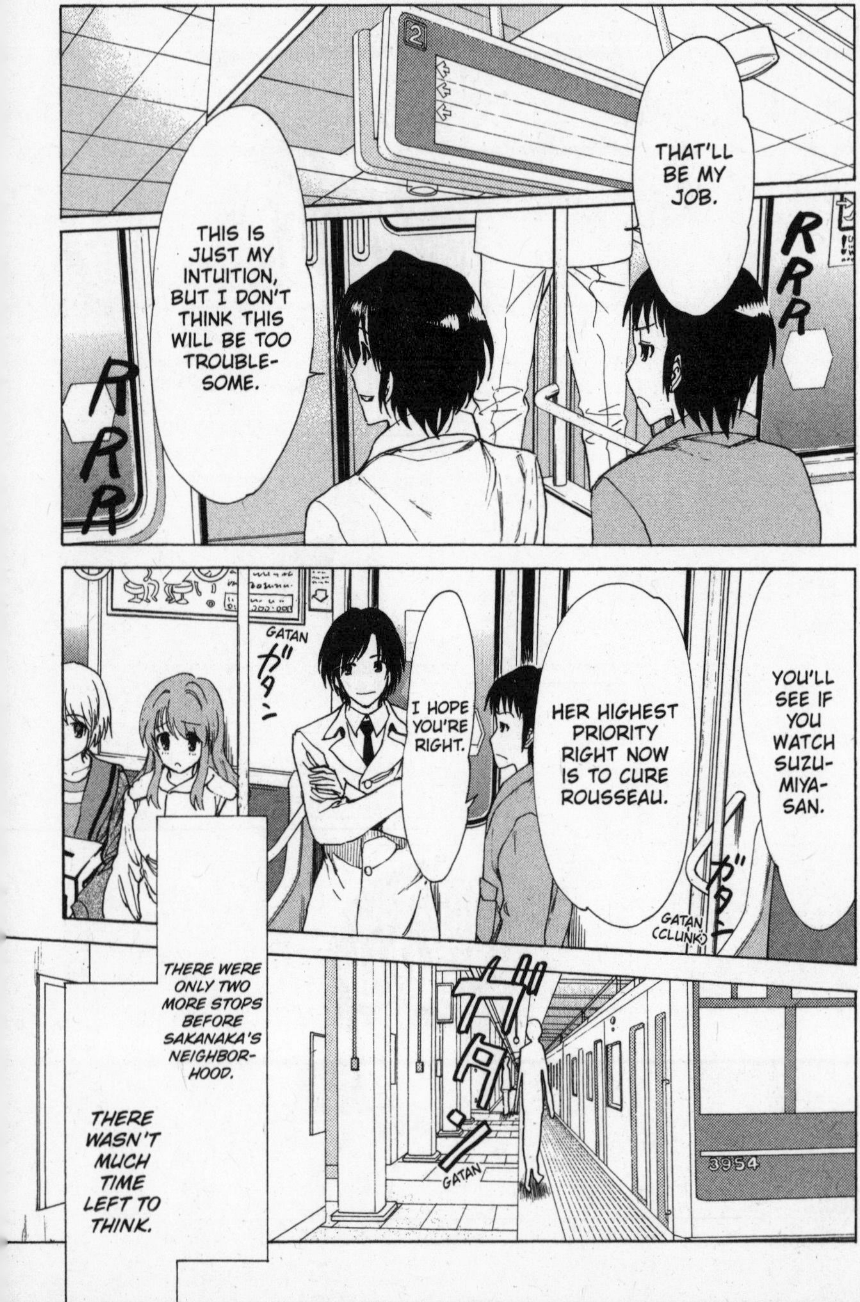
RRR
THAT'LL BE MY JOB.
THIS IS JUST MY INTUITION, BUT I DON'T THINK THIS WILL BE TOO TROUBLE-SOME.
RRR
YOU'LL SEE IF YOU WATCH SUZU-MIYA-SAN.
GATAN (CLUNK)
HER HIGHEST PRIORITY RIGHT NOW IS TO CURE ROUSSEAU.
I HOPE YOU'RE RIGHT.
GATAN
3954
GATAN
THERE WERE ONLY TWO MORE STOPS BEFORE SAKANAKA'S NEIGHBOR-HOOD.
THERE WASN'T MUCH TIME LEFT TO THINK.

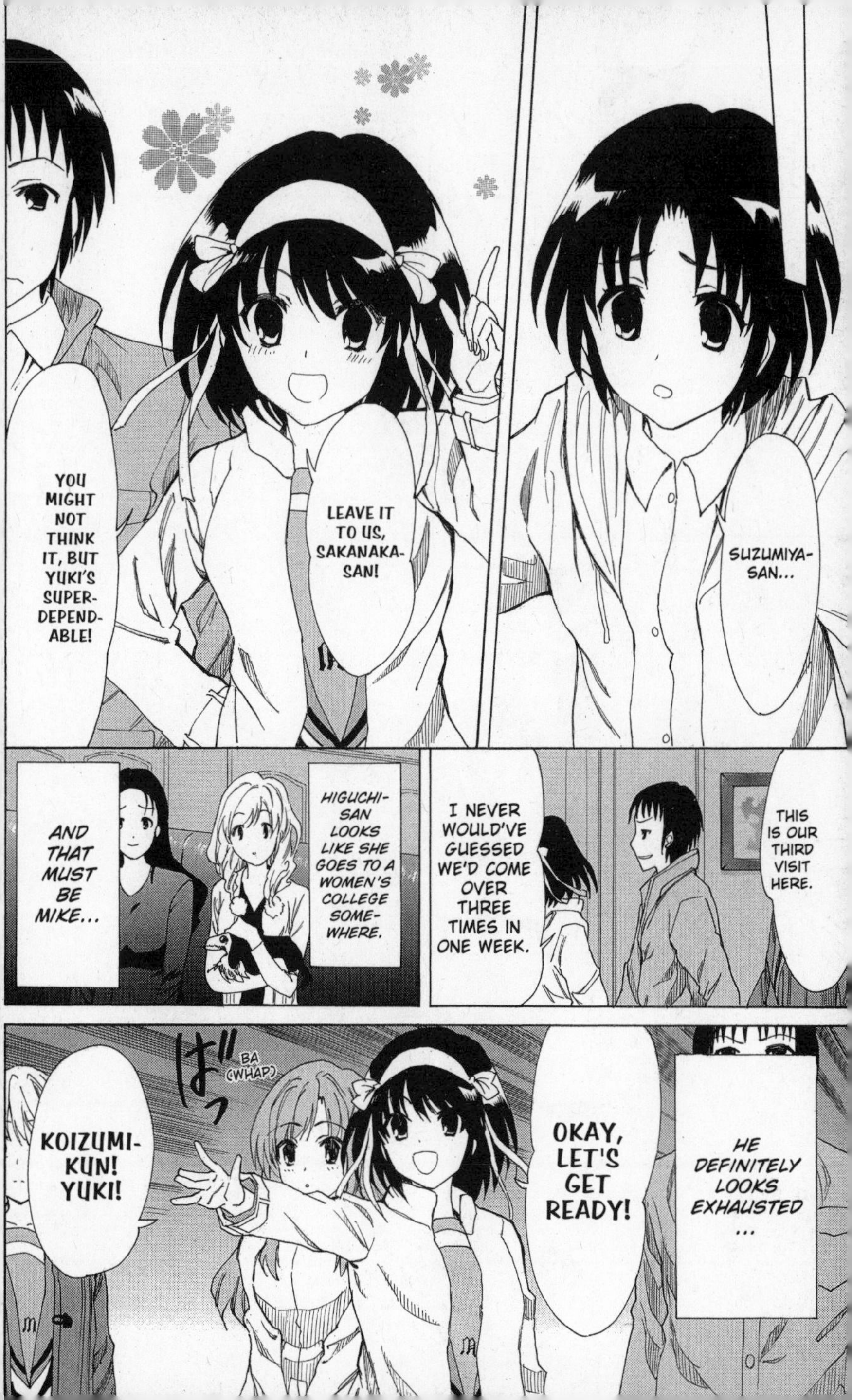
SUZUMIYA-SAN...
LEAVE IT TO US, SAKANAKA-SAN!
YOU MIGHT NOT THINK IT, BUT YUKI'S SUPER-DEPENDABLE!
THIS IS OUR THIRD VISIT HERE.
I NEVER WOULD'VE GUESSED WE'D COME OVER THREE TIMES IN ONE WEEK.
HIGUCHI-SAN LOOKS LIKE SHE GOES TO A WOMEN'S COLLEGE SOMEWHERE.
AND THAT MUST BE MIKE...
HE DEFINITELY LOOKS EXHAUSTED...
OKAY, LET'S GET READY!
ばっ
BA (WHAP)
KOIZUMI-KUN! YUKI!

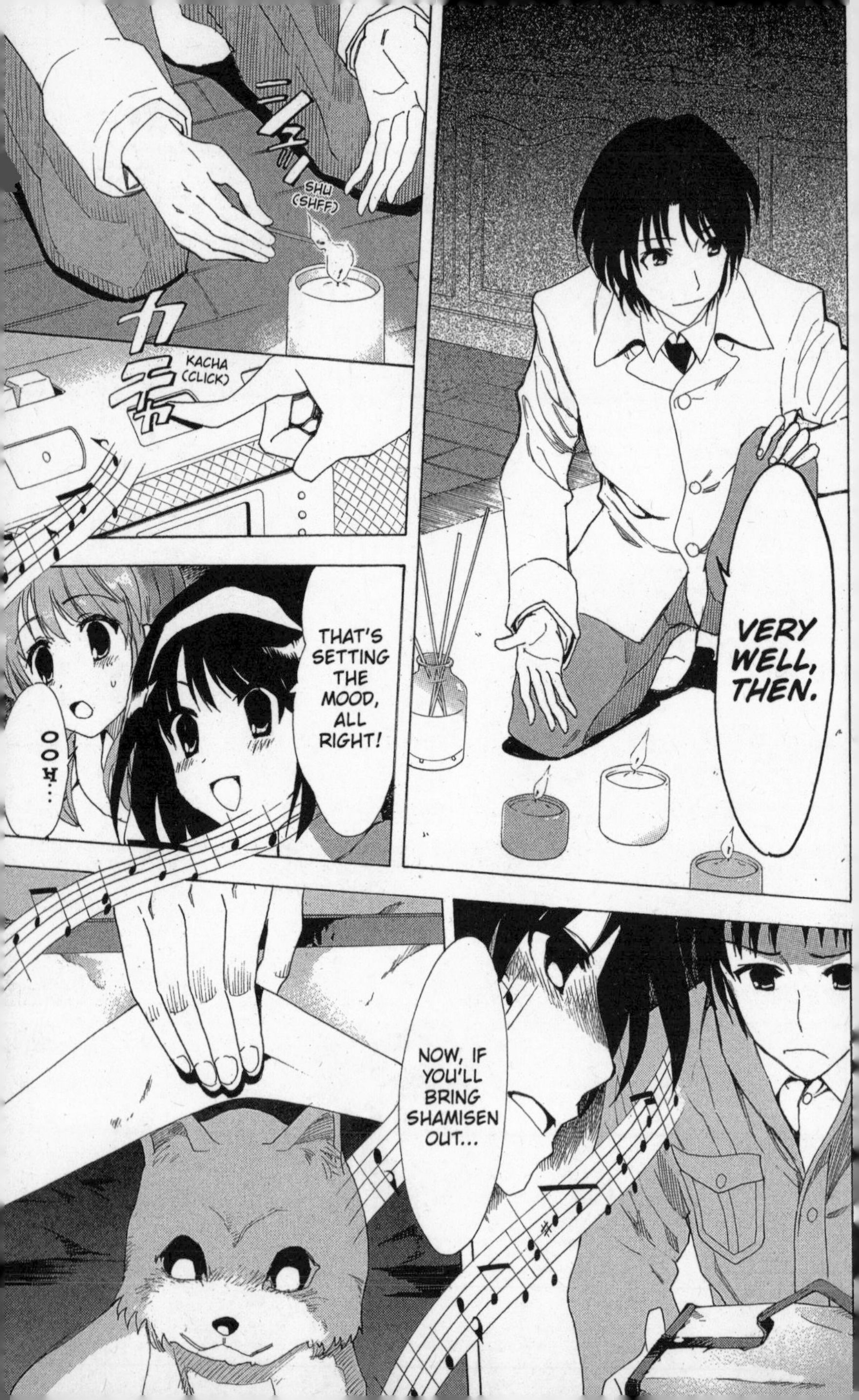
VERY WELL, THEN.
SHU (SHFF)
KACHA (CLICK)
THAT'S SETTING THE MOOD, ALL RIGHT!
OOH...
NOW, IF YOU'LL BRING SHAMISEN OUT...

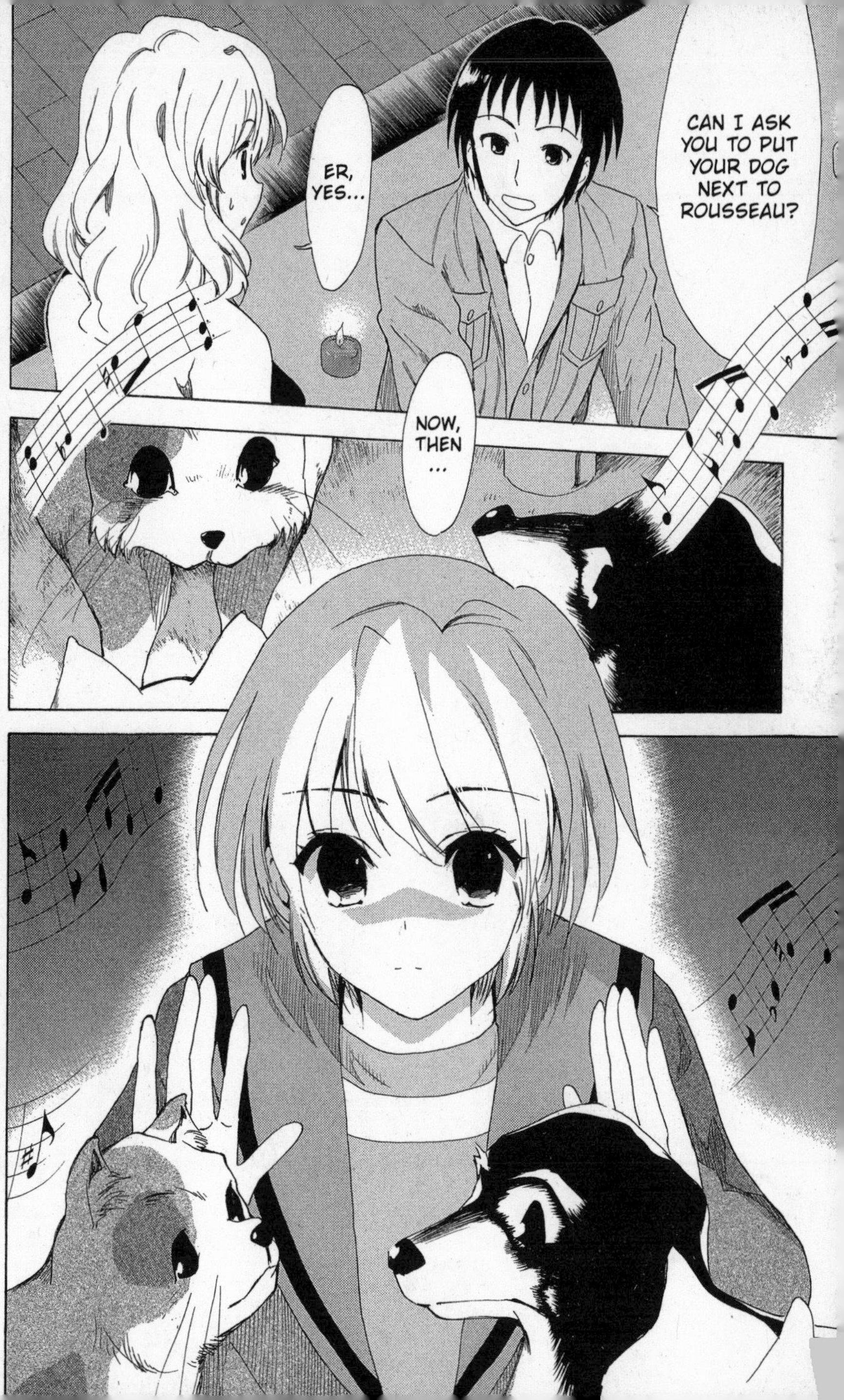
CAN I ASK YOU TO PUT YOUR DOG NEXT TO ROUSSEAU?
ER, YES...
NOW, THEN ...

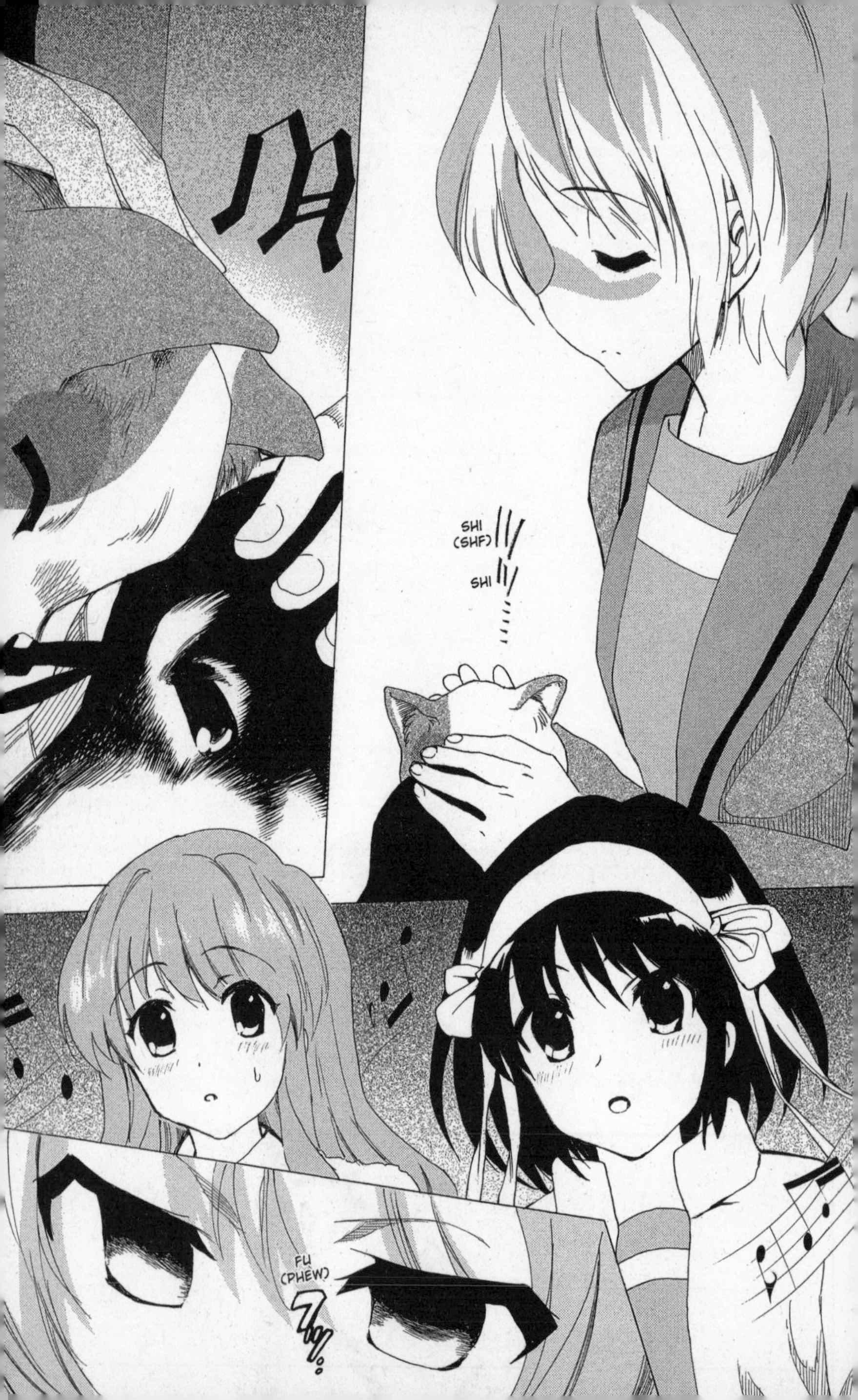
SHI
(SHF)
SHI
FU
(PHEW)

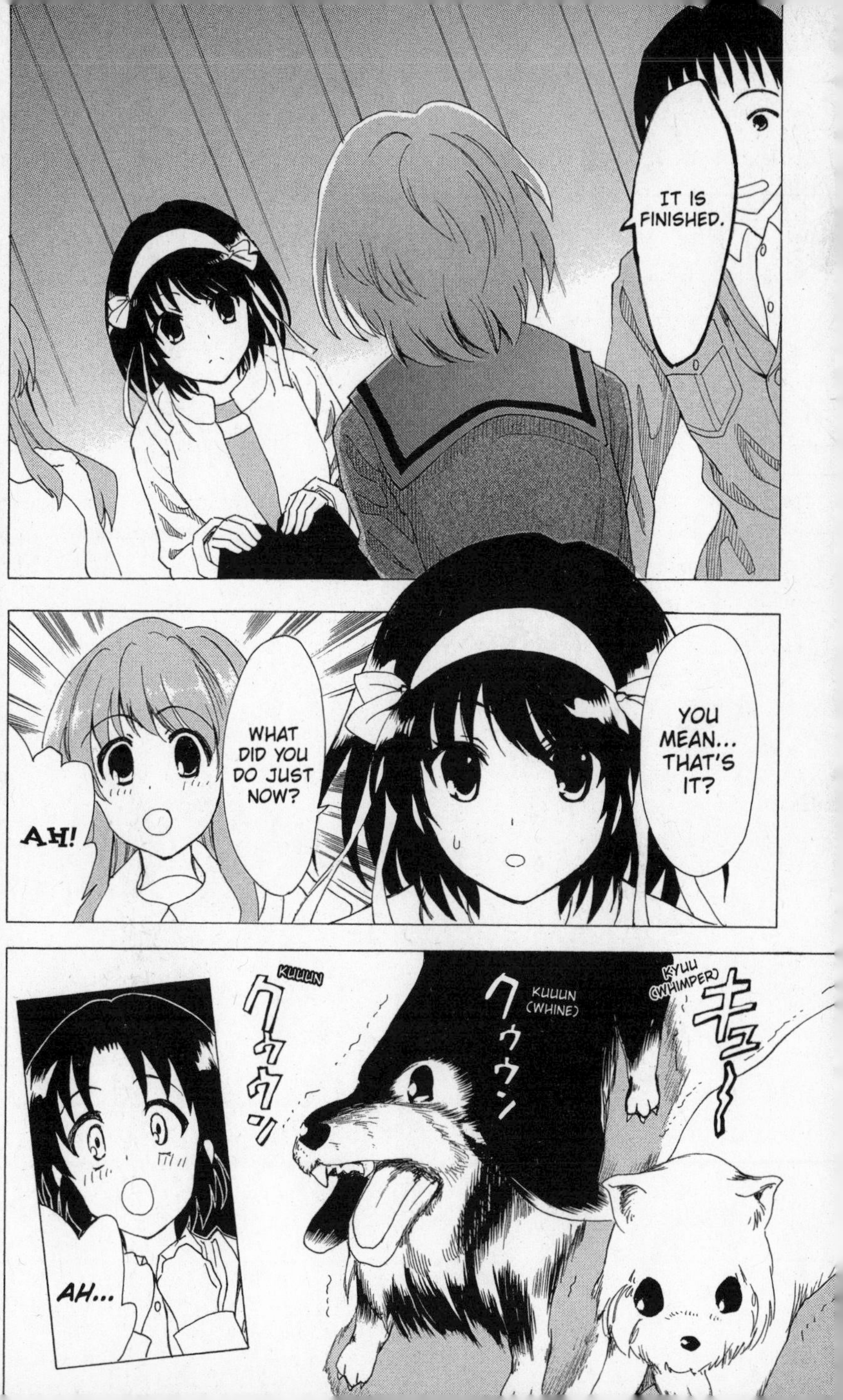
IT IS FINISHED.
YOU MEAN... THAT'S IT?
WHAT DID YOU DO JUST NOW?
AH!
キュ～
KYUU (WHIMPER)
クゥウン
KUUUN (WHINE)
クゥウウッ
KUUUN
AH...

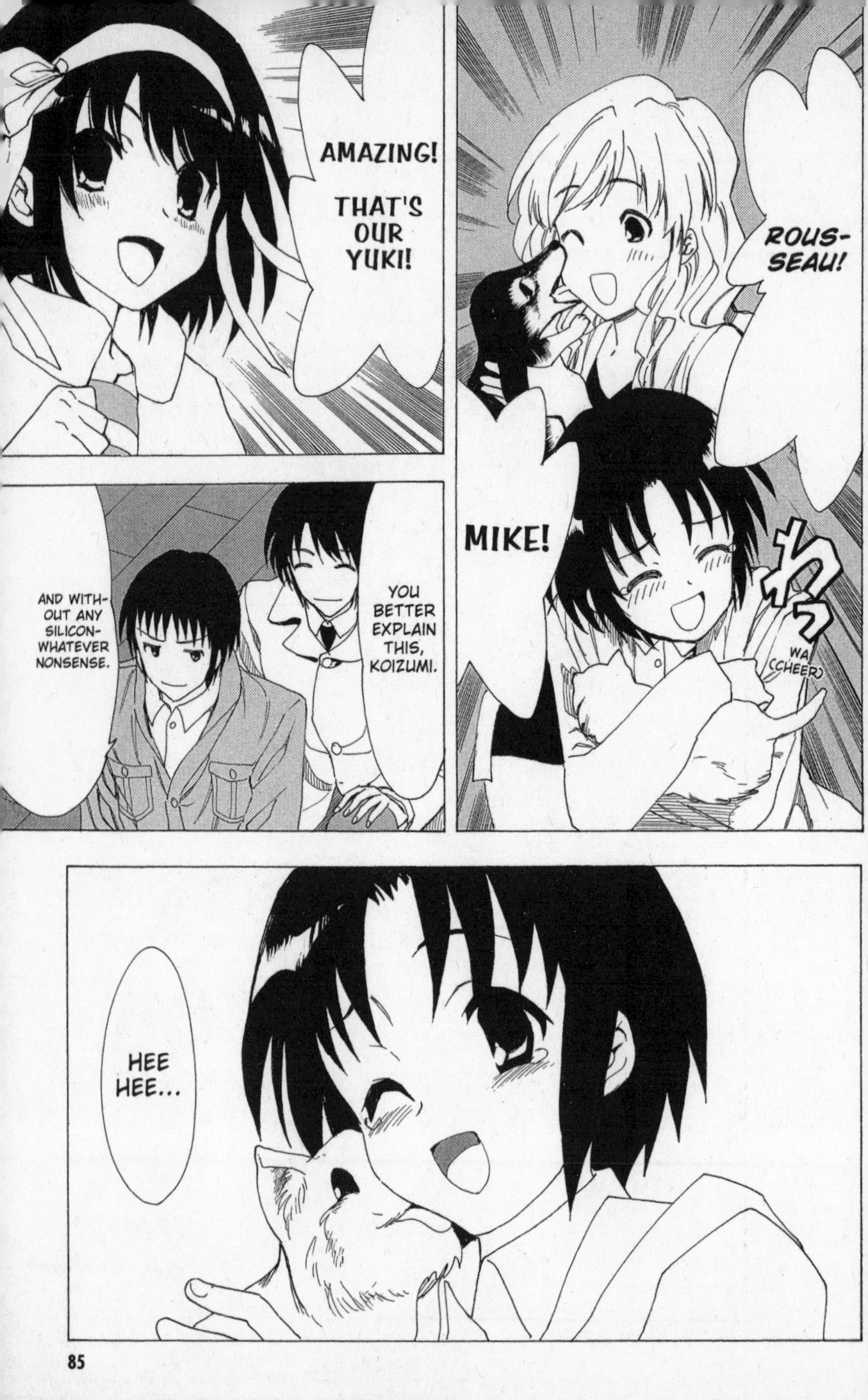
ROUS-SEAU!
MIKE!
わっ
WA (CHEER)
AMAZING!
THAT'S OUR YUKI!
YOU BETTER EXPLAIN THIS, KOIZUMI.
AND WITH-OUT ANY SILICON-WHATEVER NONSENSE.
HEE HEE...

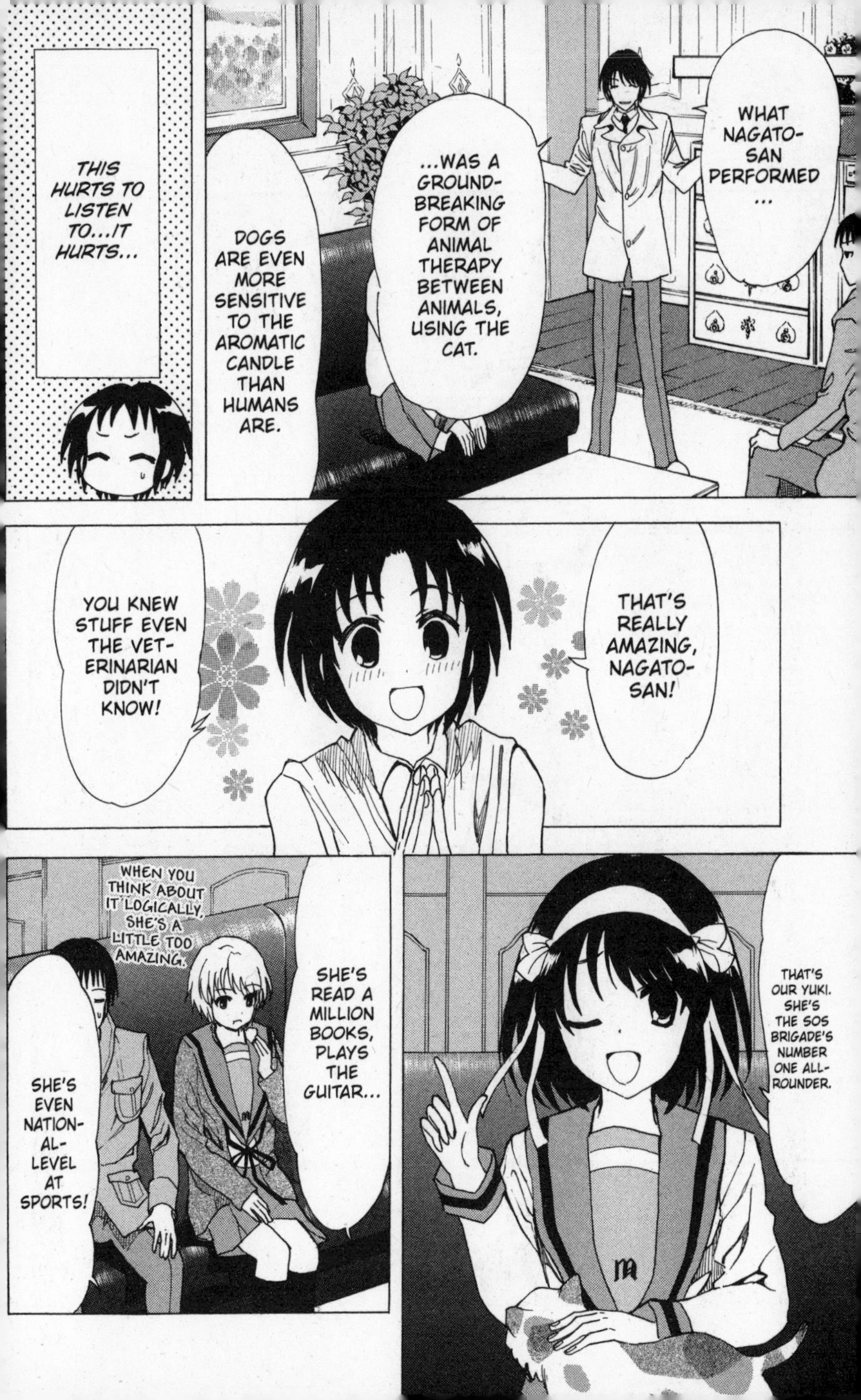
WHAT NAGATO-SAN PERFORMED...
...WAS A GROUND-BREAKING FORM OF ANIMAL THERAPY BETWEEN ANIMALS, USING THE CAT.
DOGS ARE EVEN MORE SENSITIVE TO THE AROMATIC CANDLE THAN HUMANS ARE.
THIS HURTS TO LISTEN TO...IT HURTS...
THAT'S REALLY AMAZING, NAGATO-SAN!
YOU KNEW STUFF EVEN THE VET-ERINARIAN DIDN'T KNOW!
THAT'S OUR YUKI. SHE'S THE SOS BRIGADE'S NUMBER ONE ALL-ROUNDER.
SHE'S READ A MILLION BOOKS, PLAYS THE GUITAR...
WHEN YOU THINK ABOUT IT LOGICALLY, SHE'S A LITTLE TOO AMAZING.
SHE'S EVEN NATION-AL-LEVEL AT SPORTS!

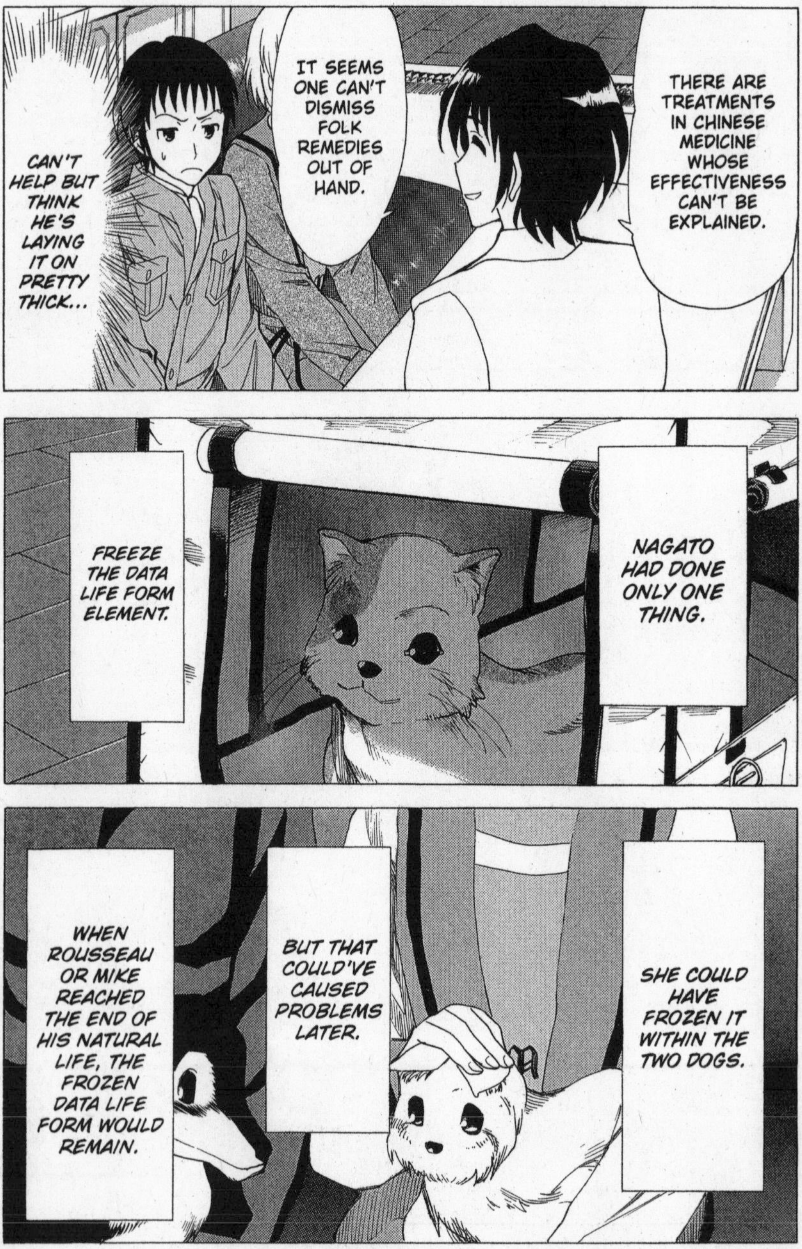
THERE ARE TREATMENTS IN CHINESE MEDICINE WHOSE EFFECTIVENESS CAN'T BE EXPLAINED.
IT SEEMS ONE CAN'T DISMISS FOLK REMEDIES OUT OF HAND.
CAN'T HELP BUT THINK HE'S LAYING IT ON PRETTY THICK...
NAGATO HAD DONE ONLY ONE THING.
FREEZE THE DATA LIFE FORM ELEMENT.
SHE COULD HAVE FROZEN IT WITHIN THE TWO DOGS.
BUT THAT COULD'VE CAUSED PROBLEMS LATER.
WHEN ROUSSEAU OR MIKE REACHED THE END OF HIS NATURAL LIFE, THE FROZEN DATA LIFE FORM WOULD REMAIN.

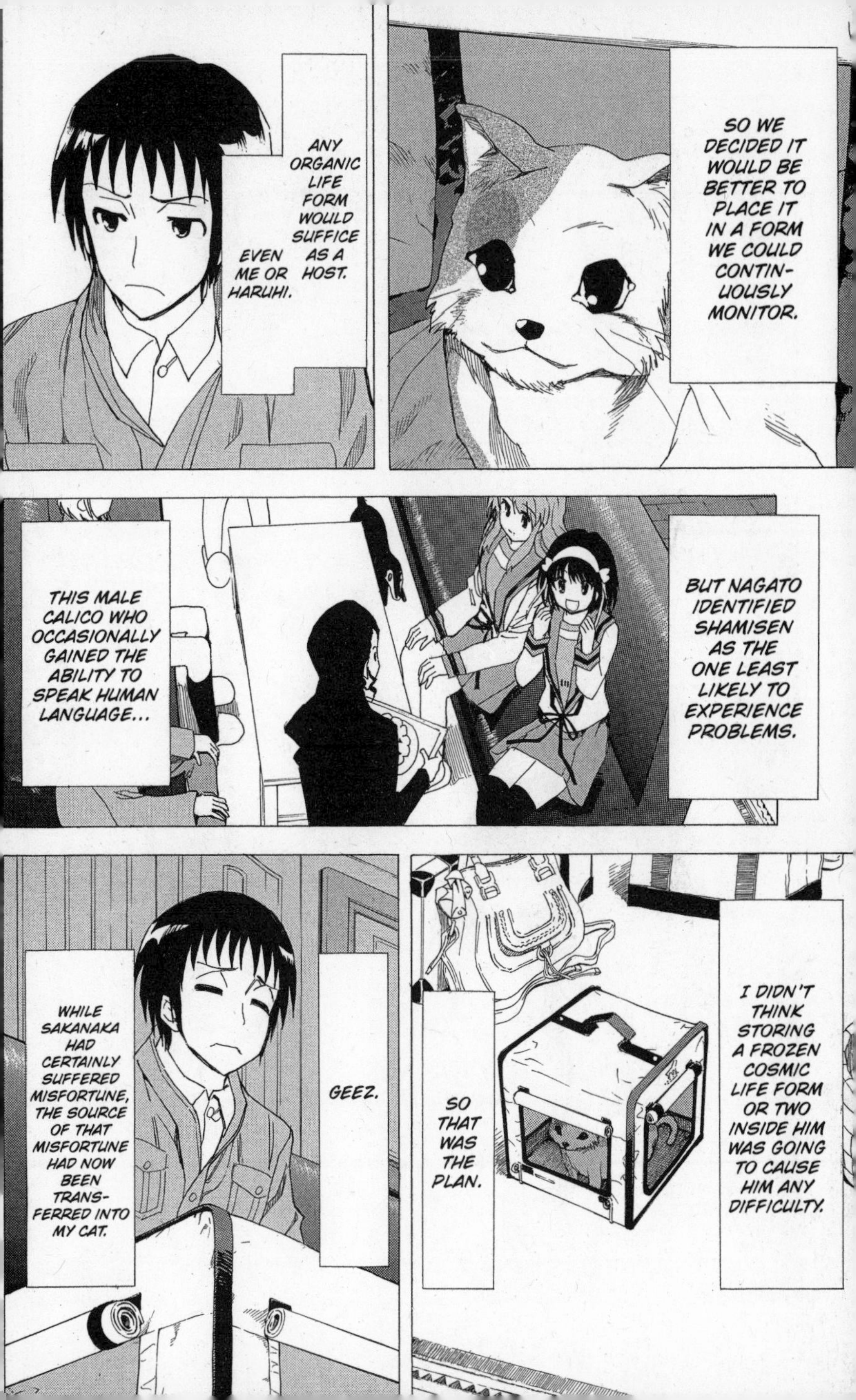
SO WE DECIDED IT WOULD BE BETTER TO PLACE IT IN A FORM WE COULD CONTIN-UOUSLY MONITOR.
ANY ORGANIC LIFE FORM WOULD SUFFICE AS A HOST.
EVEN ME OR HARUHI.
BUT NAGATO IDENTIFIED SHAMISEN AS THE ONE LEAST LIKELY TO EXPERIENCE PROBLEMS.
THIS MALE CALICO WHO OCCASIONALLY GAINED THE ABILITY TO SPEAK HUMAN LANGUAGE...
I DIDN'T THINK STORING A FROZEN COSMIC LIFE FORM OR TWO INSIDE HIM WAS GOING TO CAUSE HIM ANY DIFFICULTY.
SO THAT WAS THE PLAN.
GEEZ.
WHILE SAKANAKA HAD CERTAINLY SUFFERED MISFORTUNE, THE SOURCE OF THAT MISFORTUNE HAD NOW BEEN TRANS-FERRED INTO MY CAT.

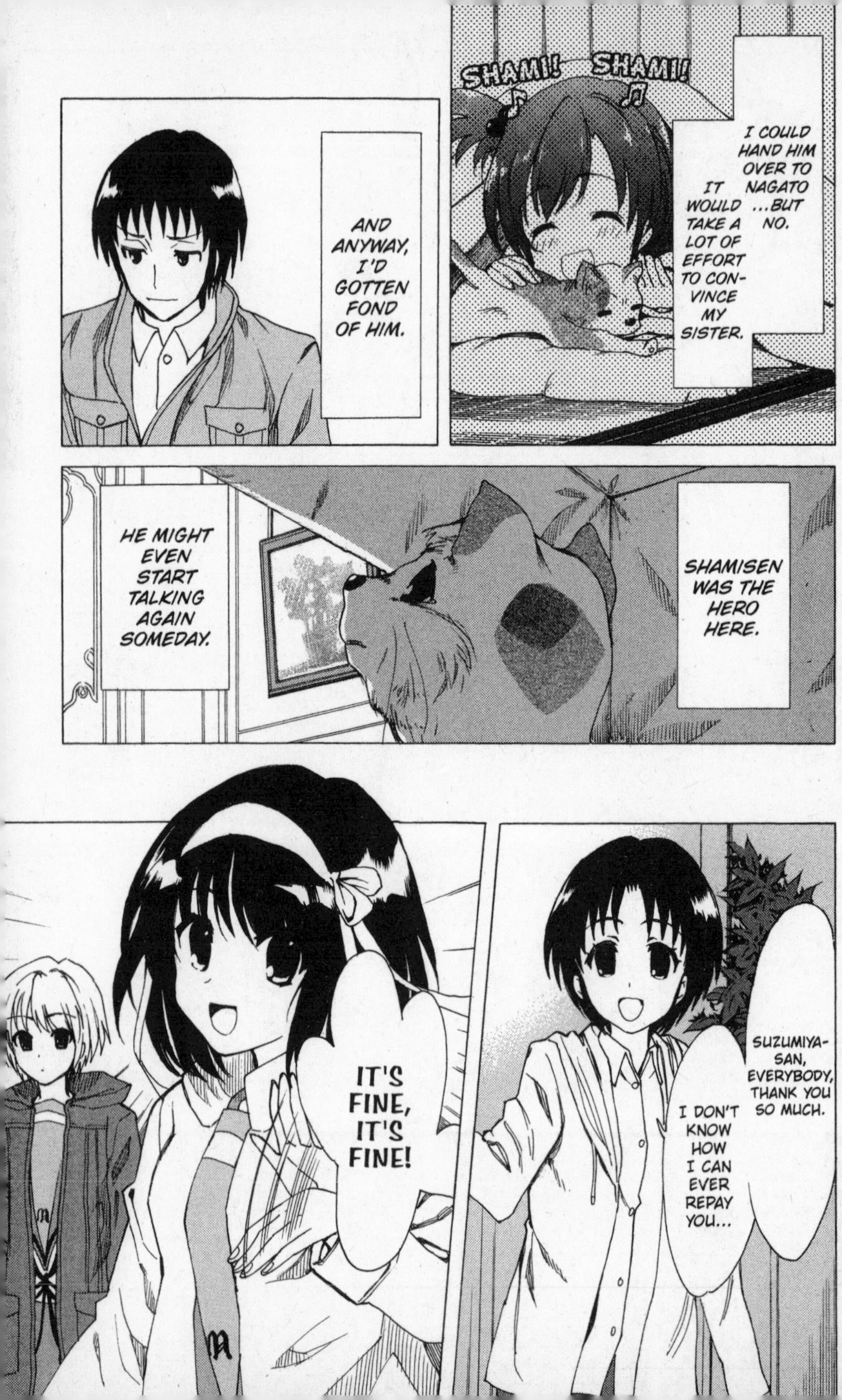
SHAMI! SHAMI!
I COULD HAND HIM OVER TO NAGATO ...BUT NO.
IT WOULD TAKE A LOT OF EFFORT TO CONVINCE MY SISTER.
AND ANYWAY, I'D GOTTEN FOND OF HIM.
SHAMISEN WAS THE HERO HERE.
HE MIGHT EVEN START TALKING AGAIN SOMEDAY.
SUZUMIYA-SAN, EVERYBODY, THANK YOU SO MUCH.
I DON'T KNOW HOW I CAN EVER REPAY YOU...
IT'S FINE, IT'S FINE!

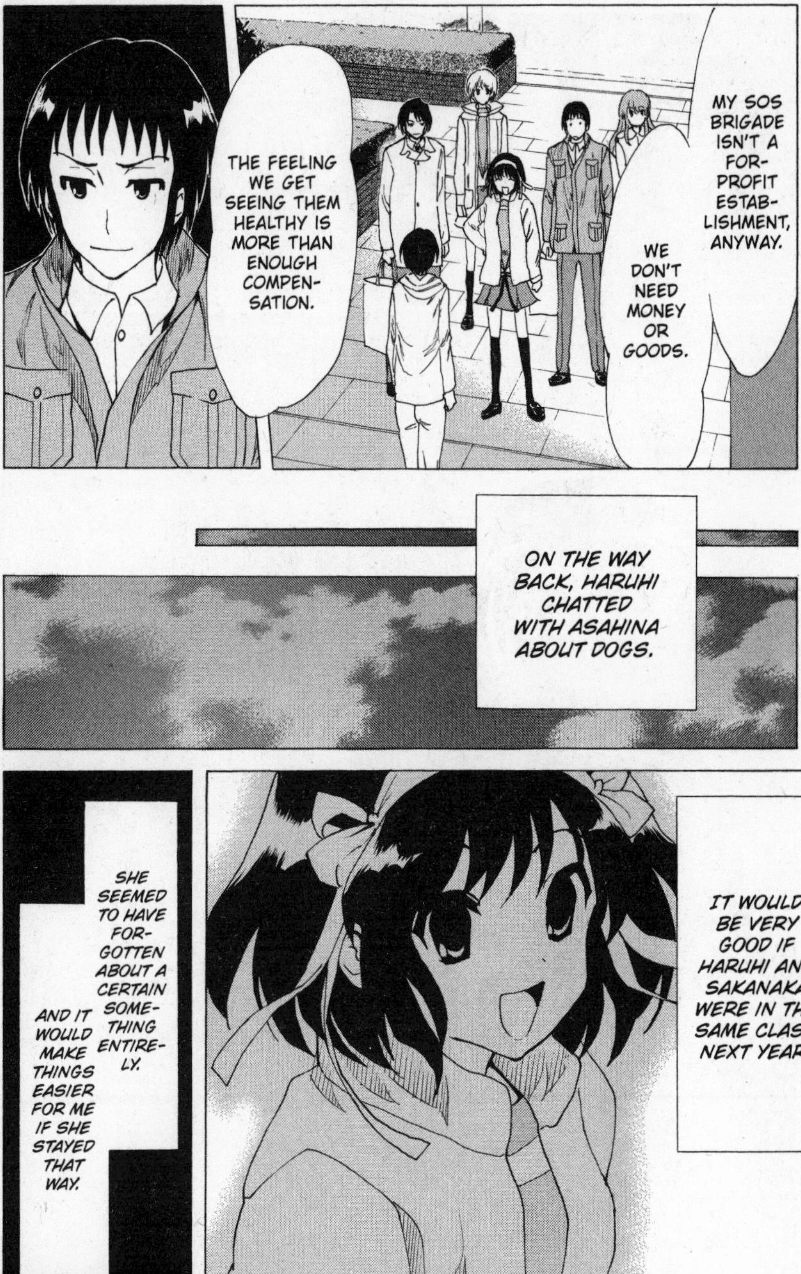
MY SOS BRIGADE ISN'T A FOR-PROFIT ESTABLISHMENT, ANYWAY.
WE DON'T NEED MONEY OR GOODS.
THE FEELING WE GET SEEING THEM HEALTHY IS MORE THAN ENOUGH COMPENSATION.
ON THE WAY BACK, HARUHI CHATTED WITH ASAHINA ABOUT DOGS.
IT WOULD BE VERY GOOD IF HARUHI AND SAKANAKA WERE IN THE SAME CLASS NEXT YEAR.
SHE SEEMED TO HAVE FORGOTTEN ABOUT A CERTAIN SOMETHING ENTIRELY.
AND IT WOULD MAKE THINGS EASIER FOR ME IF SHE STAYED THAT WAY.

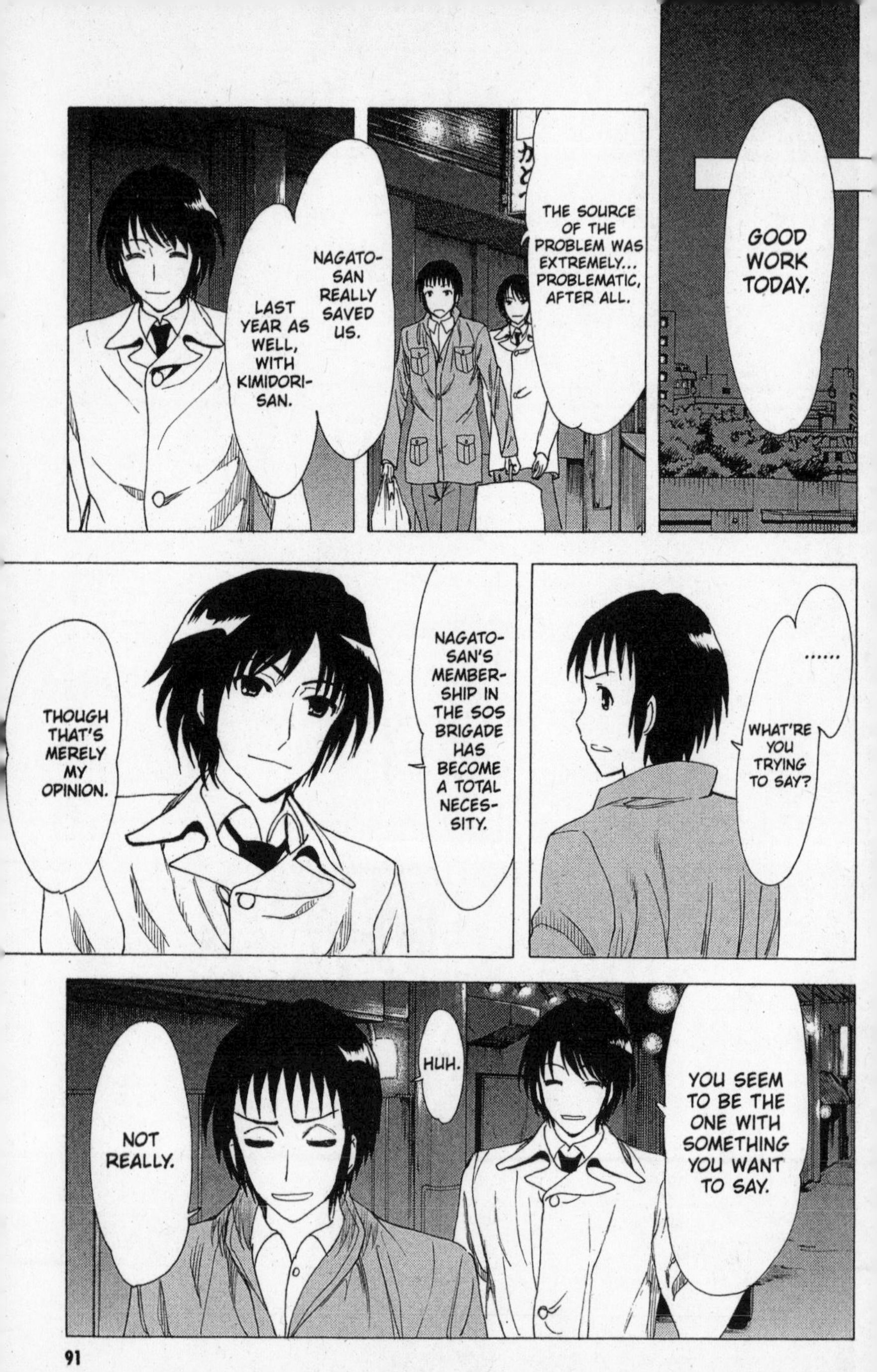
GOOD WORK TODAY.
THE SOURCE OF THE PROBLEM WAS EXTREMELY... PROBLEMATIC, AFTER ALL.
NAGATO-SAN REALLY SAVED US.
LAST YEAR AS WELL, WITH KIMIDORI-SAN.
......
WHAT'RE YOU TRYING TO SAY?
NAGATO-SAN'S MEMBERSHIP IN THE SOS BRIGADE HAS BECOME A TOTAL NECESSITY.
THOUGH THAT'S MERELY MY OPINION.
YOU SEEM TO BE THE ONE WITH SOMETHING YOU WANT TO SAY.
HUH.
NOT REALLY.

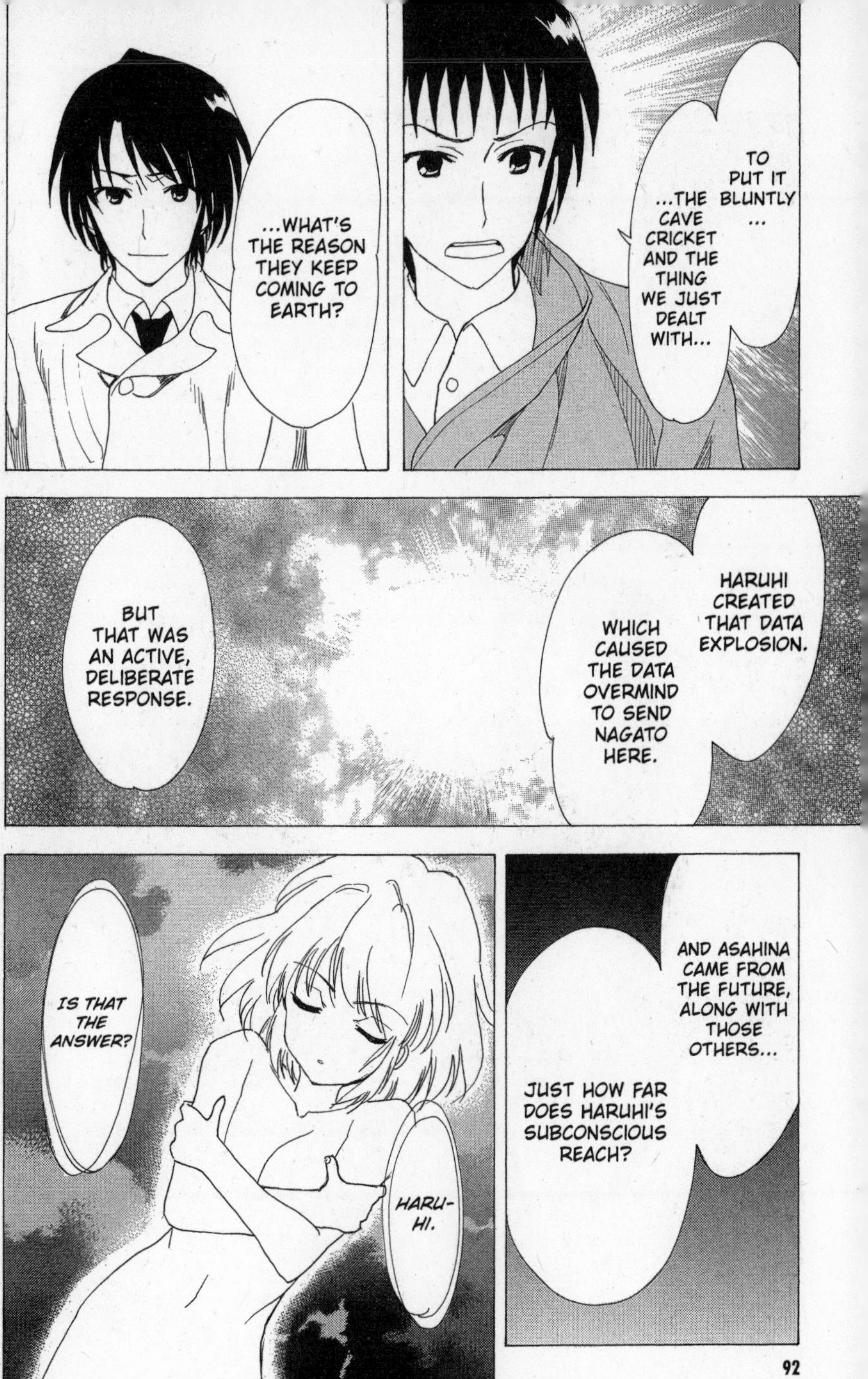
TO PUT IT BLUNTLY...
...THE CAVE CRICKET AND THE THING WE JUST DEALT WITH...
...WHAT'S THE REASON THEY KEEP COMING TO EARTH?
HARUHI CREATED THAT DATA EXPLOSION.
WHICH CAUSED THE DATA OVERMIND TO SEND NAGATO HERE.
BUT THAT WAS AN ACTIVE, DELIBERATE RESPONSE.
AND ASAHINA CAME FROM THE FUTURE, ALONG WITH THOSE OTHERS...
JUST HOW FAR DOES HARUHI'S SUBCONSCIOUS REACH?
IS THAT THE ANSWER?
HARU-HI.

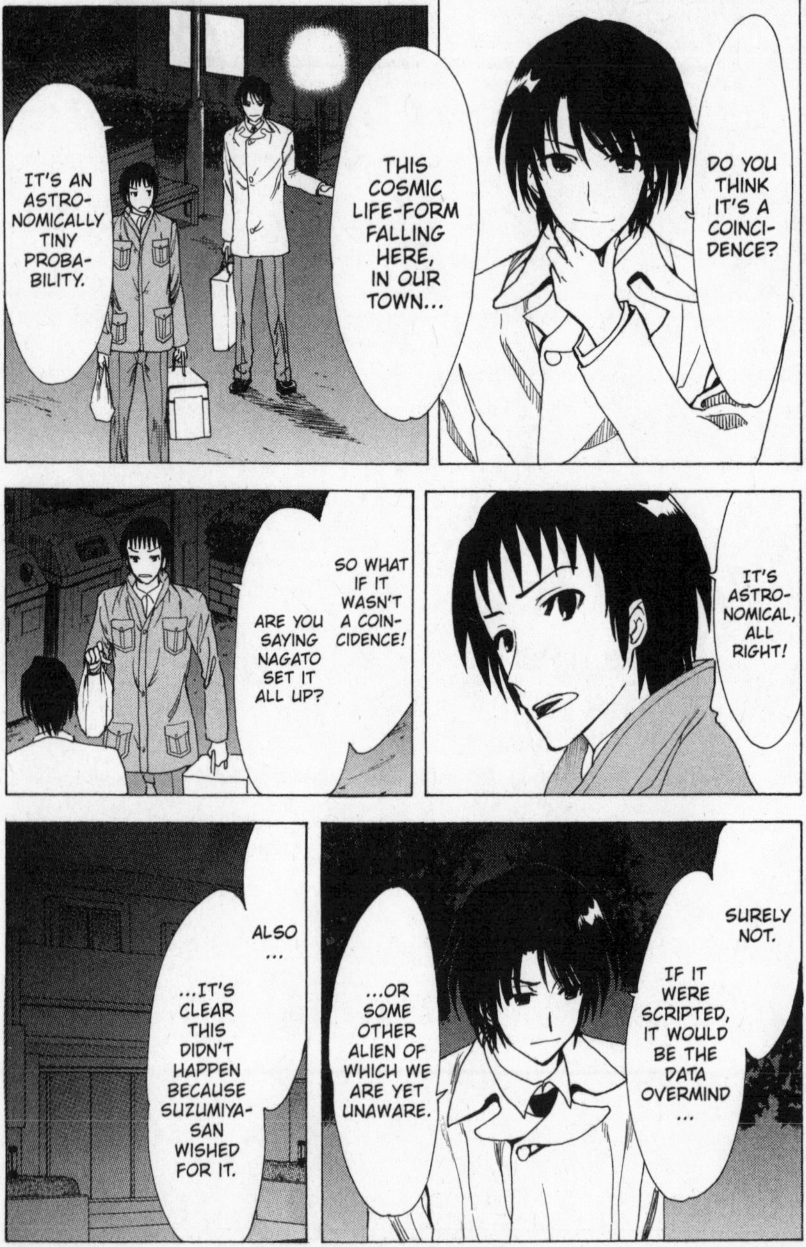
DO YOU THINK IT'S A COINCIDENCE?
THIS COSMIC LIFE-FORM FALLING HERE, IN OUR TOWN...
IT'S AN ASTRONOMICALLY TINY PROBABILITY.
IT'S ASTRONOMICAL, ALL RIGHT!
SO WHAT IF IT WASN'T A COINCIDENCE!
ARE YOU SAYING NAGATO SET IT ALL UP?
SURELY NOT.
IF IT WERE SCRIPTED, IT WOULD BE THE DATA OVERMIND...
...OR SOME OTHER ALIEN OF WHICH WE ARE YET UNAWARE.
ALSO...
...IT'S CLEAR THIS DIDN'T HAPPEN BECAUSE SUZUMIYA-SAN WISHED FOR IT.

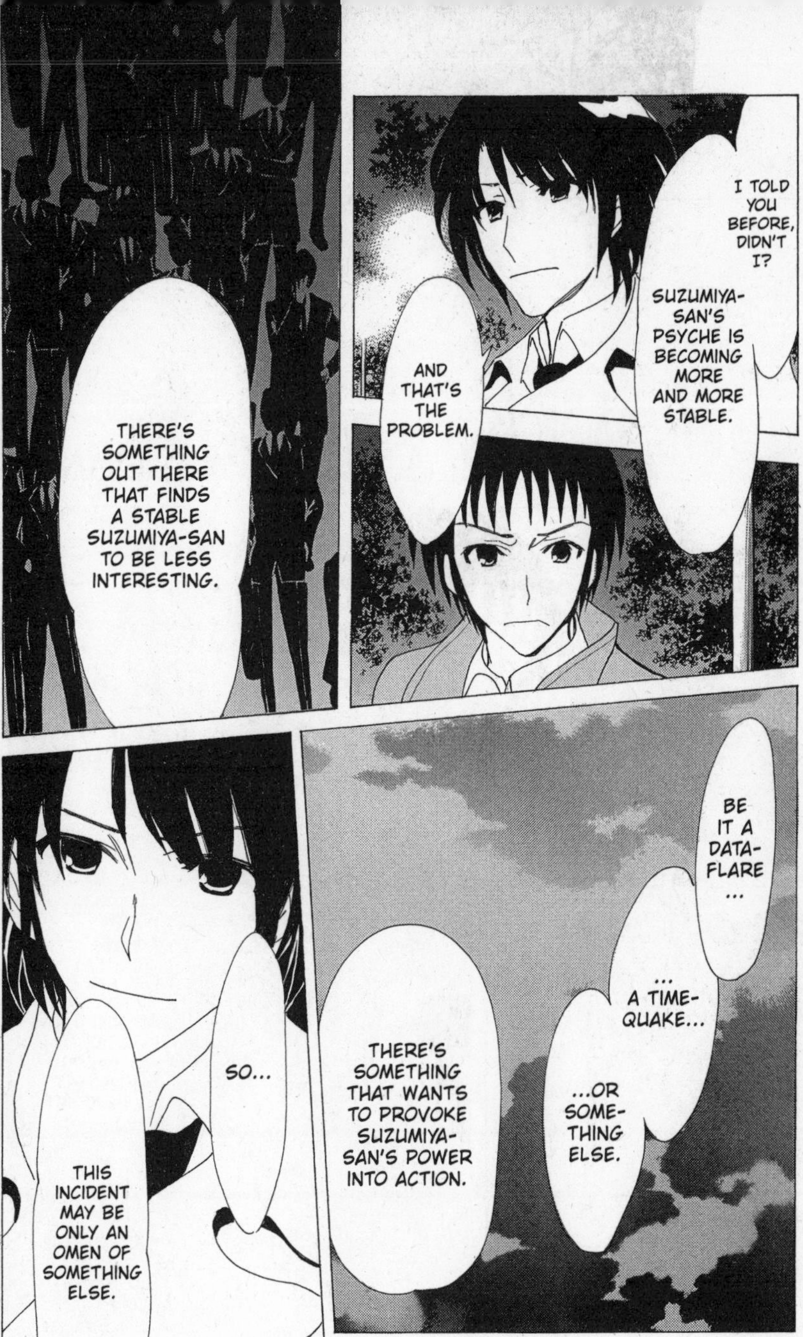
I TOLD YOU BEFORE, DIDN'T I?
SUZUMIYA-SAN'S PSYCHE IS BECOMING MORE AND MORE STABLE.
AND THAT'S THE PROBLEM.
THERE'S SOMETHING OUT THERE THAT FINDS A STABLE SUZUMIYA-SAN TO BE LESS INTERESTING.
BE IT A DATA-FLARE...
... A TIME-QUAKE...
...OR SOME-THING ELSE.
THERE'S SOMETHING THAT WANTS TO PROVOKE SUZUMIYA-SAN'S POWER INTO ACTION.
SO...
THIS INCIDENT MAY BE ONLY AN OMEN OF SOMETHING ELSE.

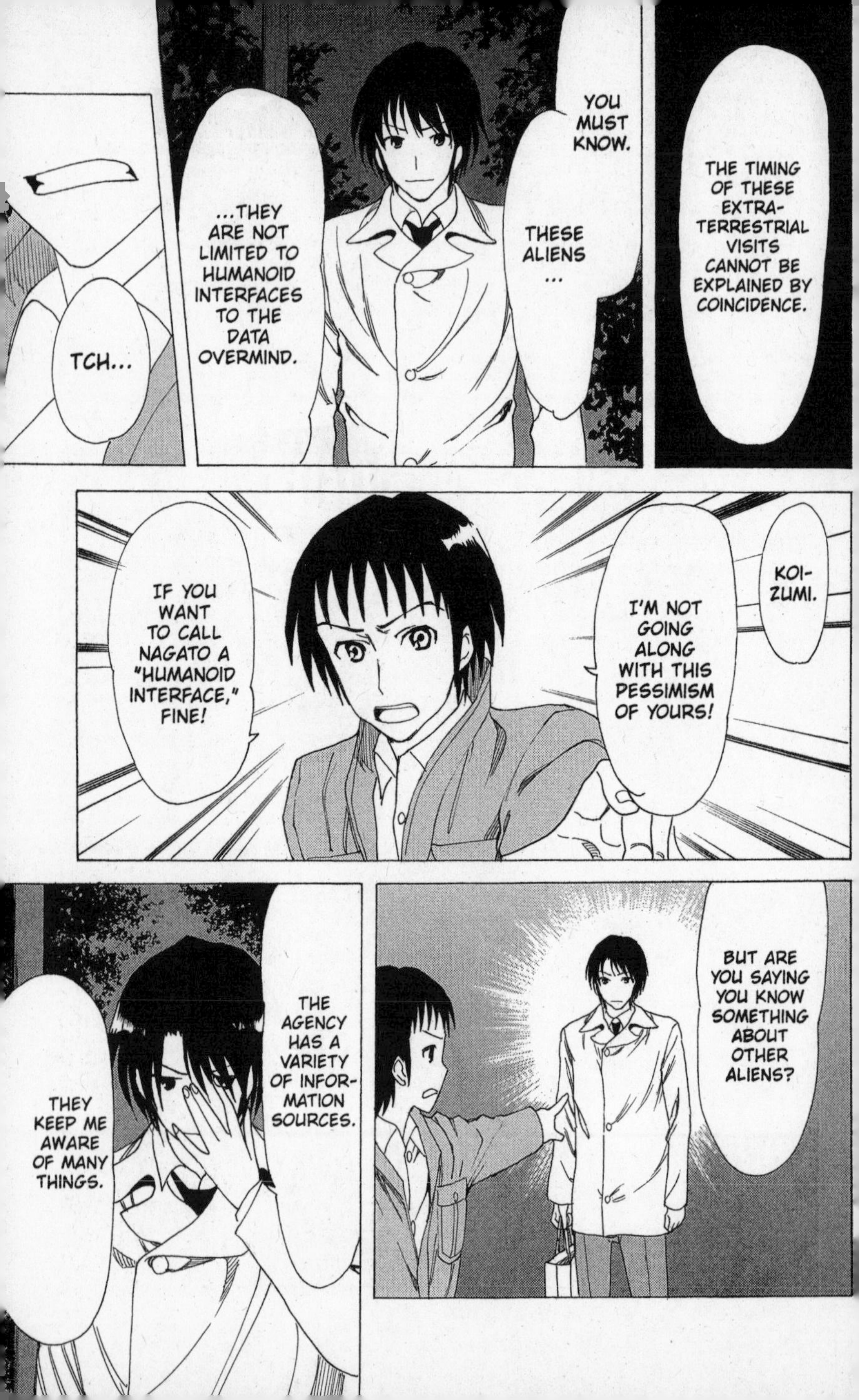
THE TIMING OF THESE EXTRA-TERRESTRIAL VISITS CANNOT BE EXPLAINED BY COINCIDENCE.
YOU MUST KNOW.
THESE ALIENS ...
...THEY ARE NOT LIMITED TO HUMANOID INTERFACES TO THE DATA OVERMIND.
TCH...
KOI-ZUMI.
I'M NOT GOING ALONG WITH THIS PESSIMISM OF YOURS!
IF YOU WANT TO CALL NAGATO A "HUMANOID INTERFACE," FINE!
BUT ARE YOU SAYING YOU KNOW SOMETHING ABOUT OTHER ALIENS?
THE AGENCY HAS A VARIETY OF INFOR-MATION SOURCES.
THEY KEEP ME AWARE OF MANY THINGS.

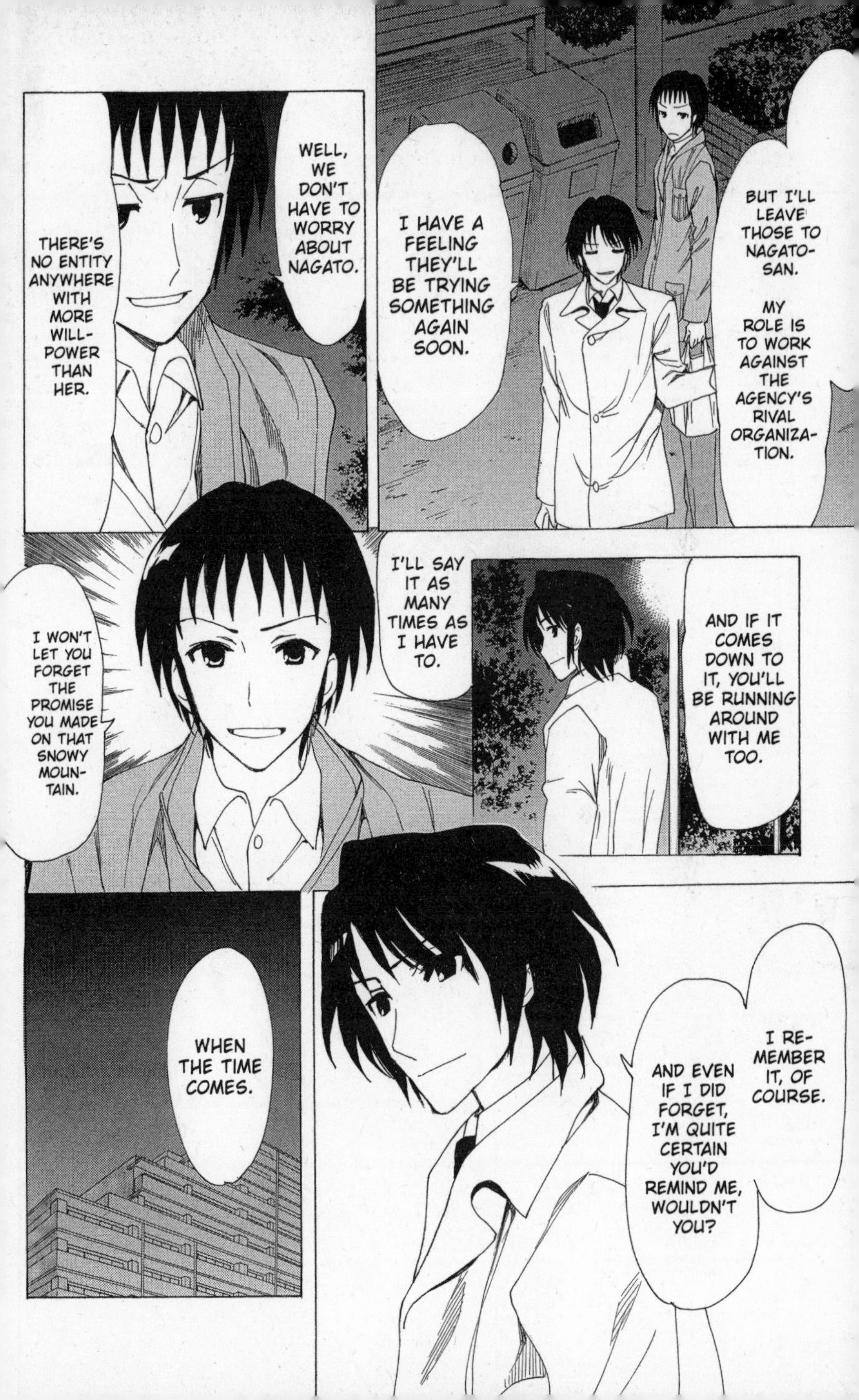
BUT I'LL LEAVE THOSE TO NAGATO-SAN.
MY ROLE IS TO WORK AGAINST THE AGENCY'S RIVAL ORGANIZATION.
I HAVE A FEELING THEY'LL BE TRYING SOMETHING AGAIN SOON.
WELL, WE DON'T HAVE TO WORRY ABOUT NAGATO.
THERE'S NO ENTITY ANYWHERE WITH MORE WILL-POWER THAN HER.
AND IF IT COMES DOWN TO IT, YOU'LL BE RUNNING AROUND WITH ME TOO.
I'LL SAY IT AS MANY TIMES AS I HAVE TO.
I WON'T LET YOU FORGET THE PROMISE YOU MADE ON THAT SNOWY MOUNTAIN.
I RE-MEMBER IT, OF COURSE.
AND EVEN IF I DID FORGET, I'M QUITE CERTAIN YOU'D REMIND ME, WOULDN'T YOU?
WHEN THE TIME COMES.

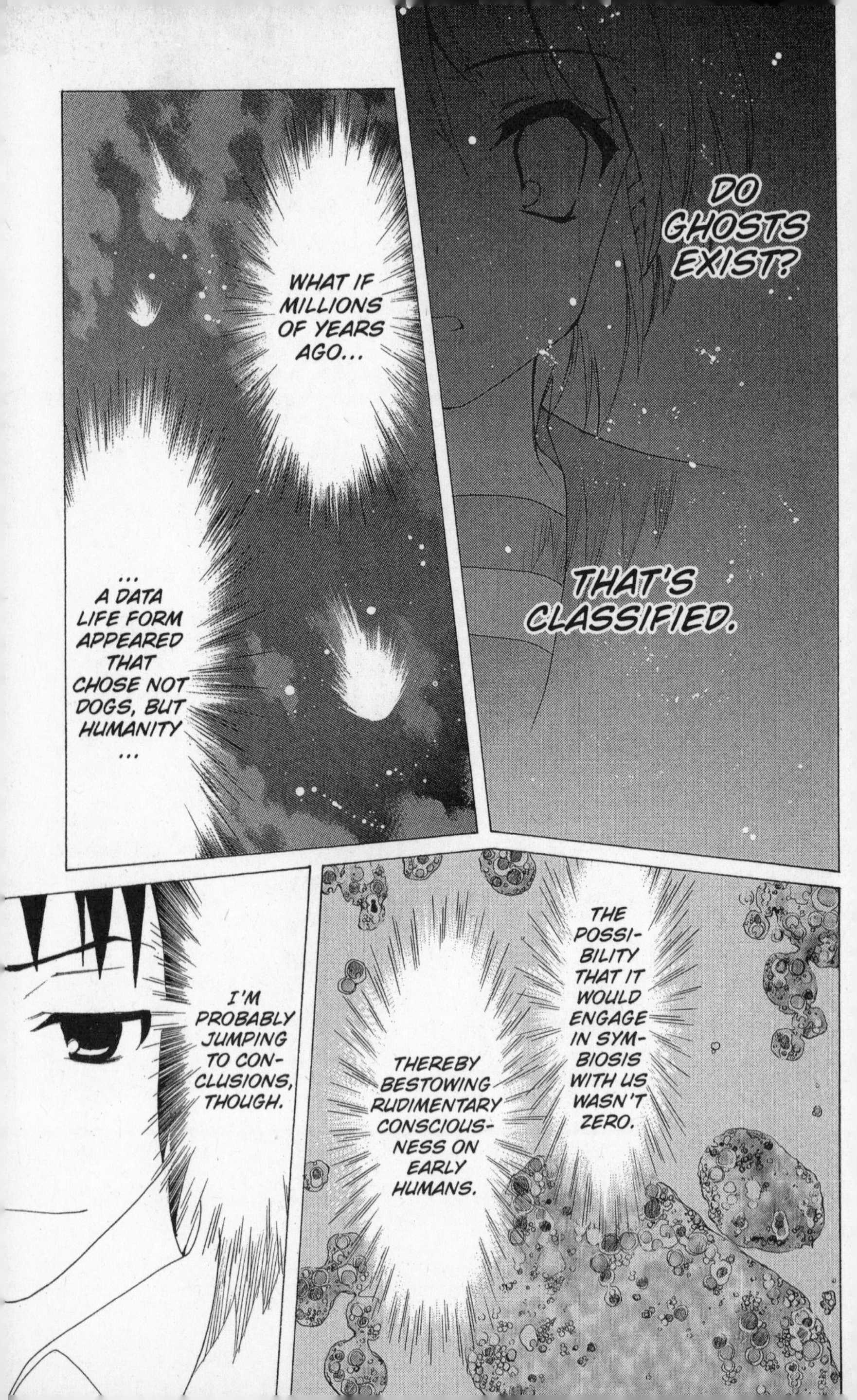
DO GHOSTS EXIST?
THAT'S CLASSIFIED.
WHAT IF MILLIONS OF YEARS AGO...
...A DATA LIFE FORM APPEARED THAT CHOSE NOT DOGS, BUT HUMANITY...
THE POSSIBILITY THAT IT WOULD ENGAGE IN SYMBIOSIS WITH US WASN'T ZERO.
THEREBY BESTOWING RUDIMENTARY CONSCIOUSNESS ON EARLY HUMANS.
I'M PROBABLY JUMPING TO CONCLUSIONS, THOUGH.

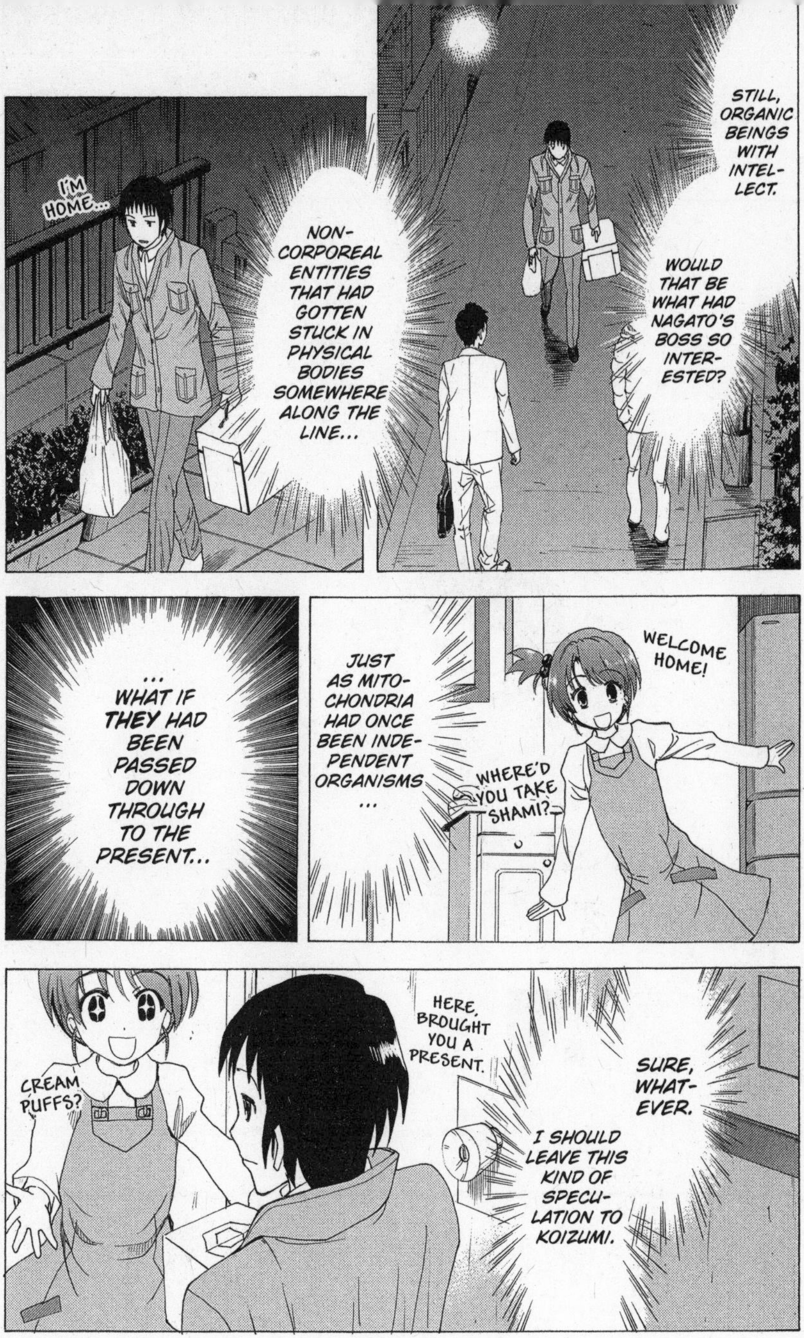
STILL, ORGANIC BEINGS WITH INTELLECT.
WOULD THAT BE WHAT HAD NAGATO'S BOSS SO INTERESTED?
NON-CORPOREAL ENTITIES THAT HAD GOTTEN STUCK IN PHYSICAL BODIES SOMEWHERE ALONG THE LINE...
I'M HOME...
WELCOME HOME!
WHERE'D YOU TAKE SHAMI?
JUST AS MITOCHONDRIA HAD ONCE BEEN INDEPENDENT ORGANISMS...
... WHAT IF **THEY** HAD BEEN PASSED DOWN THROUGH TO THE PRESENT...
HERE, BROUGHT YOU A PRESENT.
SURE, WHATEVER.
I SHOULD LEAVE THIS KIND OF SPECULATION TO KOIZUMI.
CREAM PUFFS?

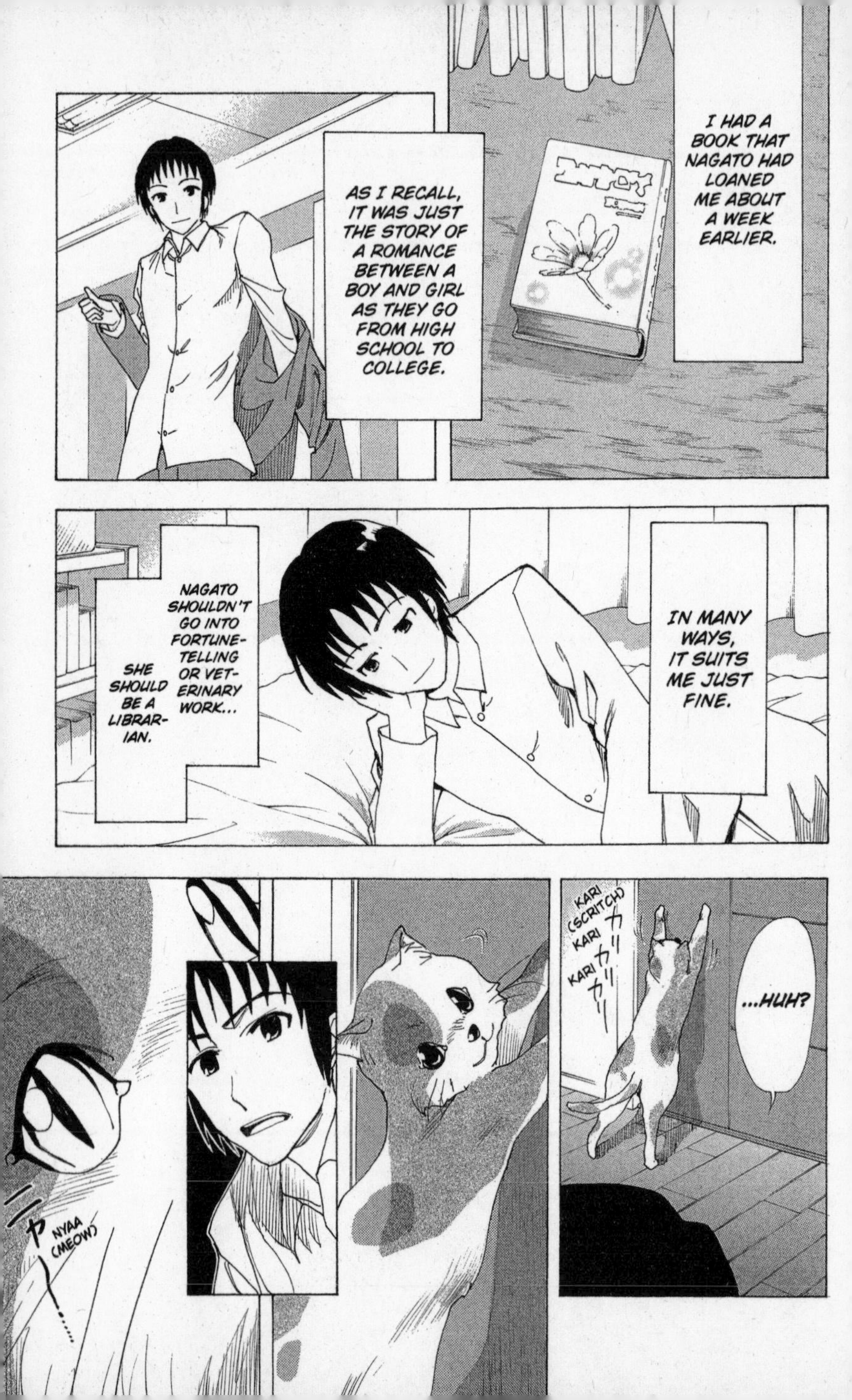
I HAD A BOOK THAT NAGATO HAD LOANED ME ABOUT A WEEK EARLIER.
AS I RECALL, IT WAS JUST THE STORY OF A ROMANCE BETWEEN A BOY AND GIRL AS THEY GO FROM HIGH SCHOOL TO COLLEGE.
IN MANY WAYS, IT SUITS ME JUST FINE.
NAGATO SHOULDN'T GO INTO FORTUNE-TELLING OR VETERINARY WORK...
SHE SHOULD BE A LIBRARIAN.
...HUH?
KARI (SCRITCH) KARI KARI
NYAA (MEOW)

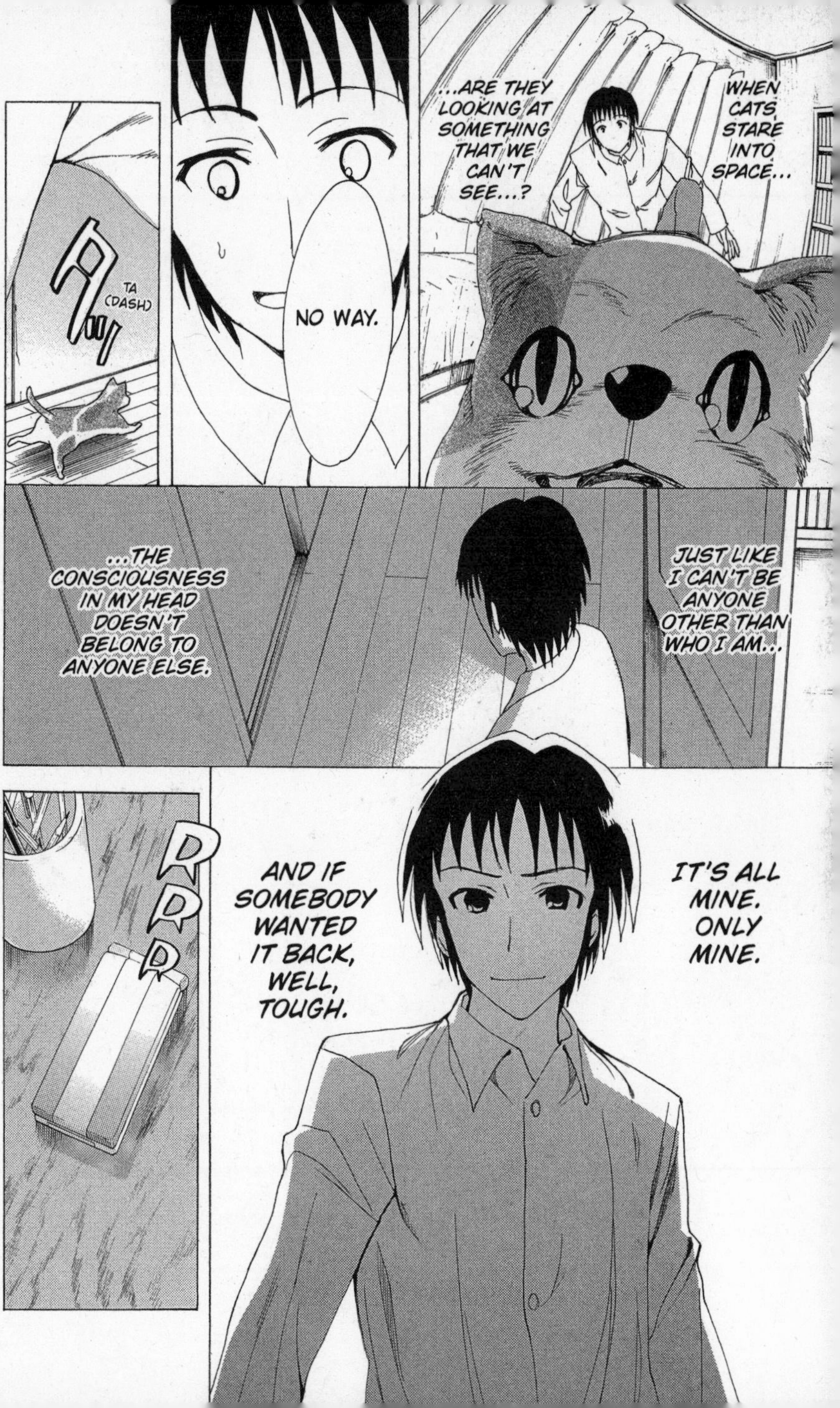
WHEN CATS STARE INTO SPACE...
...ARE THEY LOOKING AT SOMETHING THAT WE CAN'T SEE...?
NO WAY.
TA (DASH)
JUST LIKE I CAN'T BE ANYONE OTHER THAN WHO I AM...
...THE CONSCIOUSNESS IN MY HEAD DOESN'T BELONG TO ANYONE ELSE.
IT'S ALL MINE. ONLY MINE.
AND IF SOMEBODY WANTED IT BACK, WELL, TOUGH.
RRR

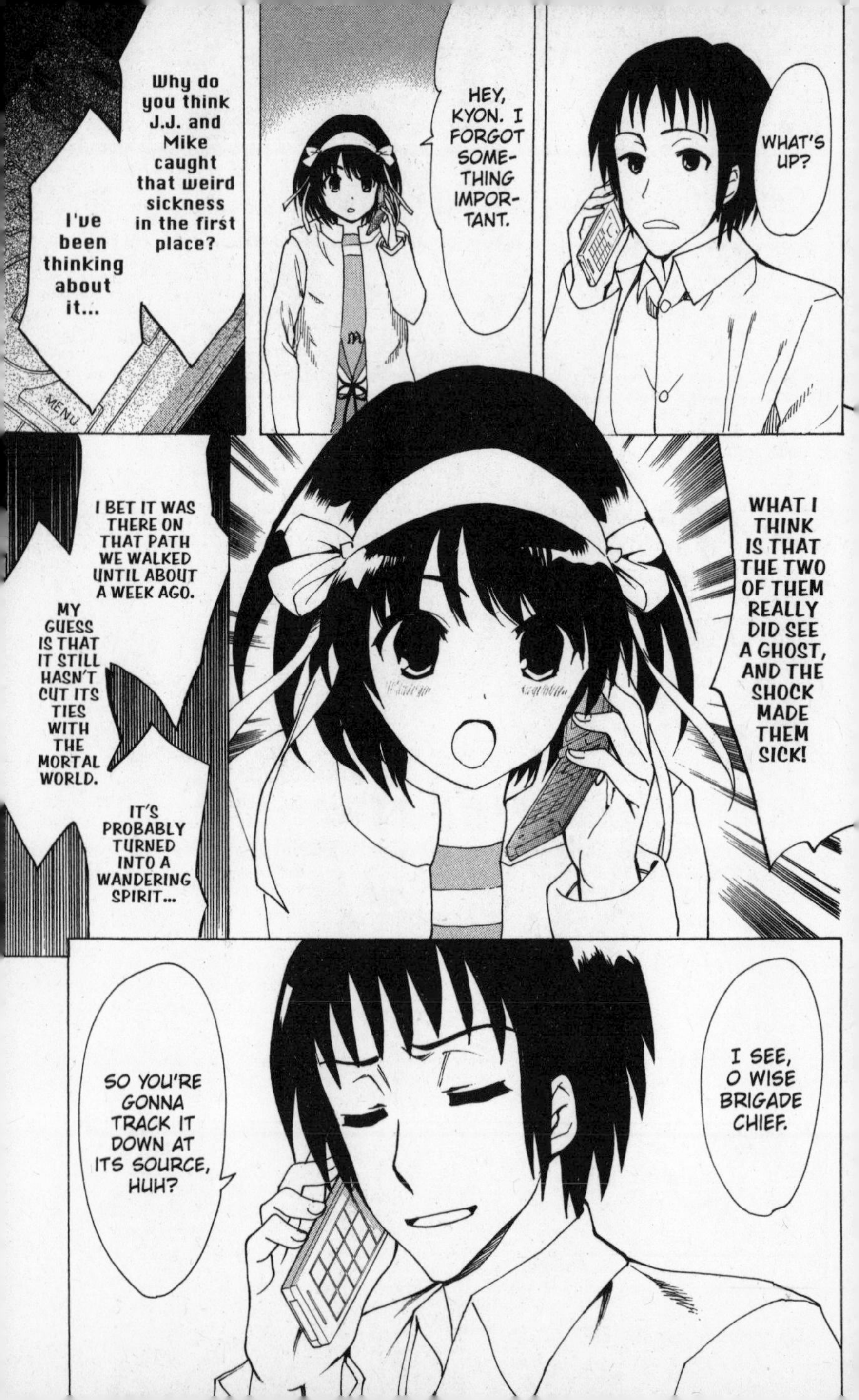
WHAT'S UP?
HEY, KYON. I FORGOT SOME-THING IMPOR-TANT.
Why do you think J.J. and Mike caught that weird sickness in the first place?
I've been thinking about it...
MENU
WHAT I THINK IS THAT THE TWO OF THEM REALLY DID SEE A GHOST, AND THE SHOCK MADE THEM SICK!
I BET IT WAS THERE ON THAT PATH WE WALKED UNTIL ABOUT A WEEK AGO.
MY GUESS IS THAT IT STILL HASN'T CUT ITS TIES WITH THE MORTAL WORLD.
IT'S PROBABLY TURNED INTO A WANDERING SPIRIT...
I SEE, O WISE BRIGADE CHIEF.
SO YOU'RE GONNA TRACK IT DOWN AT ITS SOURCE, HUH?

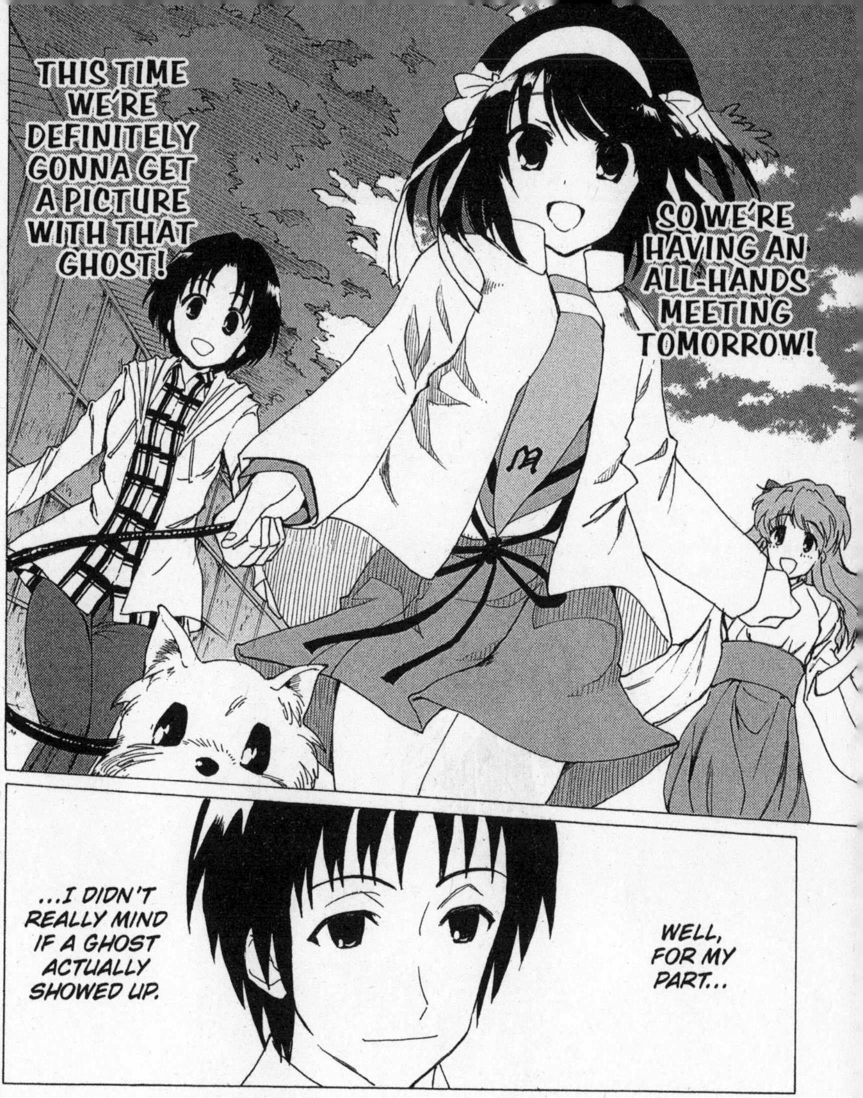
SO WE'RE HAVING AN ALL-HANDS MEETING TOMORROW!
THIS TIME WE'RE DEFINITELY GONNA GET A PICTURE WITH THAT GHOST!
WELL, FOR MY PART...
...I DIDN'T REALLY MIND IF A GHOST ACTUALLY SHOWED UP.
THE REALITY PORTRAYED IN THAT BOOK WAS FAR MORE ORDINARY THAN THE ONE THAT SURROUNDED ME.
BUT I WASN'T JEALOUS OF IT.
NOT NOW, ANYWAY.

WANDERING SHADOW III : END

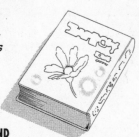

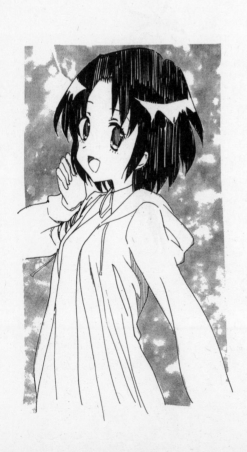

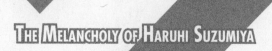
THE MELANCHOLY OF HARUHI SUZUMIYA

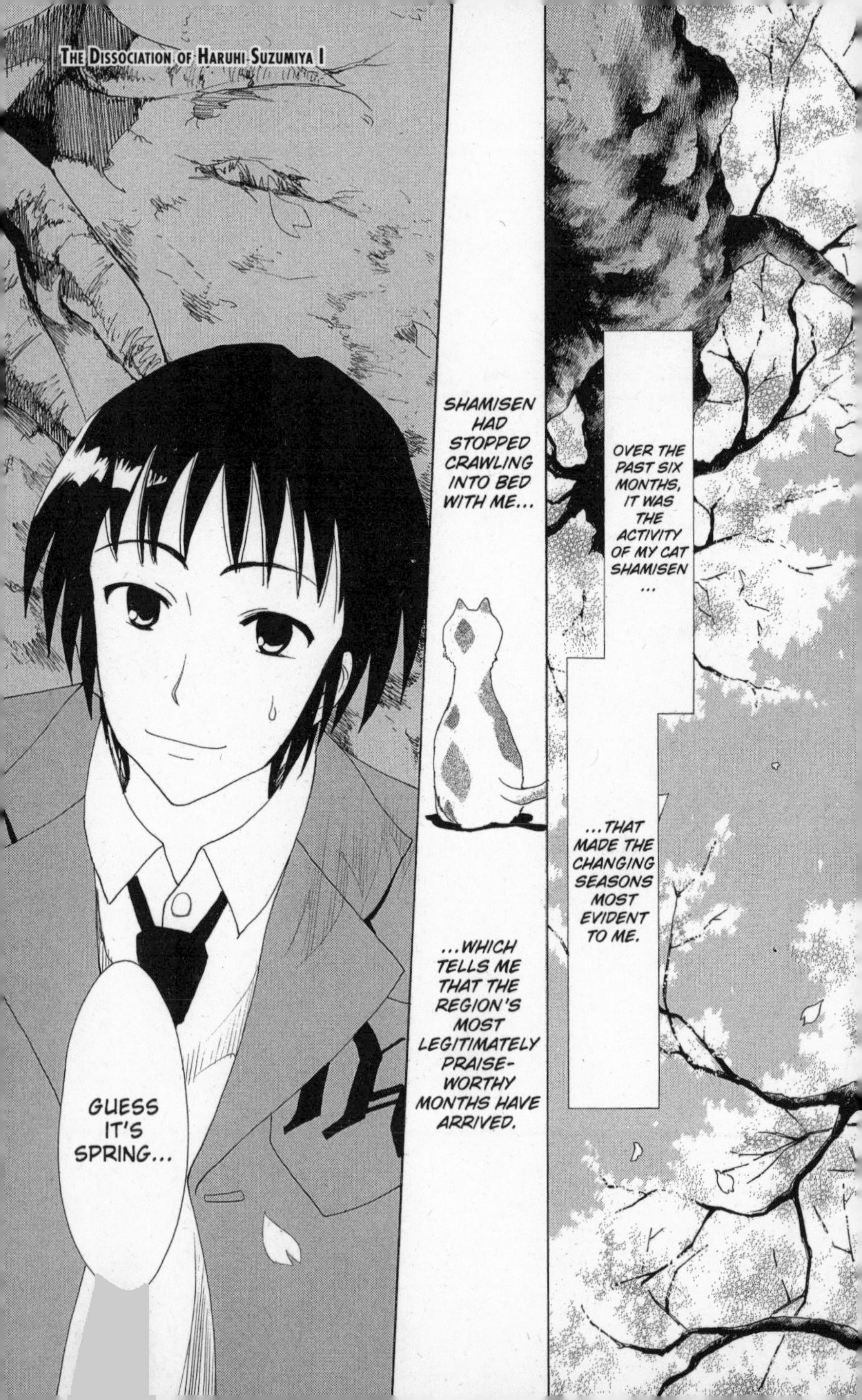
OVER THE PAST SIX MONTHS, IT WAS THE ACTIVITY OF MY CAT SHAMISEN...
...THAT MADE THE CHANGING SEASONS MOST EVIDENT TO ME.
SHAMISEN HAD STOPPED CRAWLING INTO BED WITH ME...
...WHICH TELLS ME THAT THE REGION'S MOST LEGITIMATELY PRAISE-WORTHY MONTHS HAVE ARRIVED.
GUESS IT'S SPRING...

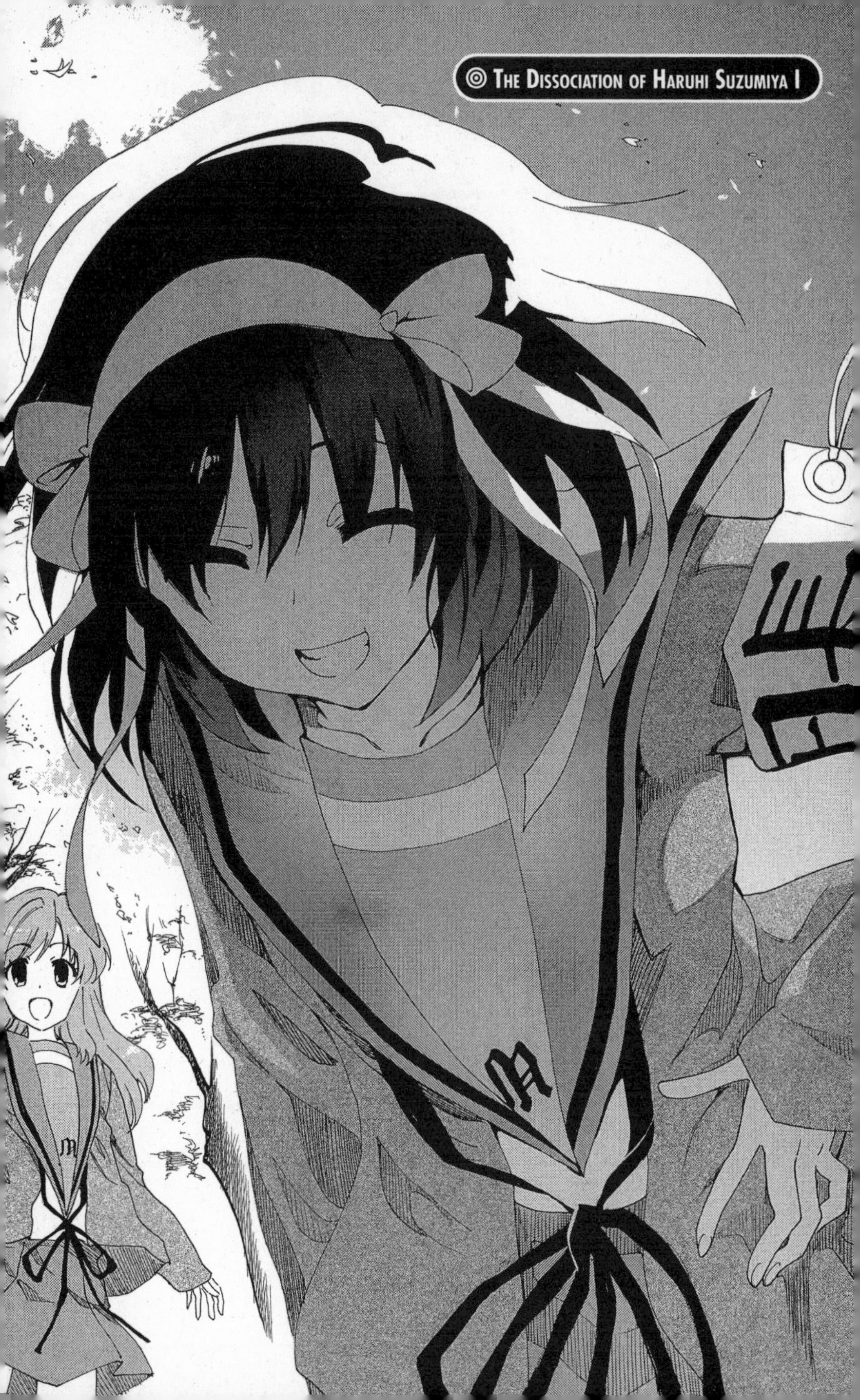
◎ The Dissociation of Haruhi Suzumiya I

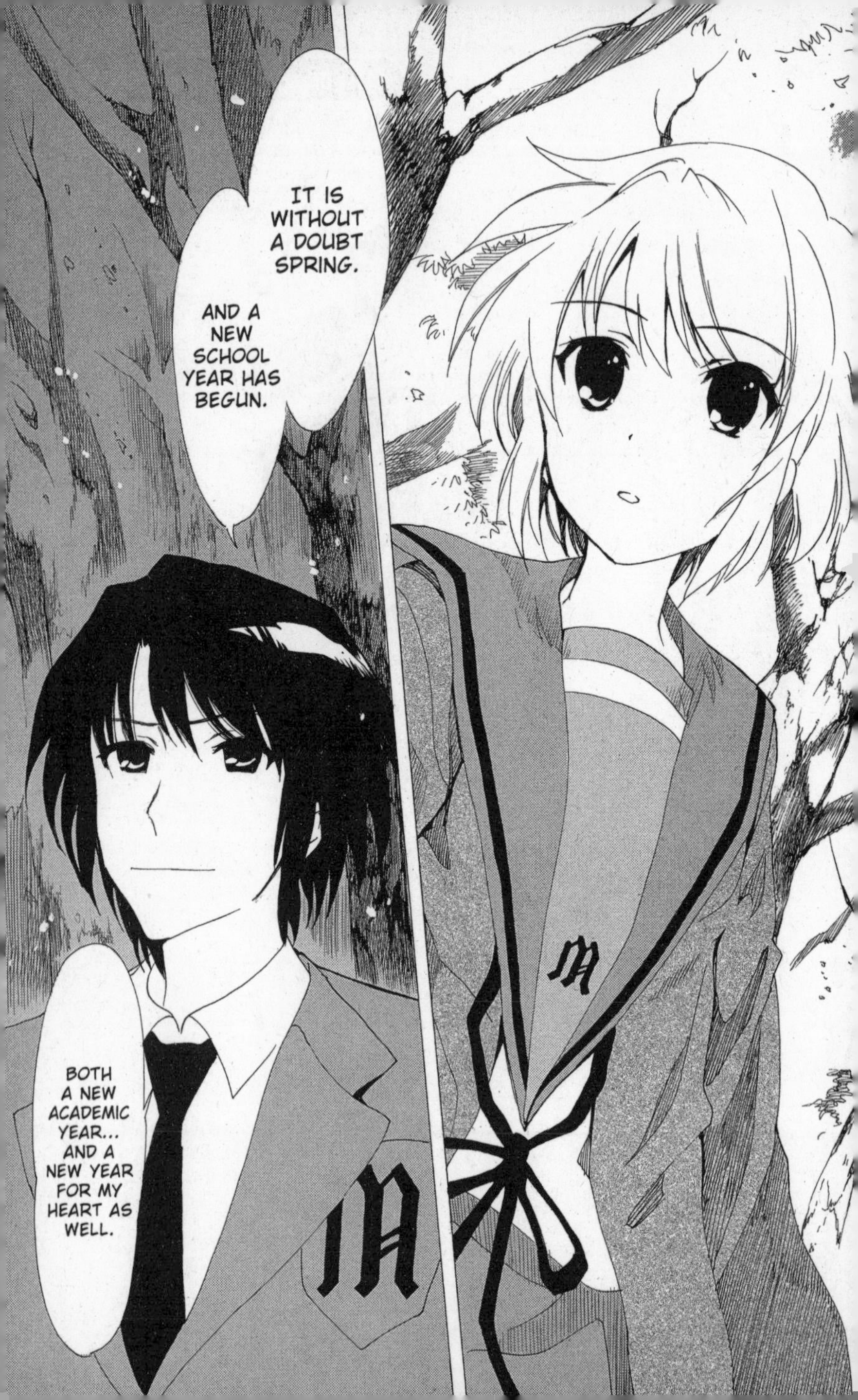
IT IS WITHOUT A DOUBT SPRING.
AND A NEW SCHOOL YEAR HAS BEGUN.
BOTH A NEW ACADEMIC YEAR... AND A NEW YEAR FOR MY HEART AS WELL.

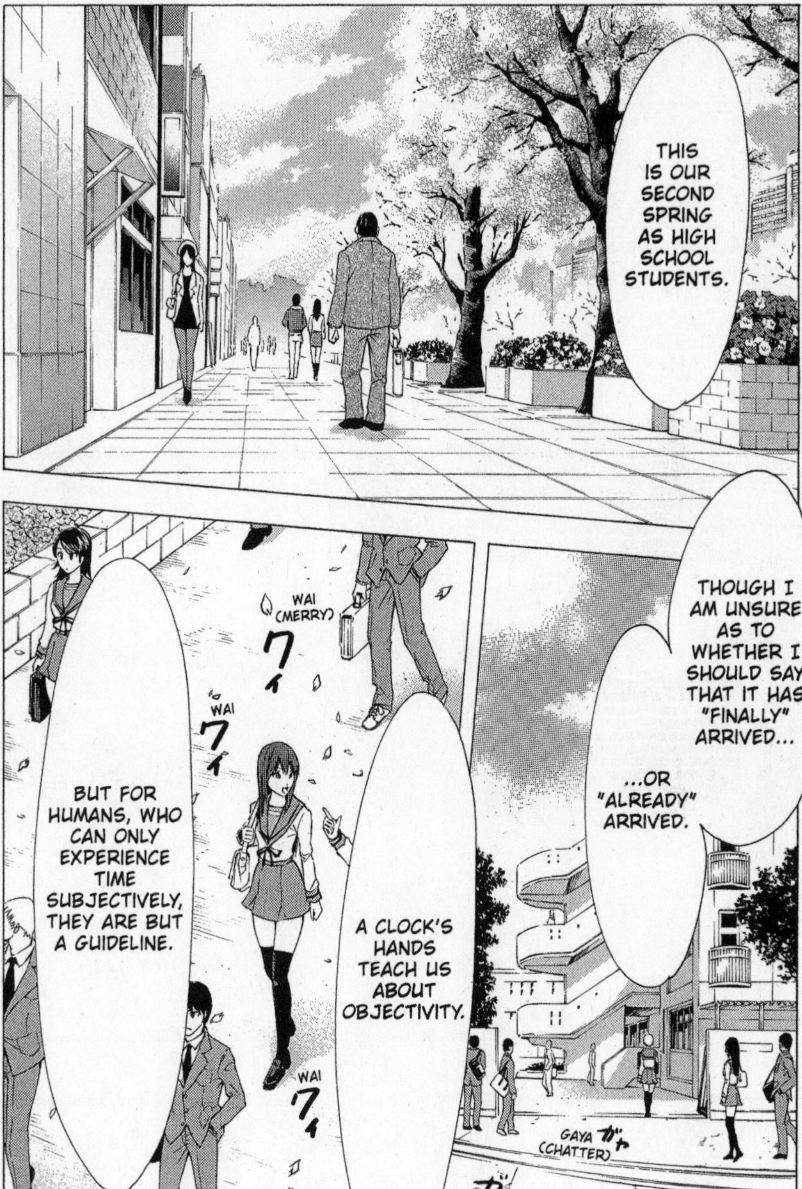
THIS IS OUR SECOND SPRING AS HIGH SCHOOL STUDENTS.
THOUGH I AM UNSURE AS TO WHETHER I SHOULD SAY THAT IT HAS "FINALLY" ARRIVED...
...OR "ALREADY" ARRIVED.
GAYA (CHATTER)
GAYA
WAI (MERRY)
WAI
A CLOCK'S HANDS TEACH US ABOUT OBJECTIVITY.
BUT FOR HUMANS, WHO CAN ONLY EXPERIENCE TIME SUBJECTIVELY, THEY ARE BUT A GUIDELINE.
WAI

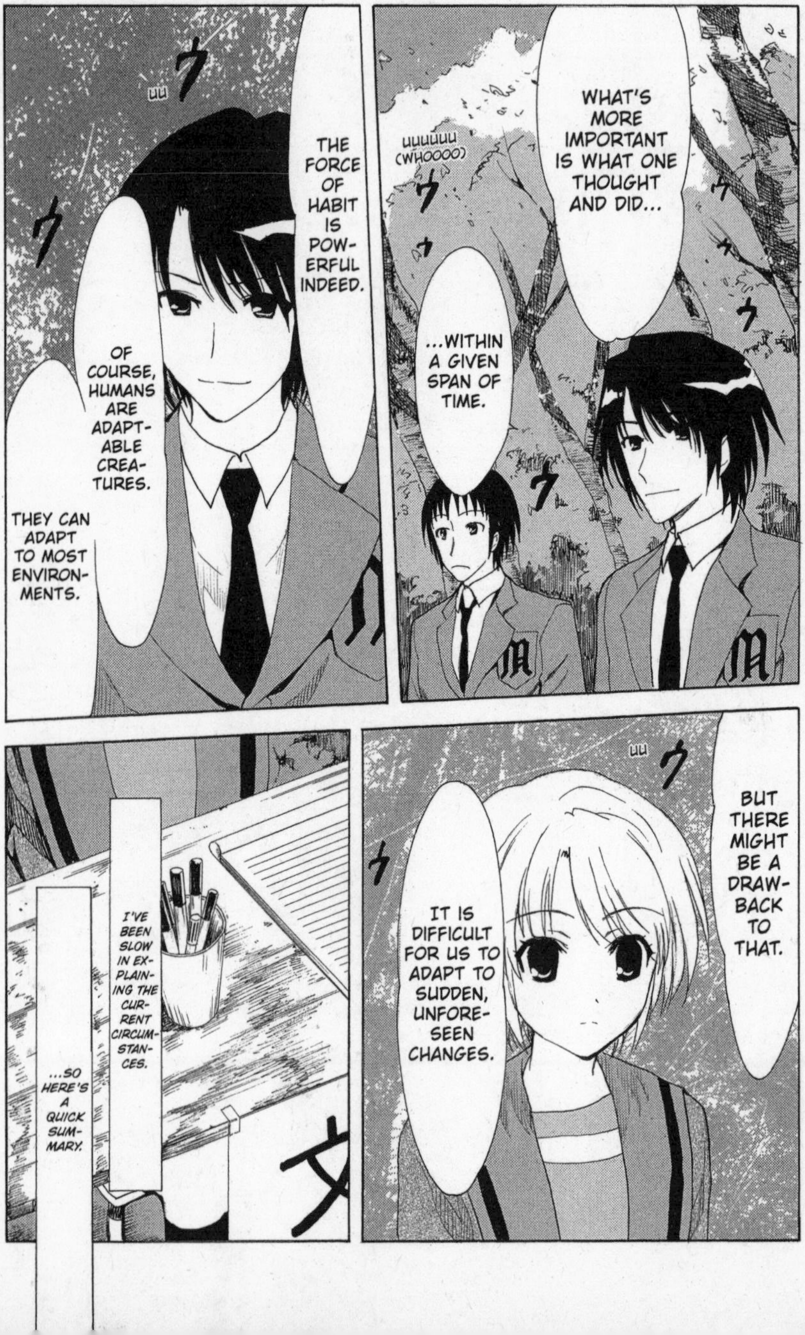
uuuuuu (WHOOOO)
WHAT'S MORE IMPORTANT IS WHAT ONE THOUGHT AND DID...
...WITHIN A GIVEN SPAN OF TIME.
uu
THE FORCE OF HABIT IS POWERFUL INDEED.
OF COURSE, HUMANS ARE ADAPTABLE CREATURES.
THEY CAN ADAPT TO MOST ENVIRONMENTS.
uu
BUT THERE MIGHT BE A DRAWBACK TO THAT.
IT IS DIFFICULT FOR US TO ADAPT TO SUDDEN, UNFORESEEN CHANGES.
I'VE BEEN SLOW IN EXPLAINING THE CURRENT CIRCUMSTANCES.
...SO HERE'S A QUICK SUMMARY.

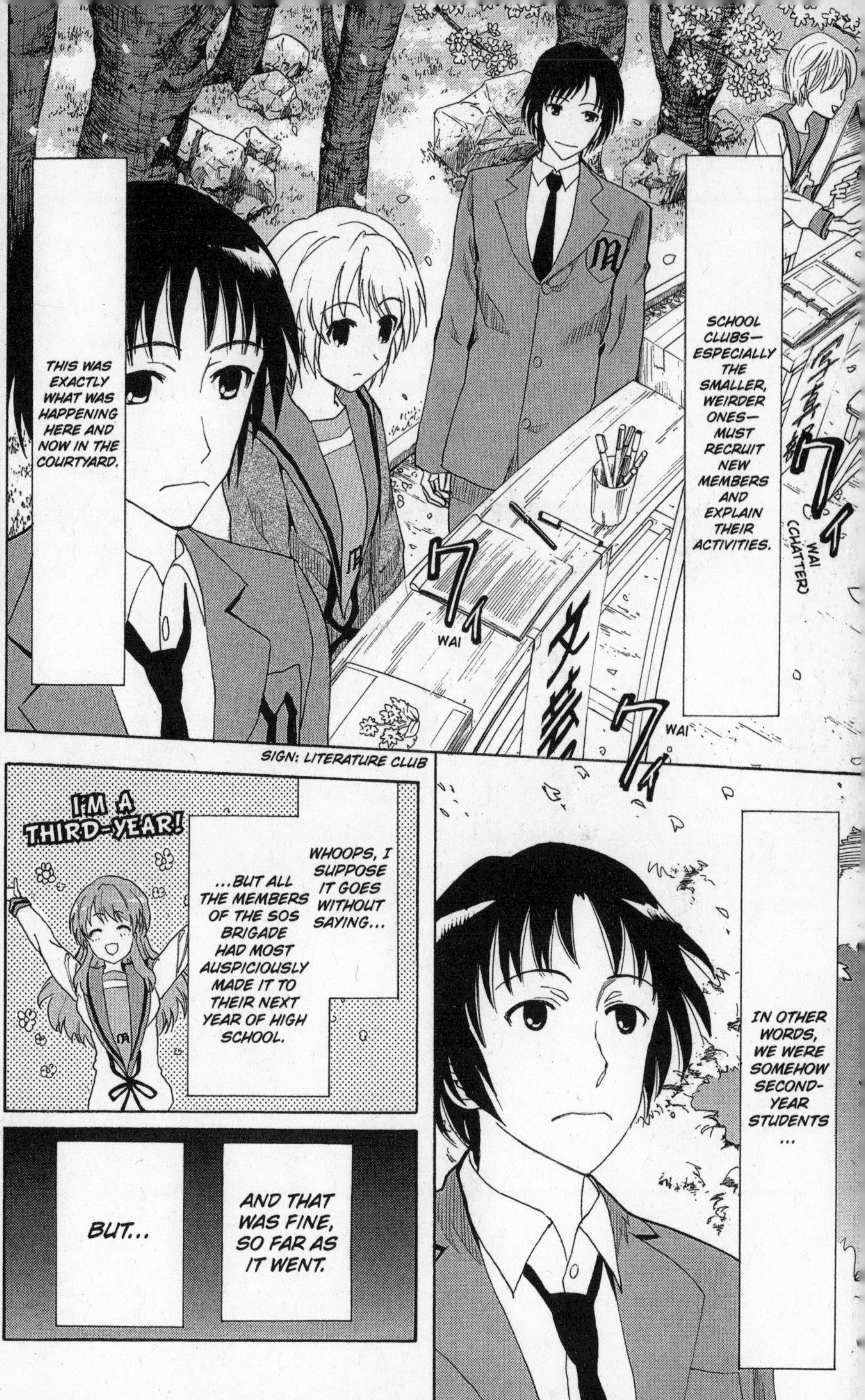
SCHOOL CLUBS—ESPECIALLY THE SMALLER, WEIRDER ONES—MUST RECRUIT NEW MEMBERS AND EXPLAIN THEIR ACTIVITIES.
WAI (CHATTER)
THIS WAS EXACTLY WHAT WAS HAPPENING HERE AND NOW IN THE COURTYARD.
WAI
WAI
SIGN: LITERATURE CLUB
IN OTHER WORDS, WE WERE SOMEHOW SECOND-YEAR STUDENTS...
WHOOPS, I SUPPOSE IT GOES WITHOUT SAYING...
...BUT ALL THE MEMBERS OF THE SOS BRIGADE HAD MOST AUSPICIOUSLY MADE IT TO THEIR NEXT YEAR OF HIGH SCHOOL.
I'M A THIRD-YEAR!
AND THAT WAS FINE, SO FAR AS IT WENT.
BUT...

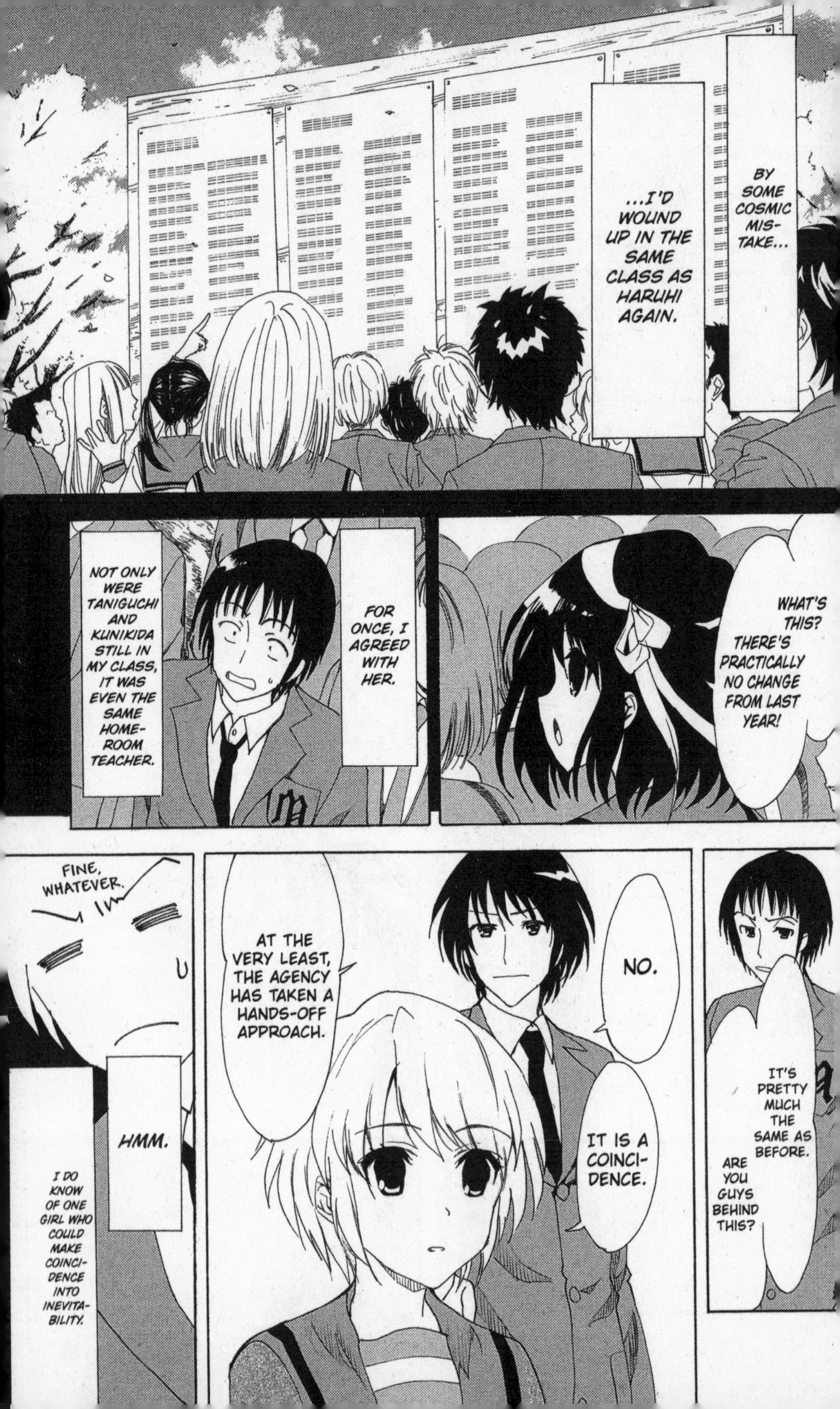
BY SOME COSMIC MIS-TAKE...
...I'D WOUND UP IN THE SAME CLASS AS HARUHI AGAIN.
WHAT'S THIS? THERE'S PRACTICALLY NO CHANGE FROM LAST YEAR!
FOR ONCE, I AGREED WITH HER.
NOT ONLY WERE TANIGUCHI AND KUNIKIDA STILL IN MY CLASS, IT WAS EVEN THE SAME HOME-ROOM TEACHER.
IT'S PRETTY MUCH THE SAME AS BEFORE.
ARE YOU GUYS BEHIND THIS?
NO.
IT IS A COINCI-DENCE.
AT THE VERY LEAST, THE AGENCY HAS TAKEN A HANDS-OFF APPROACH.
FINE, WHATEVER.
HMM.
I DO KNOW OF ONE GIRL WHO COULD MAKE COINCI-DENCE INTO INEVITA-BILITY.

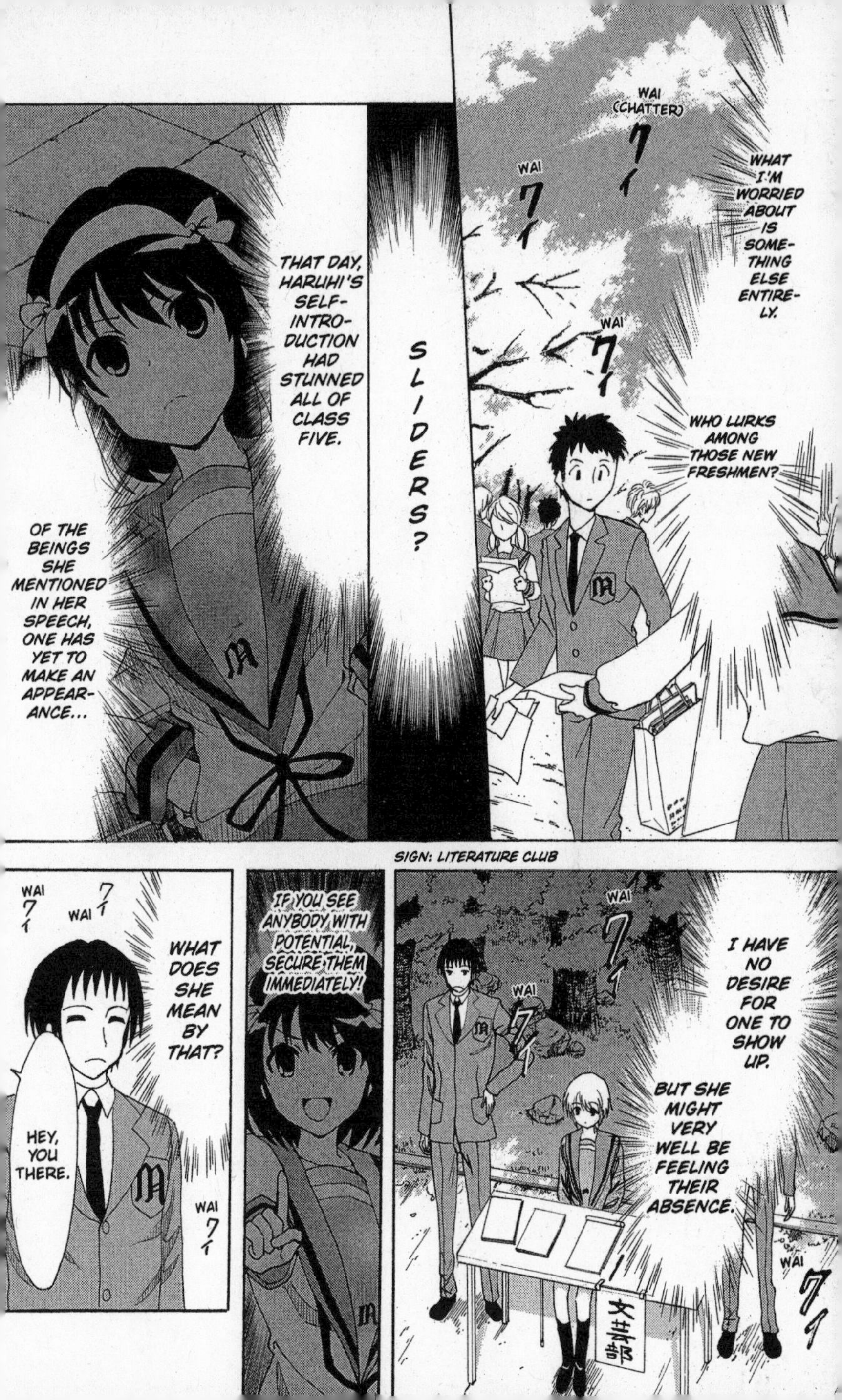

WAI (CHATTER)
ワイ
WAI
ワイ
WHAT I'M WORRIED ABOUT IS SOMETHING ELSE ENTIRELY.
WAI
ワイ
WHO LURKS AMONG THOSE NEW FRESHMEN?
SLIDERS?
THAT DAY, HARUHI'S SELF-INTRODUCTION HAD STUNNED ALL OF CLASS FIVE.
OF THE BEINGS SHE MENTIONED IN HER SPEECH, ONE HAS YET TO MAKE AN APPEARANCE...
SIGN: LITERATURE CLUB
WAI
ワイ
WAI
ワイ
I HAVE NO DESIRE FOR ONE TO SHOW UP.
BUT SHE MIGHT VERY WELL BE FEELING THEIR ABSENCE.
文芸部
WAI
ワイ
IF YOU SEE ANYBODY WITH POTENTIAL, SECURE THEM IMMEDIATELY!
WAI
ワイ
WAI
ワイ
WHAT DOES SHE MEAN BY THAT?
HEY, YOU THERE.
WAI
ワイ

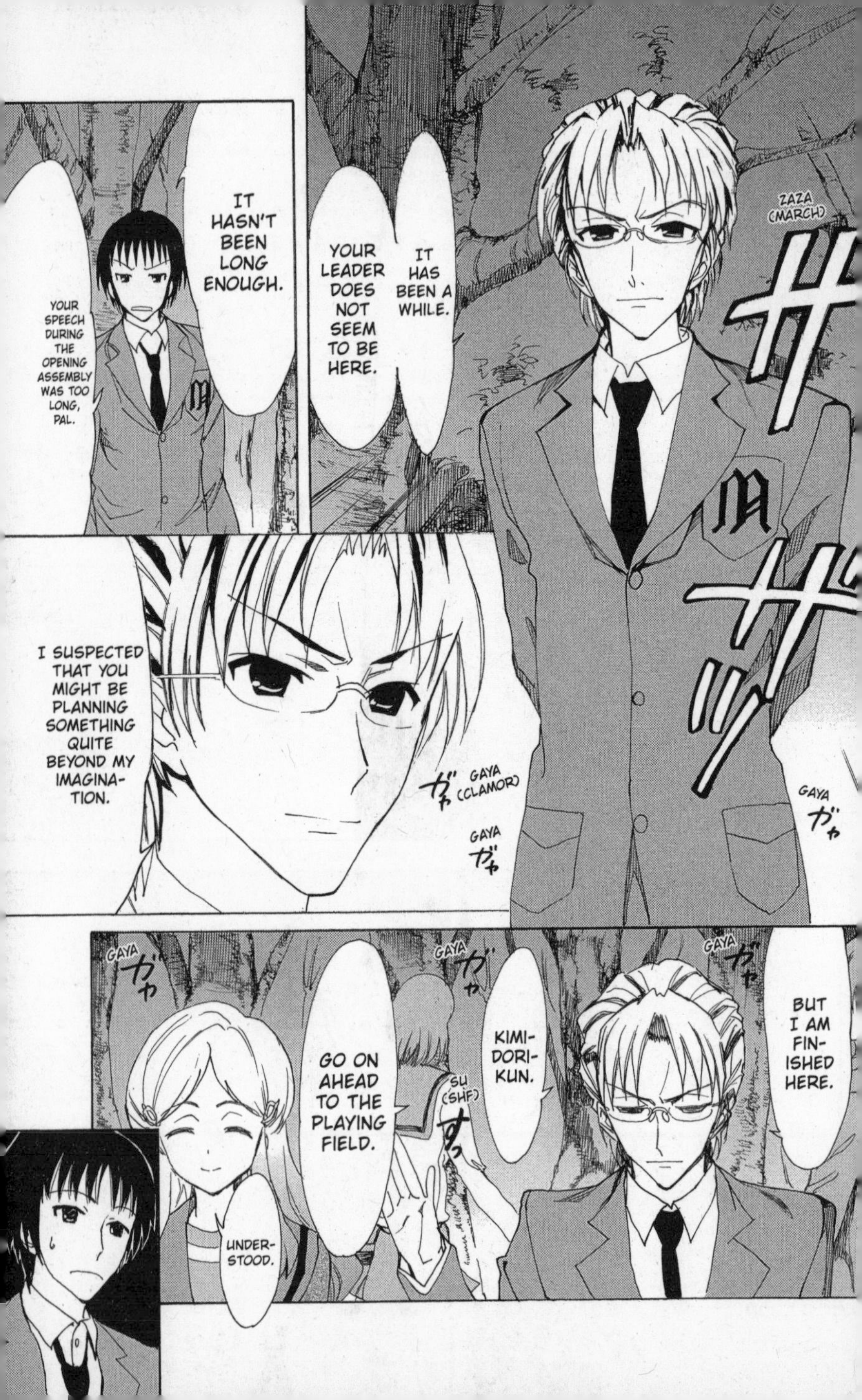
ZAZA (MARCH)
IT HAS BEEN A WHILE.
YOUR LEADER DOES NOT SEEM TO BE HERE.
GAYA
IT HASN'T BEEN LONG ENOUGH.
YOUR SPEECH DURING THE OPENING ASSEMBLY WAS TOO LONG, PAL.
I SUSPECTED THAT YOU MIGHT BE PLANNING SOMETHING QUITE BEYOND MY IMAGINATION.
GAYA (CLAMOR)
GAYA
GAYA
BUT I AM FINISHED HERE.
KIMIDORI-KUN.
GAYA
SU (SHF)
GO ON AHEAD TO THE PLAYING FIELD.
UNDERSTOOD.
GAYA

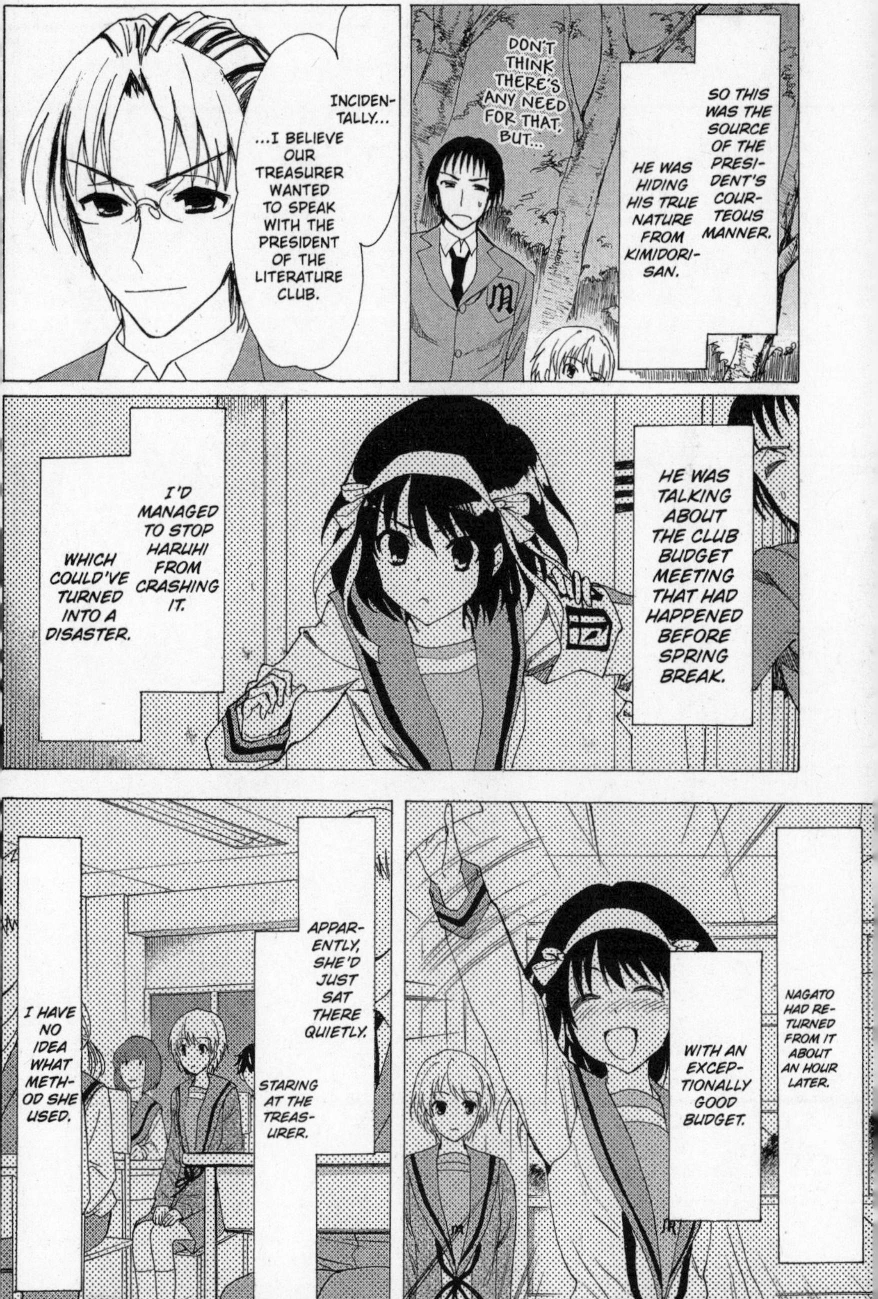
SO THIS WAS THE SOURCE OF THE PRESIDENT'S COURTEOUS MANNER.
HE WAS HIDING HIS TRUE NATURE FROM KIMIDORI-SAN.
DON'T THINK THERE'S ANY NEED FOR THAT, BUT...
INCIDENTALLY...
...I BELIEVE OUR TREASURER WANTED TO SPEAK WITH THE PRESIDENT OF THE LITERATURE CLUB.
HE WAS TALKING ABOUT THE CLUB BUDGET MEETING THAT HAD HAPPENED BEFORE SPRING BREAK.
I'D MANAGED TO STOP HARUHI FROM CRASHING IT.
WHICH COULD'VE TURNED INTO A DISASTER.
NAGATO HAD RETURNED FROM IT ABOUT AN HOUR LATER.
WITH AN EXCEPTIONALLY GOOD BUDGET.
APPARENTLY, SHE'D JUST SAT THERE QUIETLY.
STARING AT THE TREASURER.
I HAVE NO IDEA WHAT METHOD SHE USED.

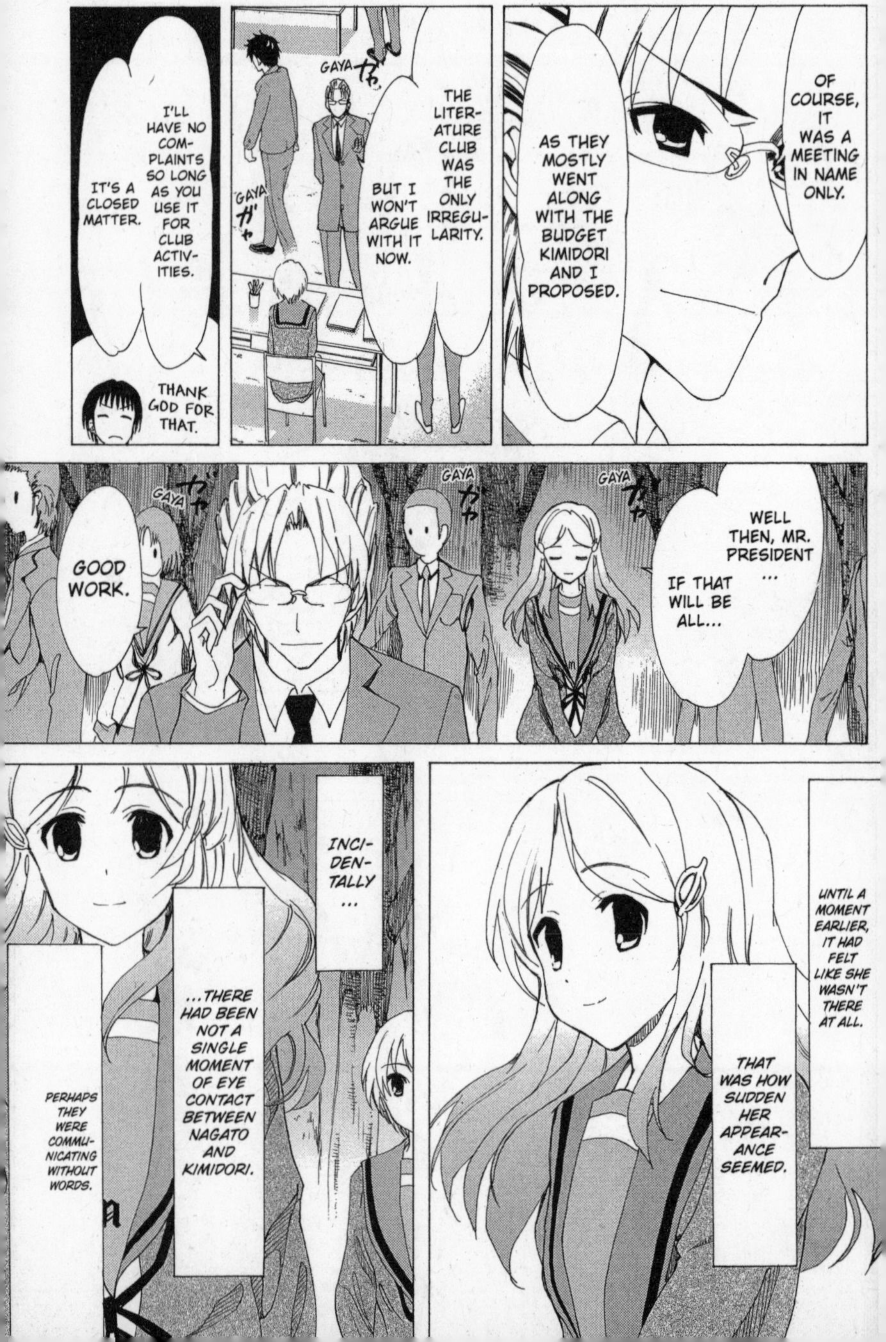
OF COURSE, IT WAS A MEETING IN NAME ONLY.
AS THEY MOSTLY WENT ALONG WITH THE BUDGET KIMIDORI AND I PROPOSED.
GAYA
GAYA
THE LITERATURE CLUB WAS THE ONLY IRREGULARITY.
BUT I WON'T ARGUE WITH IT NOW.
I'LL HAVE NO COMPLAINTS SO LONG AS YOU USE IT FOR CLUB ACTIVITIES.
IT'S A CLOSED MATTER.
THANK GOD FOR THAT.
GAYA
GAYA
WELL THEN, MR. PRESIDENT...
IF THAT WILL BE ALL...
GAYA
GAYA
GOOD WORK.
UNTIL A MOMENT EARLIER, IT HAD FELT LIKE SHE WASN'T THERE AT ALL.
THAT WAS HOW SUDDEN HER APPEARANCE SEEMED.
INCIDENTALLY...
...THERE HAD BEEN NOT A SINGLE MOMENT OF EYE CONTACT BETWEEN NAGATO AND KIMIDORI.
PERHAPS THEY WERE COMMUNICATING WITHOUT WORDS.

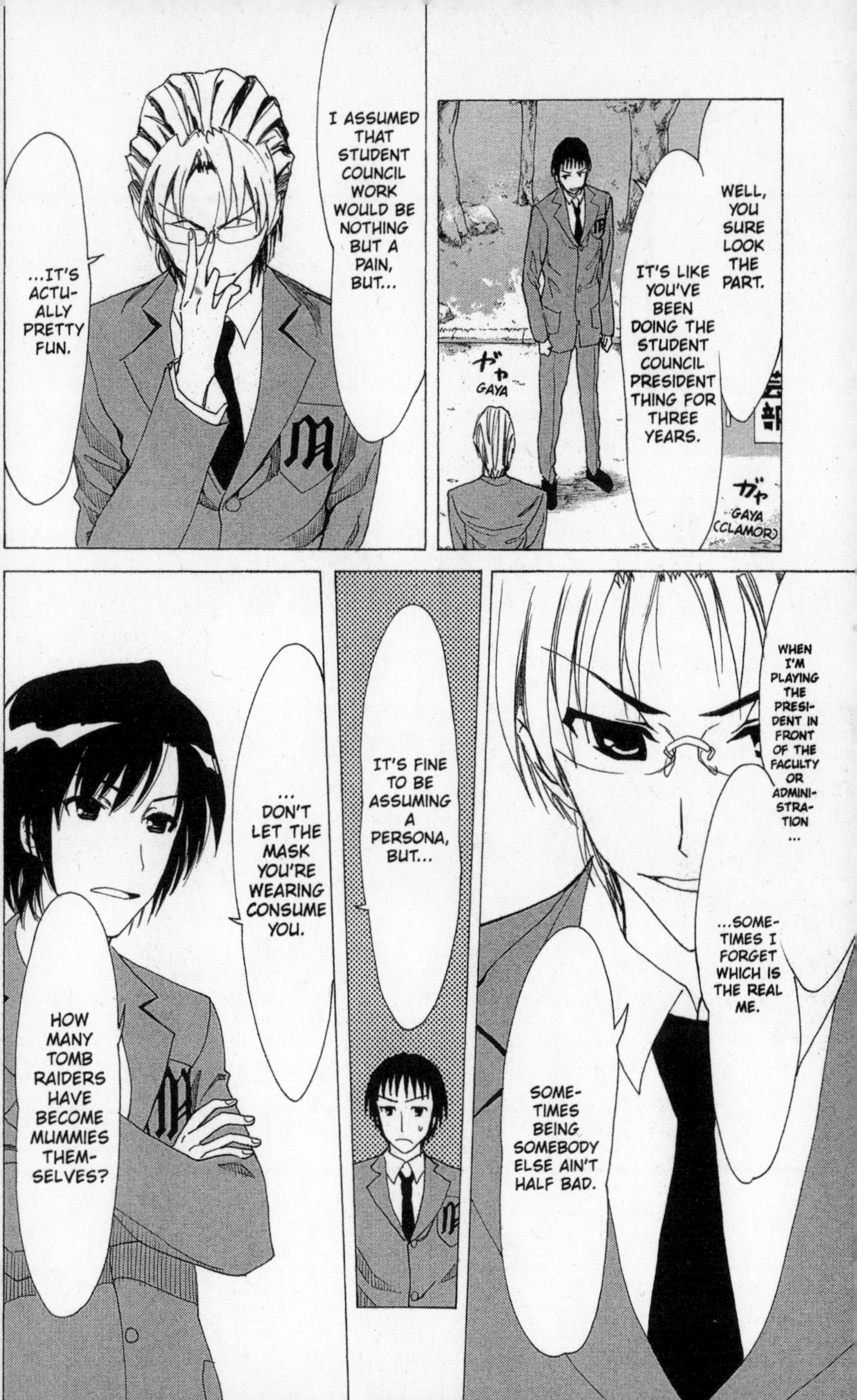
WELL, YOU SURE LOOK THE PART.
IT'S LIKE YOU'VE BEEN DOING THE STUDENT COUNCIL PRESIDENT THING FOR THREE YEARS.
ガヤ GAYA (CLAMOR)
ガヤ GAYA
I ASSUMED THAT STUDENT COUNCIL WORK WOULD BE NOTHING BUT A PAIN, BUT...
...IT'S ACTUALLY PRETTY FUN.
WHEN I'M PLAYING THE PRESIDENT IN FRONT OF THE FACULTY OR ADMINISTRATION...
...SOMETIMES I FORGET WHICH IS THE REAL ME.
SOMETIMES BEING SOMEBODY ELSE AIN'T HALF BAD.
IT'S FINE TO BE ASSUMING A PERSONA, BUT...
...DON'T LET THE MASK YOU'RE WEARING CONSUME YOU.
HOW MANY TOMB RAIDERS HAVE BECOME MUMMIES THEMSELVES?

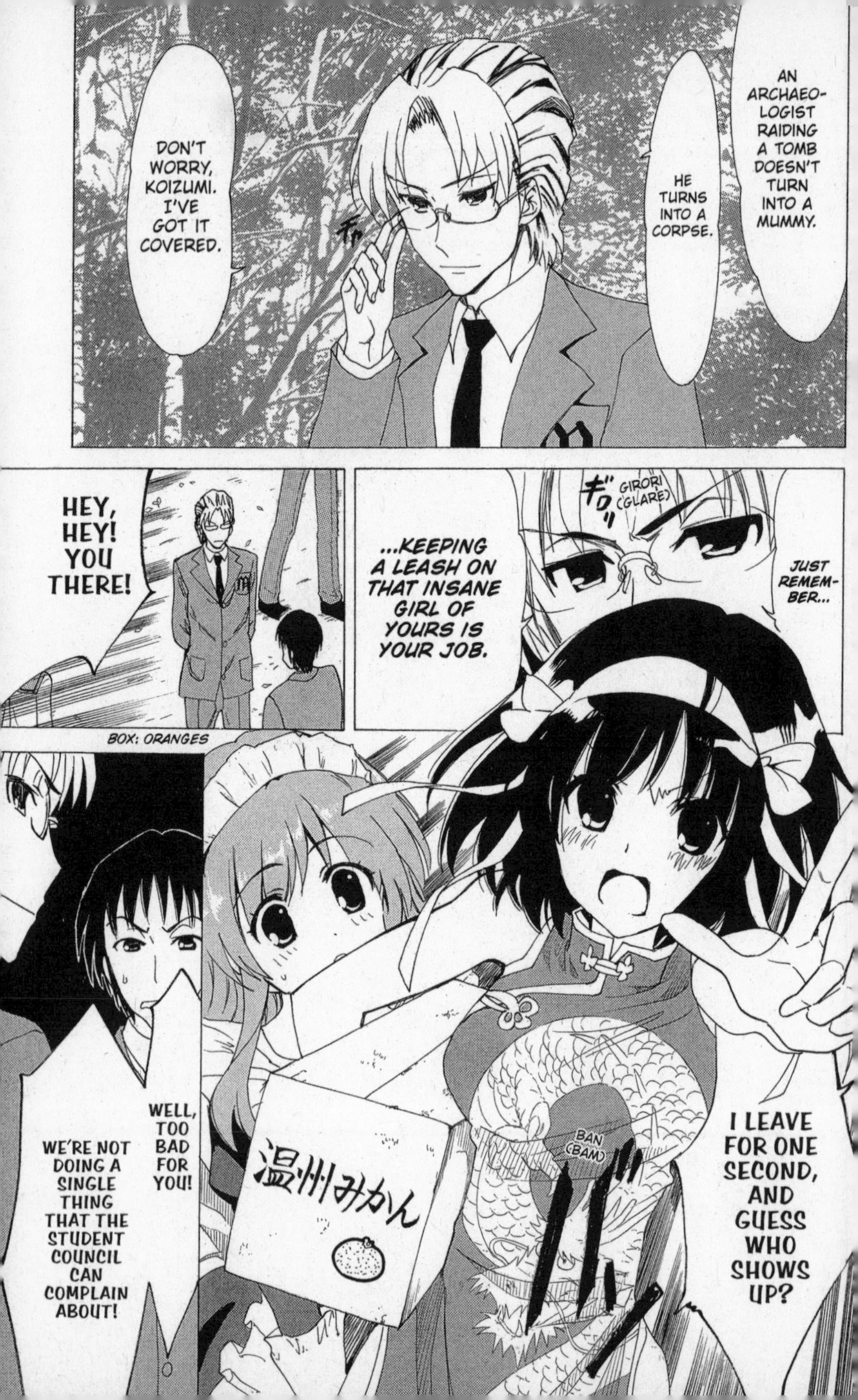
AN ARCHAEOLOGIST RAIDING A TOMB DOESN'T TURN INTO A MUMMY.
HE TURNS INTO A CORPSE.
DON'T WORRY, KOIZUMI. I'VE GOT IT COVERED.
JUST REMEMBER...
GIRORI (GLARE)
...KEEPING A LEASH ON THAT INSANE GIRL OF YOURS IS YOUR JOB.
HEY, HEY! YOU THERE!
BOX: ORANGES
I LEAVE FOR ONE SECOND, AND GUESS WHO SHOWS UP?
BAN (BAM)
温州みかん
WELL, TOO BAD FOR YOU!
WE'RE NOT DOING A SINGLE THING THAT THE STUDENT COUNCIL CAN COMPLAIN ABOUT!

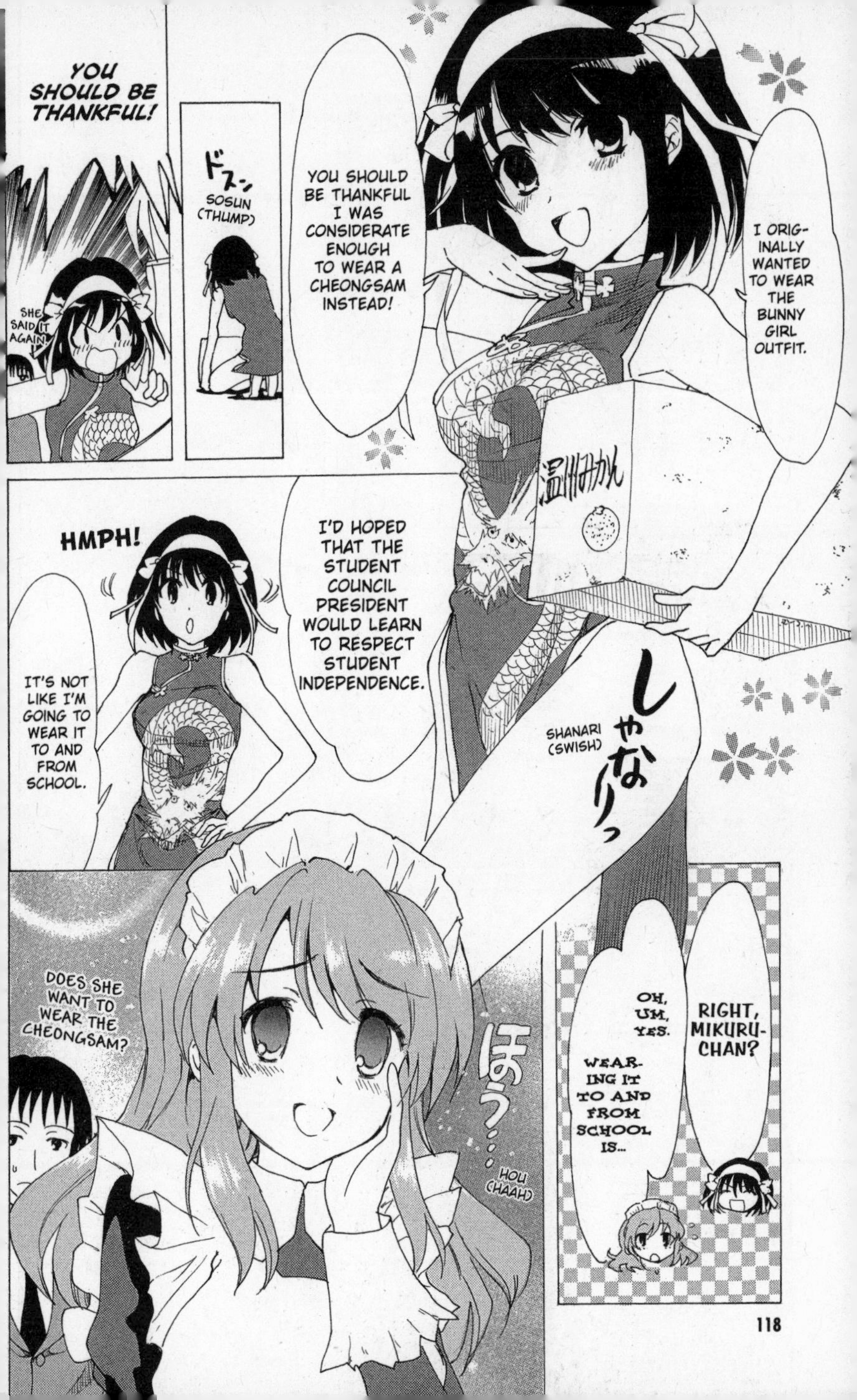
I ORIGINALLY WANTED TO WEAR THE BUNNY GIRL OUTFIT.
YOU SHOULD BE THANKFUL I WAS CONSIDERATE ENOUGH TO WEAR A CHEONGSAM INSTEAD!
ドスン
SOSUN (THUMP)
YOU SHOULD BE THANKFUL!
SHE SAID IT AGAIN.
温州みかん
I'D HOPED THAT THE STUDENT COUNCIL PRESIDENT WOULD LEARN TO RESPECT STUDENT INDEPENDENCE.
しゃなりっ
SHANARI (SWISH)
HMPH!
IT'S NOT LIKE I'M GOING TO WEAR IT TO AND FROM SCHOOL.
RIGHT, MIKURU-CHAN?
OH, UM, YES.
WEARING IT TO AND FROM SCHOOL IS...
ほう…
HOU (CHAAH)
DOES SHE WANT TO WEAR THE CHEONGSAM?

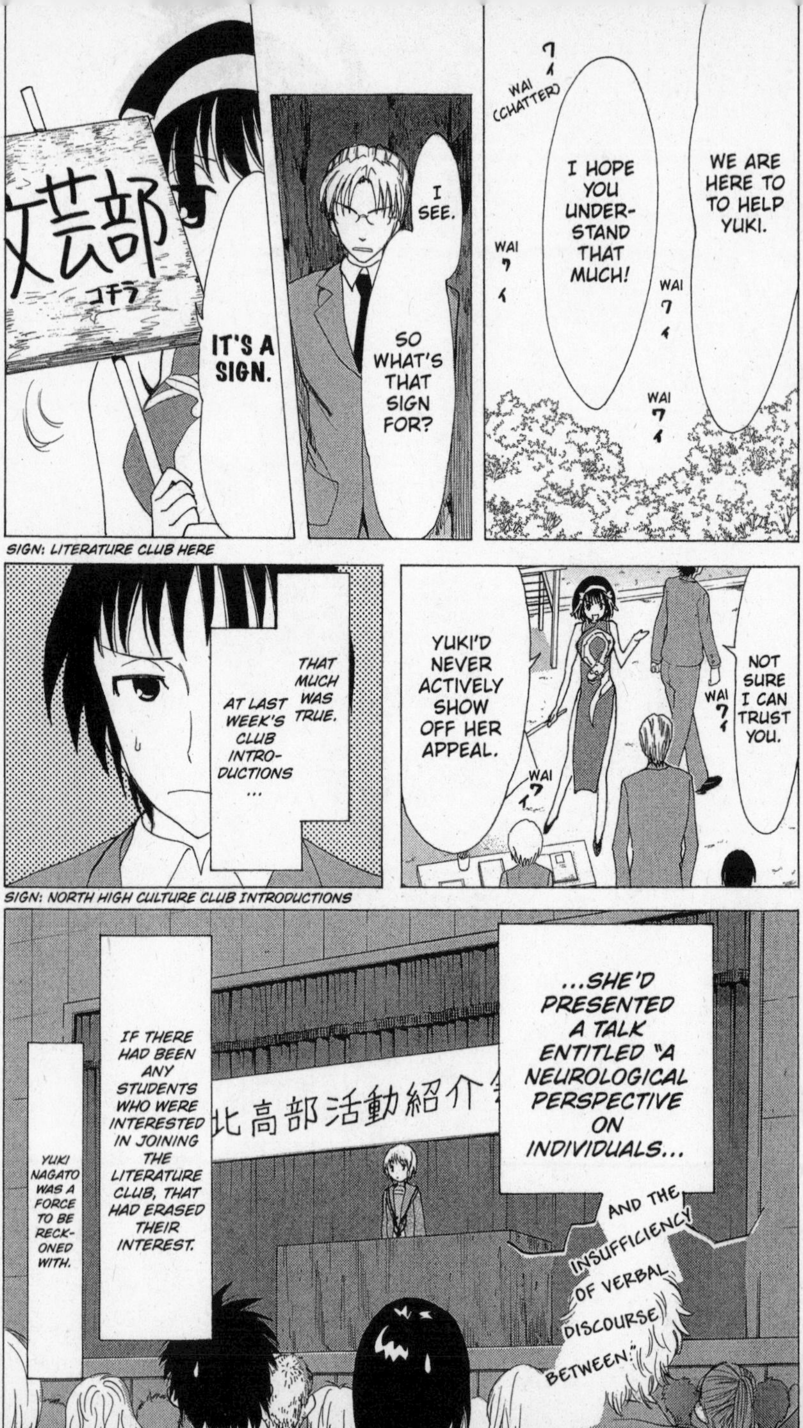
WE ARE HERE TO TO HELP YUKI.
WAI ワイ
I HOPE YOU UNDER-STAND THAT MUCH!
WAI ワイ (CHATTER)
WAI ワイ
WAI ワイ
I SEE.
SO WHAT'S THAT SIGN FOR?
文芸部
コチラ
IT'S A SIGN.
SIGN: LITERATURE CLUB HERE
NOT SURE I CAN TRUST YOU.
WAI ワイ
YUKI'D NEVER ACTIVELY SHOW OFF HER APPEAL.
WAI ワイ
THAT MUCH WAS TRUE.
AT LAST WEEK'S CLUB INTRO-DUCTIONS...
SIGN: NORTH HIGH CULTURE CLUB INTRODUCTIONS
...SHE'D PRESENTED A TALK ENTITLED "A NEUROLOGICAL PERSPECTIVE ON INDIVIDUALS...
AND THE INSUFFICIENCY OF VERBAL DISCOURSE BETWEEN:"
北高部活動紹介
IF THERE HAD BEEN ANY STUDENTS WHO WERE INTERESTED IN JOINING THE LITERATURE CLUB, THAT HAD ERASED THEIR INTEREST.
YUKI NAGATO WAS A FORCE TO BE RECK-ONED WITH.

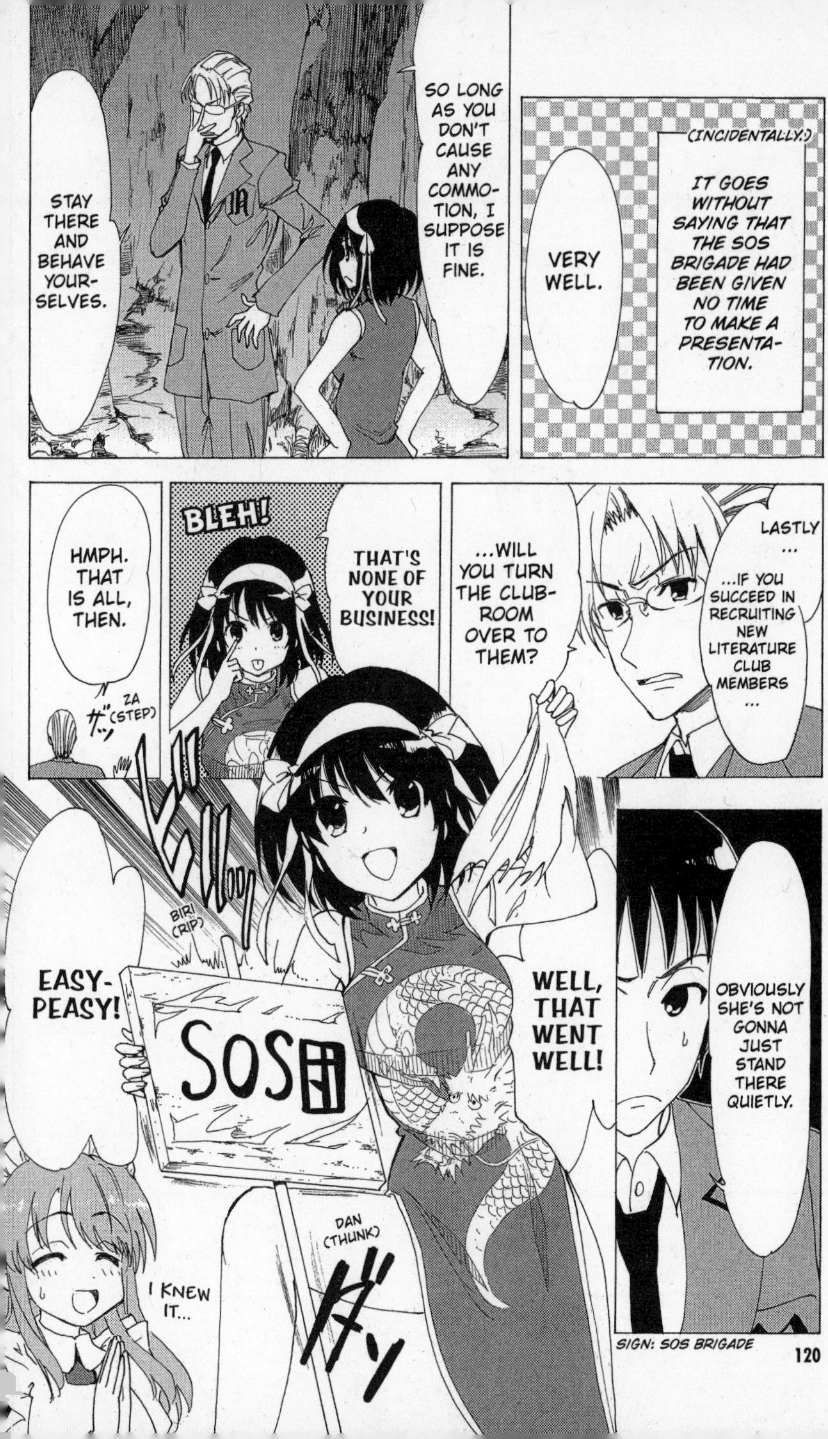
(INCIDENTALLY:)
IT GOES WITHOUT SAYING THAT THE SOS BRIGADE HAD BEEN GIVEN NO TIME TO MAKE A PRESENTATION.
VERY WELL.
SO LONG AS YOU DON'T CAUSE ANY COMMOTION, I SUPPOSE IT IS FINE.
STAY THERE AND BEHAVE YOURSELVES.
LASTLY...
...IF YOU SUCCEED IN RECRUITING NEW LITERATURE CLUB MEMBERS...
...WILL YOU TURN THE CLUBROOM OVER TO THEM?
BLEH!
THAT'S NONE OF YOUR BUSINESS!
HMPH. THAT IS ALL, THEN.
ZA (STEP)
OBVIOUSLY SHE'S NOT GONNA JUST STAND THERE QUIETLY.
WELL, THAT WENT WELL!
BIRI (RIP)
EASY-PEASY!
SOS団
DAN (THUNK)
I KNEW IT...

SIGN: SOS BRIGADE

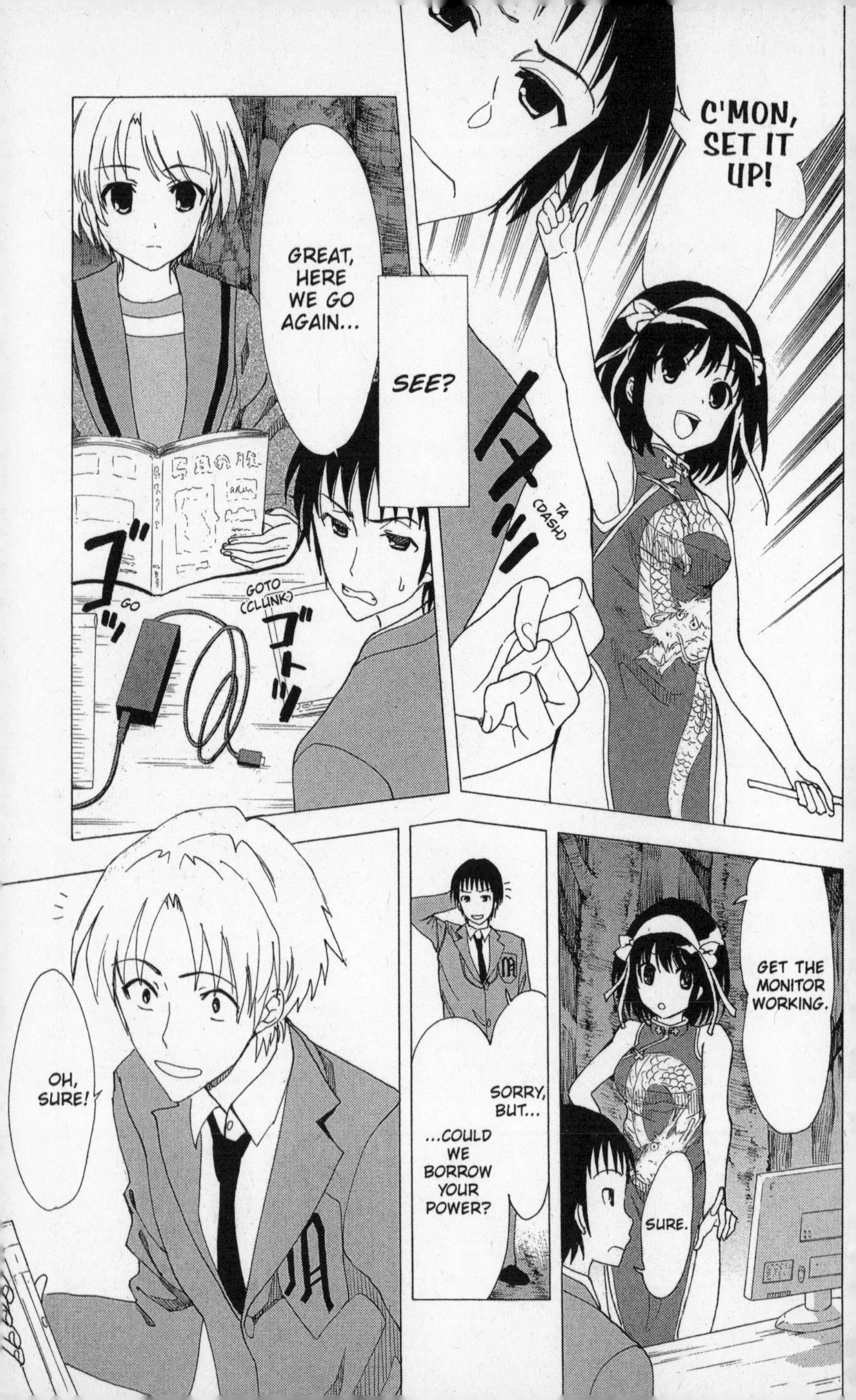
C'MON, SET IT UP!
TA (DASH)
GREAT, HERE WE GO AGAIN...
SEE?
GO
GOTO (CLUNK)
GET THE MONITOR WORKING.
SURE.
SORRY, BUT...
...COULD WE BORROW YOUR POWER?
OH, SURE!

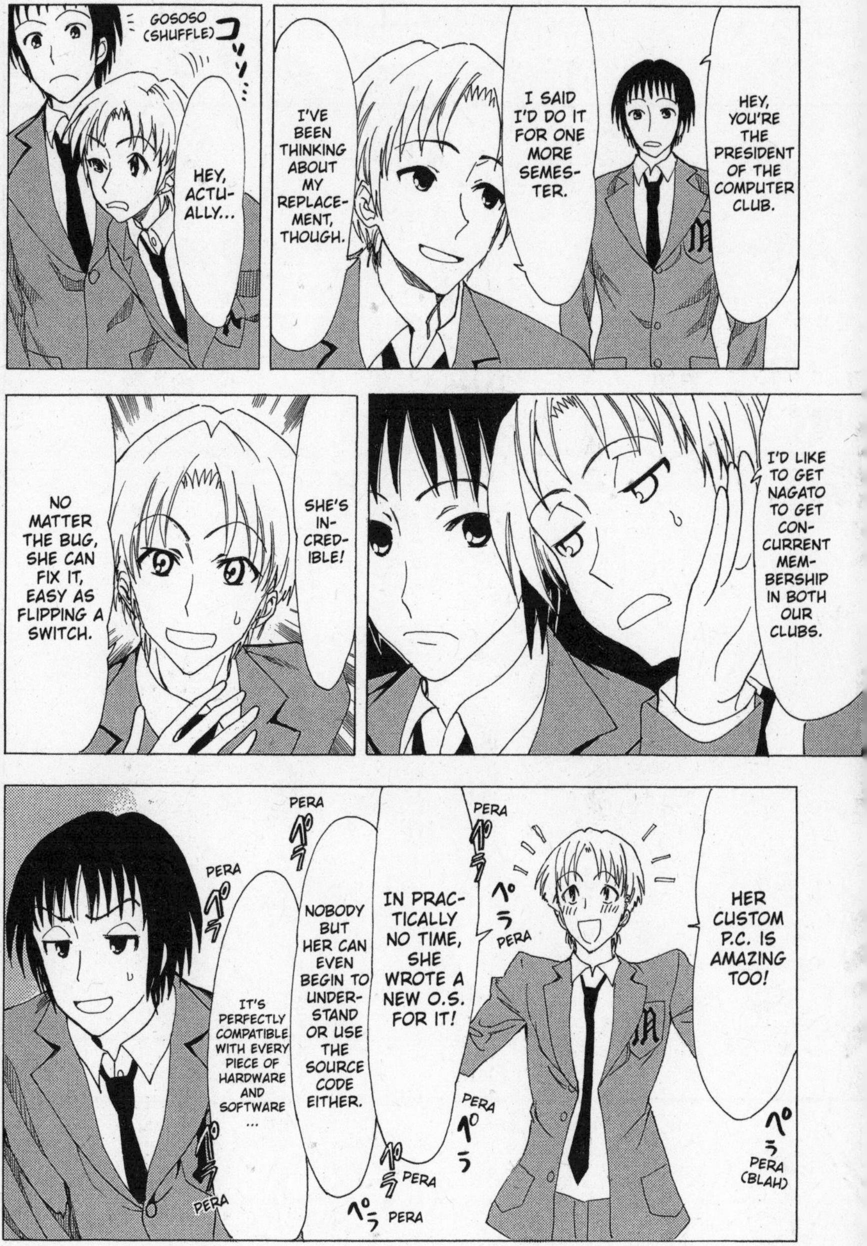
HEY, YOU'RE THE PRESIDENT OF THE COMPUTER CLUB.
I SAID I'D DO IT FOR ONE MORE SEMES-TER.
I'VE BEEN THINKING ABOUT MY REPLACE-MENT, THOUGH.
GOSOSO (SHUFFLE)
HEY, ACTU-ALLY...
I'D LIKE TO GET NAGATO TO GET CON-CURRENT MEM-BERSHIP IN BOTH OUR CLUBS.
SHE'S IN-CRED-IBLE!
NO MATTER THE BUG, SHE CAN FIX IT, EASY AS FLIPPING A SWITCH.
HER CUSTOM P.C. IS AMAZING TOO!
PERA (BLAH)
PERA
PERA
IN PRAC-TICALLY NO TIME, SHE WROTE A NEW O.S. FOR IT!
PERA
PERA
PERA
NOBODY BUT HER CAN EVEN BEGIN TO UNDER-STAND OR USE THE SOURCE CODE EITHER.
PERA
PERA
IT'S PERFECTLY COMPATIBLE WITH EVERY PIECE OF HARDWARE AND SOFTWARE ...
PERA

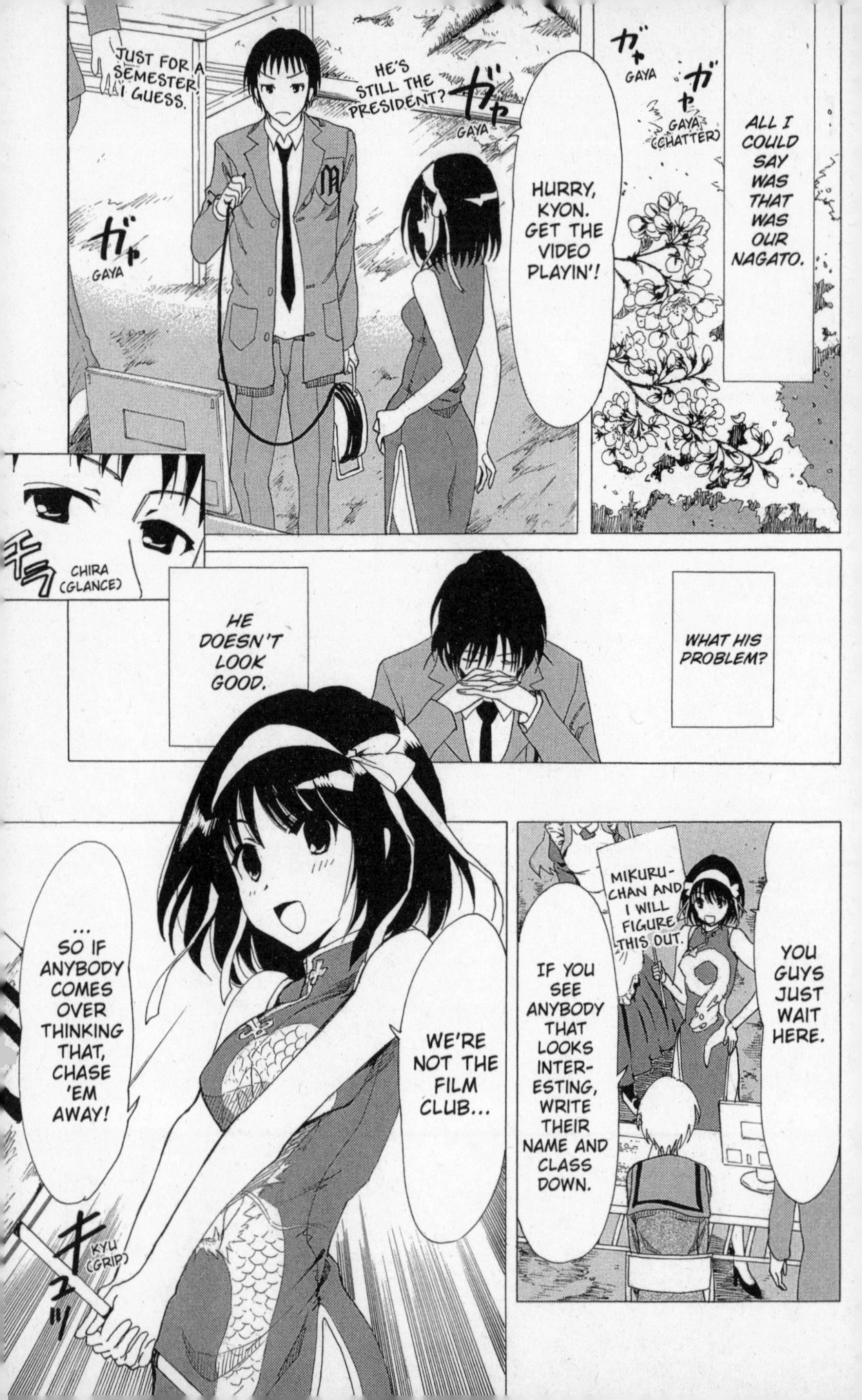
ALL I COULD SAY WAS THAT WAS OUR NAGATO.
GAYA
GAYA (CHATTER)
HURRY, KYON. GET THE VIDEO PLAYIN'!
HE'S STILL THE PRESIDENT?
GAYA
JUST FOR A SEMESTER I GUESS.
GAYA
CHIRA (GLANCE)
WHAT HIS PROBLEM?
HE DOESN'T LOOK GOOD.
YOU GUYS JUST WAIT HERE.
MIKURU-CHAN AND I WILL FIGURE THIS OUT.
IF YOU SEE ANYBODY THAT LOOKS INTER-ESTING, WRITE THEIR NAME AND CLASS DOWN.
WE'RE NOT THE FILM CLUB...
...SO IF ANYBODY COMES OVER THINKING THAT, CHASE 'EM AWAY!
KYU (GRIP)

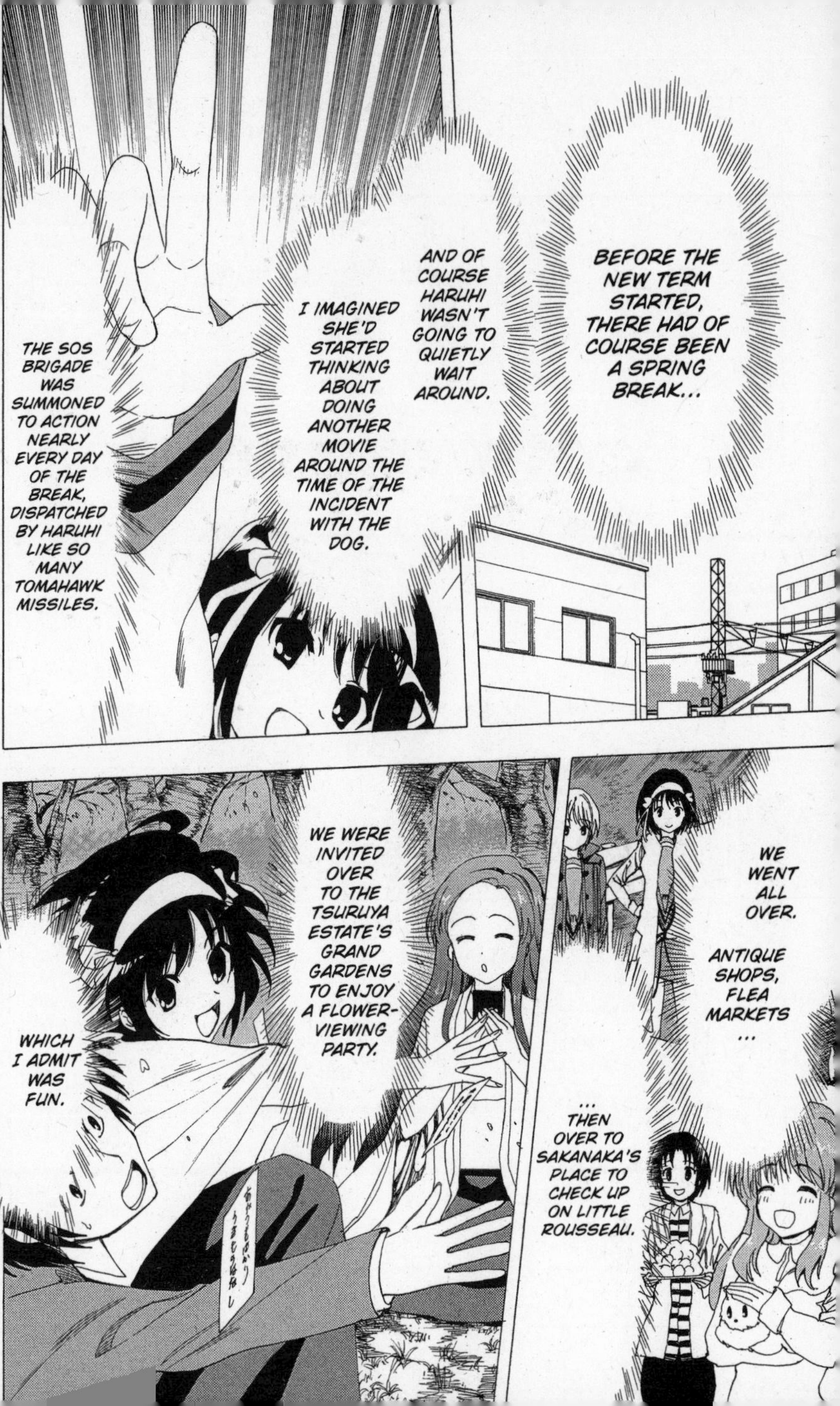
BEFORE THE NEW TERM STARTED, THERE HAD OF COURSE BEEN A SPRING BREAK...
AND OF COURSE HARUHI WASN'T GOING TO QUIETLY WAIT AROUND.
I IMAGINED SHE'D STARTED THINKING ABOUT DOING ANOTHER MOVIE AROUND THE TIME OF THE INCIDENT WITH THE DOG.
THE SOS BRIGADE WAS SUMMONED TO ACTION NEARLY EVERY DAY OF THE BREAK, DISPATCHED BY HARUHI LIKE SO MANY TOMAHAWK MISSILES.
WE WENT ALL OVER.
ANTIQUE SHOPS, FLEA MARKETS...
...THEN OVER TO SAKANAKA'S PLACE TO CHECK UP ON LITTLE ROUSSEAU.
WE WERE INVITED OVER TO THE TSURUYA ESTATE'S GRAND GARDENS TO ENJOY A FLOWER-VIEWING PARTY.
WHICH I ADMIT WAS FUN.

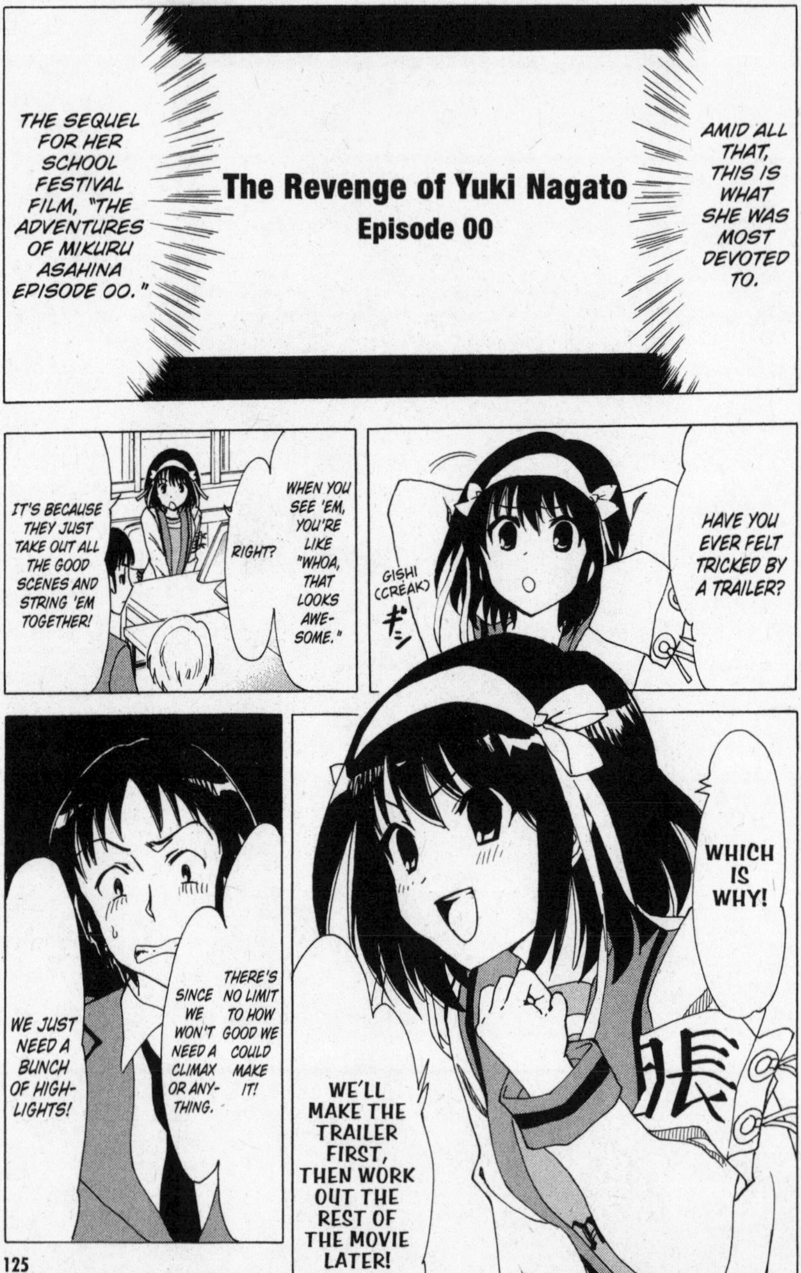
AMID ALL THAT, THIS IS WHAT SHE WAS MOST DEVOTED TO.
The Revenge of Yuki Nagato
Episode 00
THE SEQUEL FOR HER SCHOOL FESTIVAL FILM, "THE ADVENTURES OF MIKURU ASAHINA EPISODE 00."
HAVE YOU EVER FELT TRICKED BY A TRAILER?
GISHI (CREAK)
ギシ
WHEN YOU SEE 'EM, YOU'RE LIKE "WHOA, THAT LOOKS AWE-SOME."
RIGHT?
IT'S BECAUSE THEY JUST TAKE OUT ALL THE GOOD SCENES AND STRING 'EM TOGETHER!
WHICH IS WHY!
WE'LL MAKE THE TRAILER FIRST, THEN WORK OUT THE REST OF THE MOVIE LATER!
張
THERE'S NO LIMIT TO HOW GOOD WE COULD MAKE IT!
SINCE WE WON'T NEED A CLIMAX OR ANY-THING.
WE JUST NEED A BUNCH OF HIGH-LIGHTS!

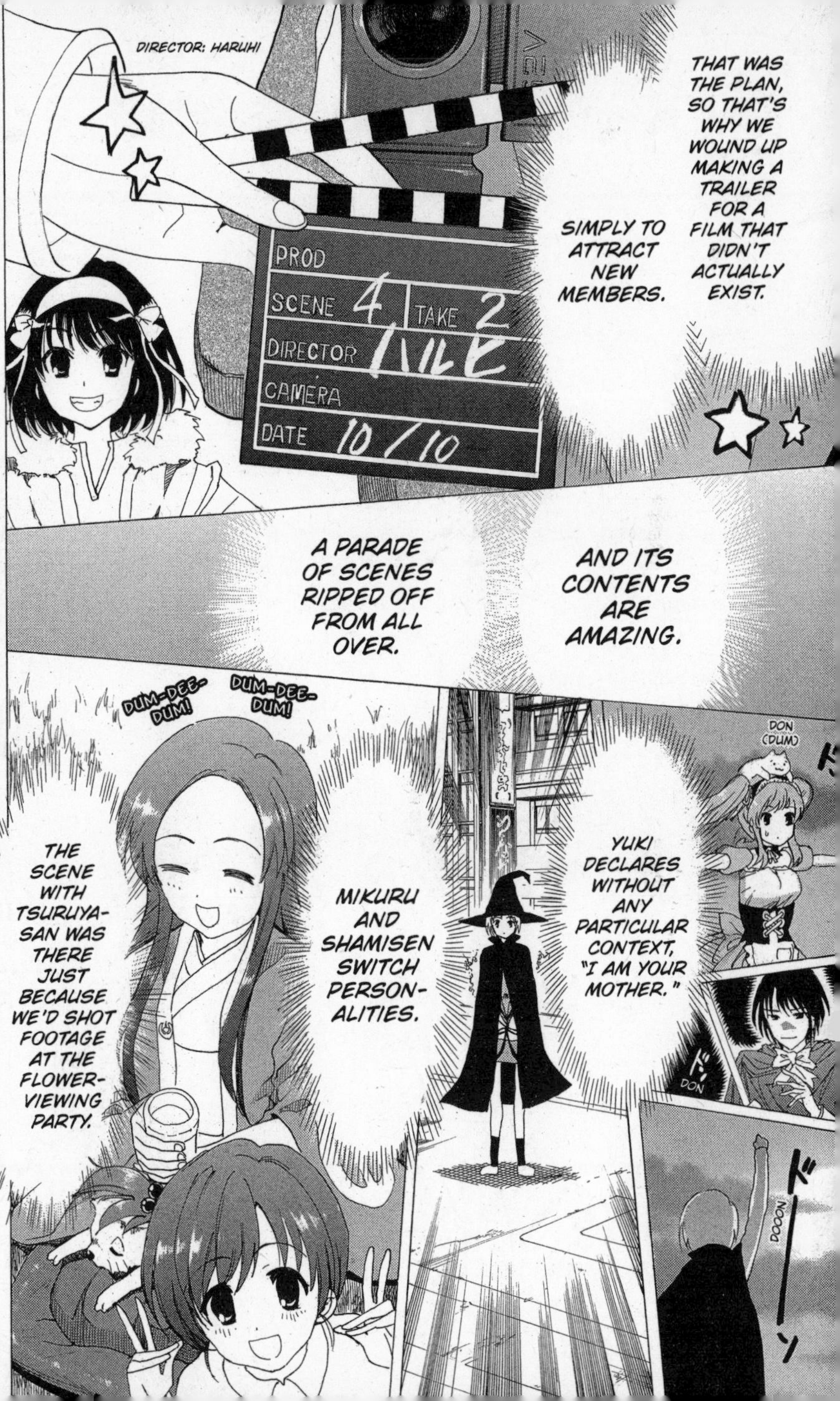
THAT WAS THE PLAN, SO THAT'S WHY WE WOUND UP MAKING A TRAILER FOR A FILM THAT DIDN'T ACTUALLY EXIST.
SIMPLY TO ATTRACT NEW MEMBERS.
PROD
SCENE 4 TAKE 2
DIRECTOR ハルヒ
CAMERA
DATE 10/10
DIRECTOR: HARUHI
AND ITS CONTENTS ARE AMAZING.
A PARADE OF SCENES RIPPED OFF FROM ALL OVER.
DON (DUM)
YUKI DECLARES WITHOUT ANY PARTICULAR CONTEXT, "I AM YOUR MOTHER."
DON
DOOON
MIKURU AND SHAMISEN SWITCH PERSON-ALITIES.
DUM-DEE-DUM!
DUM-DEE-DUM!
THE SCENE WITH TSURUYA-SAN WAS THERE JUST BECAUSE WE'D SHOT FOOTAGE AT THE FLOWER-VIEWING PARTY.

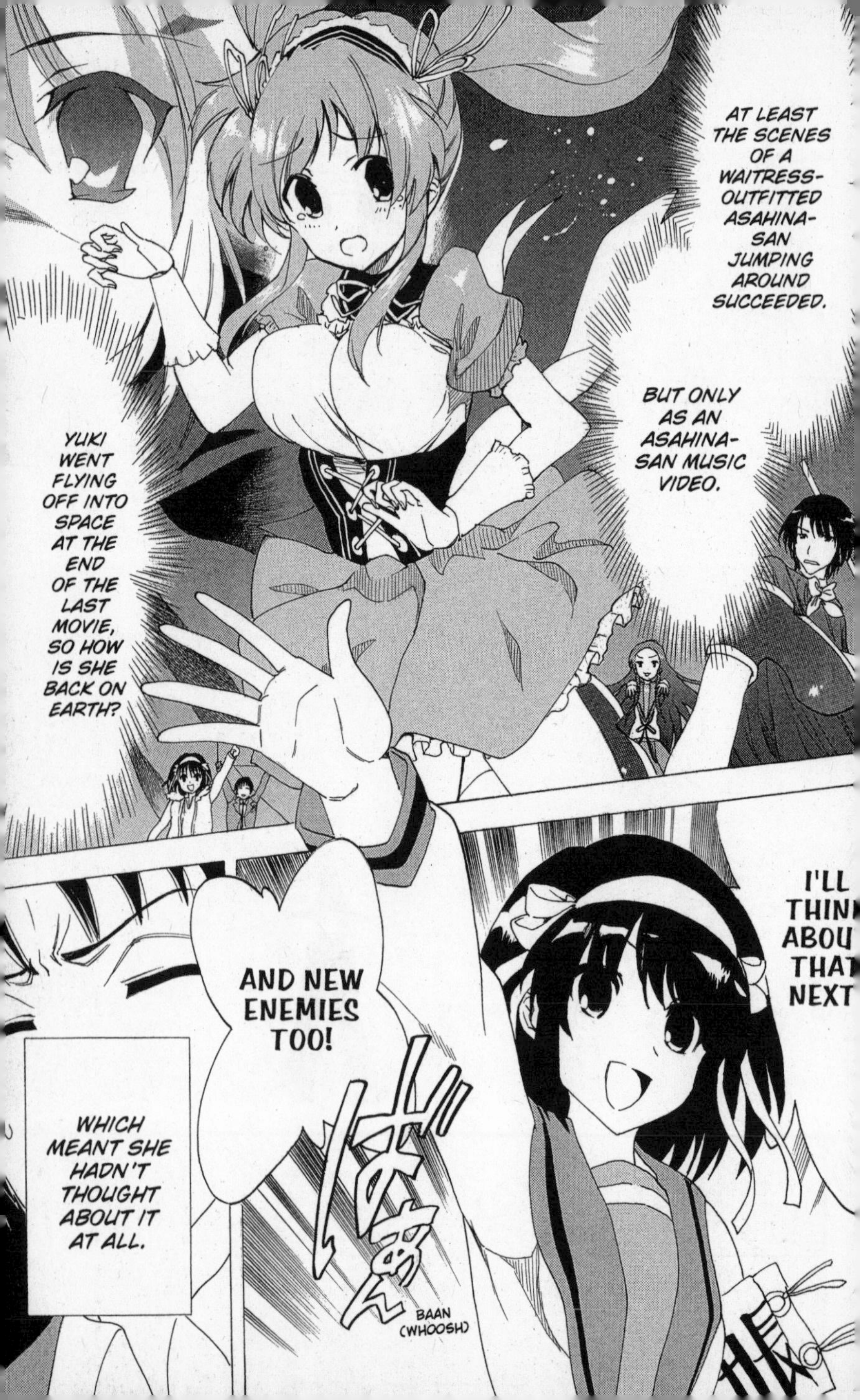
AT LEAST THE SCENES OF A WAITRESS-OUTFITTED ASAHINA-SAN JUMPING AROUND SUCCEEDED.
BUT ONLY AS AN ASAHINA-SAN MUSIC VIDEO.
YUKI WENT FLYING OFF INTO SPACE AT THE END OF THE LAST MOVIE, SO HOW IS SHE BACK ON EARTH?
I'LL THINK ABOUT THAT NEXT
AND NEW ENEMIES TOO!
BAAN (WHOOSH)
WHICH MEANT SHE HADN'T THOUGHT ABOUT IT AT ALL.

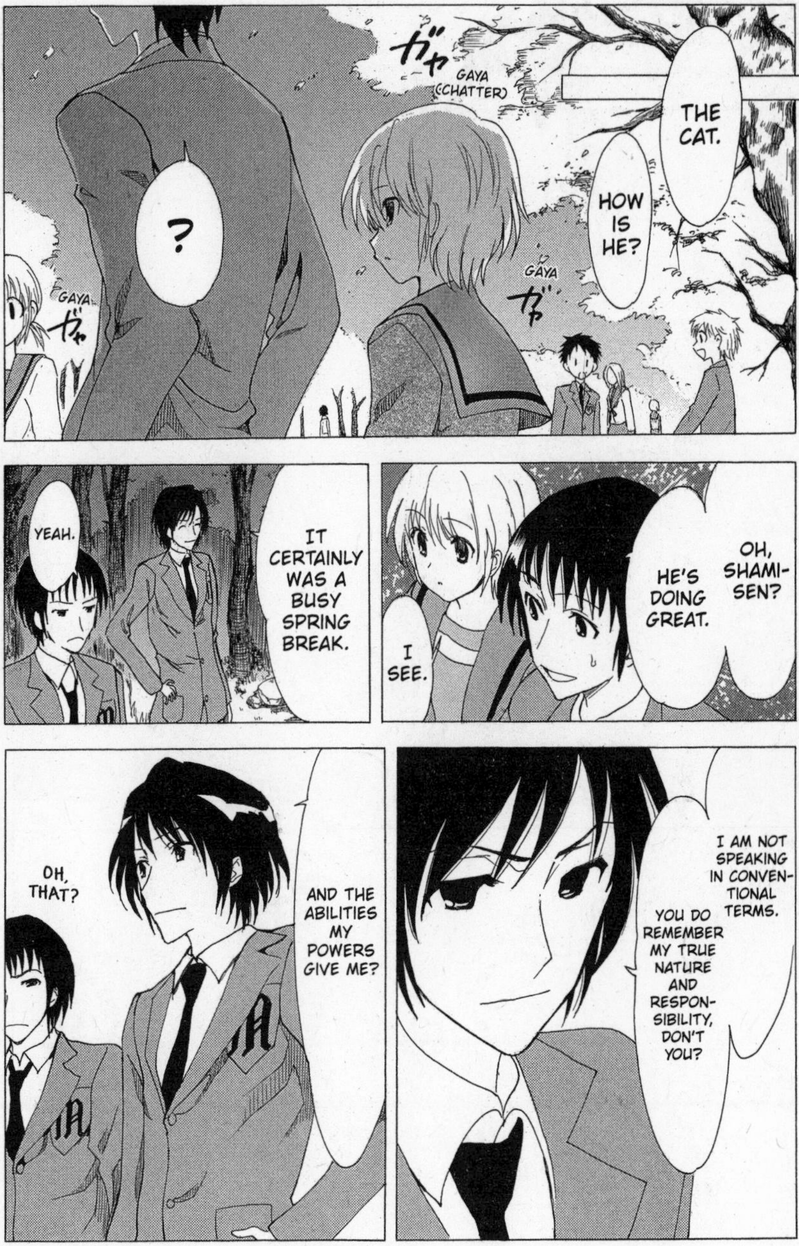
THE CAT.
HOW IS HE?
ガヤ
GAYA (CHATTER)
ガヤ
GAYA
?
ガヤ
GAYA
OH, SHAMI-SEN?
HE'S DOING GREAT.
I SEE.
IT CERTAINLY WAS A BUSY SPRING BREAK.
YEAH.
I AM NOT SPEAKING IN CONVEN-TIONAL TERMS.
YOU DO REMEMBER MY TRUE NATURE AND RESPON-SIBILITY, DON'T YOU?
AND THE ABILITIES MY POWERS GIVE ME?
OH, THAT?

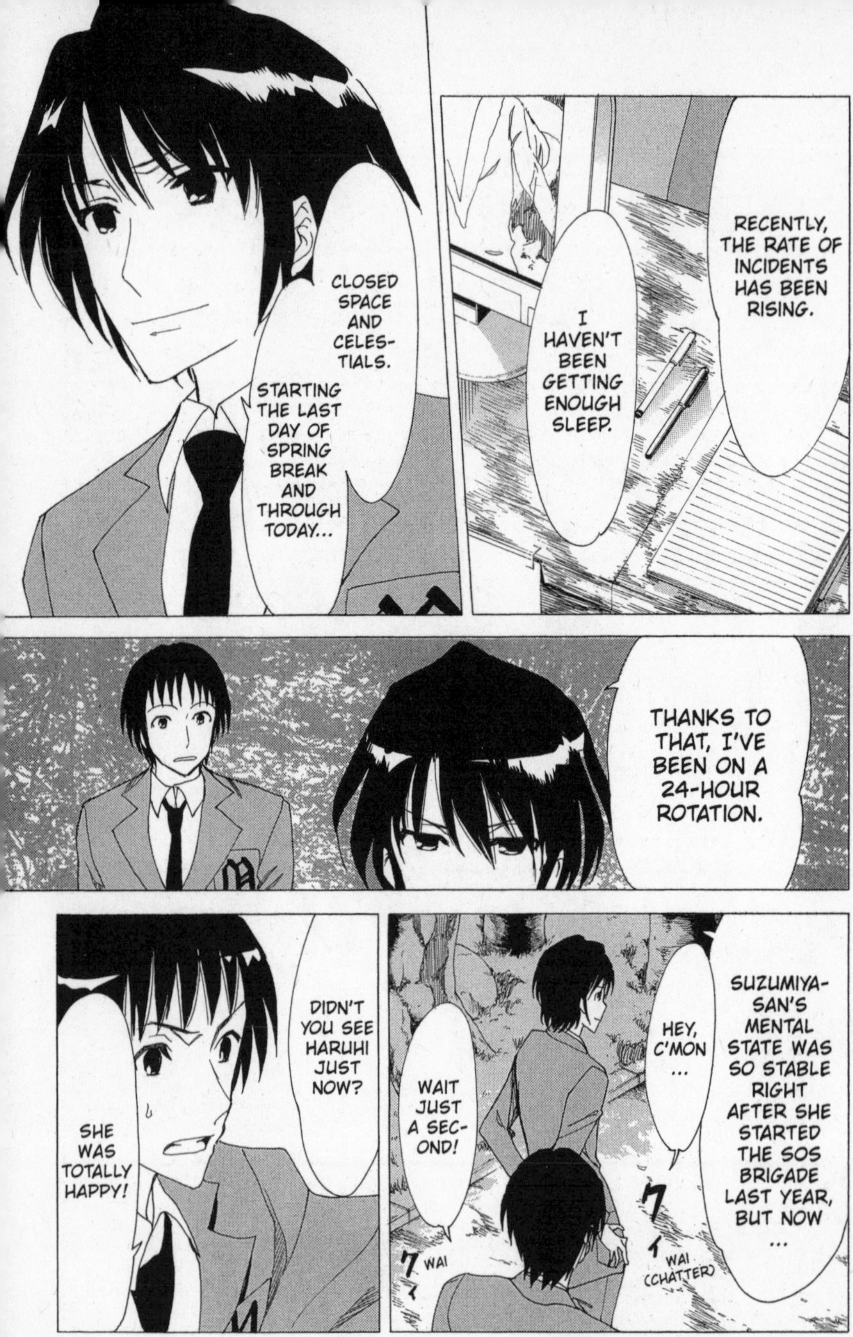
RECENTLY, THE RATE OF INCIDENTS HAS BEEN RISING.
I HAVEN'T BEEN GETTING ENOUGH SLEEP.
CLOSED SPACE AND CELESTIALS.
STARTING THE LAST DAY OF SPRING BREAK AND THROUGH TODAY...
THANKS TO THAT, I'VE BEEN ON A 24-HOUR ROTATION.
SUZUMIYA-SAN'S MENTAL STATE WAS SO STABLE RIGHT AFTER SHE STARTED THE SOS BRIGADE LAST YEAR, BUT NOW...
HEY, C'MON...
WAIT JUST A SECOND!
WAI (CHATTER)
WAI
DIDN'T YOU SEE HARUHI JUST NOW?
SHE WAS TOTALLY HAPPY!

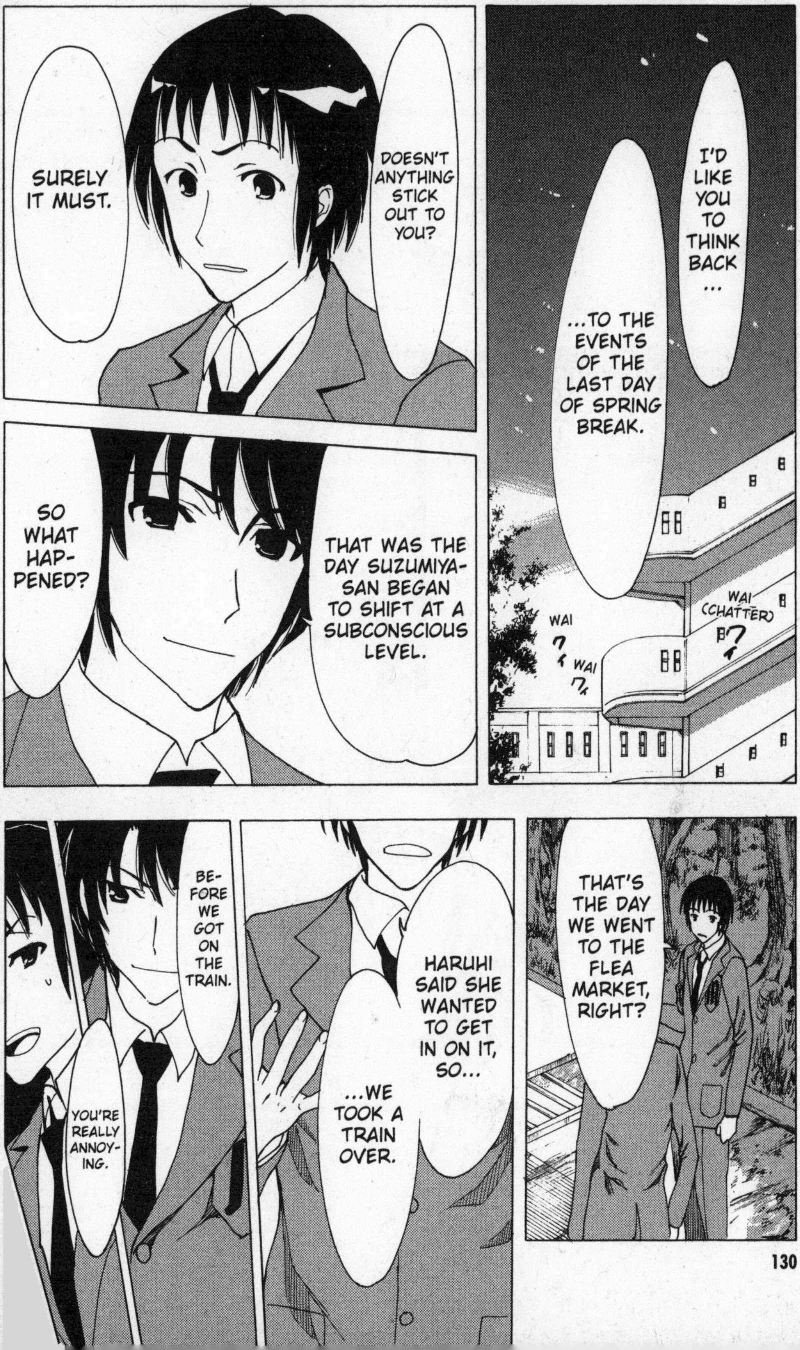
I'D LIKE YOU TO THINK BACK...
...TO THE EVENTS OF THE LAST DAY OF SPRING BREAK.
WAI
WAI
WAI (CHATTER)
DOESN'T ANYTHING STICK OUT TO YOU?
SURELY IT MUST.
THAT WAS THE DAY SUZUMIYA-SAN BEGAN TO SHIFT AT A SUBCONSCIOUS LEVEL.
SO WHAT HAP-PENED?
THAT'S THE DAY WE WENT TO THE FLEA MARKET, RIGHT?
HARUHI SAID SHE WANTED TO GET IN ON IT, SO...
...WE TOOK A TRAIN OVER.
BE-FORE WE GOT ON THE TRAIN.
YOU'RE REALLY ANNOY-ING.

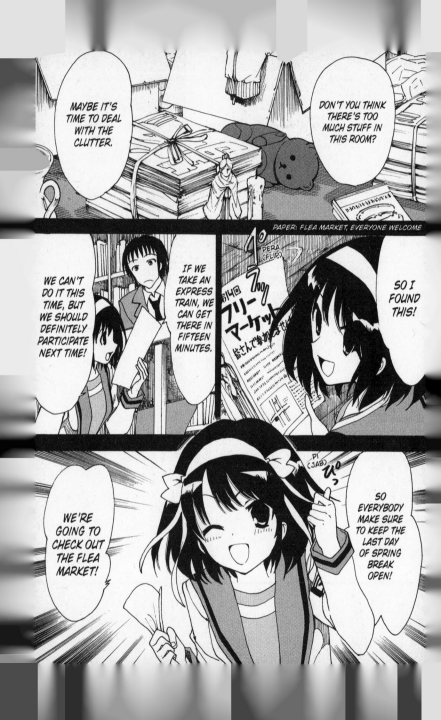

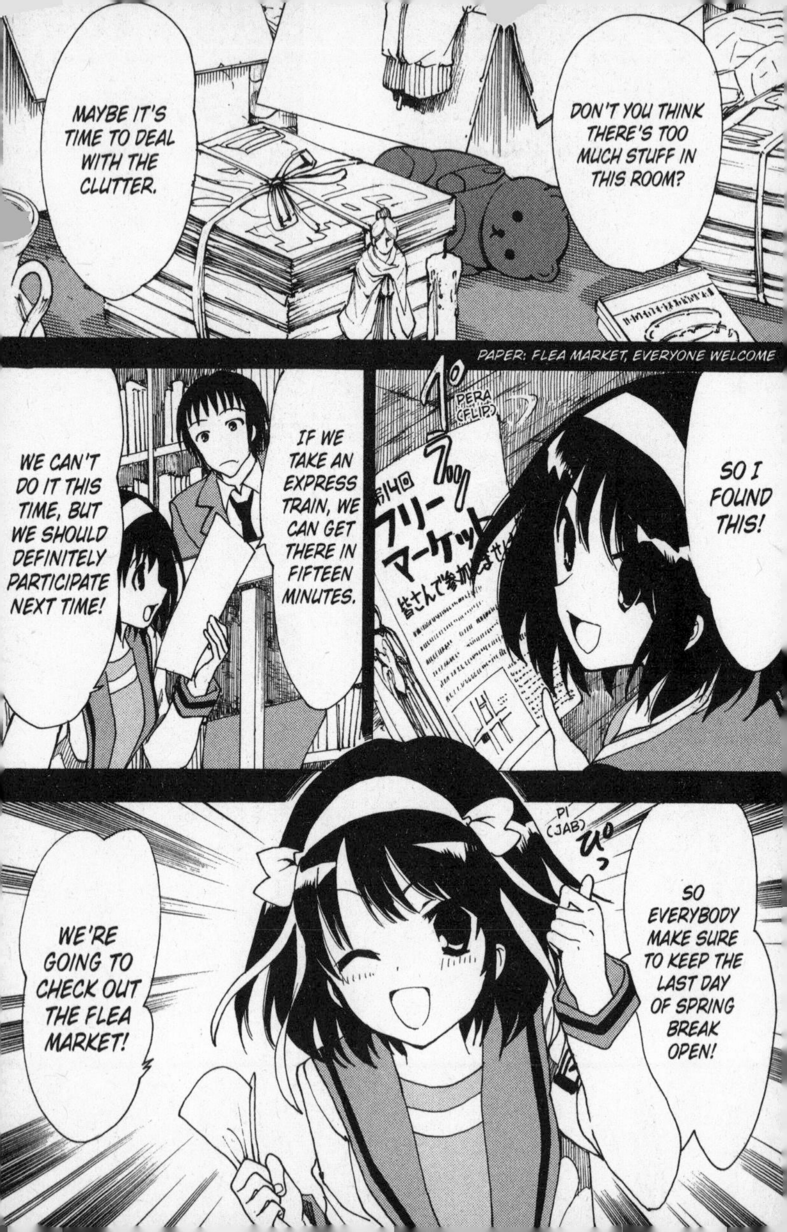
DON'T YOU THINK THERE'S TOO MUCH STUFF IN THIS ROOM?
MAYBE IT'S TIME TO DEAL WITH THE CLUTTER.
PAPER: FLEA MARKET, EVERYONE WELCOME
PERA (FLIP)
SO I FOUND THIS!
第14回
フリーマーケット
IF WE TAKE AN EXPRESS TRAIN, WE CAN GET THERE IN FIFTEEN MINUTES.
WE CAN'T DO IT THIS TIME, BUT WE SHOULD DEFINITELY PARTICIPATE NEXT TIME!
PI (JAB)
SO EVERYBODY MAKE SURE TO KEEP THE LAST DAY OF SPRING BREAK OPEN!
WE'RE GOING TO CHECK OUT THE FLEA MARKET!

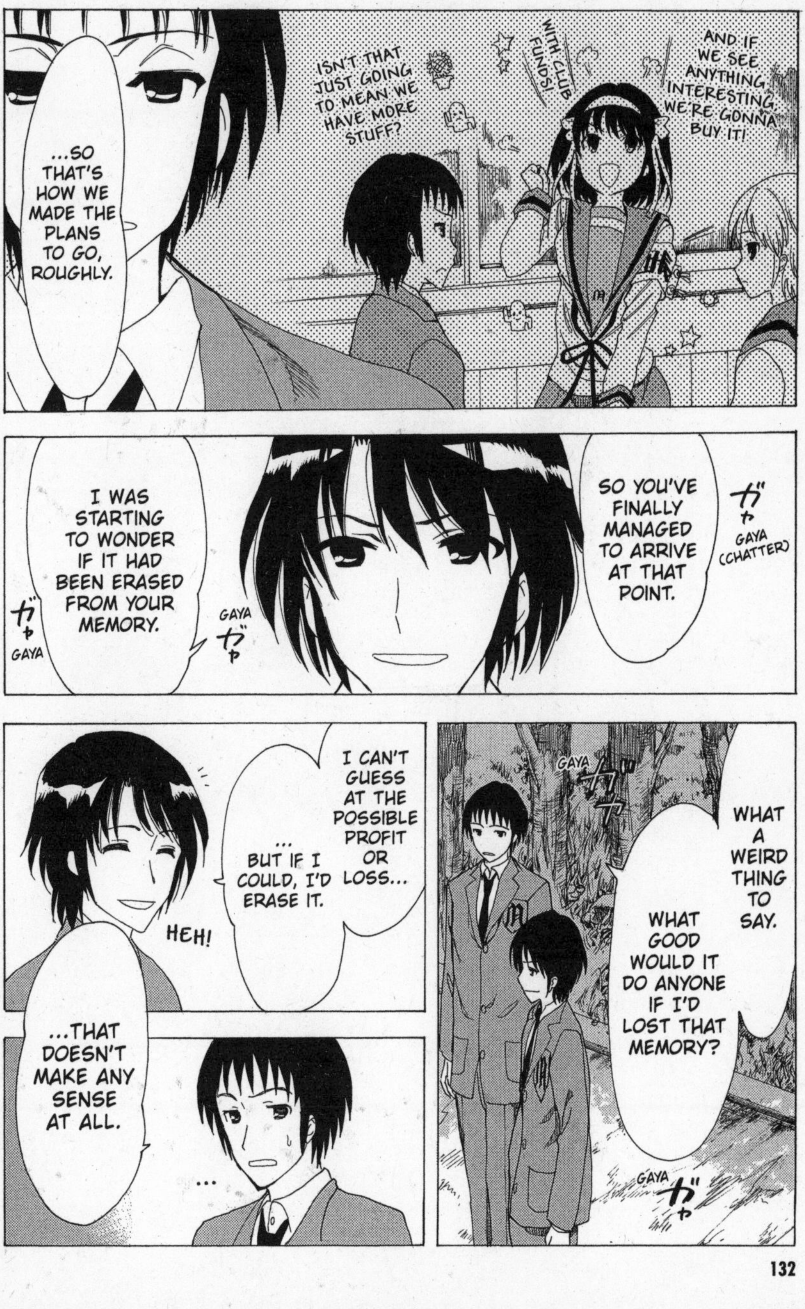
AND IF WE SEE ANYTHING INTERESTING, WE'RE GONNA BUY IT!
WITH CLUB FUNDS!
ISN'T THAT JUST GOING TO MEAN WE HAVE MORE STUFF?
...SO THAT'S HOW WE MADE THE PLANS TO GO, ROUGHLY.
ガヤ GAYA (CHATTER)
SO YOU'VE FINALLY MANAGED TO ARRIVE AT THAT POINT.
ガヤ GAYA
I WAS STARTING TO WONDER IF IT HAD BEEN ERASED FROM YOUR MEMORY.
ガヤ GAYA
ガヤ GAYA
WHAT A WEIRD THING TO SAY.
WHAT GOOD WOULD IT DO ANYONE IF I'D LOST THAT MEMORY?
ガヤ GAYA
I CAN'T GUESS AT THE POSSIBLE PROFIT OR LOSS...
... BUT IF I COULD, I'D ERASE IT.
HEH!
...THAT DOESN'T MAKE ANY SENSE AT ALL.
...

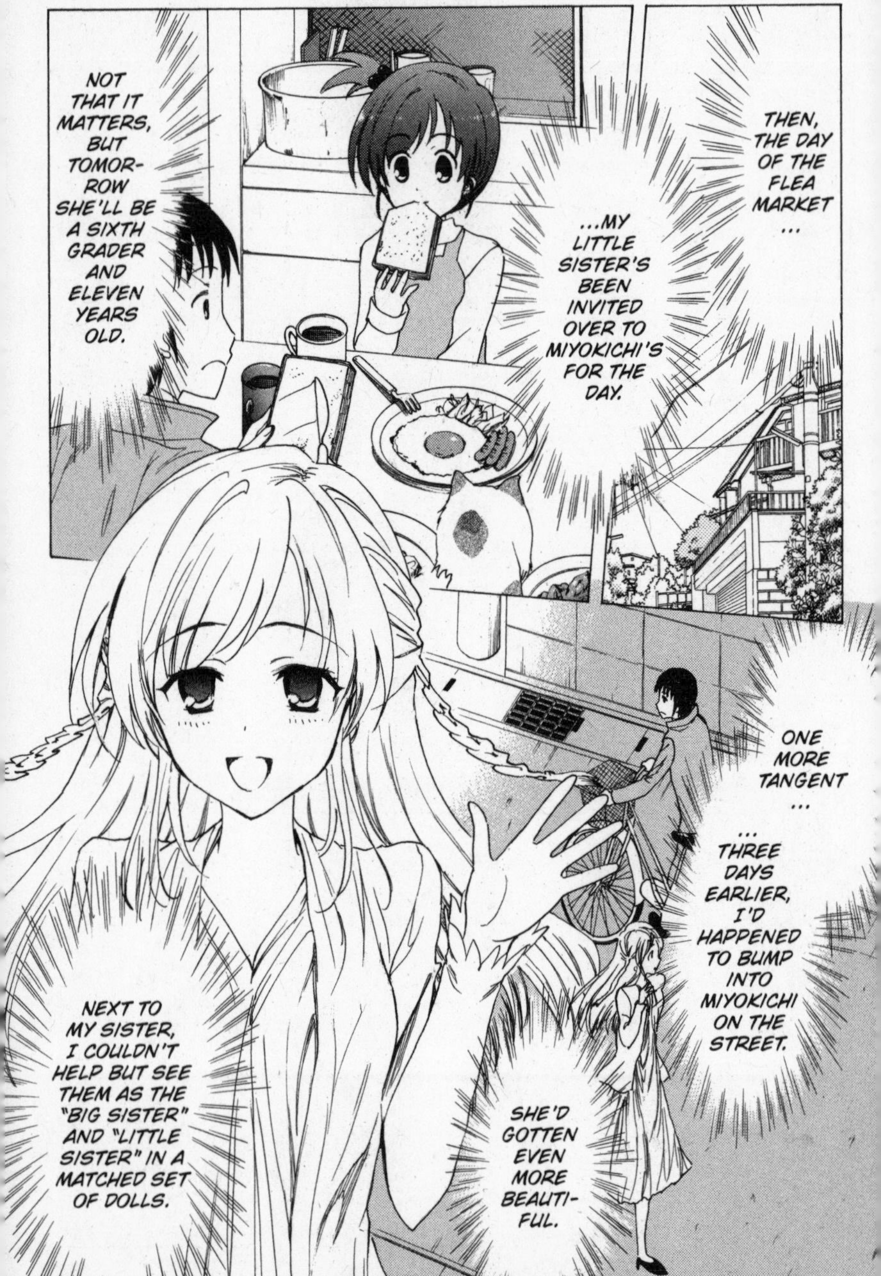
THEN, THE DAY OF THE FLEA MARKET...
...MY LITTLE SISTER'S BEEN INVITED OVER TO MIYOKICHI'S FOR THE DAY.
NOT THAT IT MATTERS, BUT TOMORROW SHE'LL BE A SIXTH GRADER AND ELEVEN YEARS OLD.
ONE MORE TANGENT...
...THREE DAYS EARLIER, I'D HAPPENED TO BUMP INTO MIYOKICHI ON THE STREET.
SHE'D GOTTEN EVEN MORE BEAUTIFUL.
NEXT TO MY SISTER, I COULDN'T HELP BUT SEE THEM AS THE "BIG SISTER" AND "LITTLE SISTER" IN A MATCHED SET OF DOLLS.

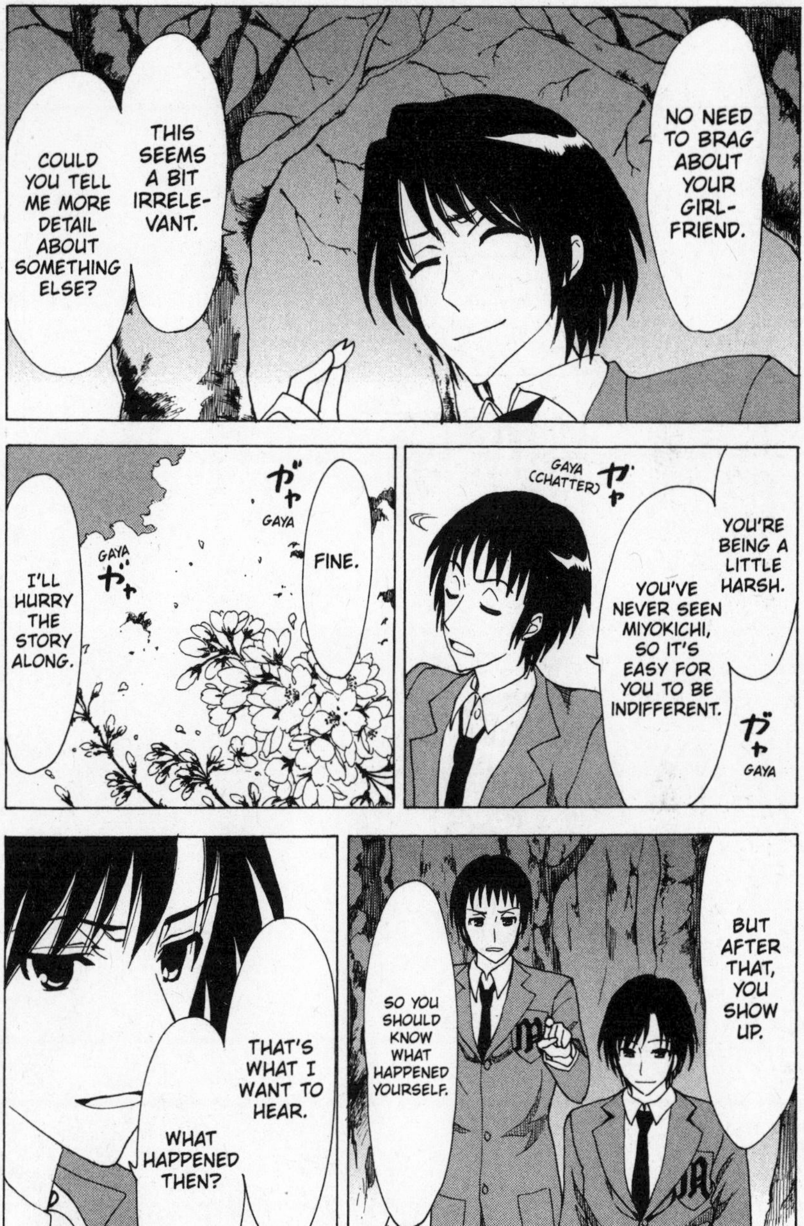
NO NEED TO BRAG ABOUT YOUR GIRLFRIEND.
THIS SEEMS A BIT IRRELEVANT.
COULD YOU TELL ME MORE DETAIL ABOUT SOMETHING ELSE?
ガヤ
GAYA (CHATTER)
YOU'RE BEING A LITTLE HARSH.
YOU'VE NEVER SEEN MIYOKICHI, SO IT'S EASY FOR YOU TO BE INDIFFERENT.
ガヤ
GAYA
ガヤ
GAYA
FINE.
ガヤ
GAYA
I'LL HURRY THE STORY ALONG.
BUT AFTER THAT, YOU SHOW UP.
SO YOU SHOULD KNOW WHAT HAPPENED YOURSELF.
THAT'S WHAT I WANT TO HEAR.
WHAT HAPPENED THEN?

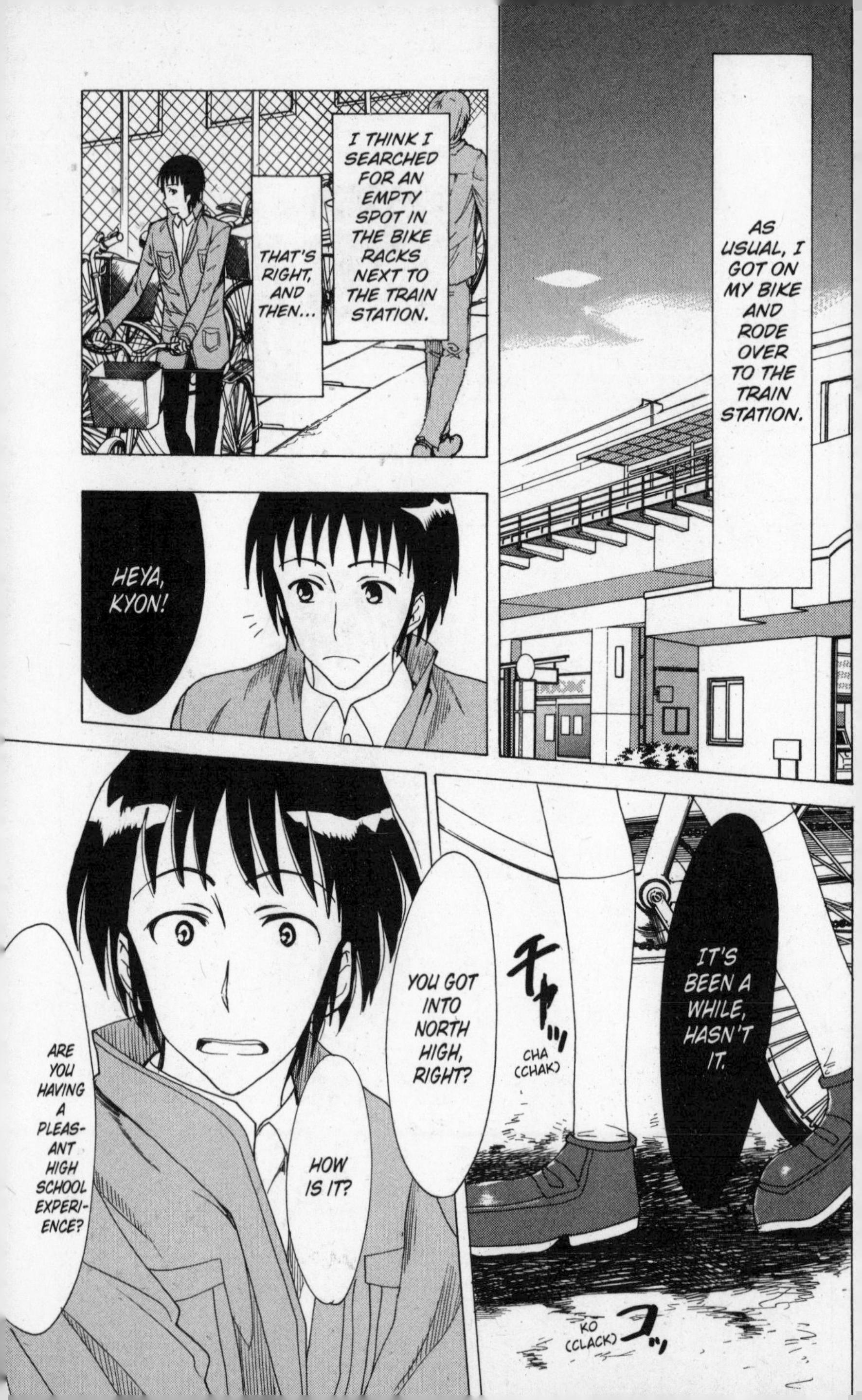
AS USUAL, I GOT ON MY BIKE AND RODE OVER TO THE TRAIN STATION.
I THINK I SEARCHED FOR AN EMPTY SPOT IN THE BIKE RACKS NEXT TO THE TRAIN STATION.
THAT'S RIGHT, AND THEN...
HEYA, KYON!
IT'S BEEN A WHILE, HASN'T IT.
CHA (CHAK)
KO (CLACK)
YOU GOT INTO NORTH HIGH, RIGHT?
HOW IS IT?
ARE YOU HAVING A PLEASANT HIGH SCHOOL EXPERIENCE?

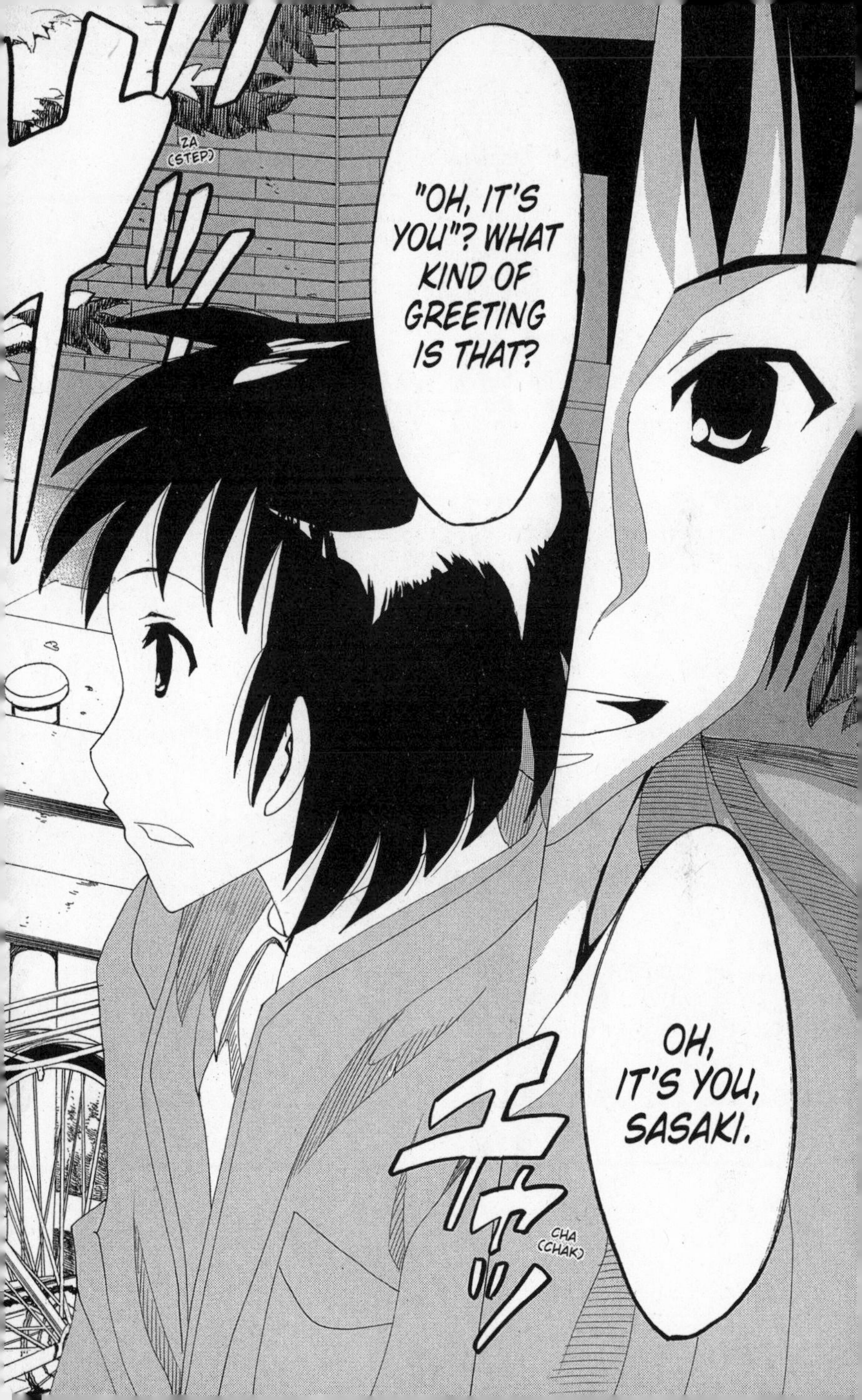
ZA
(STEP)
OH, IT'S YOU, SASAKI.
CHA
(CHAK)
"OH, IT'S YOU"? WHAT KIND OF GREETING IS THAT?

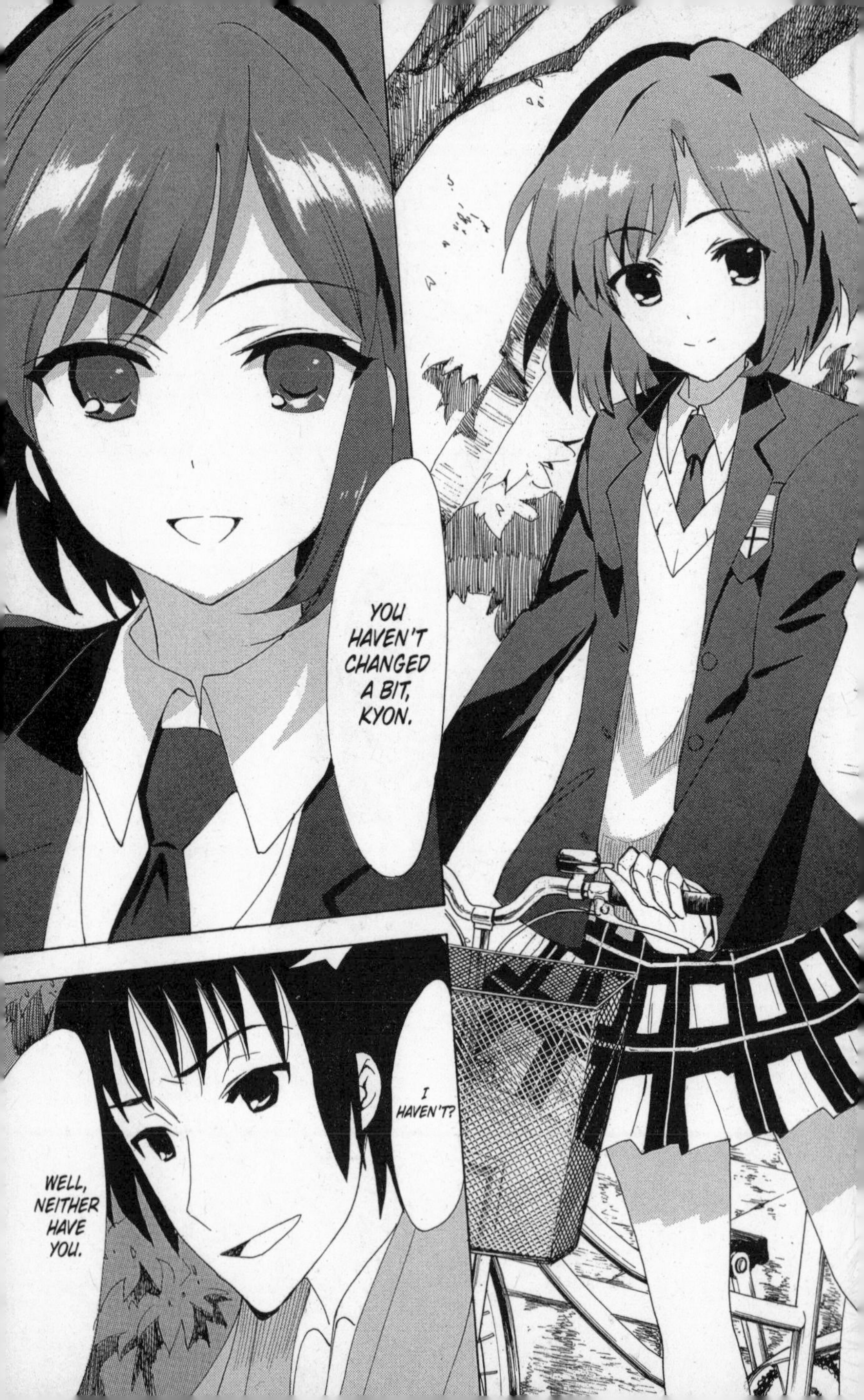
YOU HAVEN'T CHANGED A BIT, KYON.
I HAVEN'T?
WELL, NEITHER HAVE YOU.

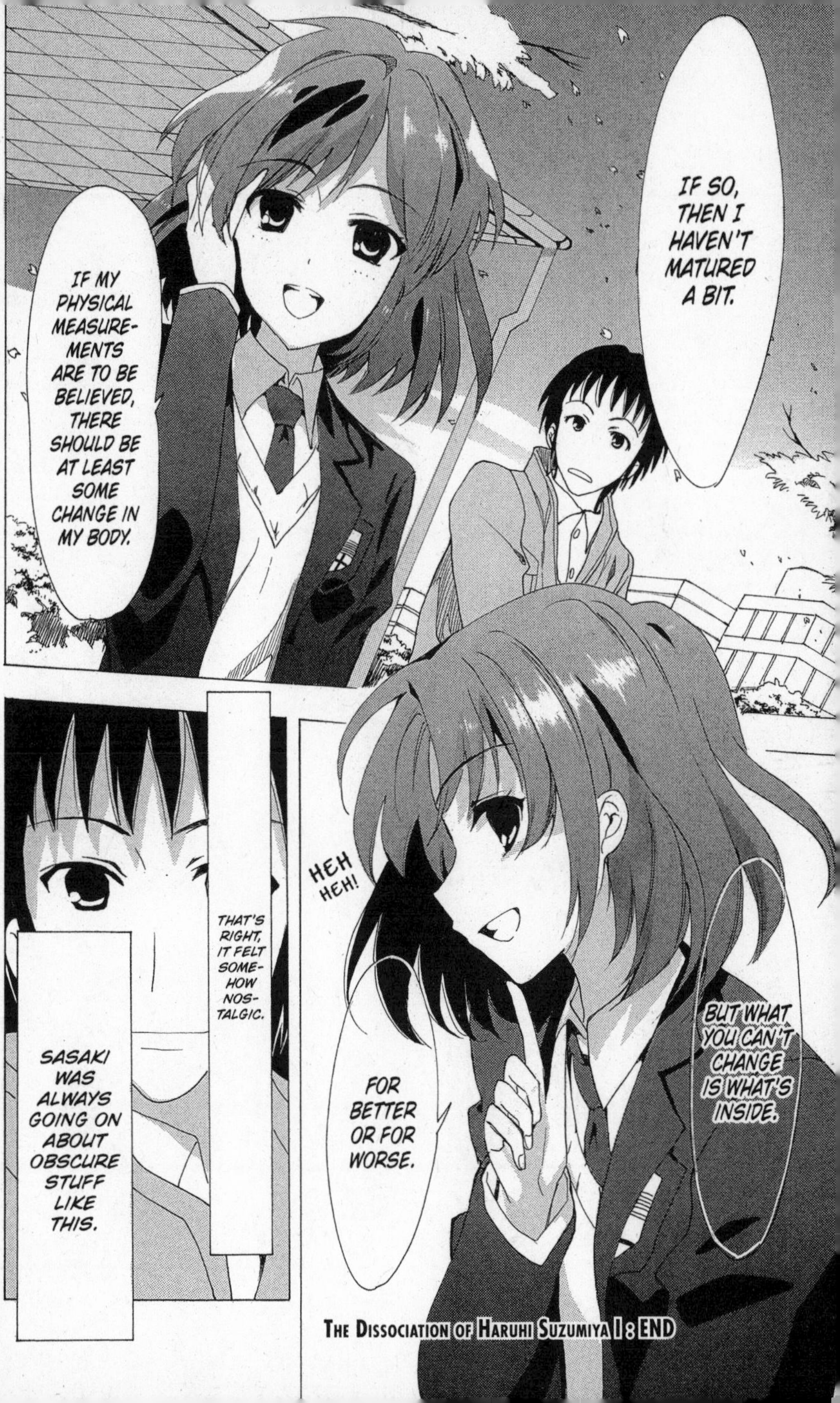
IF SO, THEN I HAVEN'T MATURED A BIT.
IF MY PHYSICAL MEASURE-MENTS ARE TO BE BELIEVED, THERE SHOULD BE AT LEAST SOME CHANGE IN MY BODY.
BUT WHAT YOU CAN'T CHANGE IS WHAT'S INSIDE.
HEH HEH!
FOR BETTER OR FOR WORSE.
THAT'S RIGHT, IT FELT SOME-HOW NOS-TALGIC.
SASAKI WAS ALWAYS GOING ON ABOUT OBSCURE STUFF LIKE THIS.
THE DISSOCIATION OF HARUHI SUZUMIYA I : END

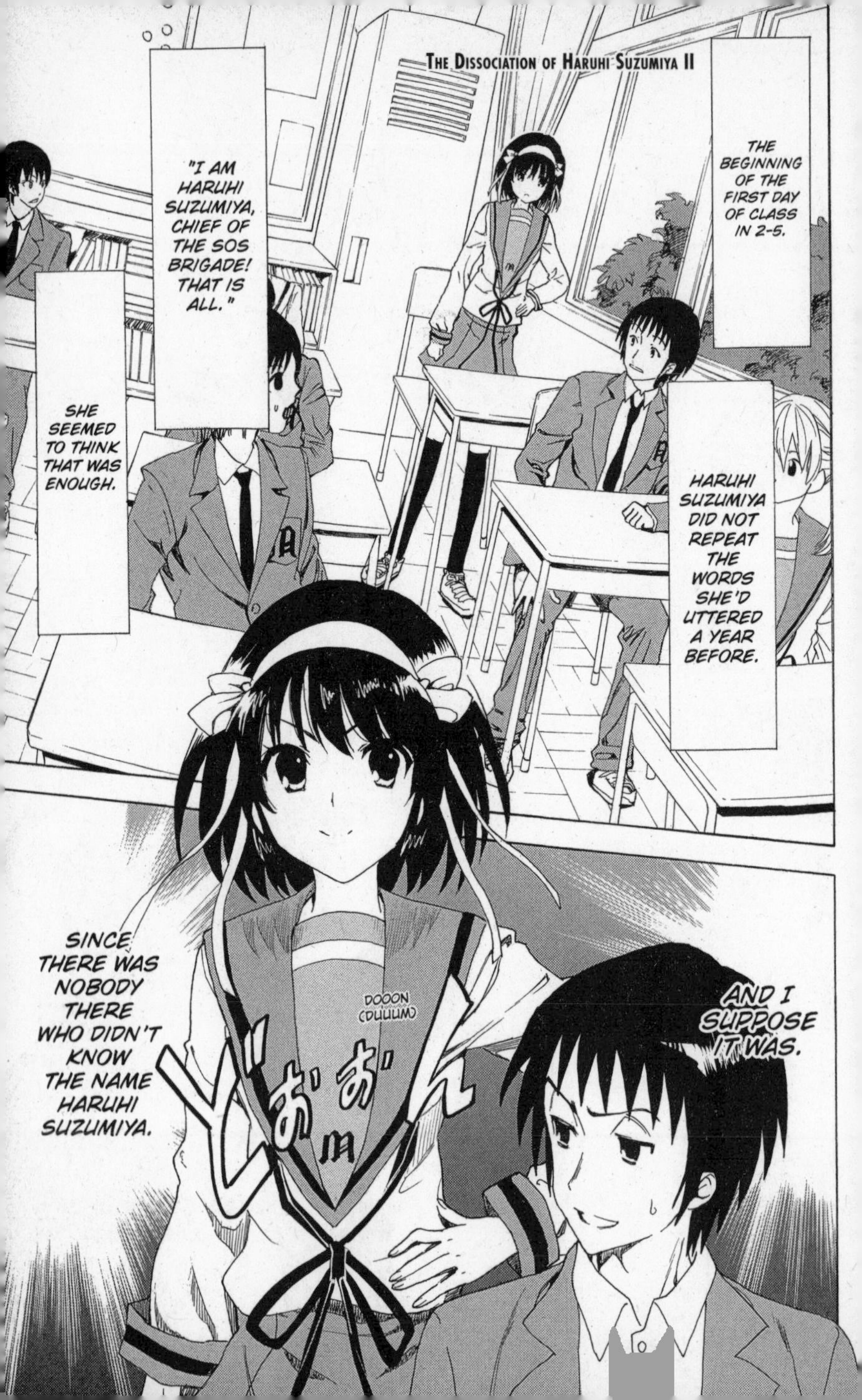
The Dissociation of Haruhi Suzumiya II
THE BEGINNING OF THE FIRST DAY OF CLASS IN 2-5.
"I AM HARUHI SUZUMIYA, CHIEF OF THE SOS BRIGADE! THAT IS ALL."
SHE SEEMED TO THINK THAT WAS ENOUGH.
HARUHI SUZUMIYA DID NOT REPEAT THE WORDS SHE'D UTTERED A YEAR BEFORE.
AND I SUPPOSE IT WAS.
DOOON (DUUUM)
SINCE THERE WAS NOBODY THERE WHO DIDN'T KNOW THE NAME HARUHI SUZUMIYA.

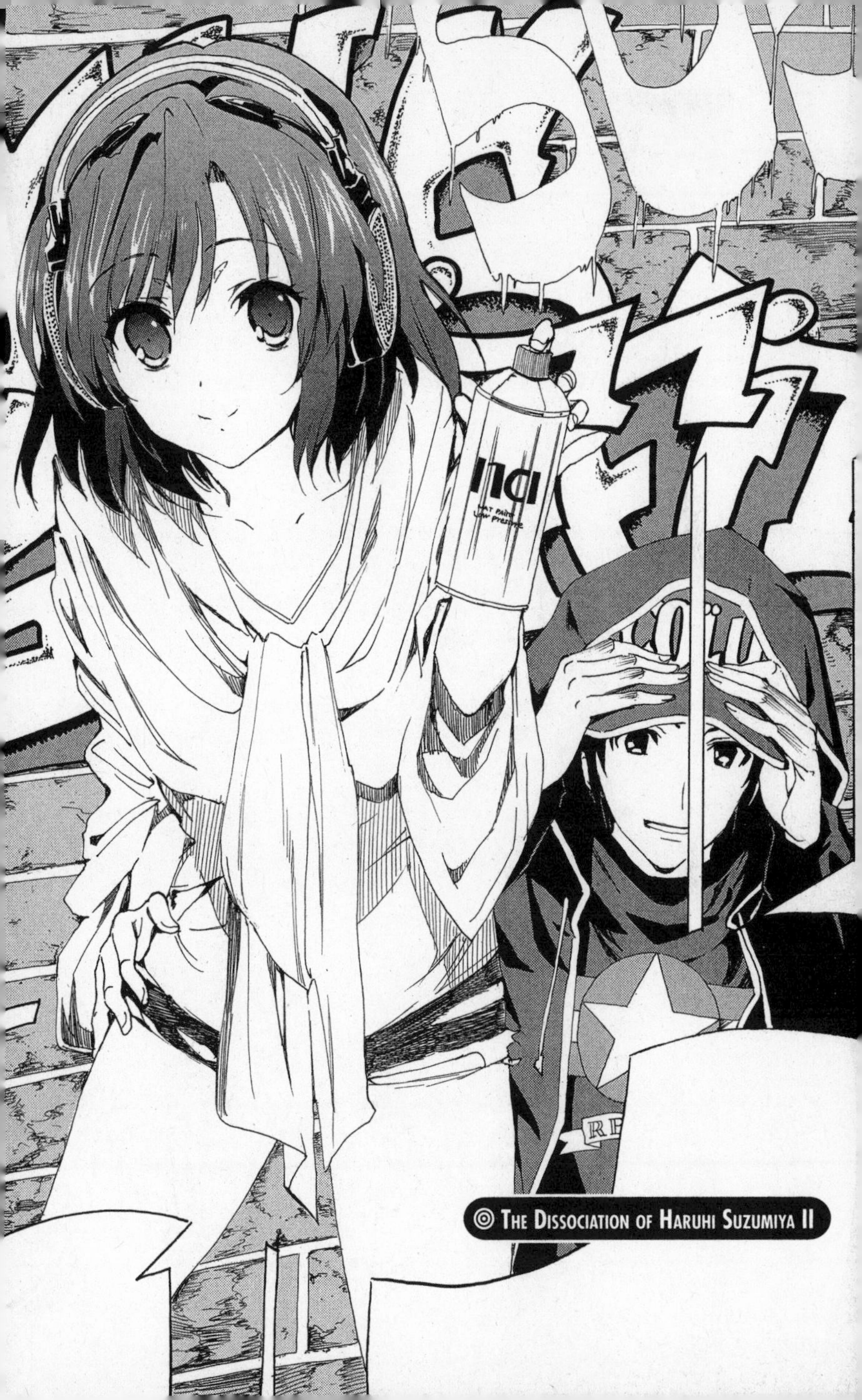

WAT Paint
Low pressure
RE
◎ The Dissociation of Haruhi Suzumiya II

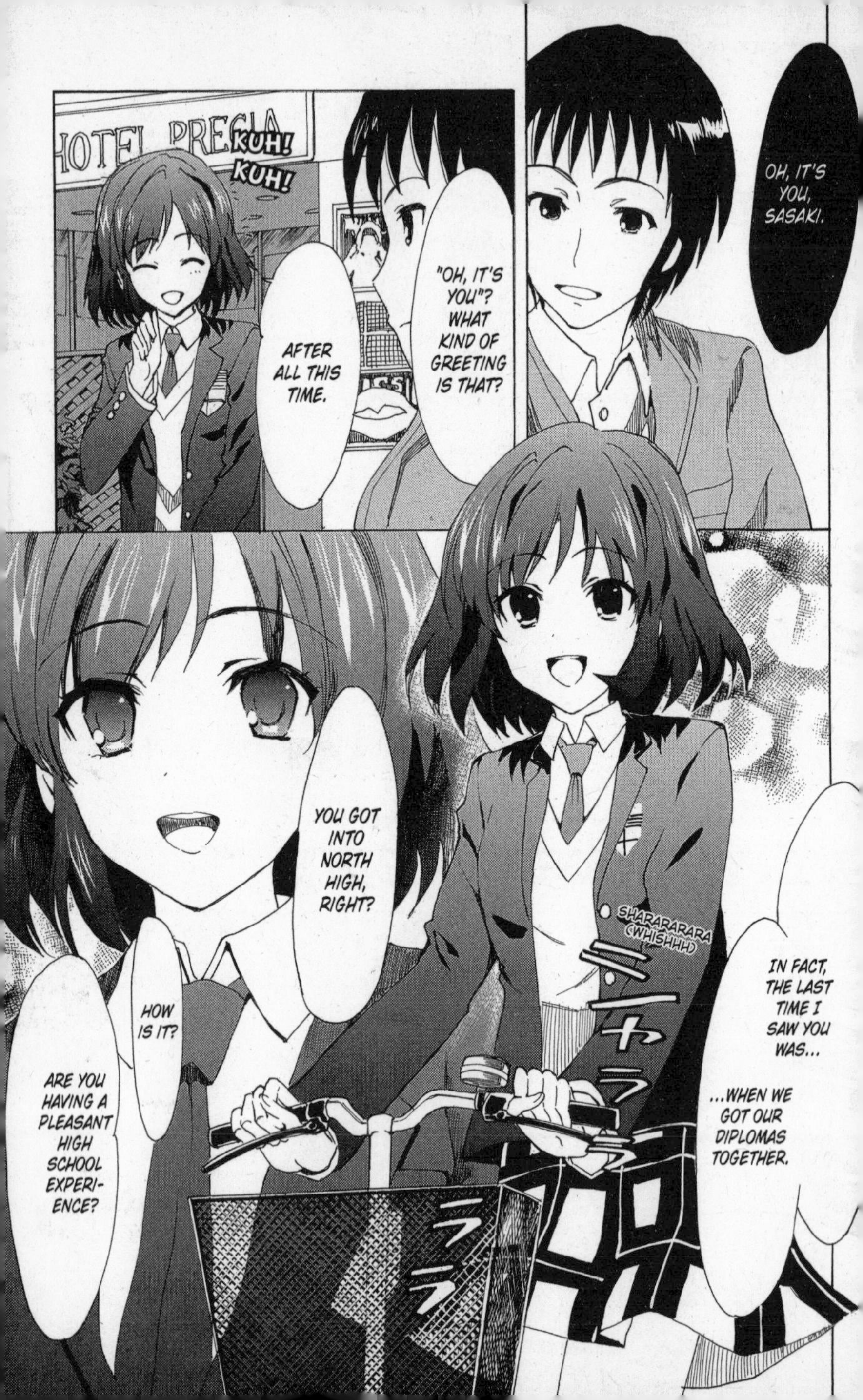
OH, IT'S YOU, SASAKI.
"OH, IT'S YOU"? WHAT KIND OF GREETING IS THAT?
AFTER ALL THIS TIME.
KUH! KUH!
HOTEL PREGIA
IN FACT, THE LAST TIME I SAW YOU WAS...
...WHEN WE GOT OUR DIPLOMAS TOGETHER.
SHARARARARA (WHISHHH)
YOU GOT INTO NORTH HIGH, RIGHT?
HOW IS IT?
ARE YOU HAVING A PLEASANT HIGH SCHOOL EXPERI-ENCE?

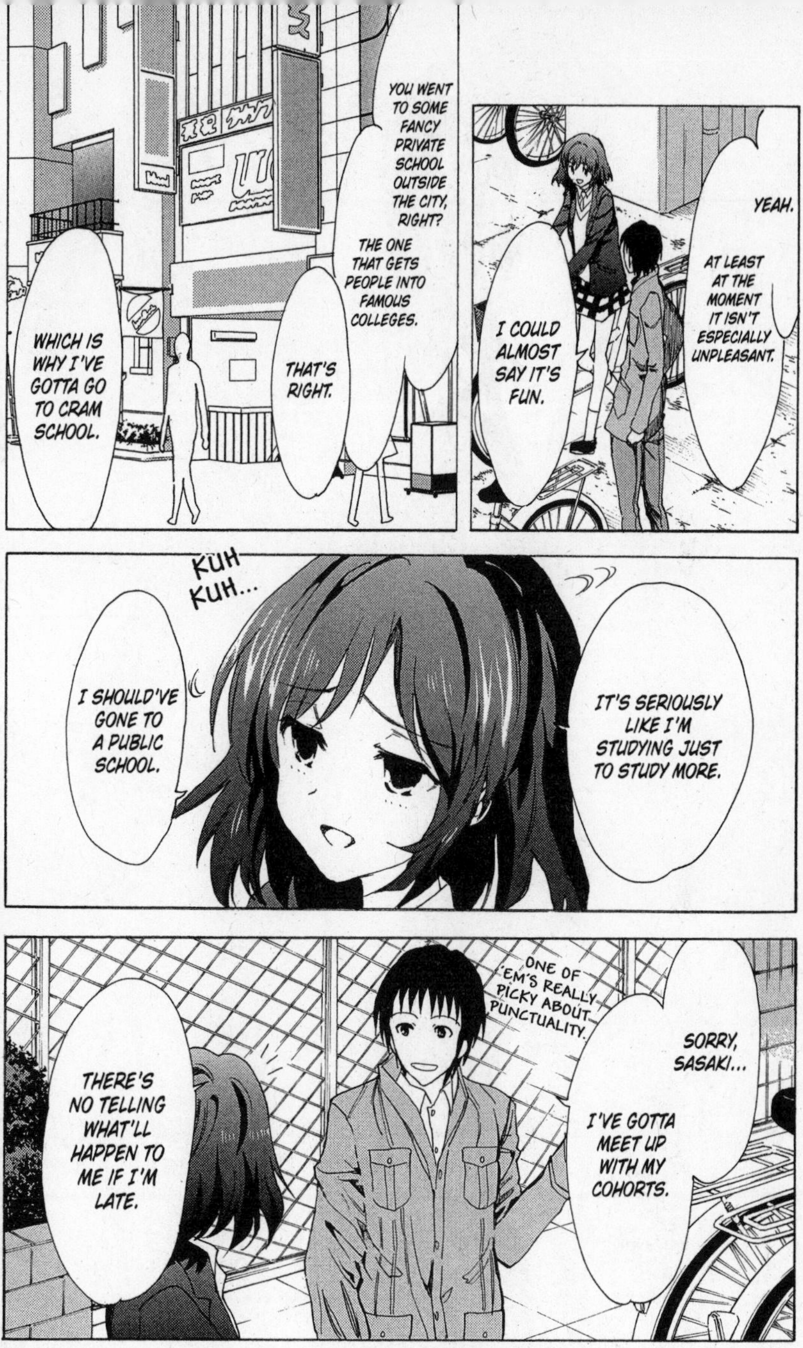
YEAH.
AT LEAST AT THE MOMENT IT ISN'T ESPECIALLY UNPLEASANT.
I COULD ALMOST SAY IT'S FUN.
YOU WENT TO SOME FANCY PRIVATE SCHOOL OUTSIDE THE CITY, RIGHT?
THE ONE THAT GETS PEOPLE INTO FAMOUS COLLEGES.
THAT'S RIGHT.
WHICH IS WHY I'VE GOTTA GO TO CRAM SCHOOL.
IT'S SERIOUSLY LIKE I'M STUDYING JUST TO STUDY MORE.
KUH KUH...
I SHOULD'VE GONE TO A PUBLIC SCHOOL.
SORRY, SASAKI...
I'VE GOTTA MEET UP WITH MY COHORTS.
ONE OF 'EM'S REALLY PICKY ABOUT PUNCTUALITY.
THERE'S NO TELLING WHAT'LL HAPPEN TO ME IF I'M LATE.

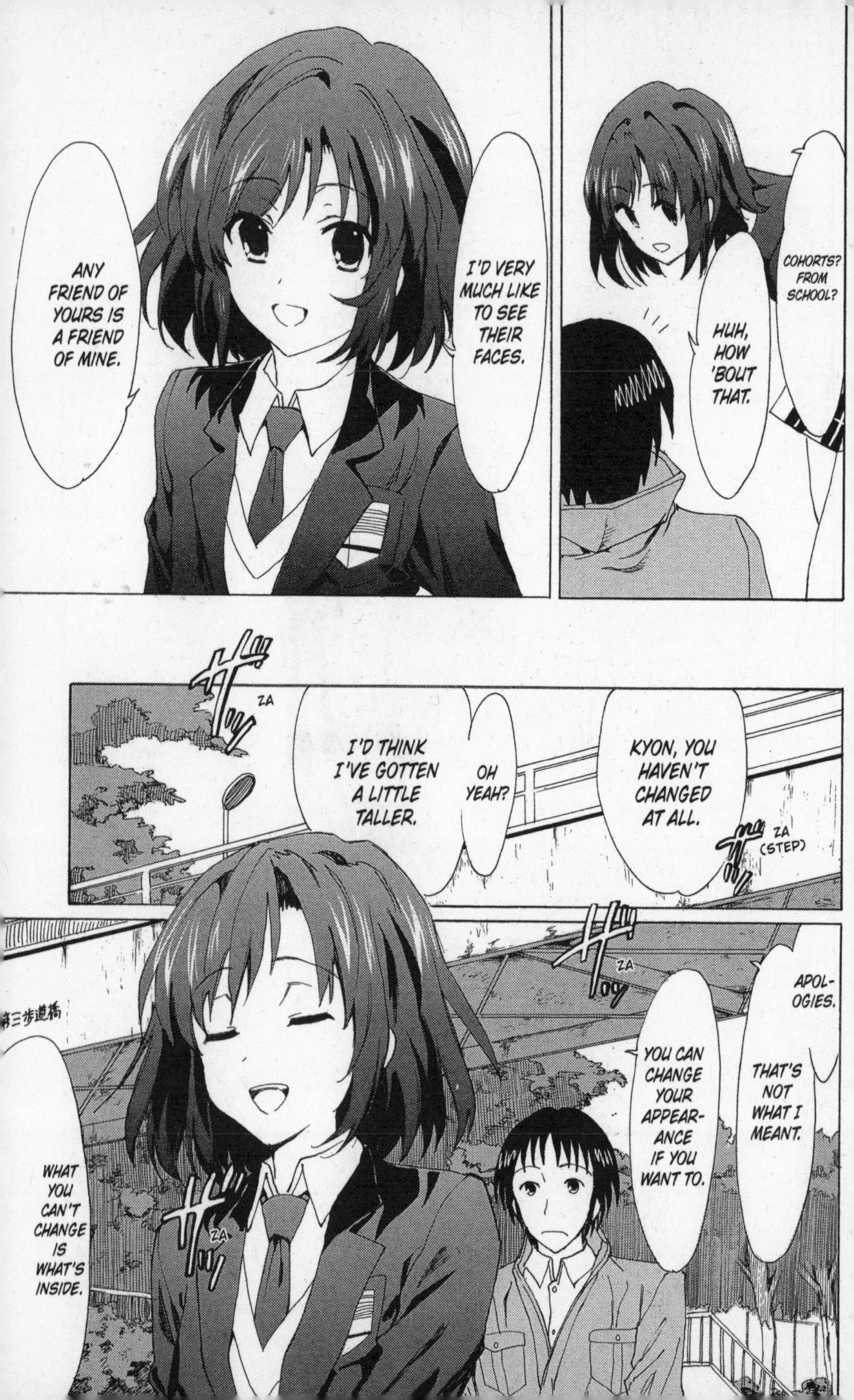
COHORTS? FROM SCHOOL?
HUH, HOW 'BOUT THAT.
I'D VERY MUCH LIKE TO SEE THEIR FACES.
ANY FRIEND OF YOURS IS A FRIEND OF MINE.
ZA (STEP)
KYON, YOU HAVEN'T CHANGED AT ALL.
OH YEAH?
I'D THINK I'VE GOTTEN A LITTLE TALLER.
ZA
APOLOGIES.
THAT'S NOT WHAT I MEANT.
YOU CAN CHANGE YOUR APPEARANCE IF YOU WANT TO.
ZA
第三歩道橋
WHAT YOU CAN'T CHANGE IS WHAT'S INSIDE.
ZA

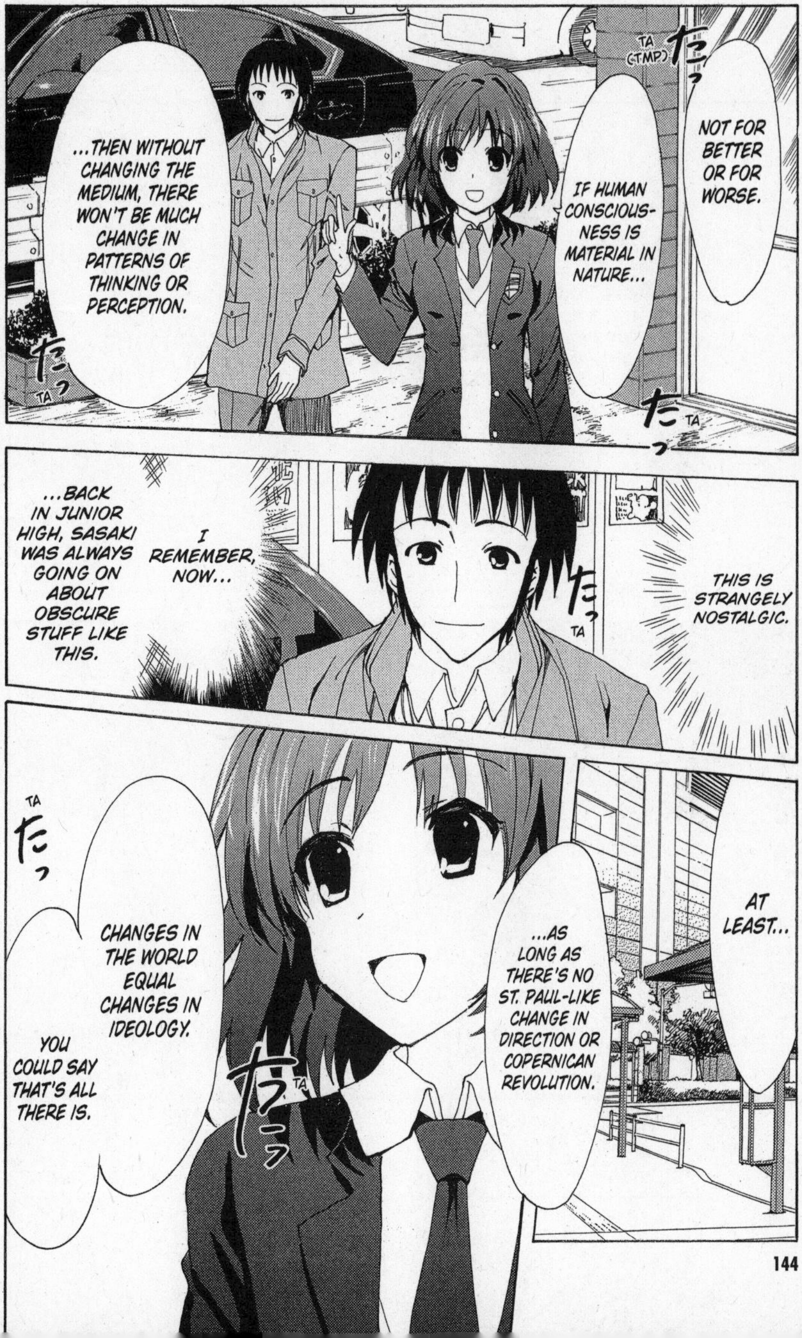
TA (TMP)
NOT FOR BETTER OR FOR WORSE.
IF HUMAN CONSCIOUS-NESS IS MATERIAL IN NATURE...
...THEN WITHOUT CHANGING THE MEDIUM, THERE WON'T BE MUCH CHANGE IN PATTERNS OF THINKING OR PERCEPTION.
TA
TA
THIS IS STRANGELY NOSTALGIC.
TA
I REMEMBER, NOW...
...BACK IN JUNIOR HIGH, SASAKI WAS ALWAYS GOING ON ABOUT OBSCURE STUFF LIKE THIS.
AT LEAST...
...AS LONG AS THERE'S NO ST. PAUL-LIKE CHANGE IN DIRECTION OR COPERNICAN REVOLUTION.
TA
CHANGES IN THE WORLD EQUAL CHANGES IN IDEOLOGY.
TA
YOU COULD SAY THAT'S ALL THERE IS.

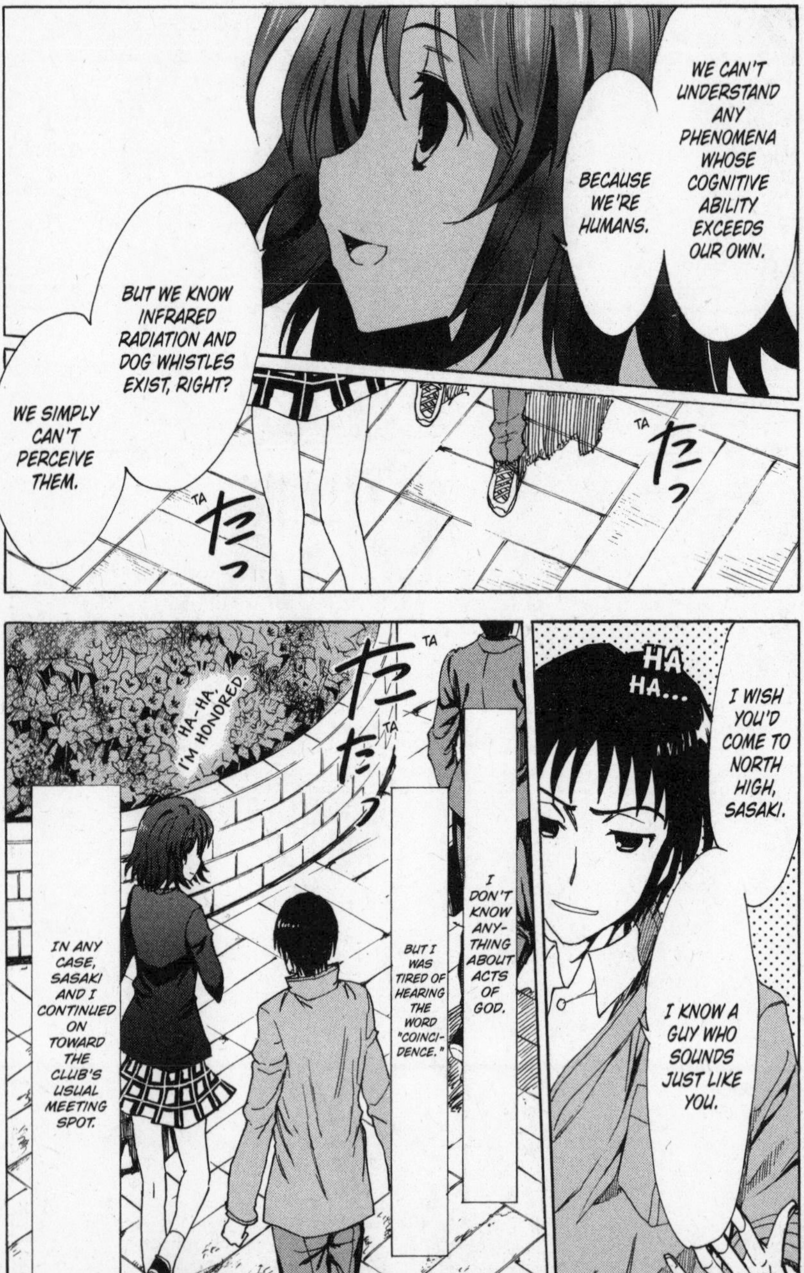
WE CAN'T UNDERSTAND ANY PHENOMENA WHOSE COGNITIVE ABILITY EXCEEDS OUR OWN.
BECAUSE WE'RE HUMANS.
BUT WE KNOW INFRARED RADIATION AND DOG WHISTLES EXIST, RIGHT?
TA たっ
WE SIMPLY CAN'T PERCEIVE THEM.
TA たっ
HA HA...
I WISH YOU'D COME TO NORTH HIGH, SASAKI.
I KNOW A GUY WHO SOUNDS JUST LIKE YOU.
TA たっ
TA たっ
HA-HA, I'M HONORED.
I DON'T KNOW ANY-THING ABOUT ACTS OF GOD.
BUT I WAS TIRED OF HEARING THE WORD "COINCI-DENCE."
IN ANY CASE, SASAKI AND I CONTINUED ON TOWARD THE CLUB'S USUAL MEETING SPOT.

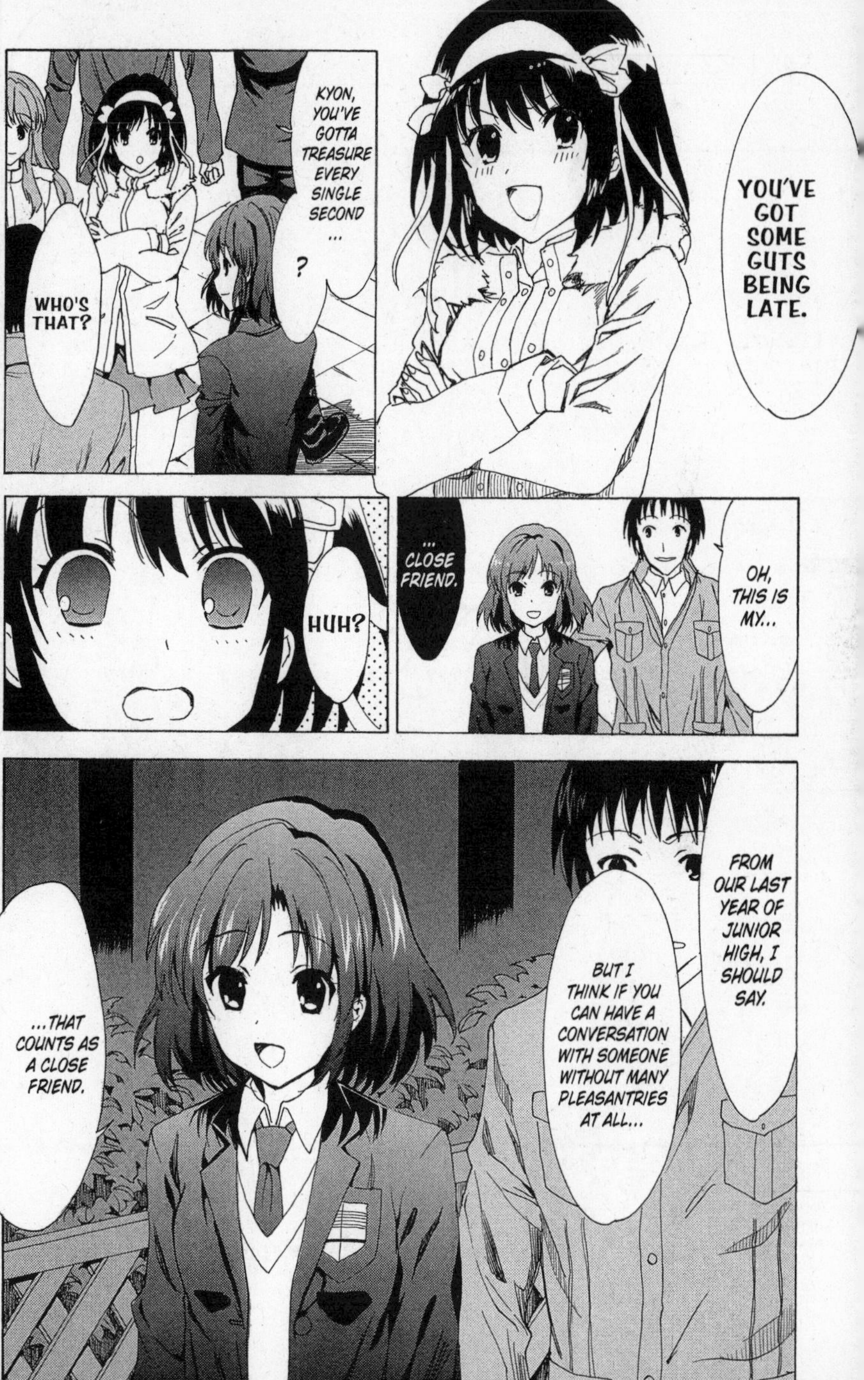
YOU'VE GOT SOME GUTS BEING LATE.
KYON, YOU'VE GOTTA TREASURE EVERY SINGLE SECOND ...
?
WHO'S THAT?
OH, THIS IS MY...
... CLOSE FRIEND.
HUH?
FROM OUR LAST YEAR OF JUNIOR HIGH, I SHOULD SAY.
BUT I THINK IF YOU CAN HAVE A CONVERSATION WITH SOMEONE WITHOUT MANY PLEASANTRIES AT ALL...
...THAT COUNTS AS A CLOSE FRIEND.

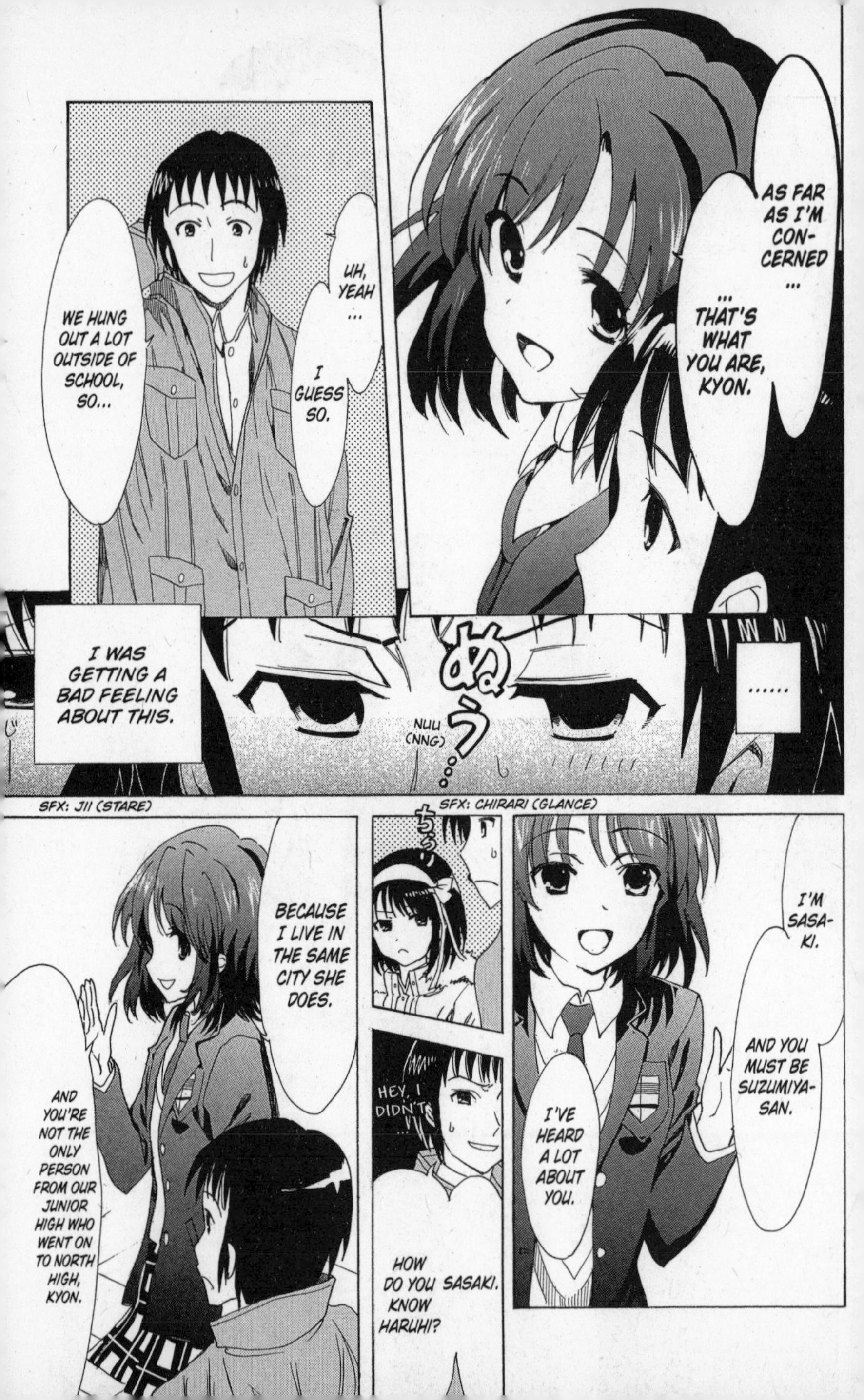
AS FAR AS I'M CONCERNED ...
... THAT'S WHAT YOU ARE, KYON.
UH, YEAH ...
I GUESS SO.
WE HUNG OUT A LOT OUTSIDE OF SCHOOL, SO...
......
ぬう
NUU (NNG)
I WAS GETTING A BAD FEELING ABOUT THIS.
SFX: JII (STARE)
I'M SASAKI.
AND YOU MUST BE SUZUMIYA-SAN.
I'VE HEARD A LOT ABOUT YOU.
SFX: CHIRARI (GLANCE)
HEY, I DIDN'T ...!!
SASAKI.
HOW DO YOU KNOW HARUHI?
BECAUSE I LIVE IN THE SAME CITY SHE DOES.
AND YOU'RE NOT THE ONLY PERSON FROM OUR JUNIOR HIGH WHO WENT ON TO NORTH HIGH, KYON.

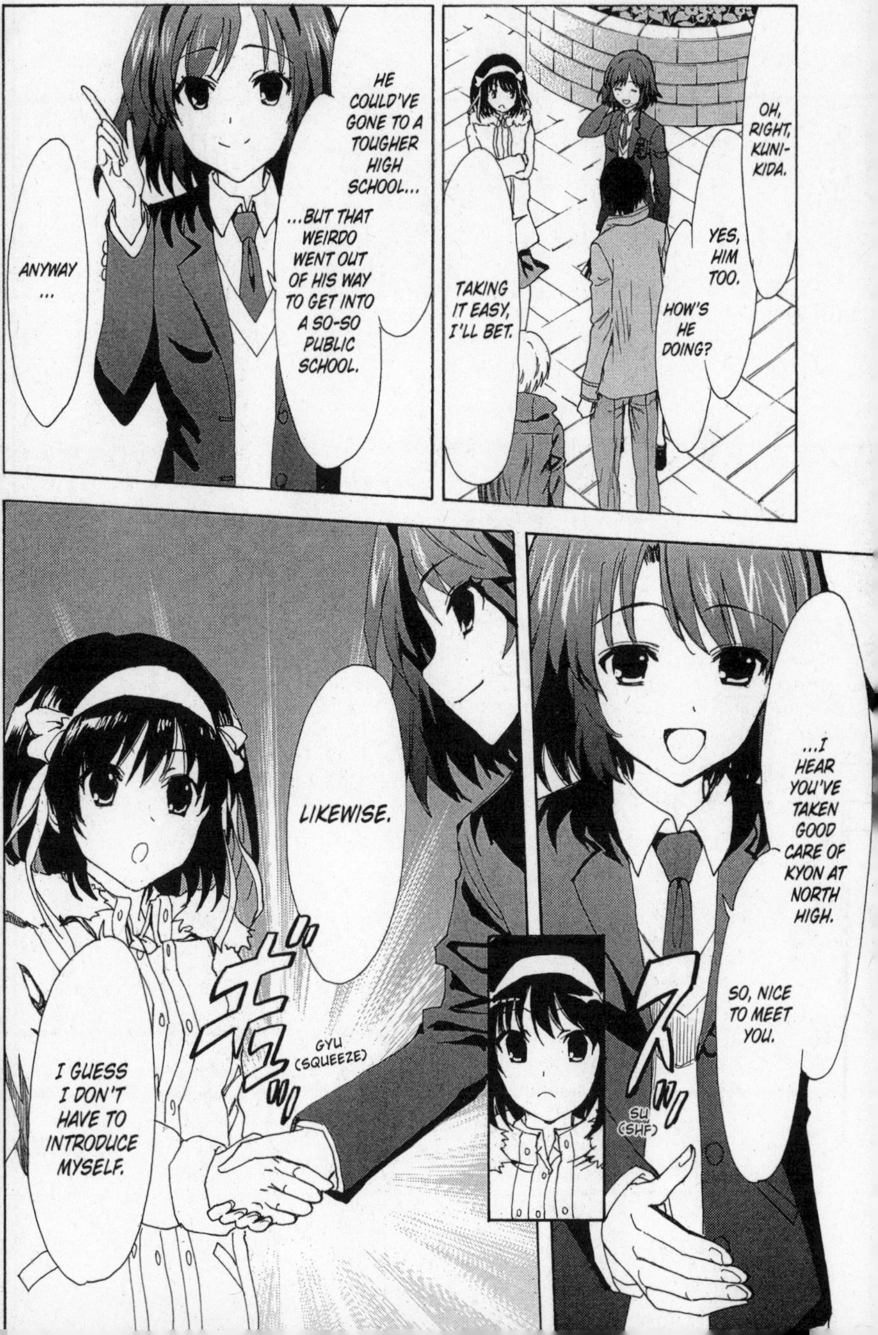
OH, RIGHT, KUNI-KIDA.
YES, HIM TOO.
HOW'S HE DOING?
TAKING IT EASY, I'LL BET.
HE COULD'VE GONE TO A TOUGHER HIGH SCHOOL...
...BUT THAT WEIRDO WENT OUT OF HIS WAY TO GET INTO A SO-SO PUBLIC SCHOOL.
ANYWAY ...
...I HEAR YOU'VE TAKEN GOOD CARE OF KYON AT NORTH HIGH.
SO, NICE TO MEET YOU.
SU (SHF)
LIKEWISE.
GYU (SQUEEZE)
I GUESS I DON'T HAVE TO INTRODUCE MYSELF.

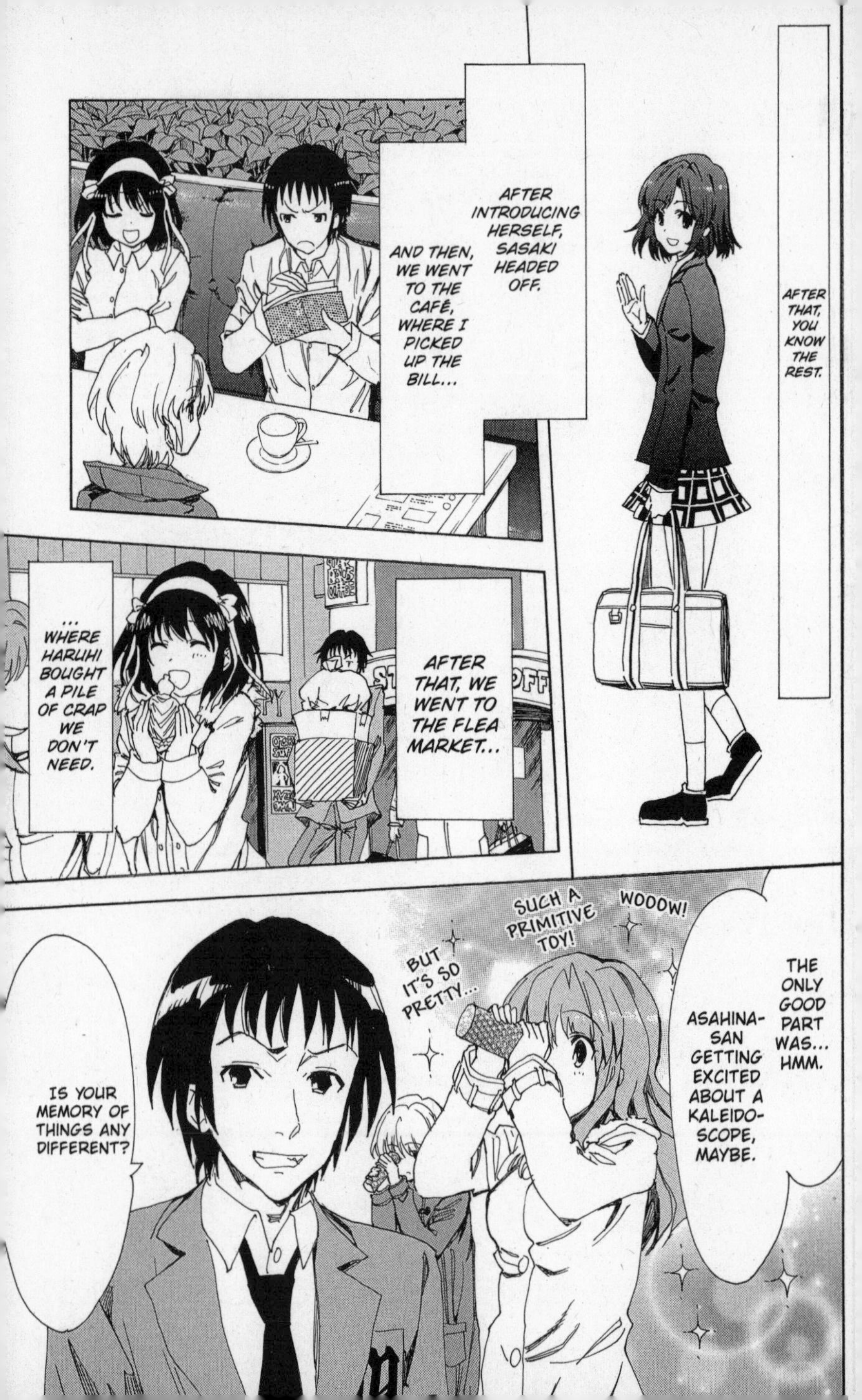

AFTER THAT, YOU KNOW THE REST.
AFTER INTRODUCING HERSELF, SASAKI HEADED OFF.
AND THEN, WE WENT TO THE CAFÉ, WHERE I PICKED UP THE BILL...
AFTER THAT, WE WENT TO THE FLEA MARKET...
... WHERE HARUHI BOUGHT A PILE OF CRAP WE DON'T NEED.
THE ONLY GOOD PART WAS... HMM.
ASAHINA-SAN GETTING EXCITED ABOUT A KALEIDO-SCOPE, MAYBE.
WOOOW!
SUCH A PRIMITIVE TOY!
BUT IT'S SO PRETTY...
IS YOUR MEMORY OF THINGS ANY DIFFERENT?

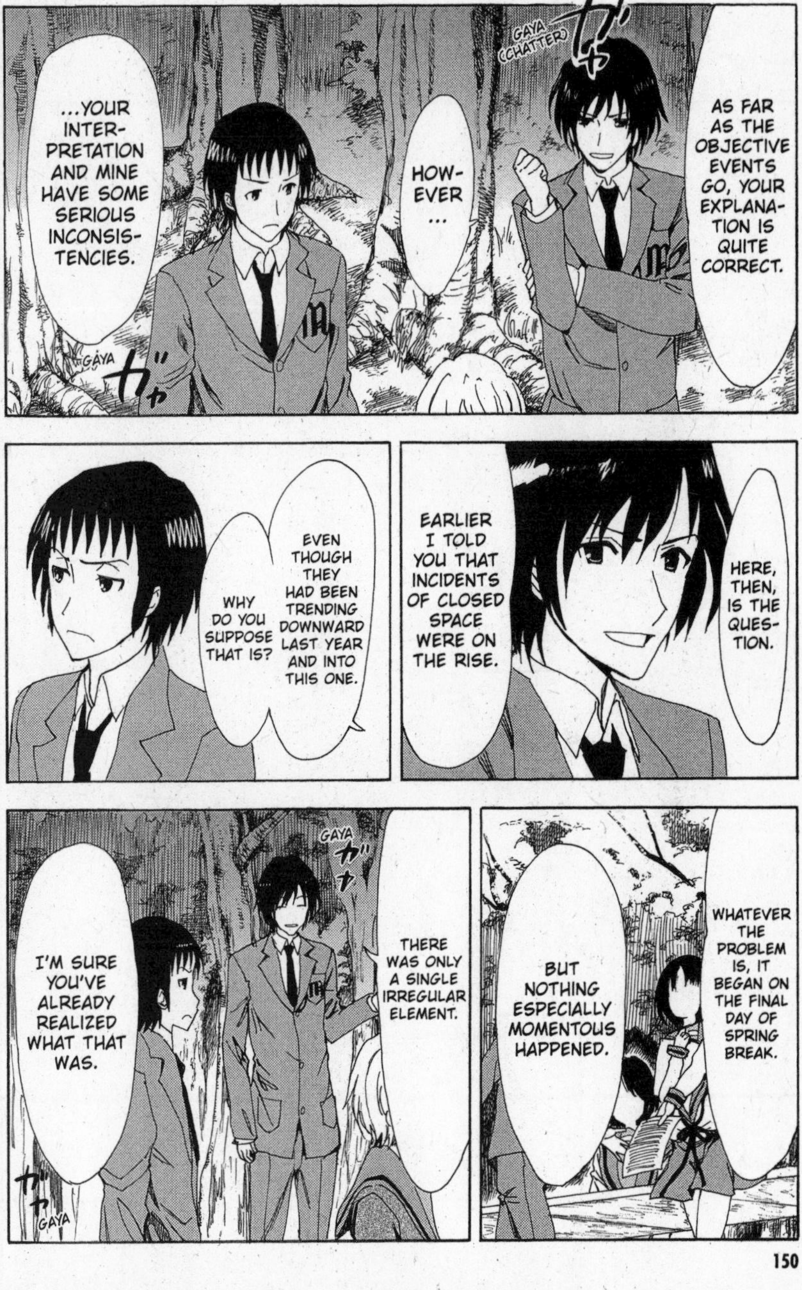
AS FAR AS THE OBJECTIVE EVENTS GO, YOUR EXPLANATION IS QUITE CORRECT.
GAYA (CHATTER)
HOW-EVER ...
...YOUR INTER-PRETATION AND MINE HAVE SOME SERIOUS INCONSIS-TENCIES.
GAYA
HERE, THEN, IS THE QUES-TION.
EARLIER I TOLD YOU THAT INCIDENTS OF CLOSED SPACE WERE ON THE RISE.
EVEN THOUGH THEY HAD BEEN TRENDING DOWNWARD LAST YEAR AND INTO THIS ONE.
WHY DO YOU SUPPOSE THAT IS?
WHATEVER THE PROBLEM IS, IT BEGAN ON THE FINAL DAY OF SPRING BREAK.
BUT NOTHING ESPECIALLY MOMENTOUS HAPPENED.
GAYA
THERE WAS ONLY A SINGLE IRREGULAR ELEMENT.
I'M SURE YOU'VE ALREADY REALIZED WHAT THAT WAS.
GAYA

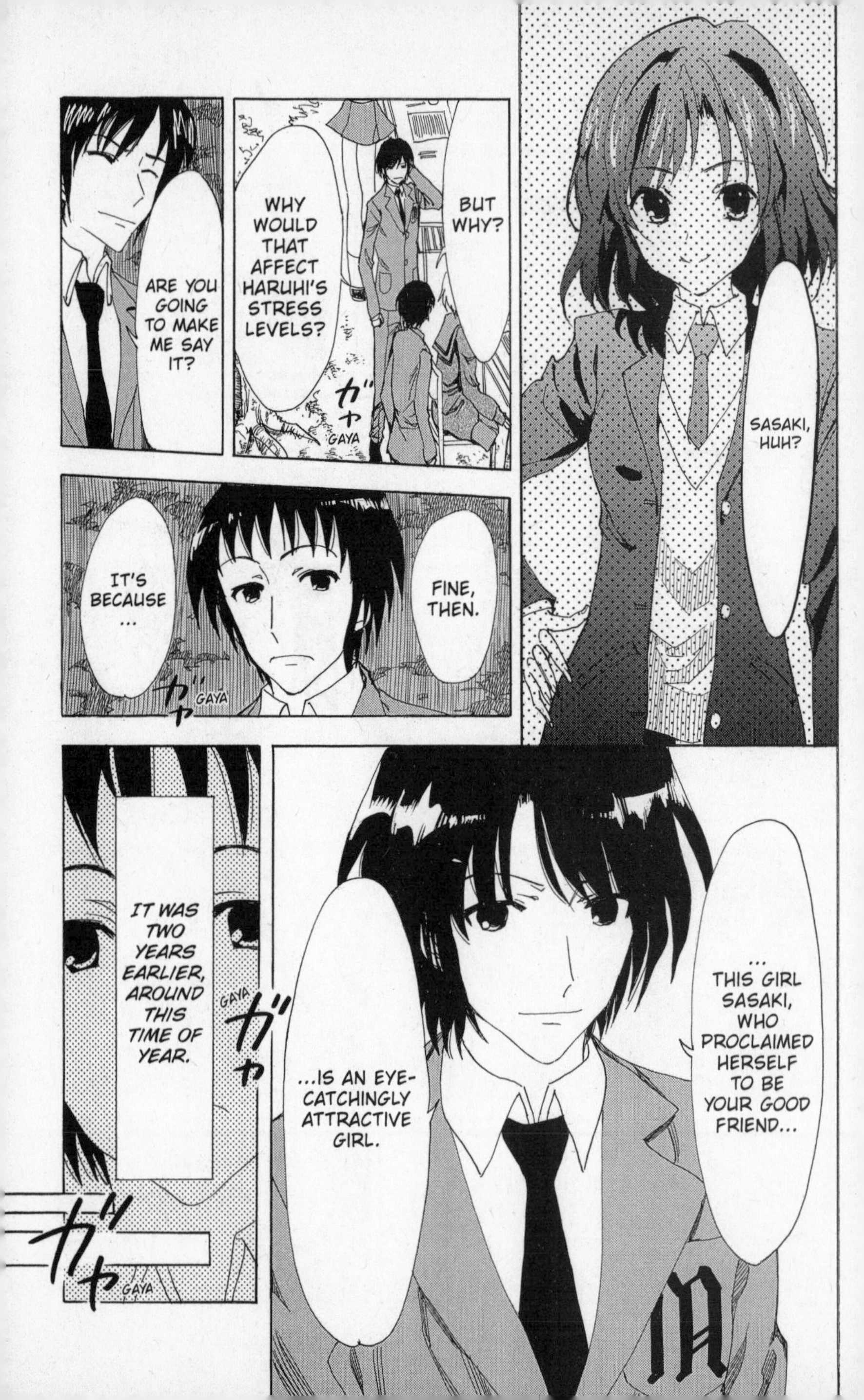
SASAKI, HUH?
BUT WHY?
WHY WOULD THAT AFFECT HARUHI'S STRESS LEVELS?
ガヤ GAYA
ARE YOU GOING TO MAKE ME SAY IT?
FINE, THEN.
IT'S BECAUSE ...
ガヤ GAYA
... THIS GIRL SASAKI, WHO PROCLAIMED HERSELF TO BE YOUR GOOD FRIEND...
...IS AN EYE-CATCHINGLY ATTRACTIVE GIRL.
ガヤ GAYA
IT WAS TWO YEARS EARLIER, AROUND THIS TIME OF YEAR.
ガヤ GAYA

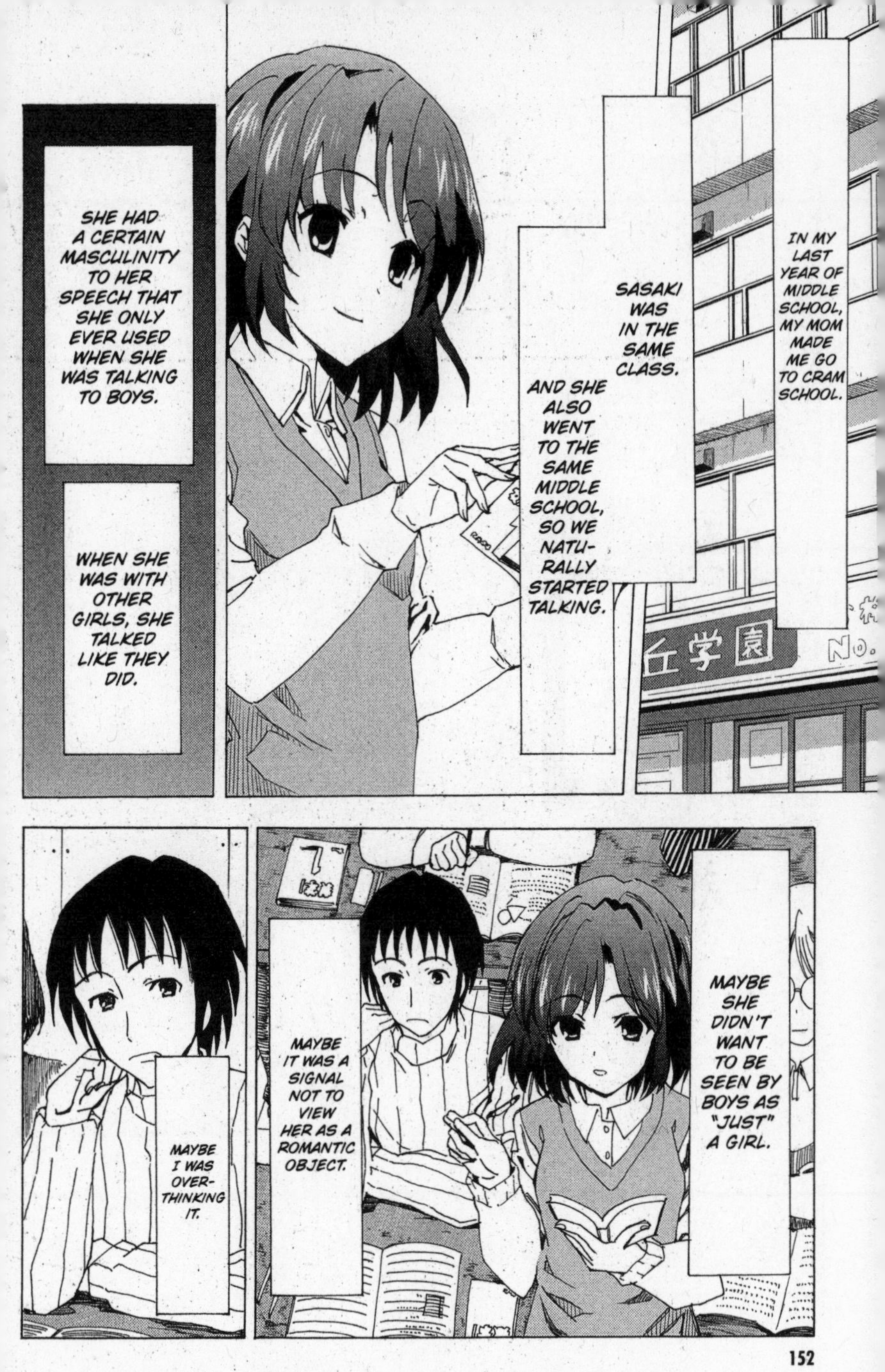

IN MY LAST YEAR OF MIDDLE SCHOOL, MY MOM MADE ME GO TO CRAM SCHOOL.
SASAKI WAS IN THE SAME CLASS.
AND SHE ALSO WENT TO THE SAME MIDDLE SCHOOL, SO WE NATU-RALLY STARTED TALKING.
丘学園
SHE HAD A CERTAIN MASCULINITY TO HER SPEECH THAT SHE ONLY EVER USED WHEN SHE WAS TALKING TO BOYS.
WHEN SHE WAS WITH OTHER GIRLS, SHE TALKED LIKE THEY DID.
MAYBE SHE DIDN'T WANT TO BE SEEN BY BOYS AS "JUST" A GIRL.
MAYBE IT WAS A SIGNAL NOT TO VIEW HER AS A ROMANTIC OBJECT.
MAYBE I WAS OVER-THINKING IT.

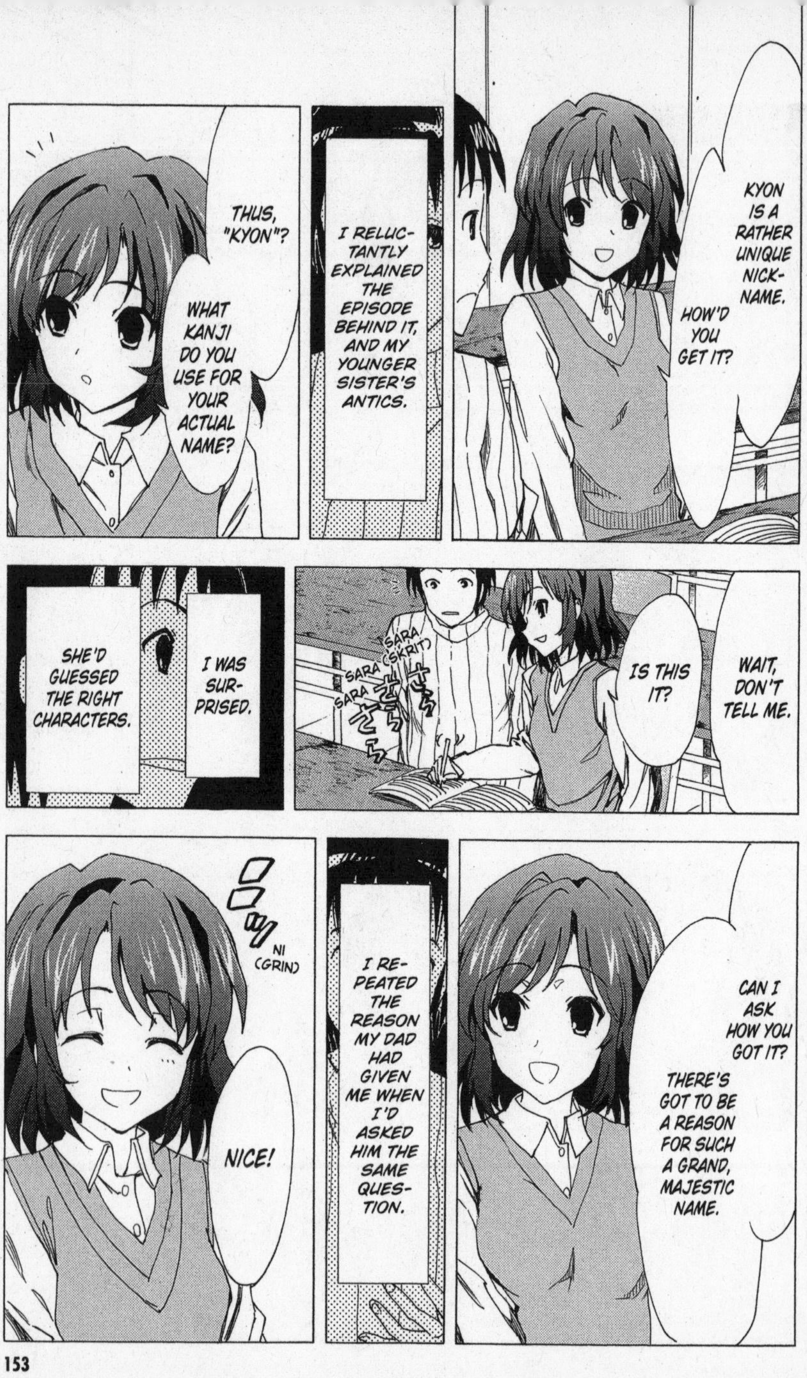
KYON IS A RATHER UNIQUE NICKNAME.
HOW'D YOU GET IT?
I RELUCTANTLY EXPLAINED THE EPISODE BEHIND IT, AND MY YOUNGER SISTER'S ANTICS.
THUS, "KYON"?
WHAT KANJI DO YOU USE FOR YOUR ACTUAL NAME?
WAIT, DON'T TELL ME.
IS THIS IT?
SARA SARA SARA (SKRIT)
I WAS SURPRISED.
SHE'D GUESSED THE RIGHT CHARACTERS.
CAN I ASK HOW YOU GOT IT?
THERE'S GOT TO BE A REASON FOR SUCH A GRAND, MAJESTIC NAME.
I REPEATED THE REASON MY DAD HAD GIVEN ME WHEN I'D ASKED HIM THE SAME QUESTION.
NI (GRIN)
NICE!

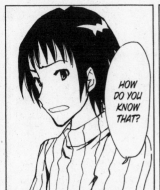

GOTTA SAY, THOUGH, I LIKE "KYON" BETTER.
SEEMS LIKE YOU'RE NOT A HUGE FAN OF YOUR NICKNAME.
HOW DO YOU KNOW THAT?
BECAUSE YOU RESPOND MORE QUICKLY WHEN CALLED BY YOUR REAL NAME THAN BY YOUR NICKNAME.
がたん
GATAN (CLUNK)
ABOUT POINT TWO SECONDS QUICKER.
THAT'S BECAUSE THE ONLY TIME PEOPLE CALLED ME BY MY REAL NAME WAS WHEN IT WAS SERIOUS.
STILL, "POINT TWO SECONDS"?
THAT'S ABOUT HOW LONG IT TAKES YOU TO ACT ON INFORMATION YOU'VE PROCESSED.
WHEN SOMEONE CALLS YOU "KYON," YOU'RE ABOUT THAT MUCH SLOWER.
WHICH MADE ME WONDER IF YOU DIDN'T LIKE IT, DEEP DOWN.

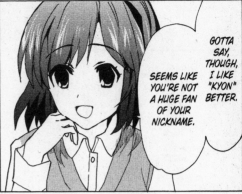

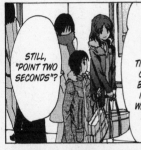

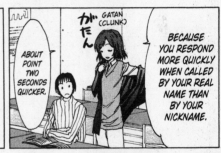

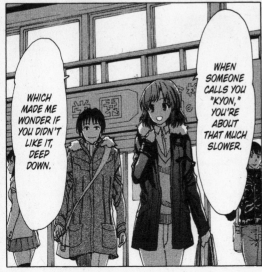

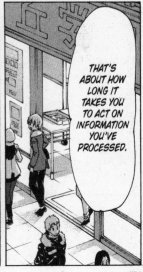

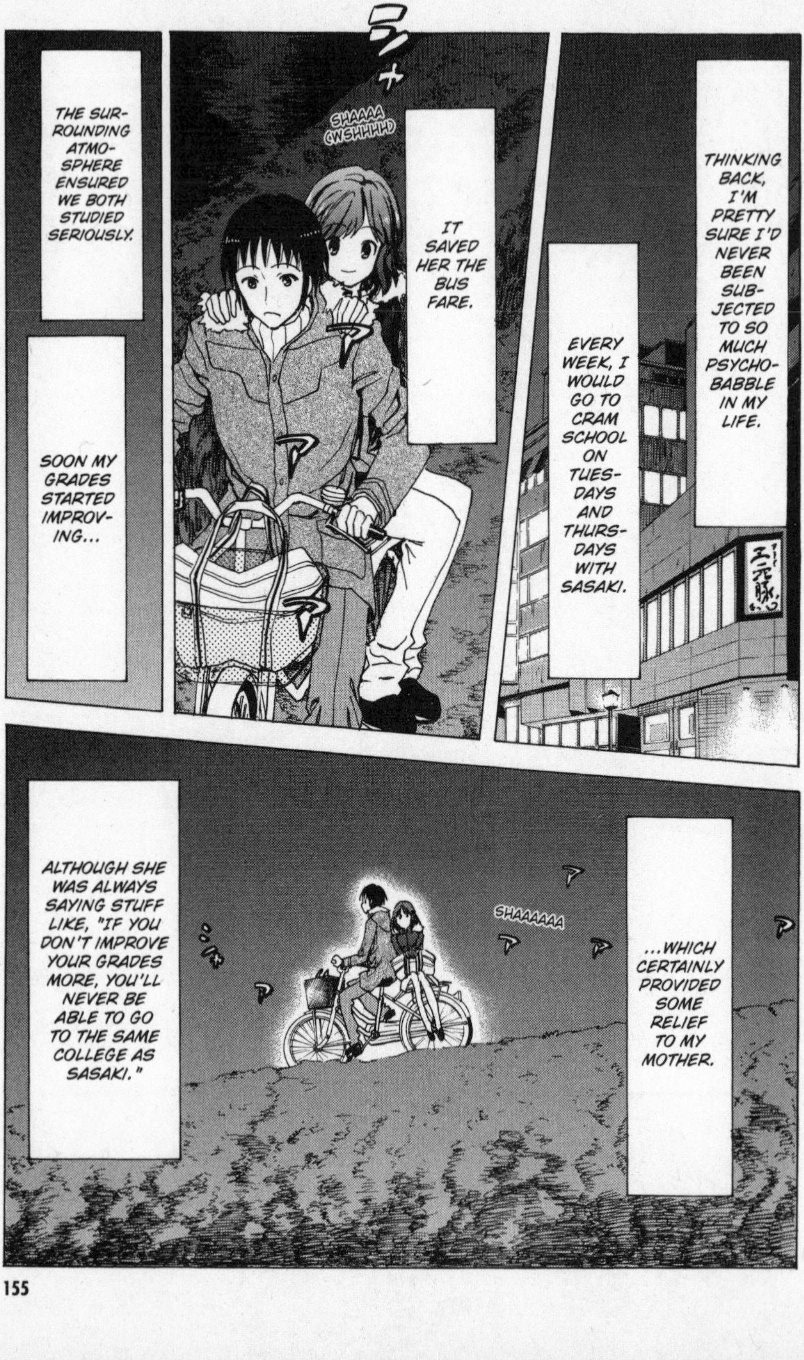
THINKING BACK, I'M PRETTY SURE I'D NEVER BEEN SUBJECTED TO SO MUCH PSYCHOBABBLE IN MY LIFE.
EVERY WEEK, I WOULD GO TO CRAM SCHOOL ON TUESDAYS AND THURSDAYS WITH SASAKI.
IT SAVED HER THE BUS FARE.
SHAAAA (WSHHHH)
THE SURROUNDING ATMOSPHERE ENSURED WE BOTH STUDIED SERIOUSLY.
SOON MY GRADES STARTED IMPROVING...
...WHICH CERTAINLY PROVIDED SOME RELIEF TO MY MOTHER.
SHAAAAAA
ALTHOUGH SHE WAS ALWAYS SAYING STUFF LIKE, "IF YOU DON'T IMPROVE YOUR GRADES MORE, YOU'LL NEVER BE ABLE TO GO TO THE SAME COLLEGE AS SASAKI."

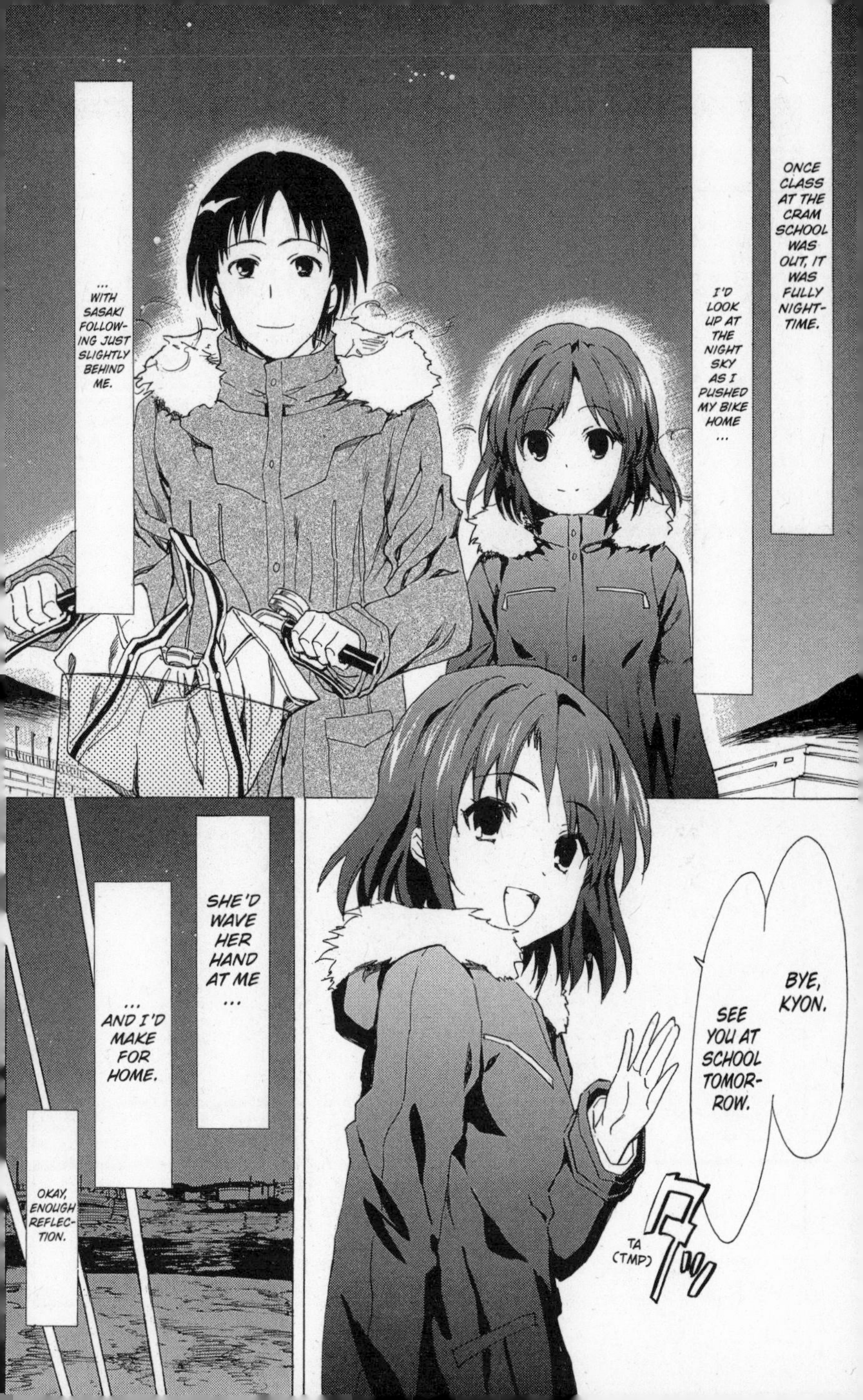
ONCE CLASS AT THE CRAM SCHOOL WAS OUT, IT WAS FULLY NIGHT-TIME.
I'D LOOK UP AT THE NIGHT SKY AS I PUSHED MY BIKE HOME ...
... WITH SASAKI FOLLOW-ING JUST SLIGHTLY BEHIND ME.
BYE, KYON.
SEE YOU AT SCHOOL TOMOR-ROW.
TA (TMP)
SHE'D WAVE HER HAND AT ME ...
... AND I'D MAKE FOR HOME.
OKAY, ENOUGH REFLEC-TION.

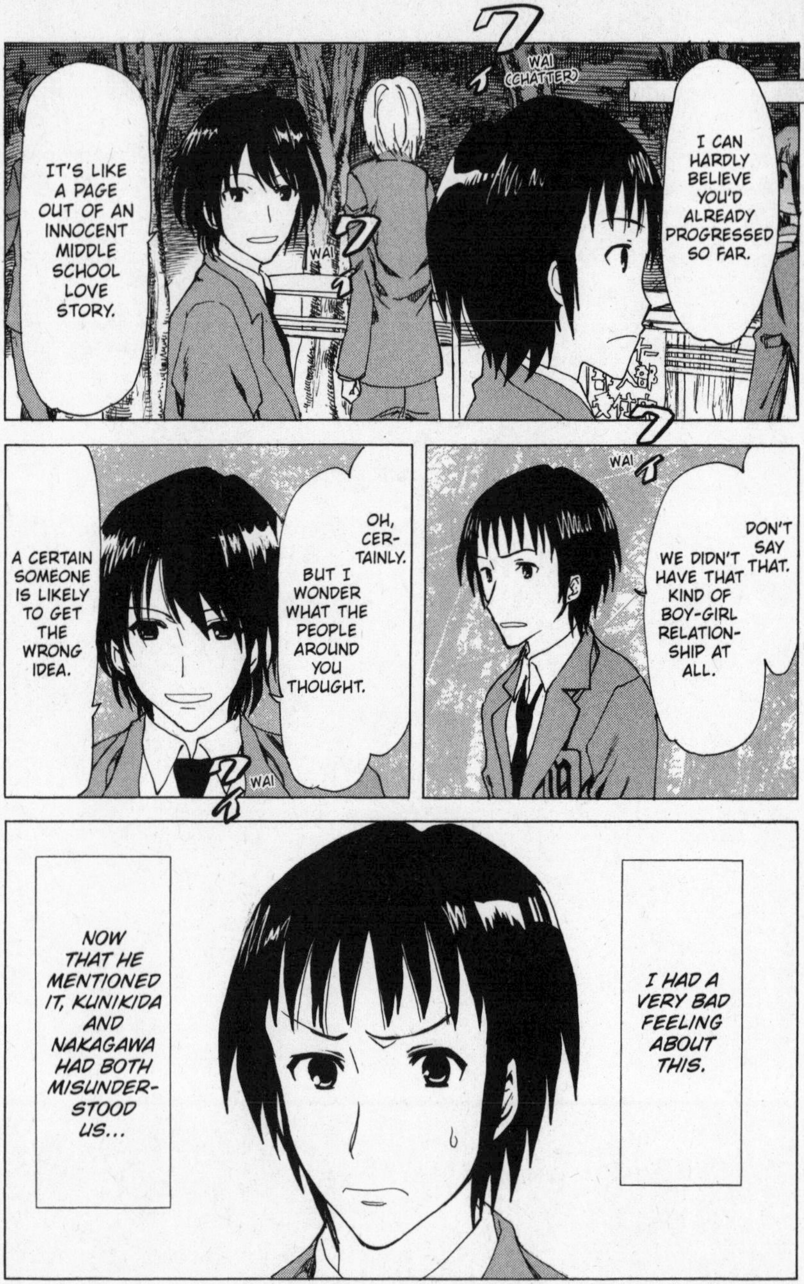
I CAN HARDLY BELIEVE YOU'D ALREADY PROGRESSED SO FAR.
WAI (CHATTER)
IT'S LIKE A PAGE OUT OF AN INNOCENT MIDDLE SCHOOL LOVE STORY.
WAI
DON'T SAY THAT.
WE DIDN'T HAVE THAT KIND OF BOY-GIRL RELATION-SHIP AT ALL.
WAI
OH, CER-TAINLY.
BUT I WONDER WHAT THE PEOPLE AROUND YOU THOUGHT.
A CERTAIN SOMEONE IS LIKELY TO GET THE WRONG IDEA.
WAI
I HAD A VERY BAD FEELING ABOUT THIS.
NOW THAT HE MENTIONED IT, KUNIKIDA AND NAKAGAWA HAD BOTH MISUNDER-STOOD US...

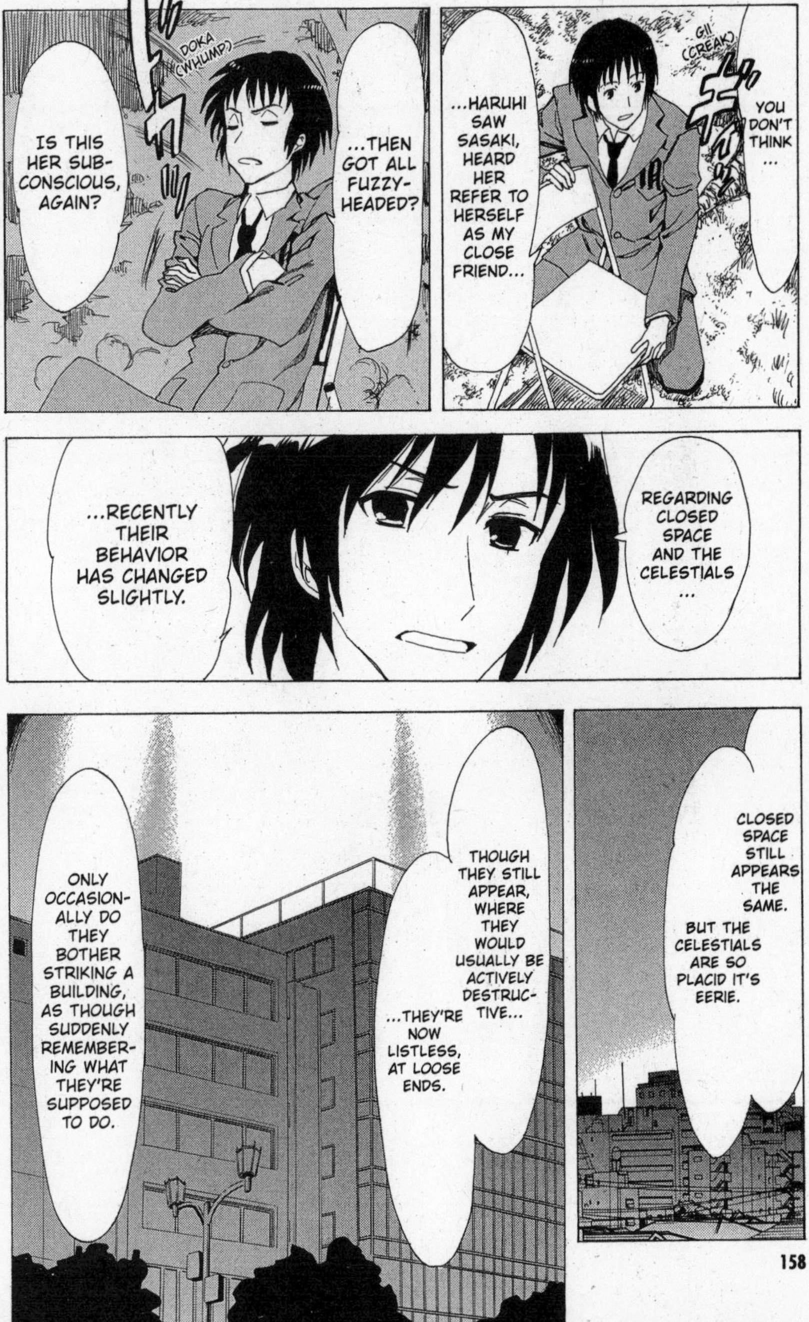
YOU DON'T THINK ...
GII (CREAK)
...HARUHI SAW SASAKI, HEARD HER REFER TO HERSELF AS MY CLOSE FRIEND...
...THEN GOT ALL FUZZY-HEADED?
DOKA (WHUMP)
IS THIS HER SUB-CONSCIOUS, AGAIN?
REGARDING CLOSED SPACE AND THE CELESTIALS ...
...RECENTLY THEIR BEHAVIOR HAS CHANGED SLIGHTLY.
CLOSED SPACE STILL APPEARS THE SAME.
BUT THE CELESTIALS ARE SO PLACID IT'S EERIE.
THOUGH THEY STILL APPEAR, WHERE THEY WOULD USUALLY BE ACTIVELY DESTRUC-TIVE...
...THEY'RE NOW LISTLESS, AT LOOSE ENDS.
ONLY OCCASION-ALLY DO THEY BOTHER STRIKING A BUILDING, AS THOUGH SUDDENLY REMEMBER-ING WHAT THEY'RE SUPPOSED TO DO.

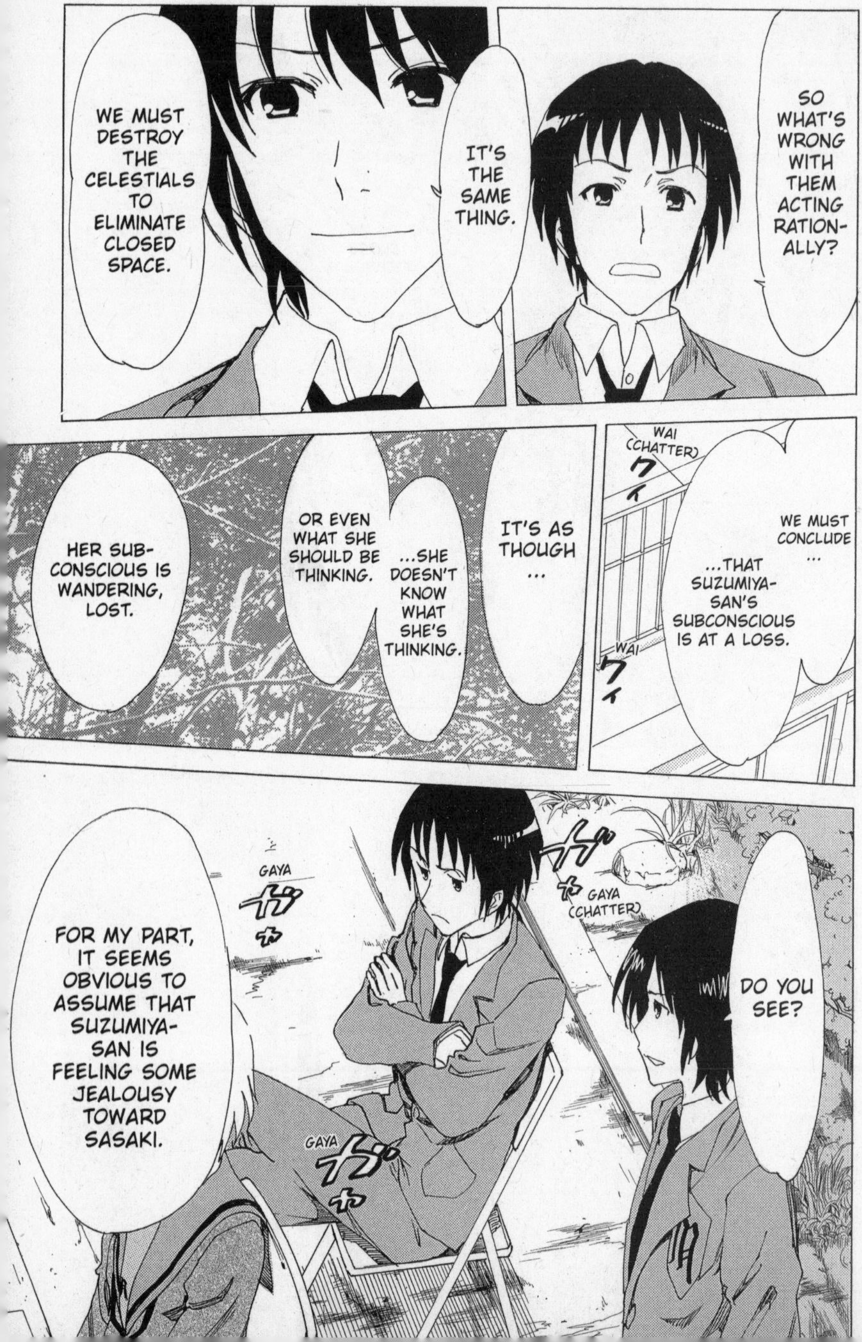
SO WHAT'S WRONG WITH THEM ACTING RATIONALLY?
IT'S THE SAME THING.
WE MUST DESTROY THE CELESTIALS TO ELIMINATE CLOSED SPACE.
WAI (CHATTER)
WE MUST CONCLUDE ...
...THAT SUZUMIYA-SAN'S SUBCONSCIOUS IS AT A LOSS.
WAI
IT'S AS THOUGH ...
...SHE DOESN'T KNOW WHAT SHE'S THINKING.
OR EVEN WHAT SHE SHOULD BE THINKING.
HER SUB-CONSCIOUS IS WANDERING, LOST.
DO YOU SEE?
GAYA (CHATTER)
GAYA
FOR MY PART, IT SEEMS OBVIOUS TO ASSUME THAT SUZUMIYA-SAN IS FEELING SOME JEALOUSY TOWARD SASAKI.
GAYA

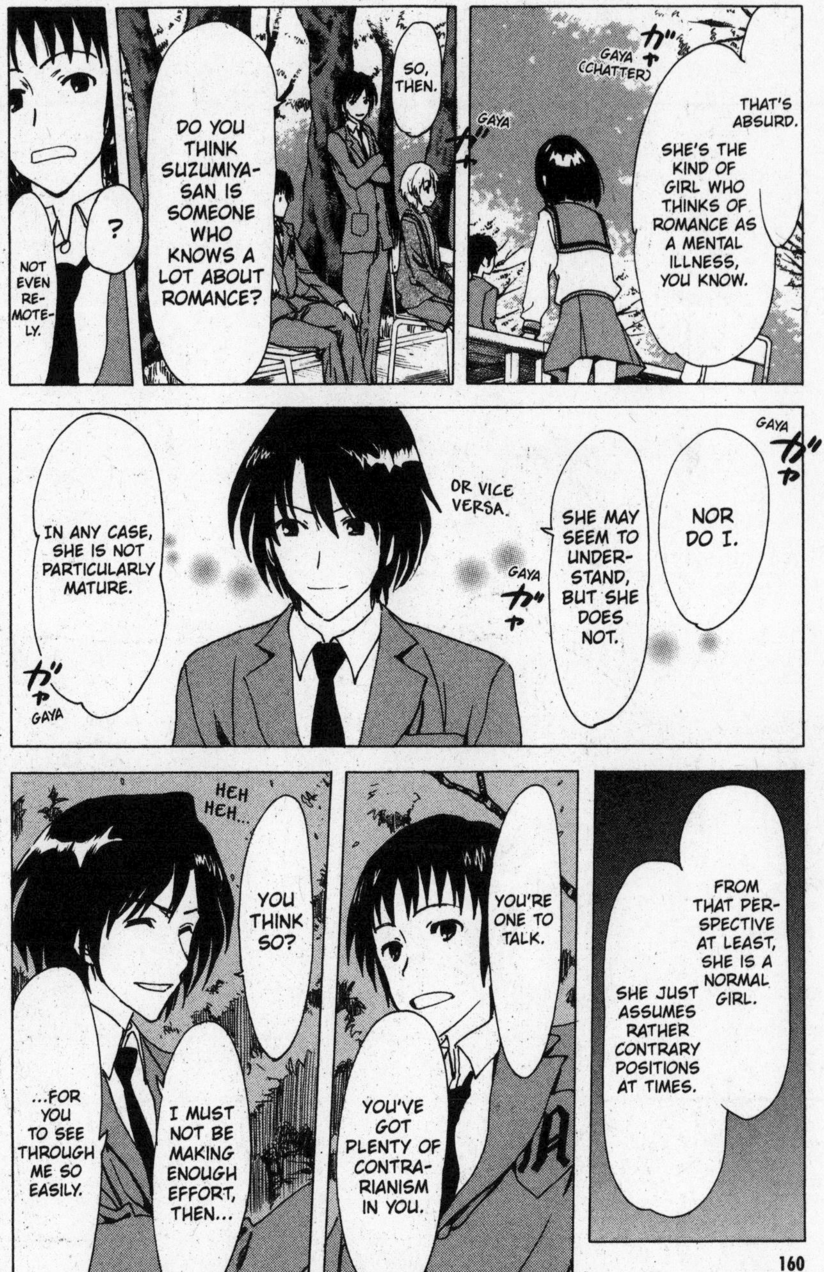
GAYA (CHATTER)
GAYA
THAT'S ABSURD.
SHE'S THE KIND OF GIRL WHO THINKS OF ROMANCE AS A MENTAL ILLNESS, YOU KNOW.
SO, THEN.
DO YOU THINK SUZUMIYA-SAN IS SOMEONE WHO KNOWS A LOT ABOUT ROMANCE?
?
NOT EVEN RE-MOTE-LY.
GAYA
NOR DO I.
SHE MAY SEEM TO UNDER-STAND, BUT SHE DOES NOT.
GAYA
OR VICE VERSA.
IN ANY CASE, SHE IS NOT PARTICULARLY MATURE.
GAYA
FROM THAT PER-SPECTIVE AT LEAST, SHE IS A NORMAL GIRL.
SHE JUST ASSUMES RATHER CONTRARY POSITIONS AT TIMES.
YOU'RE ONE TO TALK.
YOU'VE GOT PLENTY OF CONTRA-RIANISM IN YOU.
HEH HEH...
YOU THINK SO?
I MUST NOT BE MAKING ENOUGH EFFORT, THEN...
...FOR YOU TO SEE THROUGH ME SO EASILY.

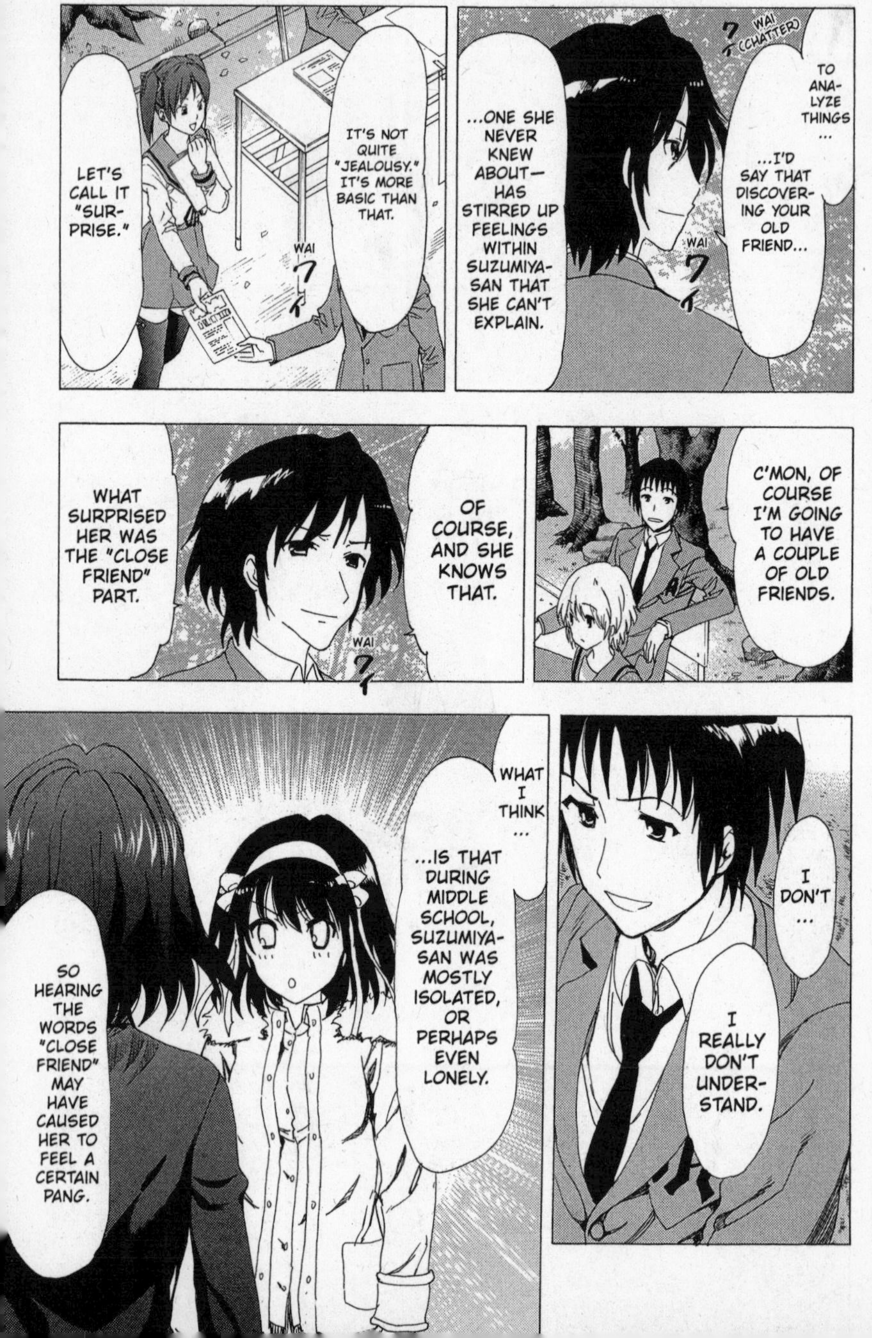
WAI (CHATTER)
TO ANALYZE THINGS...
...I'D SAY THAT DISCOVERING YOUR OLD FRIEND...
WAI
...ONE SHE NEVER KNEW ABOUT—HAS STIRRED UP FEELINGS WITHIN SUZUMIYA-SAN THAT SHE CAN'T EXPLAIN.
IT'S NOT QUITE "JEALOUSY." IT'S MORE BASIC THAN THAT.
WAI
LET'S CALL IT "SURPRISE."
C'MON, OF COURSE I'M GOING TO HAVE A COUPLE OF OLD FRIENDS.
OF COURSE, AND SHE KNOWS THAT.
WAI
WHAT SURPRISED HER WAS THE "CLOSE FRIEND" PART.
I DON'T...
I REALLY DON'T UNDERSTAND.
WHAT I THINK...
...IS THAT DURING MIDDLE SCHOOL, SUZUMIYA-SAN WAS MOSTLY ISOLATED, OR PERHAPS EVEN LONELY.
SO HEARING THE WORDS "CLOSE FRIEND" MAY HAVE CAUSED HER TO FEEL A CERTAIN PANG.

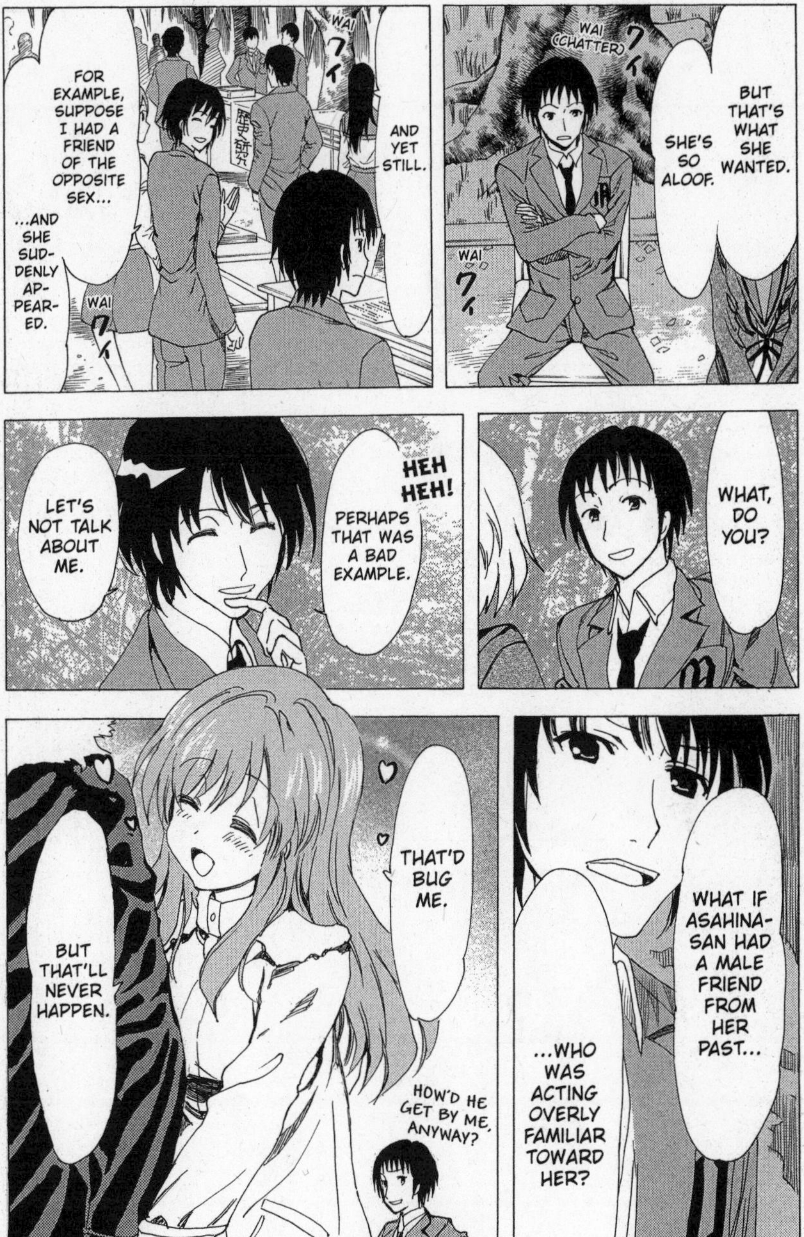
WAI (CHATTER) ワイ
BUT THAT'S WHAT SHE WANTED.
SHE'S SO ALOOF.
WAI ワイ
WAI ワイ
AND YET STILL.
FOR EXAMPLE, SUPPOSE I HAD A FRIEND OF THE OPPOSITE SEX...
...AND SHE SUDDENLY APPEARED.
WAI ワイ
WHAT, DO YOU?
HEH HEH!
PERHAPS THAT WAS A BAD EXAMPLE.
LET'S NOT TALK ABOUT ME.
WHAT IF ASAHINA-SAN HAD A MALE FRIEND FROM HER PAST...
...WHO WAS ACTING OVERLY FAMILIAR TOWARD HER?
THAT'D BUG ME.
BUT THAT'LL NEVER HAPPEN.
HOW'D HE GET BY ME, ANYWAY?

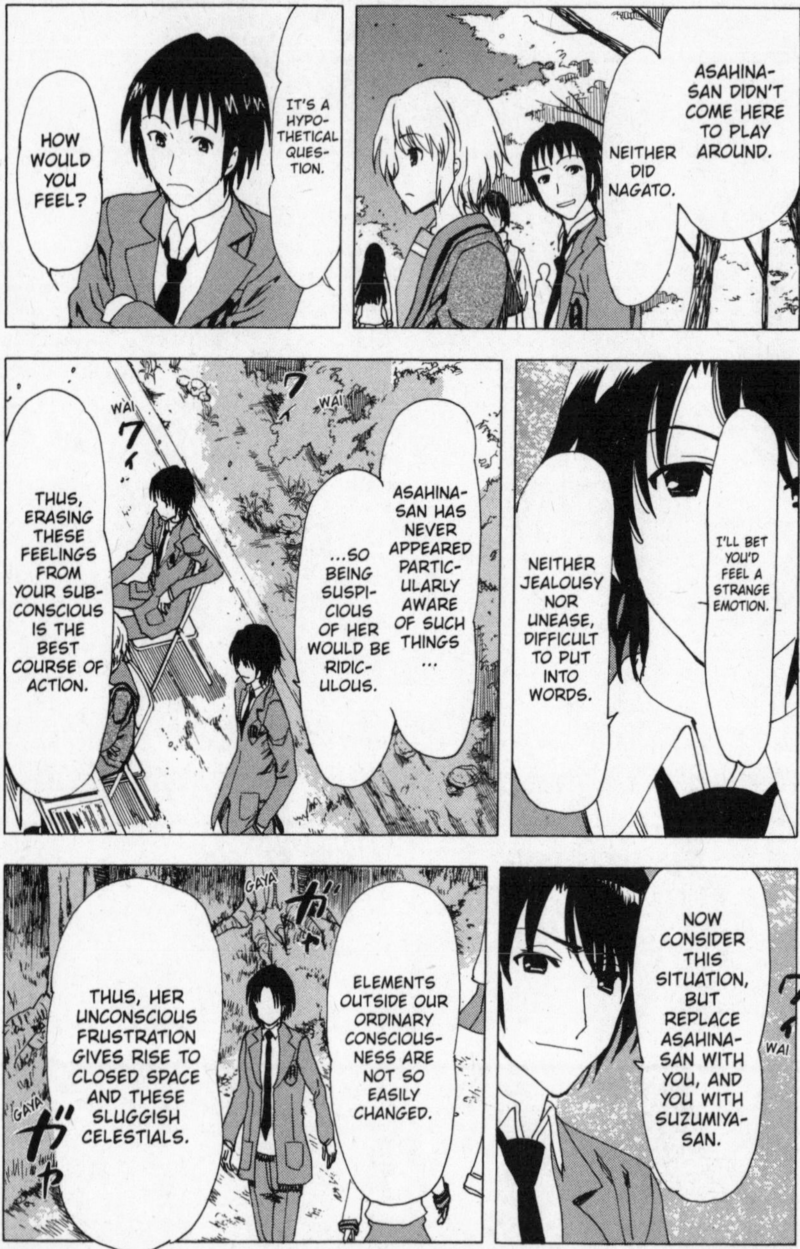
ASAHINA-SAN DIDN'T COME HERE TO PLAY AROUND.
NEITHER DID NAGATO.
IT'S A HYPOTHETICAL QUESTION.
HOW WOULD YOU FEEL?
I'LL BET YOU'D FEEL A STRANGE EMOTION.
NEITHER JEALOUSY NOR UNEASE, DIFFICULT TO PUT INTO WORDS.
WAI
ASAHINA-SAN HAS NEVER APPEARED PARTICULARLY AWARE OF SUCH THINGS...
...SO BEING SUSPICIOUS OF HER WOULD BE RIDICULOUS.
WAI
THUS, ERASING THESE FEELINGS FROM YOUR SUBCONSCIOUS IS THE BEST COURSE OF ACTION.
NOW CONSIDER THIS SITUATION, BUT REPLACE ASAHINA-SAN WITH YOU, AND YOU WITH SUZUMIYA-SAN.
WAI
GAYA
ELEMENTS OUTSIDE OUR ORDINARY CONSCIOUSNESS ARE NOT SO EASILY CHANGED.
THUS, HER UNCONSCIOUS FRUSTRATION GIVES RISE TO CLOSED SPACE AND THESE SLUGGISH CELESTIALS.
GAYA

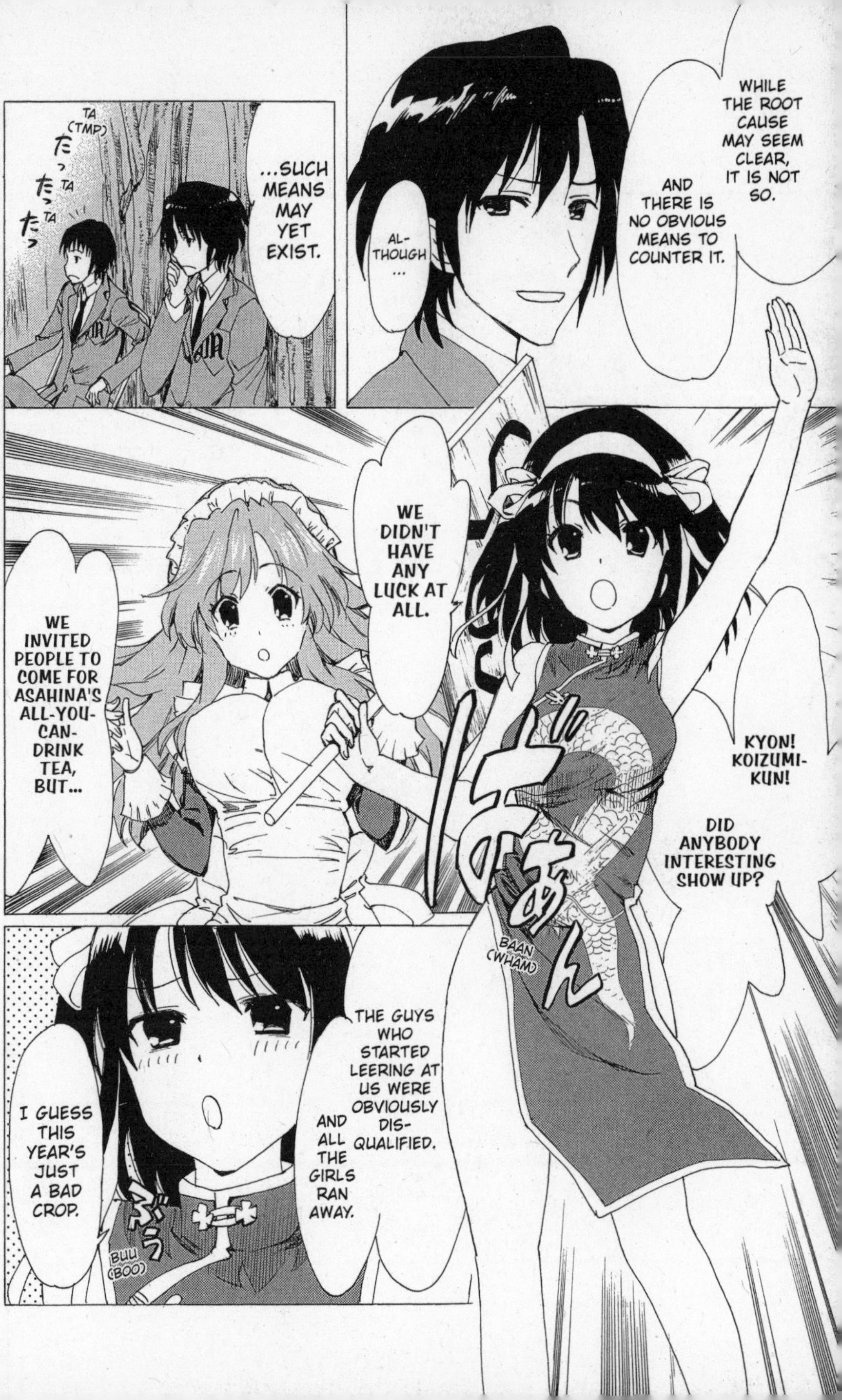
WHILE THE ROOT CAUSE MAY SEEM CLEAR, IT IS NOT SO.
AND THERE IS NO OBVIOUS MEANS TO COUNTER IT.
AL-THOUGH...
...SUCH MEANS MAY YET EXIST.
たっ TA (TMP)
たっ TA
たっ TA
KYON! KOIZUMI-KUN!
DID ANYBODY INTERESTING SHOW UP?
ばぁん BAAN (WHAM)
WE DIDN'T HAVE ANY LUCK AT ALL.
WE INVITED PEOPLE TO COME FOR ASAHINA'S ALL-YOU-CAN-DRINK TEA, BUT...
THE GUYS WHO STARTED LEERING AT US WERE OBVIOUSLY DIS-QUALIFIED.
AND ALL THE GIRLS RAN AWAY.
I GUESS THIS YEAR'S JUST A BAD CROP.
ぶぅ BUU (BOO)

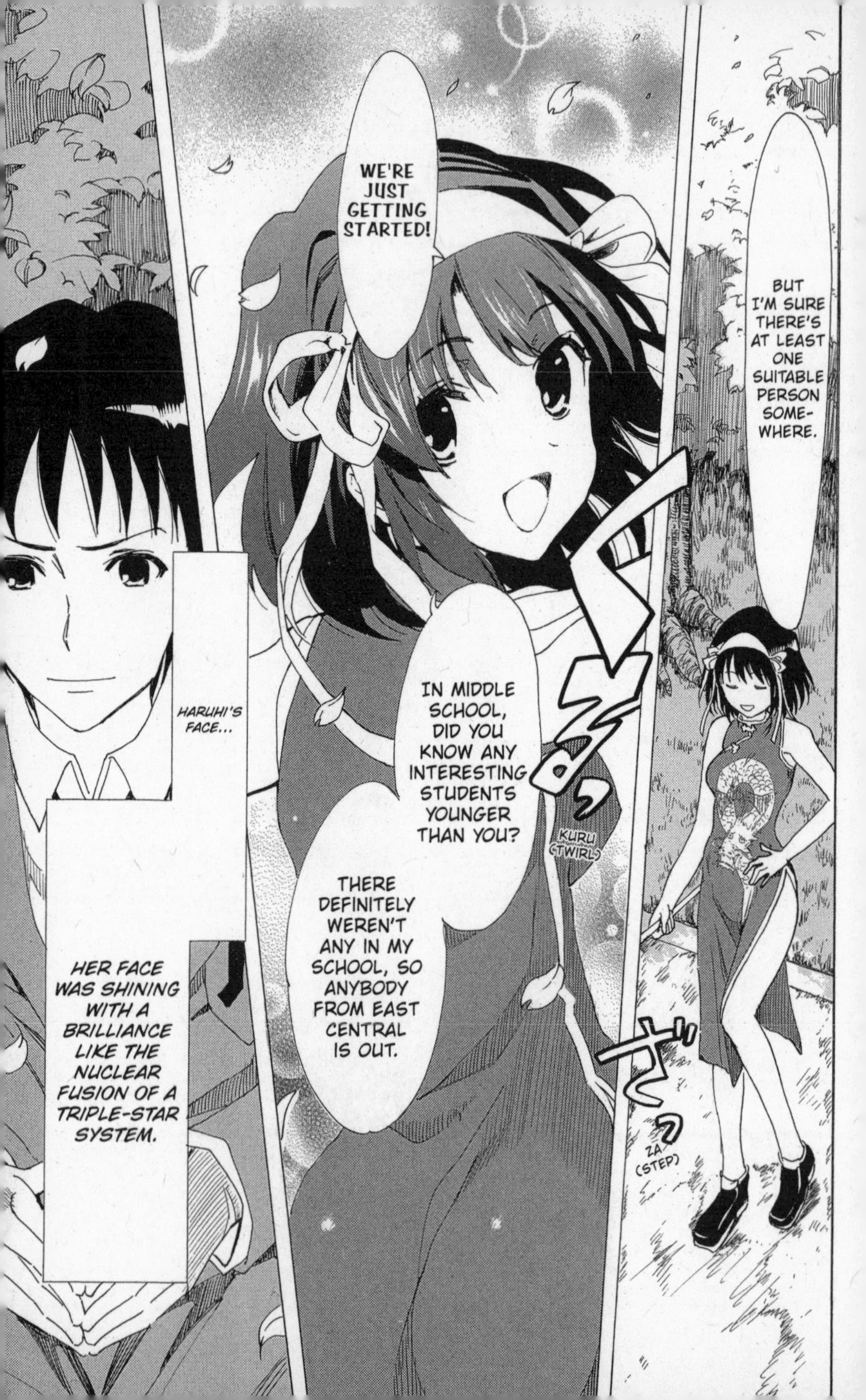
BUT I'M SURE THERE'S AT LEAST ONE SUITABLE PERSON SOME-WHERE.
ZA (STEP)
WE'RE JUST GETTING STARTED!
KURU (TWIRL)
IN MIDDLE SCHOOL, DID YOU KNOW ANY INTERESTING STUDENTS YOUNGER THAN YOU?
THERE DEFINITELY WEREN'T ANY IN MY SCHOOL, SO ANYBODY FROM EAST CENTRAL IS OUT.
HARUHI'S FACE...
HER FACE WAS SHINING WITH A BRILLIANCE LIKE THE NUCLEAR FUSION OF A TRIPLE-STAR SYSTEM.

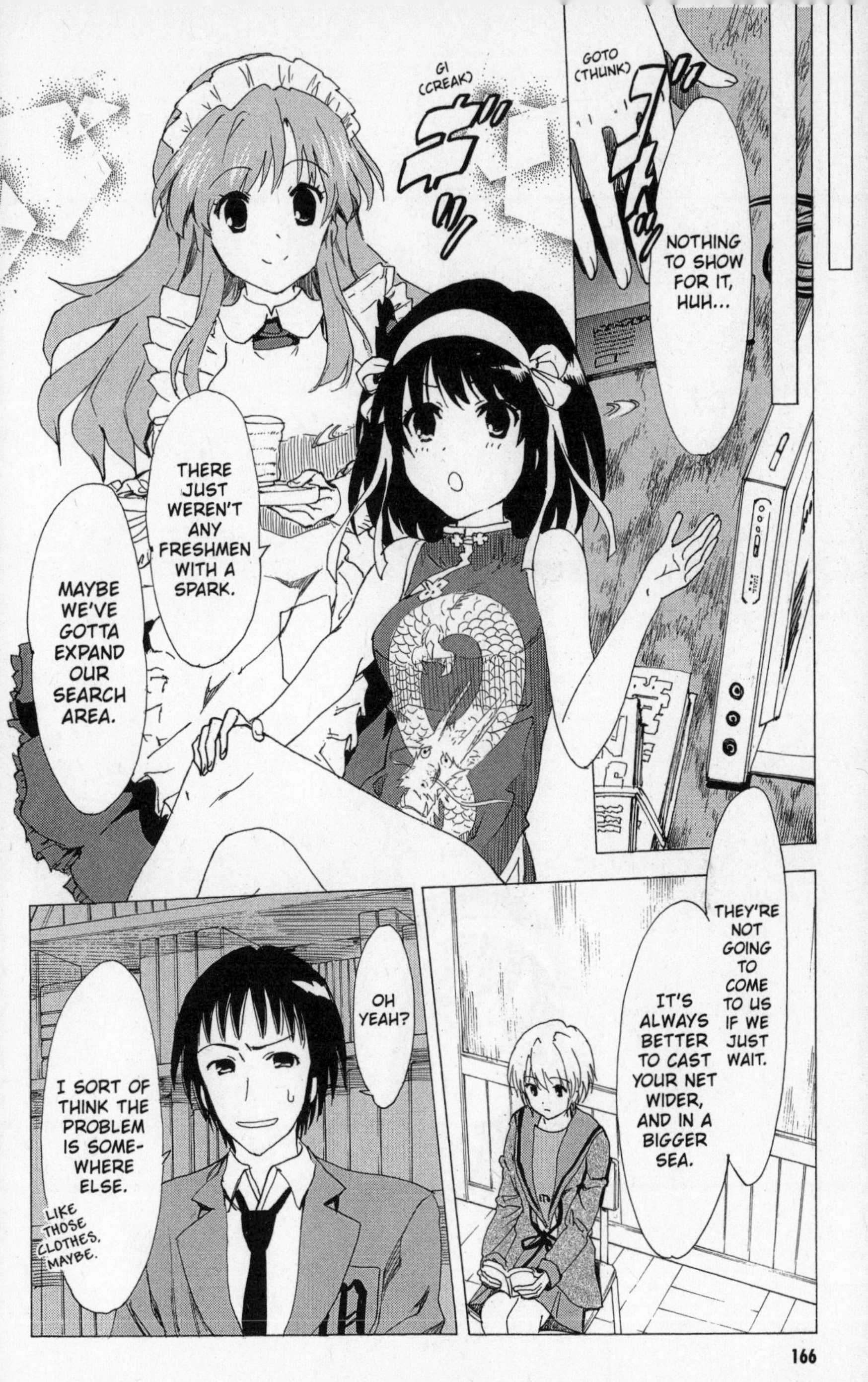
GOTO (THUNK)
NOTHING TO SHOW FOR IT, HUH...
GI (CREAK)
THERE JUST WEREN'T ANY FRESHMEN WITH A SPARK.
MAYBE WE'VE GOTTA EXPAND OUR SEARCH AREA.
THEY'RE NOT GOING TO COME TO US IF WE JUST WAIT.
IT'S ALWAYS BETTER TO CAST YOUR NET WIDER, AND IN A BIGGER SEA.
OH YEAH?
I SORT OF THINK THE PROBLEM IS SOME-WHERE ELSE.
LIKE THOSE CLOTHES, MAYBE.

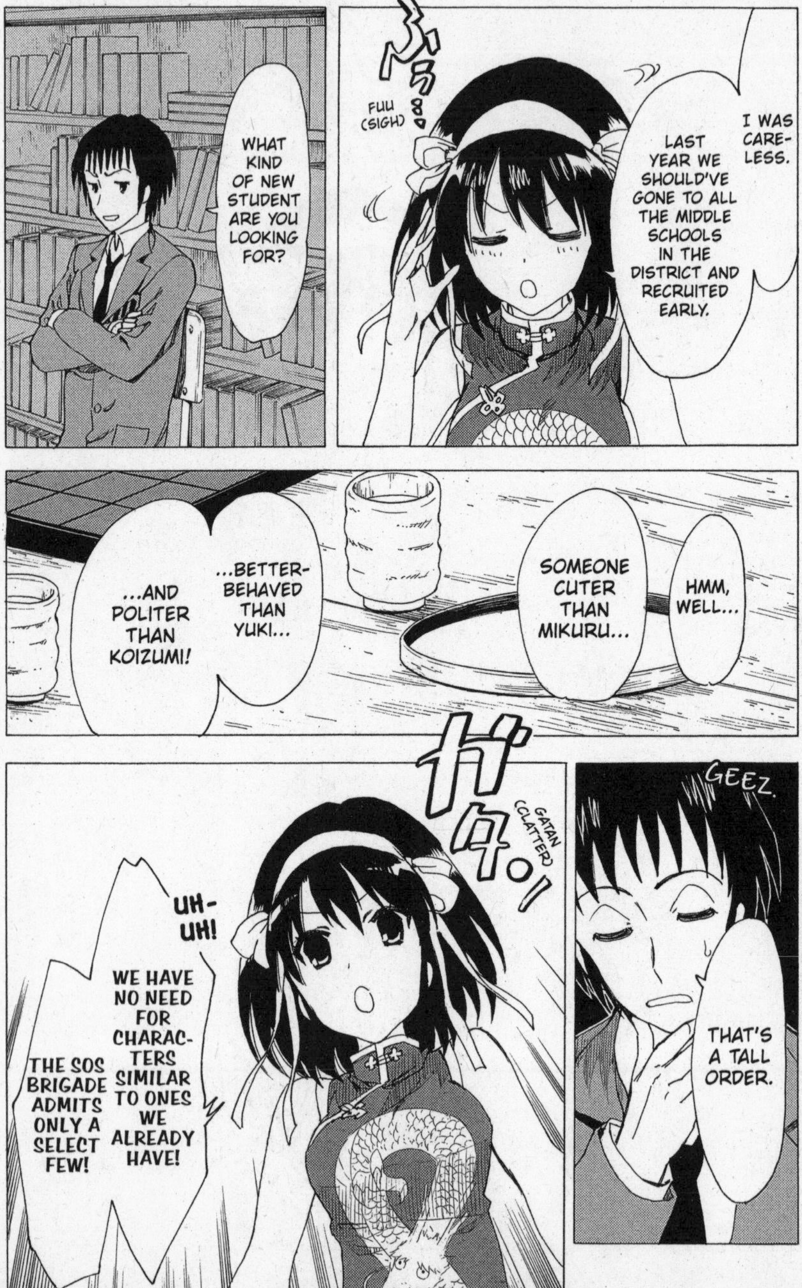
I WAS CARE-LESS.
LAST YEAR WE SHOULD'VE GONE TO ALL THE MIDDLE SCHOOLS IN THE DISTRICT AND RECRUITED EARLY.
FUU (SIGH)
WHAT KIND OF NEW STUDENT ARE YOU LOOKING FOR?
HMM, WELL...
SOMEONE CUTER THAN MIKURU...
...BETTER-BEHAVED THAN YUKI...
...AND POLITER THAN KOIZUMI!
GEEZ.
THAT'S A TALL ORDER.
GATAN (CLATTER)
UH-UH!
WE HAVE NO NEED FOR CHARAC-TERS SIMILAR TO ONES WE ALREADY HAVE!
THE SOS BRIGADE ADMITS ONLY A SELECT FEW!

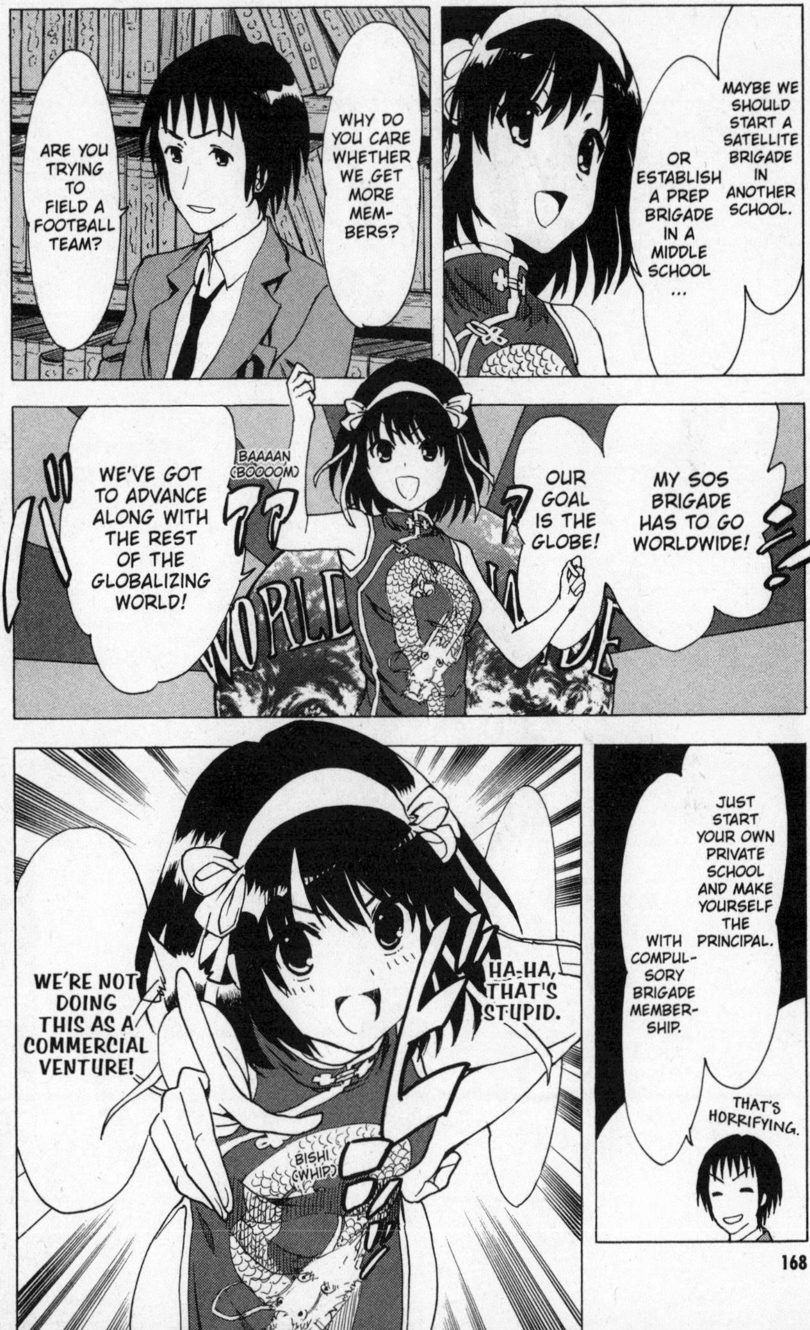
MAYBE WE SHOULD START A SATELLITE BRIGADE IN ANOTHER SCHOOL.
OR ESTABLISH A PREP BRIGADE IN A MIDDLE SCHOOL ...
WHY DO YOU CARE WHETHER WE GET MORE MEM-BERS?
ARE YOU TRYING TO FIELD A FOOTBALL TEAM?
MY SOS BRIGADE HAS TO GO WORLDWIDE!
OUR GOAL IS THE GLOBE!
BAAAAN (BOOOOM)
WE'VE GOT TO ADVANCE ALONG WITH THE REST OF THE GLOBALIZING WORLD!
WORLDWIDE
JUST START YOUR OWN PRIVATE SCHOOL AND MAKE YOURSELF THE PRINCIPAL.
WITH COMPUL-SORY BRIGADE MEMBER-SHIP.
THAT'S HORRIFYING.
HA-HA, THAT'S STUPID.
WE'RE NOT DOING THIS AS A COMMERCIAL VENTURE!
BISHI (WHIP)

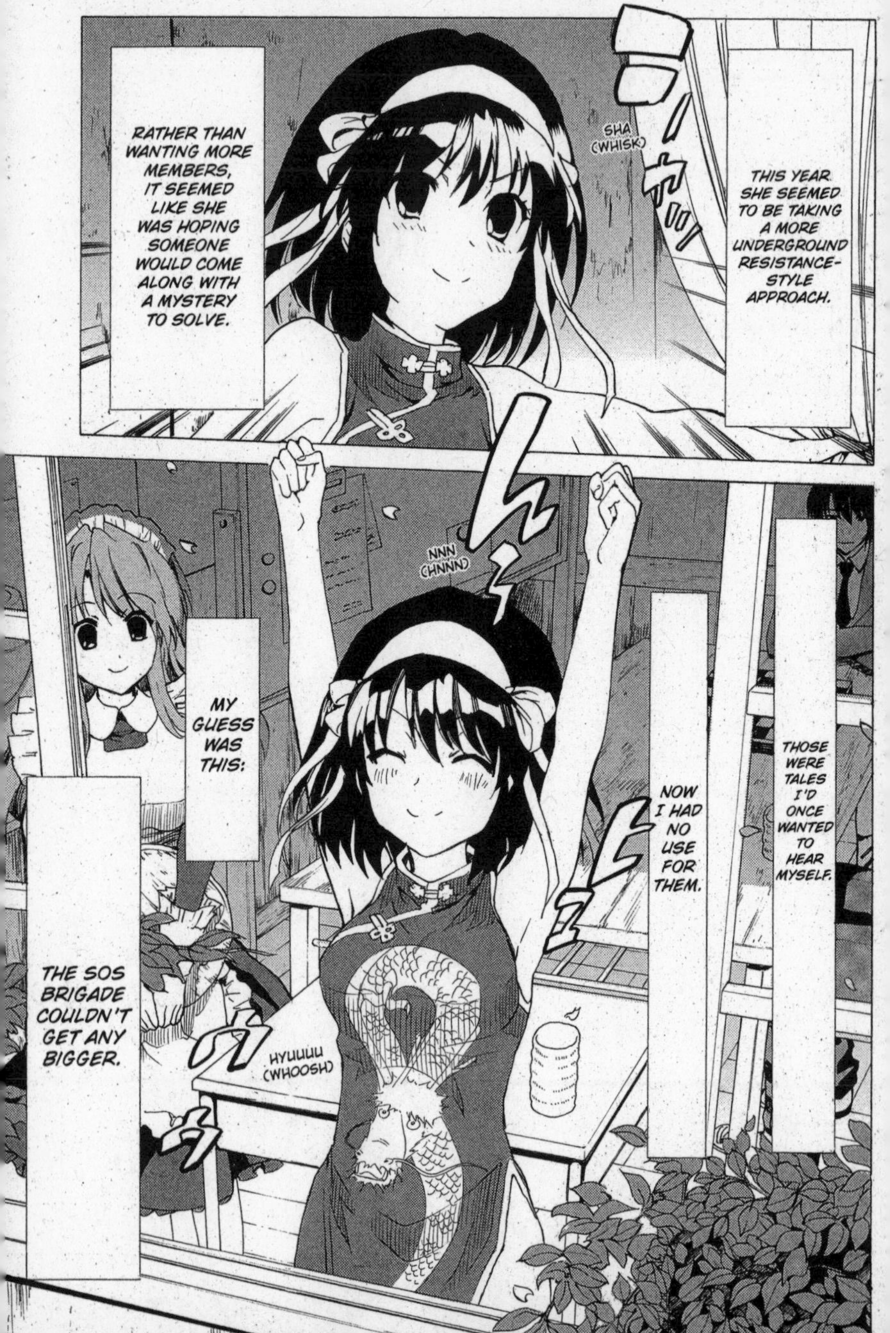
THIS YEAR SHE SEEMED TO BE TAKING A MORE UNDERGROUND RESISTANCE-STYLE APPROACH.
SHA (WHISK)
RATHER THAN WANTING MORE MEMBERS, IT SEEMED LIKE SHE WAS HOPING SOMEONE WOULD COME ALONG WITH A MYSTERY TO SOLVE.
THOSE WERE TALES I'D ONCE WANTED TO HEAR MYSELF.
NOW I HAD NO USE FOR THEM.
NNN (HNNN)
MY GUESS WAS THIS:
THE SOS BRIGADE COULDN'T GET ANY BIGGER.
HYUUUU (WHOOSH)

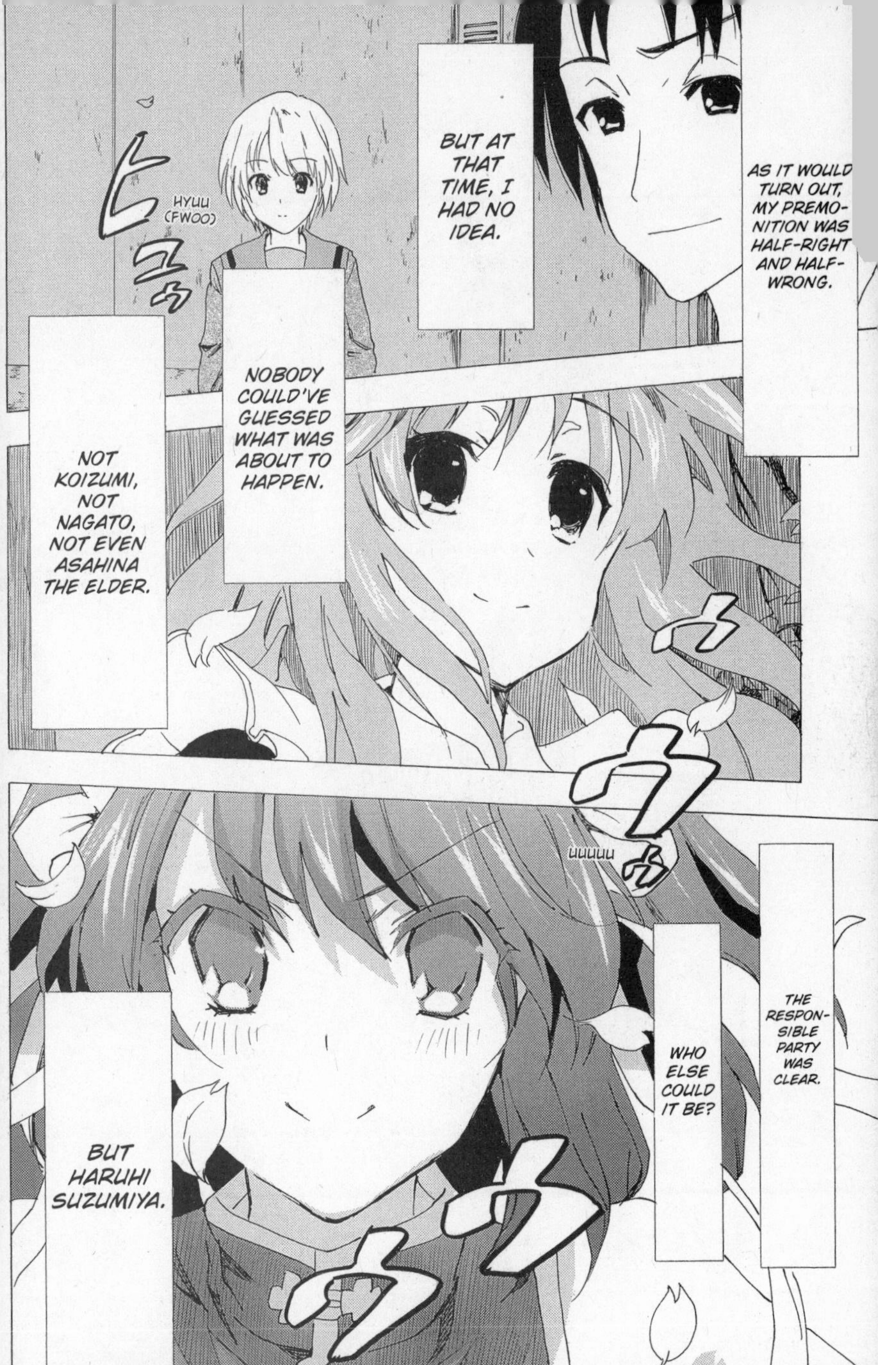
AS IT WOULD TURN OUT, MY PREMONITION WAS HALF-RIGHT AND HALF-WRONG.
BUT AT THAT TIME, I HAD NO IDEA.
HYUU (FWOO)
NOBODY COULD'VE GUESSED WHAT WAS ABOUT TO HAPPEN.
NOT KOIZUMI, NOT NAGATO, NOT EVEN ASAHINA THE ELDER.
uuuuu
THE RESPONSIBLE PARTY WAS CLEAR.
WHO ELSE COULD IT BE?
BUT HARUHI SUZUMIYA.
THE DISSOCIATION OF HARUHI SUZUMIYA II : END

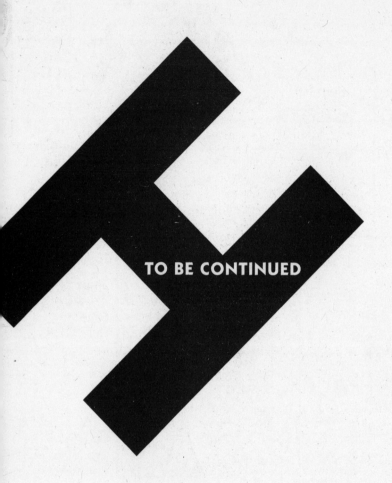

TO BE CONTINUED

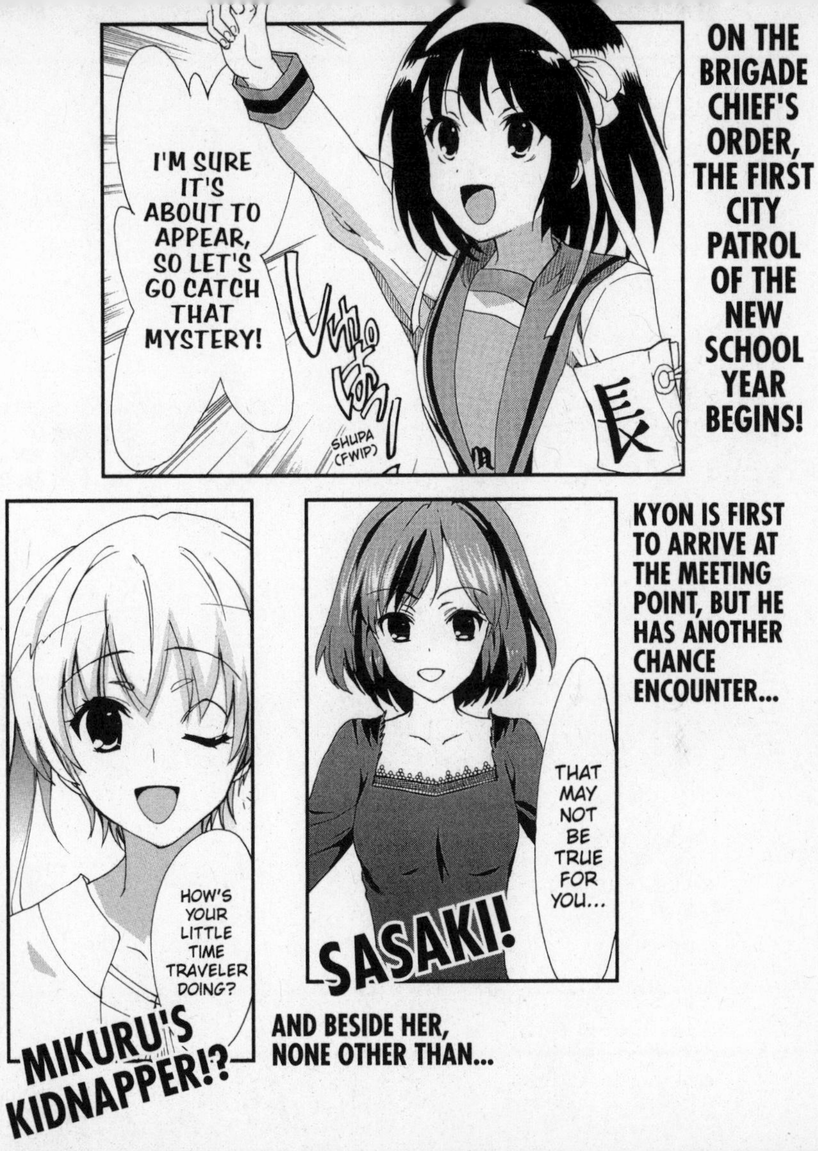
ON THE BRIGADE CHIEF'S ORDER, THE FIRST CITY PATROL OF THE NEW SCHOOL YEAR BEGINS!
I'M SURE IT'S ABOUT TO APPEAR, SO LET'S GO CATCH THAT MYSTERY!
SHUPA (FWIP)
長
KYON IS FIRST TO ARRIVE AT THE MEETING POINT, BUT HE HAS ANOTHER CHANCE ENCOUNTER...
THAT MAY NOT BE TRUE FOR YOU...
SASAKI!
AND BESIDE HER, NONE OTHER THAN...
HOW'S YOUR LITTLE TIME TRAVELER DOING?
MIKURU'S KIDNAPPER!?

AND ONE OTHER...

IS SHE A GHOST?
OR SOMETHING LIKE ONE.

SHE'S NOT HUMAN!!

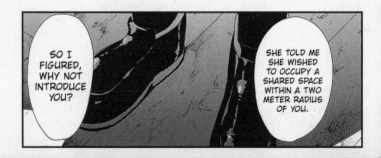

SHE TOLD ME SHE WISHED TO OCCUPY A SHARED SPACE WITHIN A TWO METER RADIUS OF YOU.
SO I FIGURED, WHY NOT INTRODUCE YOU?

MYSTERIOUS INDIVIDUALS APPEARING
ONE AFTER THE OTHER...

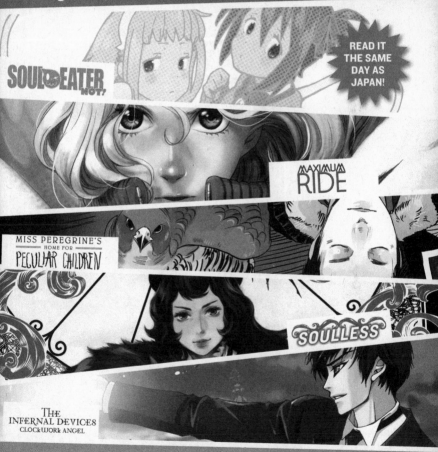
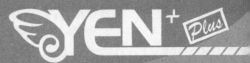

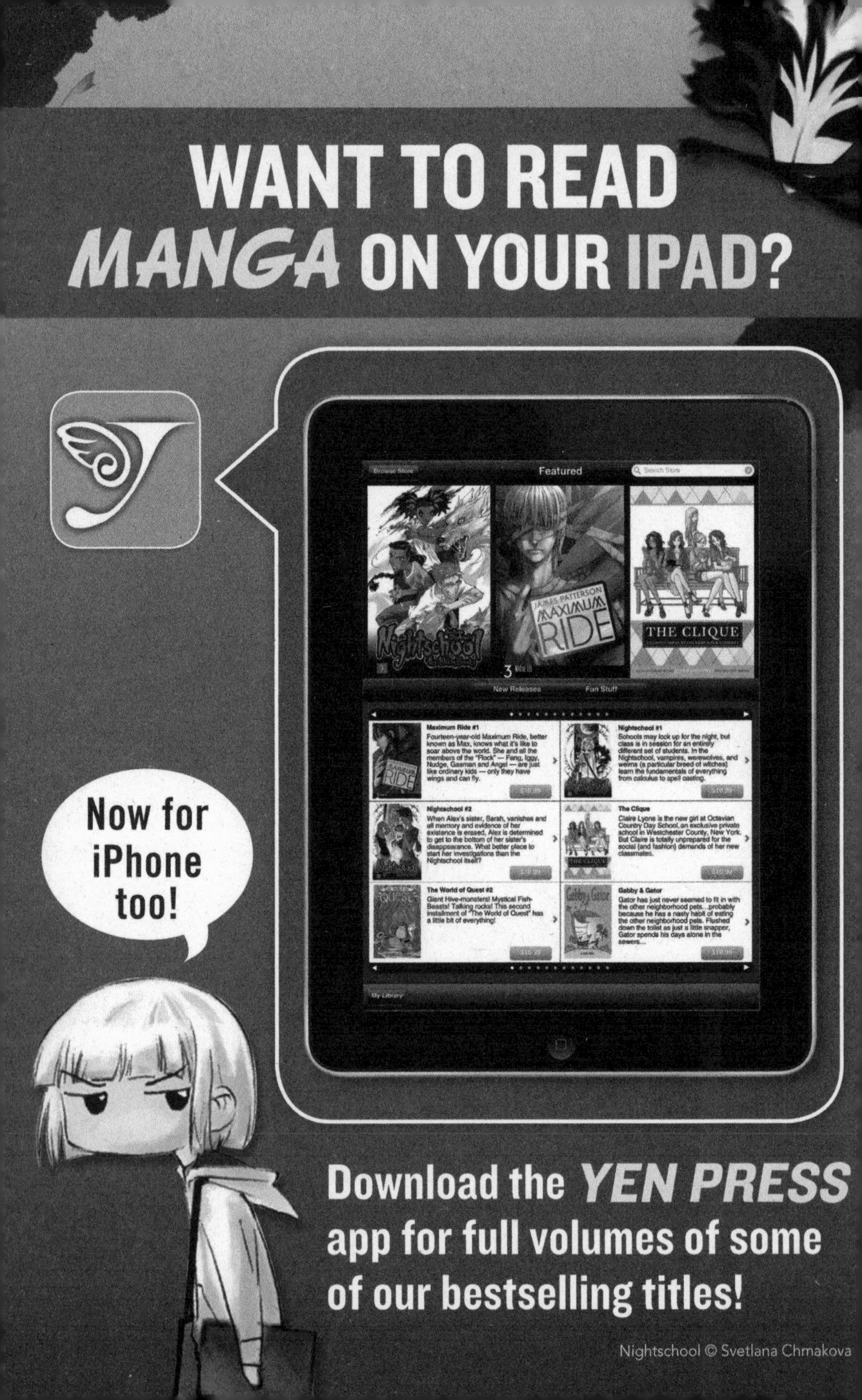
WANT TO READ
MANGA ON YOUR IPAD?
Now for iPhone too!
Download the YEN PRESS app for full volumes of some of our bestselling titles!
Nightschool © Svetlana Chmakova

ENJOY EVERYTHING.

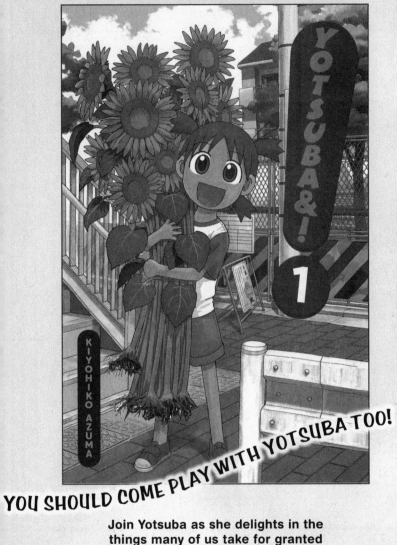

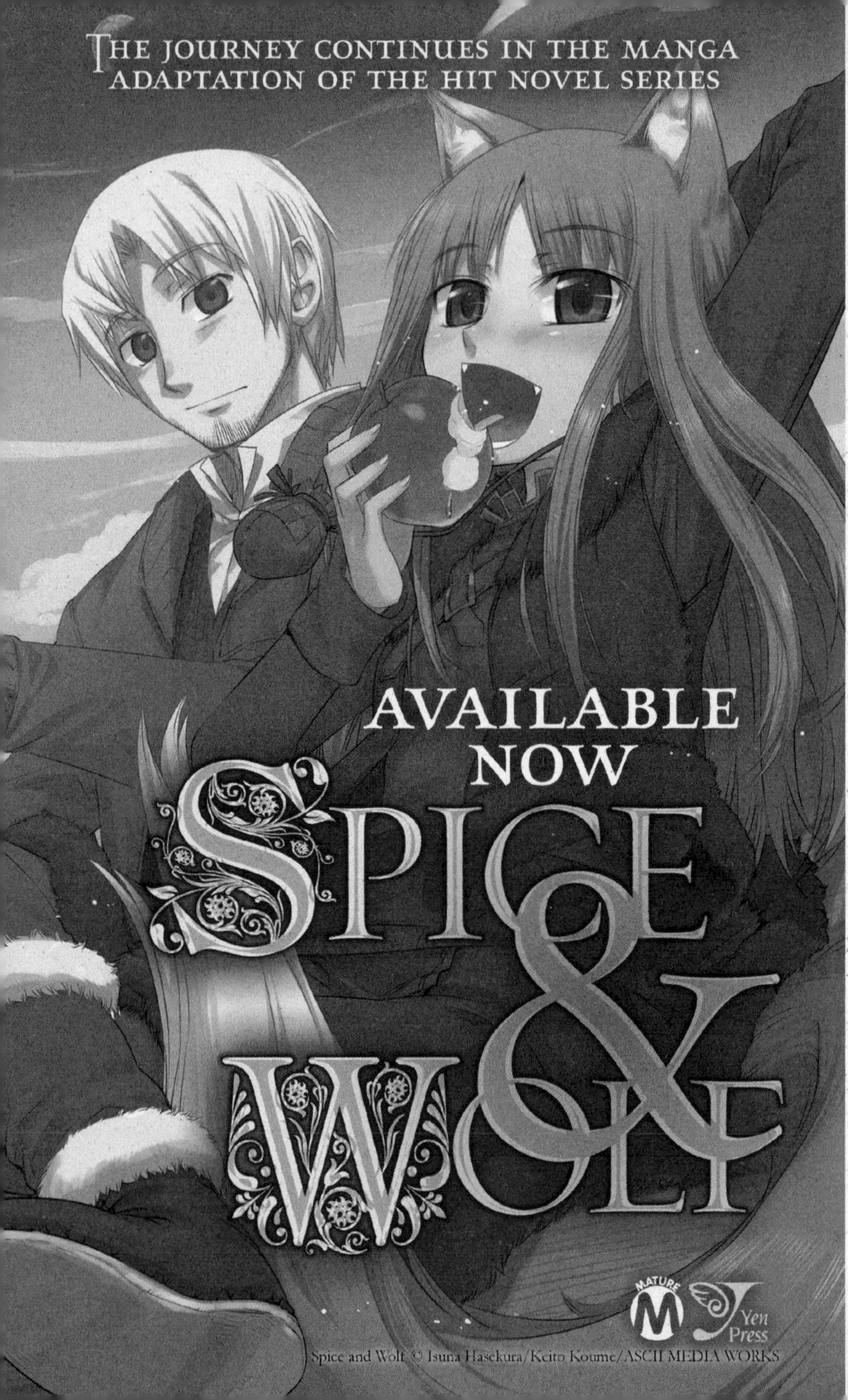
THE JOURNEY CONTINUES IN THE MANGA
ADAPTATION OF THE HIT NOVEL SERIES
AVAILABLE
NOW
SPICE
&
WOLF
MATURE
M
Yen
Press
Spice and Wolf © Isuna Hasekura/Keito Koume/ASCII MEDIA WORKS

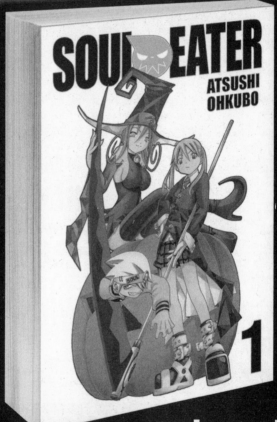

THE MELANCHOLY OF HARUHI SUZUMIYA

Original Story: Nagaru Tanigawa
Manga: Gaku Tsugano
Character Design: Noizi Ito

Translation: Paul Starr
Lettering: Alexis Eckerman

SUZUMIYA HARUHI NO YUUTSU Volume 16 © Nagaru TANIGAWA • Noizi ITO 2012 © Gaku TSUGANO 2012. First published in Japan in 2012 by KADOKAWA SHOTEN CO., LTD., Tokyo. English translation rights arranged with KADOKAWA SHOTEN CO., LTD., Tokyo through Tuttle-Mori Agency, Inc., Tokyo.

English translation © 2013 by Hachette Book Group, Inc.

Yen Press
Hachette Book Group
237 Park Avenue, New York, NY 10017

www.HachetteBookGroup.com
www.YenPress.com

Yen Press is an imprint of Hachette Book Group, Inc. The Yen Press name and logo are trademarks of Hachette Book Group, Inc.

First Yen Press Edition: October 2013

ISBN: 978-0-316-23236-4

10 9 8 7 6 5 4 3 2 1

BVG

Printed in the United States of America

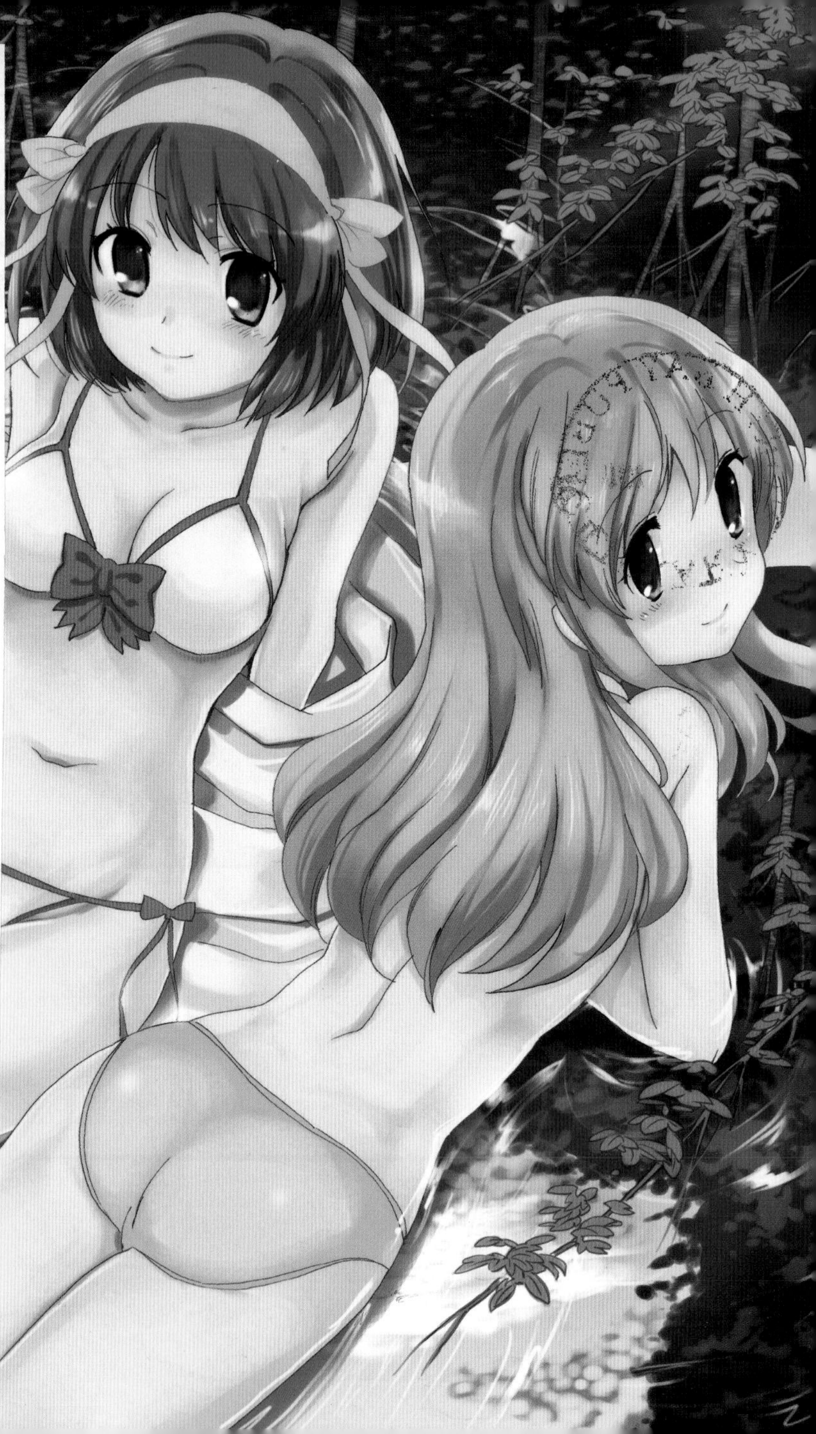

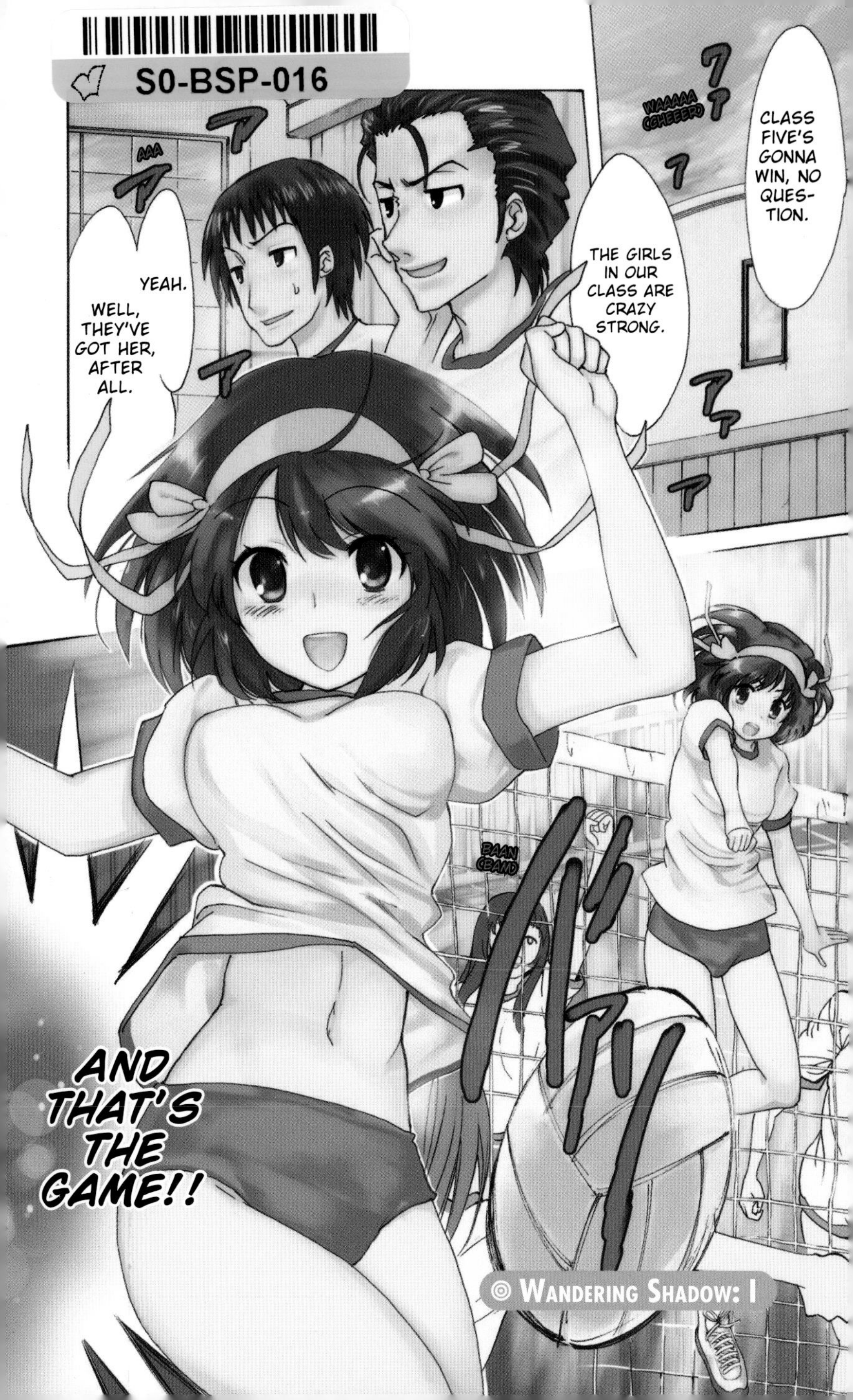
WAAAAA (CHEEEER)
CLASS FIVE'S GONNA WIN, NO QUES-TION.
THE GIRLS IN OUR CLASS ARE CRAZY STRONG.
AAA
YEAH.
WELL, THEY'VE GOT HER, AFTER ALL.
BAAN (BAM)
AND THAT'S THE GAME!!
◎ Wandering Shadow: I